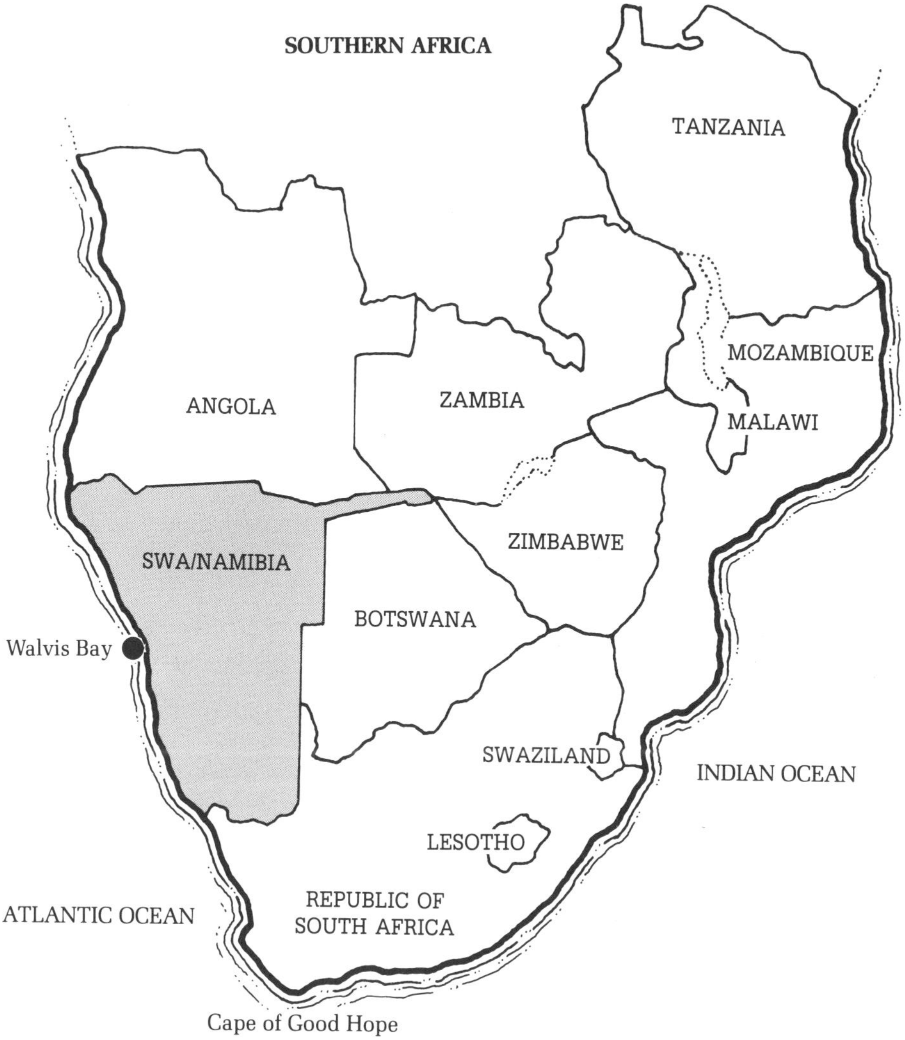
SOUTHERN AFRICA
TANZANIA
MOZAMBIQUE
MALAWI
ANGOLA
ZAMBIA
ZIMBABWE
SWA/NAMIBIA
BOTSWANA
Walvis Bay
SWAZILAND
INDIAN OCEAN
LESOTHO
REPUBLIC OF
SOUTH AFRICA
ATLANTIC OCEAN
Cape of Good Hope

Death in the Desert:
The Namibian Tragedy

by

Morgan Norval

Selous Foundation Press
Washington, D.C.

Selous Foundation Press
Publishers since 1987
Washington, D.C.

Copyright ©1989 by Morgan Norval

All rights reserved. No part of this book may be reproduced
or transmitted in any form or by any means, electronic
or mechanical, including photocopying, recording or by
any information storage and retrieval system,
without permission in writing from the publisher.

Typesetting by REF Typesetting & Publishing, Inc.
9400 Fairview Ave., Manassas, VA. 22110

Cover design, maps and illustrations by William R. Wright

Photos by Morgan Norval, Paratus and UNITA.

Library of Congress Catalog Card Number: 89-62602

ISBN: 0-944273-03-3

The paper in this book is acid-free and meets the guidelines
for permanance and durability of the committee on Production
Guidelines for Book Longevity of the Council on Library Resources.

Printed in the United States of America

First Printing

To: Allison—I said to a man who stood at the Gate of the Year, "Give me a light, that I may tread safely into the unknown." And he replied, "Go out into the darkness and put your hand into the Hand of God. That shall be to you better than light, and safer than a known way."

Acknowledgments

This book was made possible by the generosity and support of the Selous Foundation, F.M. Kirby Foundation and the following individuals: Miss Caroline Bork, Peter Cook, Mrs. Ellen Garwood, Col. & Mrs. R.H. Kreuter, Mr. & Mrs. John G. Mahler and Fitzhugh Powell.

I owe a special debt of gratitude to Ken Snowball, Fred Rindel and Dick Stephen.

A special thanks to Glenn Mackal for his prayers and encouragement.

Last, but far from least, to Bob Kvederas, whose patience, advice and editorial skills kept my nose to the grindstone without affecting our friendship.

TABLE OF CONTENTS

1. The Bear in Southern Africa 1
2. Setting the Stage 17
3. People of Namibia 21
4. Economy of Namibia 29
5. Winds of Change 41
6. SWAPO–Liberators or Terrorists? 57
7. Winds of War 67
8. First Steps Toward Self-Government 79
9. Multi Party Conference 85
10. Government of Transitional National Unity 95
11. The Deteriotating Situation 103
12. Bush War Heats Up 109
13. Operation REINDEER 125
14. Operation PROTEA 143
15. Namibianizing the War 151
16. Operation ASKARI 171
17. Joint Monitoring Commission 183
18. Civic Action 195
19. Outside Support 207
20. Aid to UNITA–Operations MODULAR, HOOPER & PACKER 215
21. Cuban Involvement in Southern Africa 227
22. Illusion of Peace 245
23. After Independence–Chaos 263
24. Repairing the Damage 281

Appendices
  A–United Nations Security Council Resolution 435 289
  B–The Windhoek Declaration of Basic Principles 291

C–Bill of Fundamental Rights and Objectives 294
D–Text, Namibia Agreement: Angola, Cuba & South Africa 300
E–Text, Cuban Troop Withdrawal: Angola & Cuba 302
F–Excerpts, SWAPO Constitution 305

Index 307

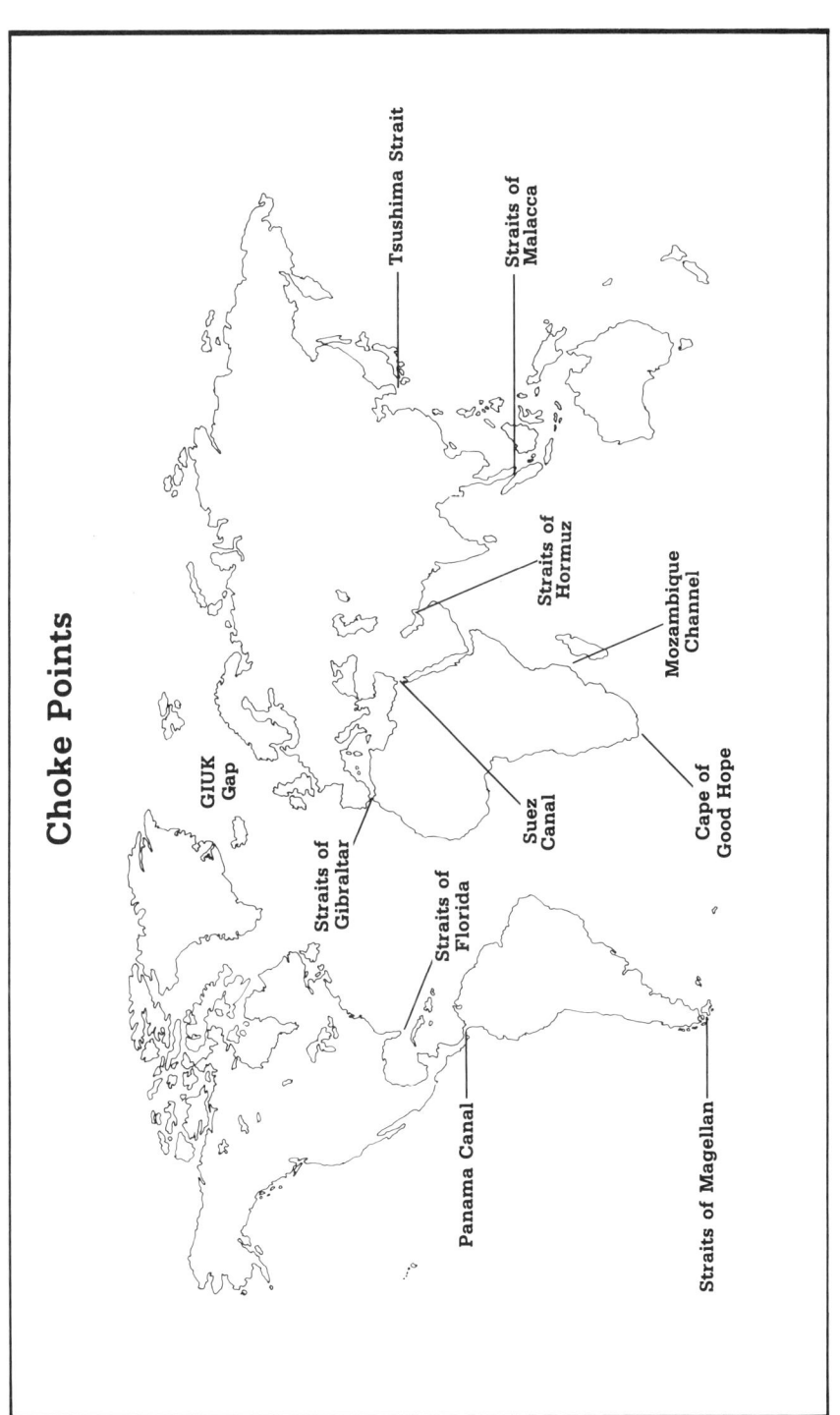

1
The Bear in Southern Africa

The situation in South West Africa/Namibia (hereafter called Namibia) is closely related to the geopolitical importance of the southern African area to the Soviet Union.[1]

The Soviet Union has never been shy about proclaiming to one and all its goal of world domination.[2] The bedrock fundamental faith of the Soviet ruling elite professes that true peace cannot exist between the socialist world and the capitalist world.[3] Marxist ideological doctrine rejects the idea of sharing the planet with any who do not accept the inevitability of their rule.[4]

Soviet imperialism doesn't require direct military confrontation to achieve its objectives. With the devious skill of Byzantine potentates and the ruthless tenacity of the Golden Horde, their spiritual ancestors,[5] the Soviets are masters of the indirect strategy, which is little understood in the West. For example, detente to the West is an end; to the Soviets, detente is a means.[6] Ceasefire to the West means the first step toward peace; ceasefire to the Soviets means the direct mode is unproductive and that a new maneuver is

---

[1] Del Pino, R., *General Del Pino Speaks,* The Cuban American Foundation, Washington, DC, 1987, p.12; see also: Norval, M., *Red Star Over Southern Africa,* Selous Fnd. Press, Washington, DC, 1988, pp.1-17.

[2] Bukovsky, V., *The Peace Movement and the Soviet Union,* The Orwell Press, New York, 1982, p.6; see also: Revel, J-F., *How Democracies Perish,* Harper & Row, New York, 1983, p.22.

[3] Gray, C.S., *The Geopolitics of Superpower,* University Press of Kentucky, Lexington, KY, 1988, p.59; see also: Bukovsky, *op. cit.,* p.7.

[4] Bukovsky, *loc. cit.*

[5] Norval, *Red Star,* pp.xv-xix.

[6] Bukovsky, *op. cit.,* p.16.

required in the continuing struggle. But most emphatically it does not mean the end of the struggle, it must go on.[7]

Circumstances permitting, the Soviets will exploit any crisis situation anywhere. They base their involvement on the degree of resistance they are likely to encounter from the West, more specifically, the United States. Their game plan is tied to their perception of the will of the U.S. to get involved. The reality of international politics vis-a-vis the Soviets and the West (United States) are as valid today as they were when stated centuries ago by the Greek historian Thucydides. He justified the Athenian sack of one of Sparta's allies, the Medians: "You know as well as we do that, when these matters are discussed on the equality of power to compel and that in fact the strong do what they have the power to do and the weak accept what they have to expect. . . . Our opinion of the gods and our knowledge of men lead us to conclude that it is a general and necessary law of nature to rule wherever one can. This is not a law that we made ourselves, nor were we the first to act upon it when it was made. We found it already in existence, and we shall leave it to exist for ever among those who come after us."[8]

Since the end of World War II, Soviet strategy has been to attack, by indirect means, the backbone of the Free World—the United States.

The Soviet actions and the counter actions by the West fit the geopolitical theories of Sir Halford Mackinder, a turn of the century British geographer and geopolitical theorist.

Mackinder's geopolitical writing is grand strategy at its best. His theory rests heavily upon the role of geography in the historically shifting power relationships that have occurred throughout man's history.

His theory described the world as a closed system composed of three areas: a continental "Pivot Area" surrounded by a partly continental and partly oceanic "Inner or Marginal Crescent" of Euro-Asia and that, in turn, is surrounded by an oceanic "Lands of Outer or Insular Crescent" of the Americas, Africa, Australia, and Japan.[9]

Mackinder characterized the Pivot Area (renamed "Heartland" by the American geopolitical theorist Nicklas Spykman) as that vast area of Euro-Asia which is inaccessible to seapower. He believed that conditions created by an extensive system of internal railroad transportation were

---

[7] Gray, *op. cit.*, p.59.

[8] Thycydides, *The Peloponnesian Wars*, trans. Rex Warner, Cassell, London, 1962, pp.360, 363.

[9] See: Mackinder, H., "The Geographical Pivot of History (1904)," in: *Democratic Ideals and Reality*, Norton, New York, 1962.

superior to those created through external seapower. This condition of expanded rail mobility would allow the Heartland to use its vast military and economic power to emerge as a powerful empire.

Mackinder further theorized the Heartland empire would expand its control over the Inner Crescent (renamed "Rimlands" by Spykman[10]) of Euro-Asia and use the vast resources of the continent for launching fleets to overwhelm the sea peoples of the Outer Crescent and acquire a global empire.

Although concern over Kaiser Wilhelm's imperialist policies in Germany prompted Mackinder's original writings, his warning was clear: whoever became the Heartland power under modern political and economical conditions could make a plausible bid for a global empire.[11] He made this clear in a 1943 article in *Foreign Affairs* that the Heartland should be considered as being essentially the Soviet Union. And that, "All things considered, the conclusion is unavoidable, that if the Soviet Union emerges from this war as conqueror of Germany, she must rank as the greatest land power on the globe. Moreover, she will be the power in the strategically strongest defensive position. The Heartland is the greatest natural fortress on earth. For the first time in history, it is manned by a garrison sufficient both in numbers and quality."[12]

Mackinder's views were the basis of the U.S. policy of containment after World War II.[13]

Containment called for a series of interlocking alliances around the Rimland oceanic edge of the Euroasian continent that would isolate or check expansion from the Heartland, i.e. the Soviet Union.[14]

Composed of people dependent upon seaborne transportation for their survival, the Rimland, or encircling allies—North Atlantic Treaty Organization (NATO), South East Asia Treaty Organization (SEATO), Australia, New Zealand and the United States (ANZUS), and the partners of the Rio de Janeiro Treaty—would not only cooperate in containing the Heartland/Soviet Union, but strive to stabilize the globe by pursuing policies dedicated

---

[10] Spykman, N., *The Geography of Peace,* Harcourt, Brace, New York, 1944, pp.37-38, 40-41.

[11] Gray, *op. cit.,* p.7.

[12] "The Real World and the Winning of the Peace," from *Democratic Ideals and Reality,* pp.272-273.

[13] See: Gaddis, J.L., *Strategies of Containment: A Critical Appraisal of Postwar American National Security Policy,* Oxford University Press, New York, 1982, p.57.

[14] See: Deibel, T.L. & Gaddis, J.L., *Containment: Concept and Policy,* Vols. I & II, National Defense University Press, Washington, DC, 1986.

to free trade, private enterprise and democratic procedure.[15]

Mackinder's thesis projected a world in which sea power (America and its allies) and land power (the Soviet Union and its satellites) were in continuous conflict.

Although Mackinder held a pessimistic view that the strategic balance in the twentieth century favored the Heartland,[16] the advantage lay with the West. Mackinder's Heartland was open to air and nuclear attack and Anglo-American navies ruled the waves. They could counter any Soviet-inspired aggression along the Pacific and Indian Ocean or Atlantic shore of Euro-Asia. This state of affairs did not last.

Since the end of World War II, Soviet strategy has been to attack, by indirect means, the backbone of the Free World—the United States.[17]

Soviet strategy is to deny the U.S. freedom of action to respond to Soviet-supported imperialism throughout the world. This strategy is part and parcel of their on-going conduct of World War III. It is not a war of massed armies, but instead, a series of terrorist acts and guerrilla insurgencies, or as the Soviets term them, "wars of national liberation," guided by the Soviet Marxist ideology.[18]

"The world today is at war," said former U.S. Secretary of Defense Caspar W. Weinberger. "It is not a global war, though it goes on around the globe. It is not war between fully mobilized armies, though it is no less destructive for all that. It is not war by the laws of war and, indeed, law itself, as an instrument of civilization, is a target of this peculiar variety of aggression. It benefits from the pernicious sophistries of those who wish to construe these wars as the efforts of sovereign people to pursue their own destinies and, as such, no business of our own."[19]

World War III, from the Soviet point of view encompassed three overlapping phases: containment or consolidation (This is a better term as it causes less confusion because our policy of containment was designed to

---

[15] See: "Alliances and Security Relationships," Deibel & Gaddis, *op. cit.*, pp.189-217.

[16] See: Gray, C.S., *The Wartime Influence of Sea Power Upon Land Power,* National Institute for Public Policy, Fairfax, VA, 1987.

[17] See: Alexander, Y. & Kucinski, R., "The International Terrorist Network"; in, Fauriol, G., editor, *Latin American Insurgencies,* National Defense University Press, Washington, DC, 1985, p.60.

[18] See: Daily, B.D. & Parker, P.J., *Soviet Strategic Deception,* Lexington Books, Lexington, MA, 1987, pp.140-142.

[19] News Release, Remarks of Casper W. Weinberger, Secretary of Defense, at the Conference on Low-Intensity Warfare, Fort McNair, Washington, DC, January 14, 1986, p.3.

prevent the spread of Soviet imperialism. Containment, from the Soviet perspective, meant to contain, or keep, their territorial acquisitions within the Soviet empire); detente—luring the West into complacency while the Soviets beef up their military and project power around the globe; and, double envelopment —encircling the People's Republic of China with a ring of Soviet diplomatic and military alliances.

Coincidentally, American policy vis-a-vis the Soviet Union's imperial tendencies is also described, by some, as going through three phases.

In his 1987 annual report to Congress, Defense Secretary Weinberger stressed three phases of containment. The first phase, the ideological one of the mid-to-late 1940's resulted in action by the U.S. to prevent "a combination of ideological appeal and internal subversion from seizing power in nations vital to U.S. interests."[20]

The Marshall Plan and Truman Doctrine were examples of first phase policies.

The second U.S. phase is associated with the 1950 National Security Council document, NSC-68, which reflected our fundamental interest in preventing the Eurasian land mass from being dominated by a hostile power.[21] NATO, SEATO, our action in the Korean and Vietnam Wars, and the inclusion of Japan's defense under the protection of the U.S. nuclear umbrella are examples of U.S. action during our second phase of containment.

"Today," said Weinberger, "we face the challenge of the third phase of containment: containment of the Soviet Union's massive military power. Having failed to achieve its ideological or geopolitical ambitions, the Soviet Union in the early 1960's launched the largest military buildup in world history."[22]

The Soviets, even though they may have been temporarily stymied by the West's actions in the early post-World War II period, still pressed on with their three stage conduct of World War III.

Each cycle, or phase, has lasted about twenty years. The first cycle, consolidation, began in 1946 and ended with the collapse of South Vietnam in 1975. The second stage, detente, as Henry Kissinger and the Western world called it, dawned in 1960 when a U.S. Presidential Review Memorandum appeared advocating accommodation with the Soviet Union. This new policy,

---

[20] Weinberger, *Annual Report*, 1987, pp.28-29.
[21] NSC-68: United States Objectives and Programs for National Security, April 14, 1950.
[22] Weinberger, *Annual Report*, 1987, pp.28-29.

which replaced the policy of containment, was aimed at preserving the global status quo and fostering interdependence by expanding trade relations with Russia.[23] U.S. efforts to reduce international tensions by accommodating the Soviet Union were accompanied by unilateral U.S. disarmament and appeasement of aggression. Unfortunately, this policy has been followed by every American administration since Johnson's.

The Cuban Missile Crisis of 1962 taught the Russians a hard lesson. Forced to retreat by overwhelming U.S. nuclear power,[24] they resolved that such a reversal would be their last. They pursued a policy of military buildup and exported subversion abroad.

Between 1964 and 1979, under the aegis of detente, the West retreated all over the globe. This retreat led to the collapse of many pro-Western hard-line, anti-communist supporters. Indo-China, Angola, Ethiopia, Mozambique, Guinea-Bissau, Rhodesia, Aden, Afghanistan, Iran, Nicaragua, Grenada, Guyana and Surinam either fell directly to Marxist regimes or became implacable foes of the United States. In addition, the U.S. either abandoned or alienated South Korea, Taiwan, South Africa, Argentina and Chile during this time.

Detente finally collapsed when the Soviets invaded Afghanistan in 1979. But while the West sought a stalemate through detente, the Soviets plotted their next move, using a public relations campaign for peaceful co-existence, eagerly trumpeted by the liberal Western media.

As a result of the widening Sino-Soviet rift, the Soviets initiated the geographical encirclement of mainland China and the third phase of World War III, double envelopment. In this endeavor they have been aided by their new vassal states of Vietnam, Cambodia and Laos and their close relations with India.

During this period they have accelerated their nuclear and naval armaments programs. While the West dozed through the period of detente, the Soviets were busy working to catch up and surpass the West in military strength. SALT I recognized American-Soviet nuclear parity. SALT II codified military Soviet nuclear superiority.

The Soviet goal is absolute nuclear superiority. Their already comfortable second strike capacity of 1980 was expanded to third strike capability by 1982. Their game plan is clear: play a conventional ninteenth century colonial

---

[23] See: Frye, Alton, "Inching Beyond Containment: Detente, Entente, Condominium-and Orchestration," in Deibel & Gaddis, *op. cit.*, pp.639-663.

[24] See: Johnson, P., *Modern Times—The World From the Twenties to the Eighties*, Harper Colphon edition, New York, 1985, p.627.

expansionist ground and naval game under the protective cover of an overwhelming twentieth century atomic umbrella.

As early as 1973, Leonid Brezhnev announced at a Communist conference in Prague that by 1985, the U.S.S.R. would achieve economic, military and political hegemony. At that time, he thought, the third and final stage of World War III, double envelopment (surround the People's Republic of China; leap-frog the U.S. containment policy by using Soviet Rimland and World Island colonies as bases to strangle the West by cutting off their access to oil and raw materials) was well advanced and would surely be completed by his target date. Brezhnev's timetable was off the mark, but the Soviets are well along the way toward their goal. This is evident by their successful colonization of parts of southern Africa and the successful satellization of Nicaragua in the backyard of the United States.

Today the Soviets have a near-global power projection system of air, naval, and technical facilities. That system is not as elaborate as the United States', but it doesn't have to be. The Soviets' Eurasian position, fitting Mackinder's thesis, and their use of ships in lieu of what might more efficiently be performed on land, act as compensating factors.[25]

The Soviets have reached global superpower status with a vengeance, seemingly having fulfilled Mackinder's prophecy.

Mackinder's thesis was based upon a historical analysis of the success of nomadic steppe people from Central Asia who ravaged the rim of Eurasia for centuries. Attilla, Genghis Khan, Batu, Timar the Lame and Babar led their horsemen around the oceanic edge of Euro-Asia from the China Sea, to the Indian Ocean and on to the Mediterranean and Adriatic. Stressing mobility and military might, these people disdained static agricultural pursuits. Instead, these tribes collected tribute from the people they had conquered.

Coincidentally, American policy vis-a-vis the Soviet Union's imperial tendencies is also described, by some, as going through three phases.

Occasionally these tribute-collecting tribes came together in a compact mass under the disciplined, central command of a dynamic leader. Then, they exploded with brief, massive bursts of energy, sending them surging out of Central Asia to savage the surrounding civilizations.

These tribes, referred to by historians as Mongols, used tactics that swept almost all before their on-rushing hordes. Feigned retreat and flanking movements were fundamental maneuvers; cunning, intrigue and treachery were standard operating procedures. Using mobility to attack and subdue one

---

[25] Harkavy, Robert E., "Soviet Conventional Power Projection and Containment," in Deibel & Gaddis, *op. cit.*, p.325.

foe at a time by radiating from Central Asia before opponents could combine was a common tactic. The Mongols also employed trade missions and diplomatic envoys as spies and propagandists. Aided by fifth-columnists, these emissaries often prepared the path of conquest through the clever use of psychological warfare and subversion, typical Mongol techniques.

Masters of mobility and deceit, these nomadic Mongols conquered and controlled the caravan routes and commercial crossroads that connected the advanced societies on the coasts of the continent. They prospered by levying tribute, not by peaceful productivity.

The modern Soviet-Mongol imperium also lives by conquest, not by peaceful productivity. The reason for this is the nature of the economic-political system the modern Mongols have adopted with a messianic zeal. That system is the totalitarian Marxist-Leninist socialism which requires expansion,[26] conquest,[27] and parasitism[28] for its survival.

Soviet parasitism has a dark ugly side in that it leads to imperialism. The parasite socialist state, as the Soviet imperium amply demonstrates, continually needs new, healthy bodies to feed upon. As it destroys one host, it moves on to destroy another. The ultimate conclusion of the socialist order is death and destruction, a goal required by its very nature.[29]

The aim of the Soviet Union is to defeat, not necessarily to destroy the West. Tribute collection, not atomic rubble, is their aim. The Soviets prefer to

---

[26] Bukovsky, V., *op. cit.*, "Was it American or Soviet troops who occupied half of Germany and built a wall in Berlin? Is it not the Soviets who still occupy Hungary, Czechoslovakia, the baltic states, not to mention Afghanistan, very much against the wishes of the people in their countries . . . ," p.22, see also: M.H. Louw, *National Security: A Modern Approach*, Institute for Strategic Studies, University of Pretoria, Pretoria, 1978, p.2.

[27] Revel, J-F, *op. cit.*, ". . . only the Soviet Union continues to grow by means of armed conquest . . . ," p.56.

[28] Rustov, Alexander, *Freedom and Dominion*, Princeton University Library, Princeton, NJ, 1980, ". . . and to the extent that bolshevism can indeed claim economic triumphs, these have been in large measure due to international capitalism, which repeatedly has furnished the credits, the machinery, blueprints and patents, the engineers and mechanics on which the Russian productive apparatus has depended . . . ," p.578; or: Chilton, David, *Productive Christians*, Institute for Christian Economics, Tyler, TX, 1981, "Socialism cannot produce wealth; it can only destroy what wealth exists. It cannot generate; it can only confiscate . . . ," p.130; or: Rushdoony, R.J., *Politics of Guilt and Envy*, Thoburn Press, Fairfax, VA, 1978, "The socialist state survives for a time by being a parasite on its people to the point of their economic destruction or by being a parasite on some richer state which contents to subsidize them, as the United States, after World War II, has done with much of the world," pp.60-61.

[29] Shafarevich, Igor, *The Socialist Phenomenon*, Harper & Row, New York, 1980, p.285.

preserve the West's productive plant in order to feed and prop up their own economy.

The curse of communism is starvation and a slave-like existence. Nevertheless, aided by certain international financiers who have loaned them over $60 billion since 1970; abetted by many multinational corporations which have sold them advanced high-level technology, or are waiting in line to do so, the USSR is seizing control of the sea lanes and strategic areas of the globe upon which the developed nations depend.[30]

They are using so-called "wars of national liberation," conducted by their Cuban and East Bloc surrogate-mercenaries, to achieve their goals.

Choke point control and tribute collection are Mongol tactical methods which the Soviets are using in large measure with naval forces.

Suddenly, the Soviets have emerged as a great naval power.[31] Realizing the importance of sea power, they have applied Mongol tactics to the maritime world by using their naval mobility to effect choke point control of the Seven Seas. Only a short time ago, the Soviet Navy was, at best, a coastal defense force.

While the United States was reducing its naval forces prior to the election of Ronald Reagan, the Soviets embarked upon a massive program of naval expansion that produced spectacular results.[32] The Soviet Pacific fleet is larger than the United States Navy—indeed, Soviet naval forces outnumber the U.S. in virtually every category except aircraft carriers.[33]

The comparative strength of the respective merchant marine fleets reflects the same trend. In 1950, the U.S. had 3,500 ships to the Soviets' 400. In 1987, the Soviets had over 7,000 to our 360.[34] In addition, the Soviet merchant fleet is modern and able to be quickly converted into military transports, as contrasted to the aging and largely outdated U.S. merchant fleet.

---

[30] See: Tedla, Aradom, "The West's Stake in Eritrea," *Journal of Defense & Diplomacy,* McLean, VA, Vol. 6, No. 3, 1988, p.4; also: "India's Strategic Surge," International Security Council's *Global Alert,* No. 3, May 2, 1988.

[31] Sieff, Martin, "Soviet Navy can tie up 16 'sea gates,' " *The Washington Times,* February 19, 1986.

[32] Gold, Philip, "Will the Soviets rule the waves of the future?", *The Washington Times,* March 10, 1988, p.F5.

[33] Morris, Robert, *Our Globe Under Siege III,* J&W Enterprises, Mantoloking, NJ, 1988, pp.37-38.

[34] Morris, *op. cit.,* p.38.

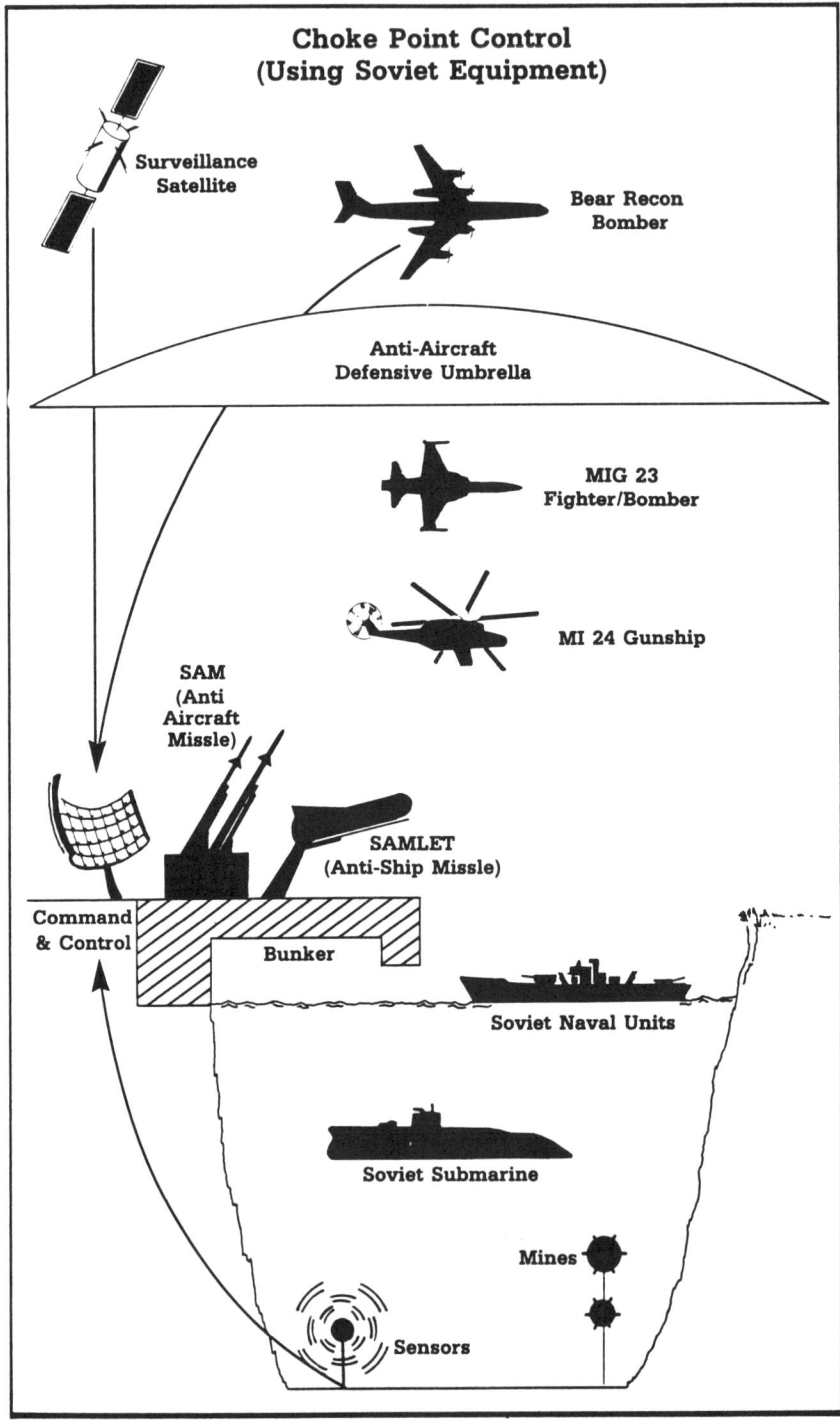

The Soviet fishing fleet is larger and more active than the fishing fleets of all other nations of the world combined.[35]

In the past, the Soviet Union, as a self-sufficient, energy and mineral independent, land power, needed nothing more. Now Soviet task forces cruise sea lanes of communication in the Pacific,[36] Indian,[37] and Atlantic Oceans[38]—sea lanes that carry oil and ores vital to the very existence of America and its allies. Even America is vulnerable, for the U.S. imports forty percent of its petroleum and many of its strategic minerals.

The tremendous increase in the size of the Soviet merchant fleet could permit its use to control trade routes in a possible new strategy of sea supremacy. It is a subtle and simple strategy: if most merchant ships carrying goods on certain trade routes are Soviet-controlled, that route is effectively dominated or choked. While the numbers in the western fleets continue to decline, the Soviets are expanding, capturing more of the shipping trade and undercutting the prices charged by their Free World competition.[39] The strategy doesn't sound too far-fetched.

Most seaborne commerce flows through fifteen funnels or choke points. Five inland seas (South China, Mediterranean, North, Norwegian and Caribbean), eight critical passage points (Malacca Straits, Ceylon, Horn of Africa, Mozambique Channel, Cape of Good Hope, Gibraltar, Cape Horn and Straits of Florida) along with two inter-oceanic canals (Suez and Panama) dominate the world's maritime traffic. These sea lanes link the industrialized states of the Western Pacific, Western Europe and Western Hemisphere. Since 1964, the Soviets have moved quietly to expand their influence in and around all fifteen of these vital choke points. They have moved to the sea with one goal: total isolation of the United States.[40]

Sea choke points are the keys to the geopolitical future of the West. Cutting off the traffic in food, the "irreducible essential" might not prove

---

[35] *Ibid.*

[36] Yamazaki, Takio, "The Soviet March toward Open Sea," *Survival in the 21st Century,* Tokyo, 1986, pp.2-5.

[37] Rudolph, Herwig, "The Indian Ocean Power Balance," *Africa Institute of SA Bulletin,* Vol. 25, nos. 9710, 1985, pp.101-107; see also: "India's Strategic Surge," *op. cit.*

[38] Max, Alphonse, "Soviet Presence Astride the Southern Sea Lanes," *The Wall Street Journal,* March 3, 1986; see also: R. Adm. Warren C. Hamm, Jr., US Navy (Ret.), "NATO's Exposed Underbelly," *U.S. Naval Institute Proceedings,* January 1988, pp.79-83.

[39] Sieff, *op. cit.,*

[40] See: Gorshkov, Admiral Sergei G., *Red Star Rising at Sea,* Naval Institute Press, Annapolis, MD, 1974, pp.123-135 and p.141.

12   Death in the Desert

fatal to the agriculturally self-sufficient. But interdicting the flow of raw materials would have an effect of global proportions—the essential industries in the West would erode and crumble.

The fall of Saigon to the communists in April 1975, followed shortly by most of Indochina, has placed U.S. containment policy in jeopardy[41] and has nearly completed the geographical encirclement of the People's Republic of China. Former U.S. naval facilities at Cam Rahn Bay and Danang now give the Soviets strategic port facilities for their Pacific fleet, with heightened danger to the West, especially to the oil and ore routes through the South China Sea to Japan, from Iran, Arabia, South Africa and South America.

Soviet power surrounds Mainland China, an ancient adversary of the Russians. A sharp sickle of Soviet bases, satellites and allies curves west, south, then east around Mainland China from the Sea of Japan to the South China Sea. The arc of the sickle includes Shikotan, Sakhalin, Sikote, Alin, North Korea, Mongolia, Siberia, Afghanistan, India and communist Indochina, beginning at the Tator Strait and stretching to Cam Rahn Bay. Only two gaps remain in this hostile perimeter, both to the south. Pro-Chinese Pakistan, threatened both by a Soviet-backed Baluchi uprising and India, and non-aligned Burma, also under communist guerrilla attack, provide Beijing with uncertain avenues to the Indian Ocean and to the markets and resources of the rest of the world.

Just south of Free China, or Taiwan, lies the South China Sea, which is dominated by Soviet carrier battle groups. To the north, from Taiwan to South Korea, lies the east China Sea—Mainland China's only access route to Western technology, food and goods. Without this access, the stifling of China could begin in short order. Ironically, Taiwanese control of the east China Sea could be the key to Red China's survival.

In Afghanistan, the Soviets have been stopped temporarily in their bid to clear their southern flank for a push toward the Persian Gulf. Volatile fundamentalist Iran becomes their next logical target. The oil of the Middle East beckons. The warm waters of the Indian Ocean call. The strategy is sound. First, insure the eastern flank in the Middle East and South Asia; second, secure the western flank by seizing Yugoslavia, and advancing to the Adriatic. This would help to destabilize Greece and neutralize Turkey.

Western Europe, almost completely dependent on the Middle East for petroleum, and hooked on natural gas from the Soviet Union; confronted with Warsaw Pact forces poised to strike and morally weakened by a

[41] See: Podhoretz, Norman, "The Rise and Fall of Containment: Informal Remarks," in Deibel & Gaddis, *op. cit.*, pp.703-719.

well-coordinated Soviet-supported campaign for nuclear disarmament, would, for their own survival and self-interest, slip into Soviet thralldom.

This is not the only threat to the West that would result from the Soviet-Mongol strategy. Most reserves of minerals essential to an industrialized society are located in southern Africa near a vital choke point. Until 1965, facilities in southern Africa that monitored mineral shipments to the West were the responsibility of the sea peoples—Great Britain and the United States. The Royal Navy, under the Simonstown agreement of 1955, had basing rights at the strategic South African port of Simonstown. The agreement also guaranteed the United States, as England's ally, access to South African port and air facilities in time of war. Thus, the sea peoples were strategically positioned to monitor and protect the vital Cape of Good Hope choke point. In addition, oil from the Persian Gulf went mainly to Japan and Western Europe by way of the South China Sea, the Suez Canal and Mediterranean. A minimal amount was exported to the United States.

By 1965, energy consumption has increased dramatically and supertankers revolutionized petroleum transport. Oil that had been moved through the Suez and Mediterranean to Western Europe came southward in supertankers along East Africa, through the Mozambique Channel, around the Cape of Good Hope and up the west coast of Africa via the South Atlantic Ocean past Angola and Guinea-Bissau, to NATO and the United States. Hostile ports-of-call soon replaced friendly naval facilities.

The Soviets have aggressively moved to the sea and are seeking to finlandize the western industrialized nations by controlling choke points and the strategic resources upon which the life and commerce of western society depend.

Eventually, the Soviets will try to establish world hegemony by indirectly confronting the U.S. through so-called "wars of national liberation" in Third World nations sitting astride vital choke points or by limiting access to vital resources.

A seminal work of communist theory, "The World Communist Movement: An Outline of Strategy and Tactics," by V.V. Zagladin, top assistant of former politburo keeper of the Marxist ideological flame, Boris Ponomarov, lucidly explains the role of national liberation movements in furthering the world goals of Soviet-Mongol imperialism.

The language is so clear and specific that the continuing debate in the West over the question of Soviet manipulation of these movements can only be explained as a triumph of Soviet propaganda.

"The social revolution," Lenin stressed, "can come only in the form of an epoch in which are combined civil war by the proletariat against the bourgeoisie in the advanced countries and a whole series of democratic and revolutionary movements, including the national-liberation movements in the underdeveloped, backward and oppressed nations."[42]

Communism's role in the development of national liberation movements was stressed by Lenin. "Revolutionary movement of peoples of the east can now develop effectively, can reach a successful issue, only in direct association with the revolutionary struggle of our Soviet republic against international imperialism."[43]

Today, Soviet theoreticians still toe the line drawn by Lenin more than six decades ago. Alexei Kozlov, writing in the Soviet weekly journal *New Times*, stressed the importance of Soviet control of revolutionary movements: "Solidarity with the liberation movements of the peoples of Asia, Africa, and Latin America is a permanent area of the collective action of the communist parties.

". . . The revolutionary democrats are guided in their activities by the doctrine of scientific socialism, by the organization and political principles of the building of the alliance with world socialism and the international Communist movement."[44]

The American Sovietologist, Dr. Peter Vanneman, told the U.S. Senate's Subcommittee on Security and Terrorism that the USSR is striving to enhance its influence in southern Africa not merely to affect events there but to influence events throughout the continent and the world. Its purpose is not merely to dominate the southern African region, but to utilize its influence there to enhance its influence elsewhere.

"In other words, Soviet activities in the southern African region reflect that regime's concern with fashioning policies for areas far from its periphery which will maximize its global influence. As a global superpower, the USSR must devise policies for far flung areas which will augment its influence in areas of its vital interests throughout the world. The problem is to exploit local conflict to expand global, continental and regional influence.

"The intensity of the continuing long range interest of the USSR in southern Africa," Dr. Vanneman told the subcommittee, "is indicated by the

---

[42] Lenin, V.I., *Collected Works*, Vol. 23, p.60.

[43] Zagladin, V., *The World Communist Movement: An Outline of Strategy and Tactics*, Progress Publishers, Moscow, USSR, 1973, pp.74-75.

[44] Kozlov, Alexei, "With Confident Stride: The International Communist Movement Today," *New Times*, No. 20, 1981.

creation of three relatively new governmental structures organized specifically to deal with that area of the world. There is a special section of the African Institute of the USSR Academy of Science that deals with 'liberation questions,' and the largest section of INU [Soviet acronym for a section of the First Directorate of the KGB, whose responsibility covers foreign intelligence], a department of the KGB dealing with propaganda, is the one for southern Africa. Finally, one of the three sections of the Soviet Foreign Ministry dealing with Africa focuses exclusively on southern Africa."[45]

Southern Africa is a storehouse of strategic minerals. Commercially exploitable reserves of many of the minerals—chrome, cobalt, ferromanganese, nickel, vanadium and titanium—are found only in southern Africa or in the Soviet Bloc. Thus, satellization of southern Africa would enable the Soviet Union to establish a communist mineral cartel with which they could economically and politically dominate the West. The Republic of South Africa, moreover, sits astride the supertanker sea routes from the Middle East. The routes run southward through the Indian Ocean along the East Africa coast, through the Mozambique Channel, and around the Cape of Good Hope before angling northward into the Atlantic Ocean. They travel past Namibia, Angola and Guinea-Bissau, terminating in the United States or Western Europe.

Thus, the political independence of southern Africa and the reintegration of South Africa into the Western world is essential to Western survival.

The Soviets have moved adeptly to isolate South Africa. Angola, Zambia, Zimbabwe and Mozambique have fallen to Soviet backed forces. The next domino to fall is Namibia. Namibia is an important way-station in the Soviet Union's grand strategy for spreading Soviet hegemony over the globe.

If the Red tide surges over southern Africa, the Soviets will have buried the treasure chest of the West.

The modern-day Mongols—the Soviets—would be in a position to collect tribute from a humble West, begging for essentials to keep its industrial base from collapsing.

The next domino, Namibia, is tottering under Soviet-sponsored

---

[45] U.S. Congress, Senate, Judiciary Committee, *Soviet, East German and Cuban Involvement in Fomenting Terrorism in Southern Africa,* Report of the Chairman of the Subcommittee on Security and Terrorism, 97th Congress, 2nd session, 1982.

guerrilla attack. We will now turn our attention to that beleaguered country.

2
Setting the Stage

Namibia, named after the desert that runs the length of its western shore, lies on the Atlantic coast of southern Africa south of the equator between the seventeenth and twenty-ninth parallels of latitude.

It is the second largest country in southern Africa, exceeded only by the Republic of South Africa. To give one an idea of its size, it encompasses over 317 thousand square miles and is approximately four times the size of England or three times the size of West Germany. This comparison does not include the 374 square mile enclave of Walvis Bay, the largest harbor on the Namibian coast which is an integral part of South Africa.

Walvis Bay's history, however, is closely interwoven in with the establishment of Namibia's predecessor, South West Africa.

During the eighteenth century, attracted by the rich marine life, especially whales and seals, living in the cold Atlantic waters off the coast of southern Africa, English and American whalers established small settlements at Swakopmund and Walvis Bay. After England had permanently seized the Cape Colony from the Dutch they made a point of "showing the flag" along the South West African coast. This was done in an attempt to scare off other nations and restrict whaling and sealing to British ships. From these two tiny settlements a small trade was established with the tribes in the interior. Trade was funneled to and shipped out of Walvis Bay. As a result, the British commissioned a small ship and stationed it at Walvis Bay to keep foreign traders out. In 1878 the British further solidified their hold on Walvis Bay by proclaiming it a British Crown Territory.

Meanwhile, the Germans, after soundly defeating the French in the Franco-Prussian War, had emerged as a premier European military power. To enhance this new prestige Germany decided it needed an overseas colonial empire. Being a latecomer to colonial grabbing, it had missed out on the best real estate. Most had already been staked out by the two dominant colonial powers—England and France.

Into the picture stepped a German trader named Adolf Luderitz who had a burning ambition to set up a German colony on the west coast of Africa. In 1883, his agent Heinrich Vogelsang established a trading post near Angra Pequena, where the Portuguese navigator Bartholmeu Dias de Novais had first stepped ashore in 1488. To this modest chunk of real estate, Luderitz audaciously added the whole coastal strip from the Orange River north to the twenty-sixth parallel of south latitude. After this bold stroke, he petitioned the German Imperial Chancellor, Prince Otto von Bismarck, for German protection of his new enterprise.

Bismarck was in a bit of a bind. On the one hand Luderitz's petition arrived coincident with a strong surge of public opinion in Germany in favor of acquiring an overseas empire. The rub, in Bismarck's opinion, was what would the British reaction be? He carefully broached the question to the British government and prolonged negotiation between the two powers over the question quickly ensued.

Fortunately for Bismarck, the British government had its hands full coping with the Mahdist threat to Egypt and the vital Suez Canal. In return for German support, the British acknowledged Germany's claim to the South West African coast, minus the Walvis Bay enclave which the British incorporated into their existing Cape Colony.

The German flag was hoisted at Angra Pequena on August 7, 1884. In 1920, after Germany had lost its colony in South West Africa, the name of the town was changed to Luderitz.

International power politics had reared its ugly head early in South West Africa/Namibia's history, and it would resurrect itself again and come to center stage during the second half of the twentieth century.

International politics isn't the only big factor in the Namibian drama. The geography of the country also plays a major role in the affairs of the country.

South West Africa/Namibia is bounded in the north by Angola and Zambia, in the east by Botswana and in the south by the Republic of South Africa. A narrow strip about 180 miles long, the Caprivi Strip, extends eastward up to the Zambezi River, separating Botswana from Zambia and touching Zimbabwe.

Geography further divides the country into four distinct regions. The Namib Desert runs along the entire Atlantic coastline and extends inland 80 to 120 kilometers.

The central portion is a mountainous plateau that rises up to over 6,000 feet above sea level and extends over almost half of the country.

On the northeastern and southeastern side of the country are extensions of the Kalahari Desert. The northern area consists of bush covered plains which make up almost a third of the country.

Water, or lack of it, plays a major role in South West Africa/Namibia. Her only rivers that flow year-round lie on her borders: the Orange River in the south, and the Cunene, Kavongo, Kwando and Zambezi Rivers in the north. Although these rivers have great potential, they are too far removed from the country's developed areas to be properly utilized. Furthermore, since many of these rivers form the borders of the country, only limited claims can be made to utilize these water resources.

All the inland rivers flow only sporadically and then only after short intense rain showers. After such brief periods of rainy activity, the rivers courses are often dry for many years.

The climate of the country is a typical desert climate, warm to very hot days with cool nights. The climate is influenced by the height of the inland plateau, the mountain ranges and the Benguela Current which flows from Antarctica up the west coast of Africa. This cold current generates a thick fog which often pushes inland for a distance of thirty miles. Its condensation provides lifegiving moisture to a wide variety of animal and plant life in the Namib Desert.

Namibia has two rainy seasons: the short minor season in October and November and the major rainy season from January to March.

However, rainfall is erratic and usually occurs as thunderstorms in the afternoon and early evening. Given the high daytime temperatures during this period of time, there is a very high evaporation rate.

The average rainfall figures vary in different parts of the country. In the Namib Desert they are very low, from 0 to 50 mm per year. The southern area has an average annual rainfall of 100 mm per year, while the Caprivi Strip has the highest annual rainfall in Namibia, between 600 to over 700 mm per year.

As can be expected, the agricultural activity, not to mention the native plant, tree and bush growth varies considerably and depends upon the amount of lifegiving water.

In this land of harsh climate and contrasting geography 1,250,000 people comprising eleven different ethnic groups (Basters, Bushmen, Caprivians, Coloureds, Damaras, Hereros, Kavangos, Namas, Tswanas, Wambos and whites) make their home.[1] Namibia's population and vast

---

[1] Wambos are also called Owambos. The area they inhabit in northern Namibia is called Owamboland. They will be referred to as Owambos throughout this book.

territory combine to give it one of the lowest population densities in the world: 1.5 persons per square kilometer.

Namibia is a comparatively prosperous country by African and Third World standards. In 1986 the Gross Domestic Product (GDP) was almost $1500 per capita.

There has been no starvation and there is ample space for more agricultural land to be developed. There is also a good labor pool that can be utilized to develop the country's rich mineral supply and exploit the enormous potential for tourism.

We will look more closely at these and other factors as we trace the agony of the Namibian saga. For the present this will serve as an introduction to the country that has become a pawn in the international power game between the Western liberal democracies and the totalitarian forces led by the Soviet Union and its Marxist-Leninist entourage.

3
People of Namibia— Ethnic Diversity

Namibia is a vast empty land with relatively few people. In fact it is one of Africa's most sparsely populated countries. The average population density of the continent of Africa is 18 persons per square kilometer while that of Namibia is only 1.5 per square kilometer.

The population of Namibia is as varied in its skills and occupations as it is in ethnic diversity. Occupations vary across the spectrum from primitive hunters and gatherers, through herders, rural farmers, traders, both semi-skilled and highly-skilled urban workers, civil servants and diverse professional workers.

The country's diversity is also shown in the languages spoken. These can be broken down into three major categories: the Bantu languages spoken by the black tribes—Owambos, Kavangos, Tswanas, Hereros and Caprivians; the Indo-Germanic languages—Afrikaans, German and English; and the Khoisan languages—Bushman and Nama. There are two official languages, Afrikaans and English, although almost ten percent of the population can speak German.

The Indo-German languages are the result of Namibia's past with its white migration, colonial history and post-World War I political history.

The Owambos were part of the great Bantu migration that burst out of the great lakes region in East Africa almost five hundred years ago. It was responsible for the settlement of the black tribes in southern Africa.

About 1550, the Owambos moved southwesterly from the lake region and settled between the Cunene and Kavango Rivers in the southern part of Angola and the northern part of Namibia. Today most of the Owambos still live in that area which, in Namibia, is known as Owamboland.

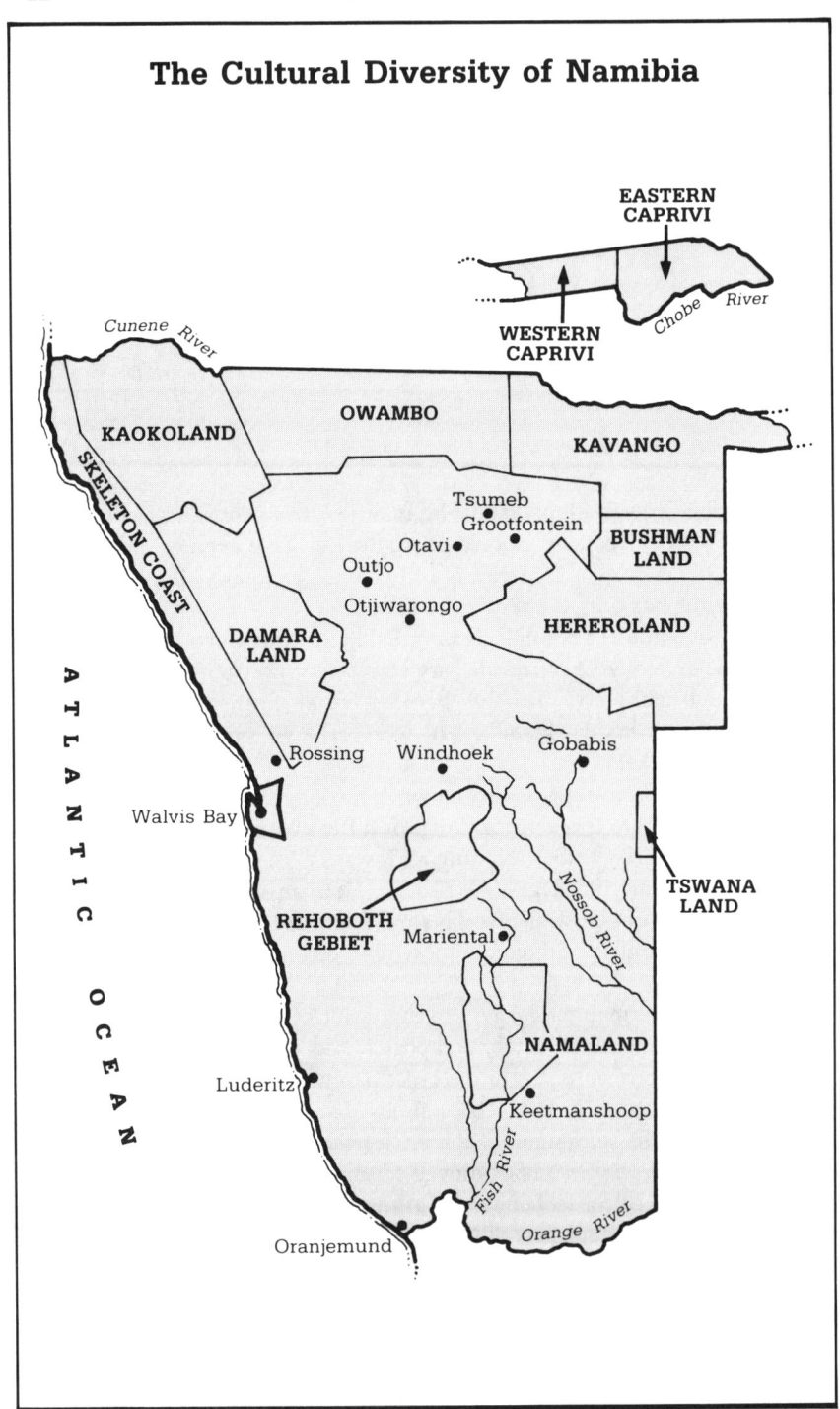

People of Namibia

The Population Table:

Ethnic Groups	Census 1981	1989 Estimate
Owambos	506,100	641,000
Kavangos	95,000	120,000
Whites	76,400	82,000
Hereros	76,300	82,000
Damaras	76,200	97,000
Namas	48,500	62,000
Coloureds	42,300	52,000
Caprivians	38,600	48,000
Bushman	29,400	37,000
Tswanas	6,700	8,000
Others	12,400	12,000
Total	1,033,200	1,288,000

(The estimates are calculated on an annual growth rate of 3% for all groups except whites and others. The projected rate for whites is 1.5% and for others nil.)

Although the Owambos are divided up into eight tribal groups only seven tribal areas are represented in Owamboland. The eight tribes are the Kwanyama, Ndongo, Kwambi, Ngandjera, Mbalanti, Kwaluudhi, Nkolonkadhi and Eunda. The biggest tribe is the Kwanyama. The Nkolonkadhi and Eunda are the smallest tribes and both share the same tribal area. Thus eight tribes but only seven tribal areas. The Owambos represent about one-half the total population of Namibia.

Although the Owambo language is one of the Bantu language group there are eight different dialects spoken. The dialects spoken by the Kwanyama and Ndonga are recognized as Owamboland's official languages.

The Owambo has taken to the world of business with a vengeance. In fact it is a strange anomaly that the Marxist terrorist organization SWAPO, with its hostility to capitalism, is an Owambo-centered movement operating from Angola. Yet their tribal brothers and sisters across the border are embracing capitalism.

The more than 10,000 roadside market stalls, *cuca* shops (named after a prize-winning Portuguese beer that was brewed in southern Angola) and other business enterprises in Owamboland bear witness to this phenomenon.

The Kavangos are distantly related to the Owambos and, like them, also came from the lakes region of East Africa. From there they moved southwesterly and settled near the Kwando River in Angola. Between 1750 and 1800 they moved south of the Kavango River and settled in present day Kavangoland in Namibia.

During this same period the Kavangos broke up into four separate tribes, the Kwangali, Mbunza, Sambiyu and Geiriku, each speaking a separate dialect.

Of the four dialects spoken in Kavangoland Kwangali is the most common.

The Kavangos are a river people, most living along the banks of the Kavango River. There they fish, tend their fields and herd their cattle.

In 1760 a Dutch elephant hunter, Jacobus Coetse, became the first known white to venture from the Cape Colony into the interior of Namibia, then known as the Transgarieb (literally means across the great river-the Orange). From 1780 on more whites, primarily traders, hunters and missionaries began arriving in Namibia in search of adventure, wealth, or to save souls.

More than a century later, in 1883, Adolf Luderitz bought Angra Pequena (present day Luderitz) and its nearby territory from a Nama chief. In 1884 SWA/Namibia officially came under German protection and became a full-fledged protectorate in 1890. German Chancellor Otto von Bismarck's policy preferred to establish trading settlements rather than colonies. Thus there was not a large migration of people from Germany to populate their newly acquired protectorate. In fact, most that went out from Germany were those necessary to run the various trading concerns or those necessary to administer the colony.

After the Governor-General of the Union of South Africa had taken over the administration of SWA/Namibia in 1921 under the League of Nations mandate, a large number of farms were sold to settlers from South Africa. Encouraged by generous financial aid, this was the last white migration to SWA/Namibia.

The whites live mainly in the urban, central and southern parts of Namibia. Afrikaans, German and English are the most common languages spoken by the whites although another common language of this group is Portuguese.

The Hereros, too, migrated to Namibia from Central Africa and settled in the Kaokoland, an arid, mountainous area in the northwest part of the country. By the eighteenth century most of them had again migrated to the south. Only the Ovahimba and Ovatjimba tribes stayed behind in the Kaokoland.

Moving south, the rest of the Hereros settled at Okahandja, Otijimbinque, the Waterberg and near Omaruru and Gobabis.

While the Owambos are primarily crop farmers, the Hereros are stock farmers. A Herero male's status and influence in his community is determined by the number of cattle he owns.

The Hereros moved south searching for better lands for grazing their cattle. This migration met that of the Namas moving north also seeking better grazing lands. This led to almost continued clashes and tribal wars between the two groups during the nineteenth century.[1]

German missionaries of the Rhenish Missionary society were the first white men to live among the Hereros in the 1840s. They imported a custom that, even today, characterizes the Herero women. The Herero women copied the Victorian style of dress worn by the wives of the Rhenish missionaries. They subsequently developed their own individual style and their colorful dresses, requiring up to twelve yards of material, and hats became the Herero women's traditional dress.

The Ovahimbas, remaining in the Kaokoland, however, still retain their traditional leather-style dress.

Although the Damaras share a language with the Namas, they differ ethnically from both the Nama and the black tribes of southern Africa. Their origin is still uncertain and open to speculation. The Damaras live scattered in small groups without a central authority. They have gained their livelihood in various ways. They have been stock herders, have planted tobacco, mined and smelted copper, and traded articles made from copper and soapstone with other tribes. Towards the end of the eighteenth century the Damaras settled at Okombahe in Damaraland where they became farmers.

The Nama today are the only true descendents of the Khoi-khoin in SWA/Namibia. The Khoi-khoin had lived from the earliest times in the southwestern parts of southern Africa.

The Namas' ancestors lived both north and south of the Orange River. Great Namaland was north of the Orange and small Namaland south of it. Both, however, spoke a common language and are stock farmers.

Namibia contains several groups of Namas. They are the Rooinasie group from Hoachanas, the Bondelswarts from Karaburg and Gibeon, the Tapnaars from the Kuiseb River and Serfontein, the Fransmanne from the

---

[1] See: Vedder, H., *South West Africa In Early Times,* Frank Cass & Co., Ltd., London, 1966.

banks of the Auab River, the Velskoendraers from northeast of Keetmanshoop, the Groot Daden from Schlip and Maltahohe, the Swartboois from Fransfontein and the Keetmanshopers from Keetmanshoop and vicinity.

In the nineteenth century the Oorlams from the Cape Province joined the Namas. The Oorlams group is subdivided into the Bethanians, the Afrikaners, the Gobabis tribe, the Bersebaners and the Witboois.

Originally the Coloureds came from the Cape Province of South Africa, although a large group are descendants of the offspring resulting from liaisons with early white settlers in Namibia. Afrikaans is the language of the majority of the Coloureds.

A small group of Coloureds are stock farmers living in the southern part of Namibia. Most, however, live in the urban areas such as Windhoek, Keetmanshoop and Luderitz, and the South African port of Walvis Bay where they are fishermen.

The Caprivians live in the long, thin, peninsula-like finger that projects eastward from Namibia until it touches Zimbabwe. The largest Caprivian tribal groups are the Masubia and Mafive. Other tribes are the Mayeyi, Matotela and Mbukushu.

Caprivians trace their descendants either through the father or the mother, depending upon which tribal group they belong to.

In the Masubia, who originally came from Zambia, descent is patrilinear. The father is the head of the family and the right of succession is limited to male descendants.

The Mafive, however, came originally from Angola and their line of descent is through the mother, who is also the head of the family.

The Caprivians have taken over a foreign language as their commmon language. That is the Lozi, a language which originally came from Barotseland in Zambia. Together with English, Lozi is used as the medium of instruction in the schools. English, however, is the most commonly used written language.

Most Caprivians are subsistence farmers and live on the banks of the Zambesi and Kwando Rivers.

The Bushmen were the earliest people to live in Namibia. They are the last survivors of a people who once lived all over southern Africa and who for centuries were the sole inhabitants of the land.

The Bushman have certain characteristics that distinguish them from other peoples of Africa. They are short of stature; have high, wide cheek-bones and pointed chins and their eyelids have a fold similar to that of the Chinese.

The Bushmen have pursued a nomadic hunter-gatherer existence that has blended in with the ecosystem in which they live: "They understood the ways of nature in the most complete manner,for they knew themselves to be part of its intricate and divinely-ordered system."[2]

The Bushmen are divided into three groups: the Haixom in the north in the area of Otavi, Tsumeb and Grootfontein; the Kung in Bushmanland and the Mbarakwengo in West Caprivi.

The Bushmen speak different dialects of the Nama or Qqu languages.

In spite of their nomadic existence some Bushmen developed artistic skills. The results were many rock paintings and engravings, such as the well-known White Lady of the Brandenberg, which are still found in the mountains and hills of Namibia.

Because of the scarcity of game and other bush food the Bushmen have been forced to adapt to a different way of life. Both the government and the private sector in Namibia are involved in an attempt to facilitate the Bushmen's leap from the Stone Age into the twentieth century.

The Basters are descendants from the inter-mixing of white stock farmers with the Oorlams. In 1868, a small number of Baster families, under the leadership of Captain Hermanus van Wyk, crossed the Orange River to settle in Namibia. In 1870, they finally settled in their present location, Rehoboth Gebiet, south of present-day Windhoek.

Although ethnologically they are a mixed group like the Coloureds, they insist on being recognized as a separate group, by virtue of their unique history and the fact they have been living in their own territory for more than a century.

At their own request and insistence members of the Rehoboth community are known as Rehoboth Basters, a name they take with pride.

The Basters speak Afrikaans and most live in or around Rehoboth. They are stock and crop farmers, although they have branched out into other sectors of the economy.

The Tswanas are the smallest ethnic group in Namibia. They speak Tswana and are related to the Tswanas of South Africa and Botswana.

The three Tswana tribes—the Batlharo, Batlhaping and Bakgalagadi—live mainly in the Aminus and Epukiro areas near the Botswana border. The rest live scattered on farms and in urban areas.

This is a brief glimpse of the people of Namibia. They have, and will continue to be, affected by events taking place in their country and places far, far away from it. All, however, from the sophisticated urban dwellers in Windhoek to the tiny, scattered Bushmen bands still eking out their

---

[2] Van Der Post & Taylor, *Testament to the Bushman,* Viking, Middlesex, 1984, p.11.

traditional primitive way of life in the Kalahari Desert, will be affected by changes and events gathering like ominous storm clouds over the desert.

The winds of change are now blowing across Namibia. Whether they bode ill or good will be looked at in some detail in the rest of the book. Whatever their effect, it will be on all the groups of people in Namibia. They will bear the burden of the future of Namibia on their shoulders.

Let us examine Namibia in more detail.

4
The Economy of Namibia

The economy of Namibia is a mixed economy. Free enterprise exists along side of direct and indirect involvement by the state. It is by no means a socialist economy nor is it a totally free-wheeling capitalist one either.

The economy is complex ranging from subsistence farming to the highly advanced technology of a modern industrial society.

Does the economy have the potential to allow Namibia to become self-sufficient after independence? That depends upon who one talks to for there are arguments pro and con.

The official line of the Transitional Government of National Unity (TGNU) is an unqualified yes: "Despite limiting factors such as a lack of perennial rivers in the interior, erratic climatic conditions, the small domestic market and low literacy level of the population, SWA/Namibia has a strong potential to develop a productive and self-sufficient economy . . ."[1]

Even SWAPO has a positive view of Namibia's economic potential. Their view of the economy is within a Marxist concept which blames capitalism for any of Namibia's real or imagined economic problems on the shaky ground of its alleged "illegal occupation" and the capitalistic economic system of Namibia. "These rather unpromising realities do not imply that turning the economy around is impossible—indeed Namibia's potential for doing so at independence would appear better than that of a majority of sub-Saharan African economies today . . ."[2]

Other voices are more cautious. Leister, Esterhuysen and Malan in *Namibia/SWA Prospectus* a monogram published by the Africa Institute of

---

[1] *SWA/Namibia Today*, Section Liaison Services of the Department of Governmental Affairs, Windhoek, March, 1988, p.100.

[2] *Namibia: Perspectives for National Reconstruction and Development,* United Nations Institute for Namibia, Lusaka, 1986, p.58.

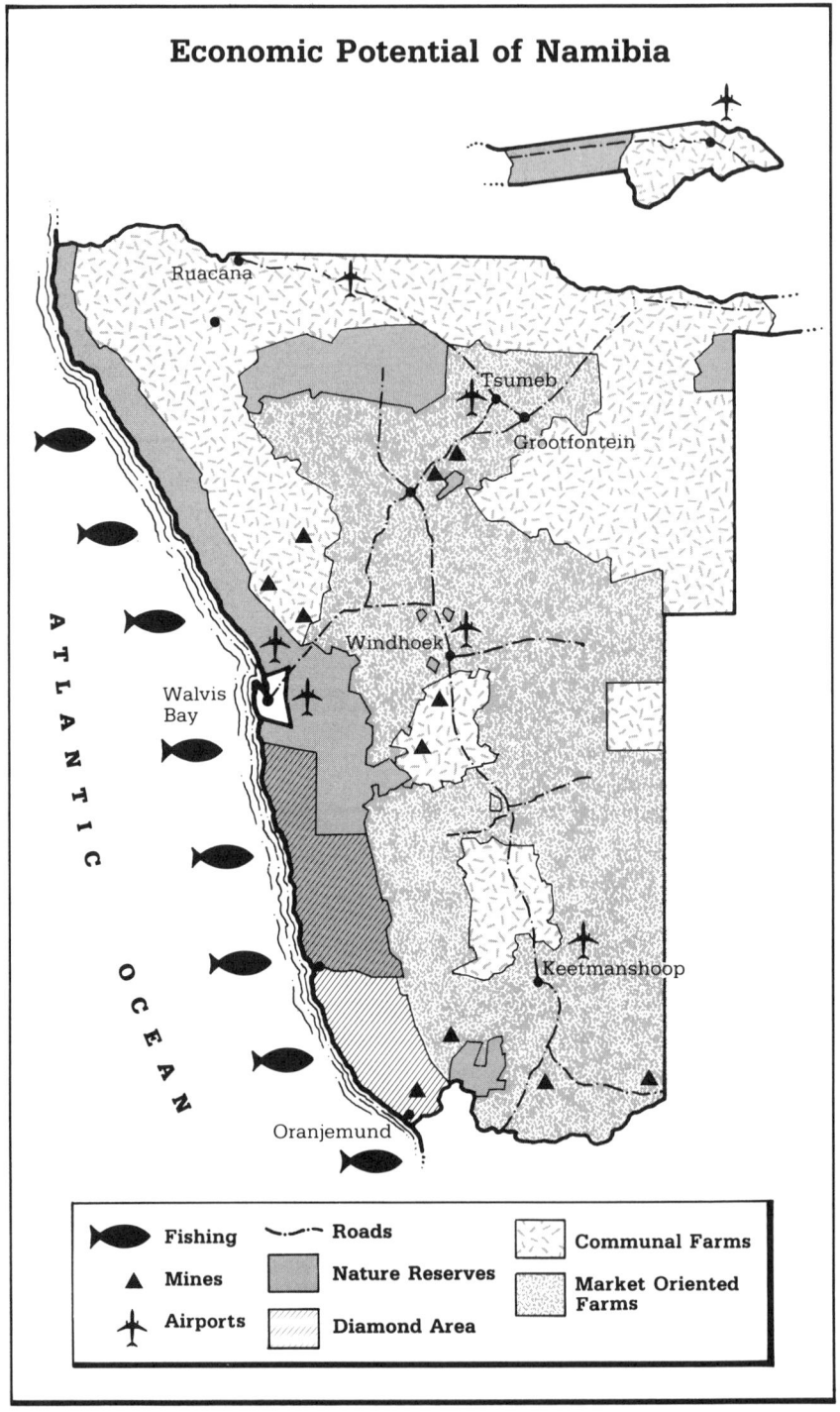

South Africa pointed out: "A realistic assessment of the economy's actual potentialities must take into account its inherent vulnerability and dependence on the outside world-features firmly rooted in ecological facts and beyond human control."[3]

What are these facts beyond human control?

The lack of water; the lack of a local source of fuel for power generation and transport; a small and scattered population; the vast distances between major population settlements—all these have the net effect of raising the costs of water, power, transport and communications well above those enabling them to compete with similar goods produced in South Africa.

". . . The prospects for building up major manufacturing and processing industries are correspondingly poor, and the country's economy is bound to remain susceptible to the vagaries associated with agricultural and other primary sector production . . ."[4]

Yet Namibia is already a comparatively prosperous country by African standards with a Gross Domestic Product (GDP) per person of about $1700 in 1980, well over twice the average for Africa as a whole. There is no starvation, nor any land shortage—there is still plenty of agricultural land to be occupied and cultivated. The heterogenous population provides a range of skills from sophisticated entrpreneurs and managers to an abundance of unskilled labor.

Namibia's economy is geared to the production of goods and services for the export market, especially agricultural and mining products. Most manufacturing goods, however, are imported into the domestic market.

Because about four-fifths of all goods produced are exported, the economy is particularly sensitive to cyclical fluctuations in international business activity, especially commodity prices. About half of all goods and services consumed are imported. The economy is thus sensitive to trends in the supplying countries.

Given Namibia's small population and limited capital resources, establishing internal manufacturing and processing industries may well be beyond its capabilities. This was pointed out in a study by the African-American Scholars Council: "Namibia cannot develop by turning inward, given the small size of the domestic market. It cannot anticipate much 'import-substituting' industrial development. Its industrial growth will have to come from processing raw materials for export. Its economy must necessarily be integrated into a wider regional or world economy. Moreover,

---

[3] *Namibia/SWA Prospectus,* Africa Institute of South Africa, Pretoria, 1980, p.35.
[4] *Ibid.*

Namibia will never fully enjoy fiscal and monetary independence. Not many countries enjoy this kind of independence and certainly not small ones."[5]

The productive capacity of the economy is based mainly on mining (primarily diamonds and uranium), agriculture (cattle and karakul sheep farming) and the fishing industry. These sections normally represent 40 percent of the gross domestic product and 90 percent of the total exports.

The relative importance of the different sectors of the Namibian economy can be measured in terms of the contributions which each made to the GDP in 1986:

Contributions as % of GDP 1986

Sector	Percentage
Agriculture & fishing	8.2
Mining & stone-quarrying	36.2
Manufacturing	4.4
Electricity & water	2.7
Construction	2.2
Wholesale & related trade, catering & accommodations	12.2
Finance, insurance, real estate & business services	6.1
Community, social & personal services	1.9
General government	17.0
Other producers	2.9
Total	100.0

Namibia is one of Africa's major mining countries—the fourth most important in Africa and the 17th in the world. The country contains the world's richest diamond fields and largest uranium mine, as well as producers of the space-age minerals germanium and lithium, silver, vanadium, tin, copper, lead, zinc and tantalum.

Thirty-three mines are active in Namibia producing thirty types of minerals.[6]

---

[5] Adams, Samuel C., "Zimbabwe and Namibia: Anticipations of economic and humanitarian needs," Southern Africa Project, African-American Scholars Council, Washington, DC, 1977, p.169.

[6] *What Mining Means to SWA/Namibia,* The Chamber of Mines of SWA/Namibia, Windhoek, 1986, p.2.

The great variety of minerals found is skewered, however, since the bulk of the exports depends upon diamonds and a few base metals. Uranium oxide from the Rossing mine east of Swakopmund is rapidly becoming Namibia's largest contributor of income in the mining sector.

Most of Namibia's mines are operated by subsidiaries of foreign multinational mining groups. The reasons for this are purely economic in spite of SWAPO's bombastic cries of "exploitation."

The diffuse nature of most known mineral deposits in Namibia as well as their geographical location in the country make heavy demands on modern technology. Thus only highly capitalized and technically proficient companies are able to carry out mining operations on the scale necessary to make the venture profitable. Since Namibia's own pool of capital and technological skills is inadequate, only outside concerns have been able to undertake this task.

Unlike the situation in most other mineral-rich countries, Namibia has mining laws designed to encourage companies to find and develop its resources. From necessity, they presently do not discriminate in any way against foreign-owned firms. This would most likely change if SWAPO took over control of the government. SWAPO's Marxist program calls for state control over such a major industry.

A prospecting license is not difficult to get although the mineral right is vested in the state, not in the land owner. A prospector has to pay the land owner for the use of his land in order to extract those minerals, however.

The government grants exclusive rights to prospect any defined area for any or all minerals, and the terms of the grant are usually flexible and not encumbered by much red tape. A prospecting title may easily be converted into a mining title if minerals are found.

The tax law encourages mineral development with low taxes levied on profits. Another feature making prospecting attractive for mining companies is the policy of allowing a new mine to recover all capital costs out of profits before starting to pay a mining tax.

Because the mining industry is almost totally export oriented, it is susceptible to fluctuating world mineral prices. The ups and downs of the world prices also effect the GDP of Namibia, as is to be expected.

The diamond mining industry is the second largest contributor to Namibia's mining income, but it is probably the best known of all Namibian enterprises.

The diamonds are found at the mouth of the Orange River, and deposited in alluvial sand and gravel that accumulate to the north of the river's mouth along the coast.

Consolidated Diamond Mines (Pty) Ltd. mines the diamonds by strip-mining methods, involving the stripping of vast quantities of overburden, about half of which is washed, treated and sifted to recover the diamonds.

To give an idea of the size of the task consider the following figures for 1982: 10 million cubic meters (18 million tons) of overburden were stripped; of that, 5.6 million cubic meters (10 million tons) were treated, sifted and inspected for diamonds. Out of all of that, 1 million carats (200 kilograms—a little over 500 pounds) of diamonds were recovered.

To accomplish that required the consumption of 134,000,000 KWH of electrical power; 7,800,000 cubic meters of fresh water; an earthmoving fleet of over 200 units, such as 35-ton dump trucks, bowl scrapers, bulldozers, front-end loaders and back-hoe excavators; a labor force of 1600 permanent and 3239 migrant laborers. No wonder diamonds are expensive!

The Rossing mine, located east of Swakopmund is the largest contributor to the country's income. The mine, which started operations in 1976, is the largest open pit uranium mine in the world.

Since 1979 an estimated average of 60 million tons of ore has been processed annually. The mine has a production capacity of 5000 tons of yellowcake uranium oxide concentrate per year.

The Tsumeb Corporation Ltd., which produces about 70 percent of the country's base minerals, is the third largest contributor to Namibia's mining income. More than 200 different minerals have been identified at Tsumeb. The minerals mined at Tsumeb include copper, silver, lead, gold, cadmium, arsenic trioxide and pyrite.

The Tsumeb-Grootfontein-Otavi mining region is the oldest in the country. Long before the arrival of the white man copper outcrops were being mined by the indigenous people. The Germans were quick to realize the area contained some of the richest deposits of base minerals in the world. They started to mine them in 1907.

Other mines owned by South Africa Iron and Steel Corporation subsidiaries include Rosh Pinah (zinc, lead and silver), Uis (tin) and Karibib (quartz, lithium and beryllium). Small quantities of lime, marble and semi-precious stones are also mined.

In 1987 the Anglo American Corporation announced that it would start mining gold near Karibib.

Minerals occurring in minor deposits in Namibia are beryllium, lithium, manganese, phosphates, semi-precious stones, tantalite and tungsten.

Although mining is the major contributor to Namibia's GDP, the effect of agriculture, the second most important sector of the economy, on the domestic economy is greater. It provides more work opportunities, profits are mostly kept in Namibia and it contributes more to regional development.

In 1986 government figures showed that 16 percent of the active labor force worked in the agricultural sector, while about 70 percent of the population was directly or indirectly dependent on agriculture for their living.[7]

Namibian agriculture consists of two sectors: a market-oriented sector with around 50,000 workers and a subsistence sector located in areas where communal land ownership is the prevailing custom. It is interesting to note that the communal land is located where there is an abundance of water. So it is the custom, not the lack of water, that keeps the productivity of the land low. Under both German and South African rule, commercial farmers were predominately settled in the arid, low-rainfall areas. The northern and north-eastern parts in the high-rainfall area and land with better crop carrying potential were reserved for the Owambo, Kavango and East Caprivi peoples, groups with the custom of communal land ownership.

The commercial farmers could only survive by adapting to the low potential of their area. Cattle and sheep were their answer although such activity requires considerable capital outlays in land, livestock, fencing and water provision.

A SWAPO government instituting a nation-wide system of communal land ownership would be a formula for disaster in Namibia, as it has proved throughout the world where Marxism has fastened its vicious grip upon a nation.

This fact is even more graphically illustrated by noting the commercial market-oriented sector produces about 80% of the total agricultural yield. Yet it is not located near abundant water sources like the communal farming areas.

Agriculture, however, is at the mercy of the elements in Namibia—the climatic conditions. Years of drought can have an adverse effect upon agricultural production in Namibia.

Agricultural exports are particularly sensitive to international marketing conditions. This, coupled with the relatively long distances between farming areas and markets with their increasing effect on costs, impose another severe constraint on Namibian agricultural development.

High standards of farm management, along with a commitment to produce and market high quality commodities, combined with access to the

---

[7] *Namibia, Facts and Figures 1988*, Internal Liaison, Department of Governmental Affairs, Windhoek, 1988.

South African market, have enabled the country's farming industry to prosper.

Namibia would enhance its agricultural sector by diversifying its production to lessen the current reliance on exports of livestock and karakul pelts. What it really needs is to lessen its current reliance on food imports.

Crop farming, at present, is primarily done in the Grootfontein-Otavi-Tsumeb triangle. The main product is maize, which is produced for the local market. It is not enough to satisfy the local domestic demand. For example, the maize harvest in 1986 was 18,500 tons which is well short of the total domestic demand of 45,000 tons per year. Namibia, as well as other countries in southern Africa, is dependent on South Africa for maize, sugar, fruit and vegetables.

A more free enterprise oriented ethos in some of the communal areas could help Namibia along the road to food self-suffiency. The north-eastern areas of the Caprivi and Kavango have great potential for crop farming. Changing the custom of communal ownership along with advanced agricultural technologies could work wonders in Namibia.

There is no doubt that Namibia stands to gain considerably once the people in the northern communal areas begin to develop the potential for commercial farming. Given their relatively easy access to the development of a 280-kilometer canal and pipeline system, over one million hectacres in Owamboland are suitable for irrigation farming. All that is needed is a change of attitude from their traditional way of farming. That is slowly starting to happen as a few farmers in Owamboland have begun to grow and market vegetables.

The fishing grounds off the coast of Namibia are considered to be among the richest in the world. The reason for this is the upwelling of the plankton-rich waters of the Benguela Current, which flows from the South Polar region northward along the western coast of Africa. The plankton provide food to a wide variety of marine life.

The backbone of the country's fishing industry is the catching and processing of pilchard, anchovy, mossbanker and mackerel and the substantial white fish resources further out to sea.

Due to the fact that Namibia's fishing waters extend for only 12 nautical miles into the sea and since the major portion of the white fish resources are found further out, over the past thirty years these resources have been heavily exploited. The biggest exploiters are the Soviet Union, Communist Poland and Spain. Their fishing activities bestow no benefits whatsoever on the people of Namibia.

Because Namibia is in a sort of a political limbo it can't take advantage of current international law to protect its fishing resources.

Both Namibia and South Africa have made several efforts to have the country's fishing zone extended to the internationally accepted 200 nautical miles recognized by the International Law of the Seas Treaty. These efforts have been resisted by the international community on the grounds that South Africa is no longer recognized, by the U.N. and most countries, as the legal overseer of Namibia and that Namibia is not a sovereign state—a real catch-22 situation.

Policing the overfishing of Namibian waters depends upon the voluntary cooperation within the framework of the International Commission for South East Atlantic Fisheries, which meets and sets quotas which the countries may catch with their fishing fleets.

In spite of this agreement, Namibian patrol vessels find ample evidence of foreign fishing fleets constantly violating the agreement. Most of the violators are from the Soviet Bloc countries.

The UN inaction further exposes that organization's customary hypocrisy on Namibia. The UN Council on Namibia, presuming itself to be the surrogate sovereign of Namibia, signed the Law of the Sea treaty which establishes the 200-mile exclusive economic zone. Yet the Council on Namibia hasn't uttered one word of protest over the inhabitants of Namibia being robbed of their fishing assets by the Soviet Union and its satellites. Instead they apparently spend their time eagerly compiling blacklists of Western companies who are supposed to be "illegally" exploiting Namibian resources.

The depressed nature of the fishing industry can be seen from the fact that of the eleven factories that processed fish at Walvis Bay and Luderitz in the sixties only seven are still in production today.

Another important aspect of the fishing industry in Namibia is the rock lobster market. The rock lobster industry, centered on Luderitz, is a labor intensive industry providing jobs for over 1,000 people.

Almost all of the catch is exported to Japan. The rest is marketed locally and to other countries as lobster tail.

In 1984 another fishing industry was started in Swakopmund. Oysters were cultivated and marketed in commercial quantities for the first time. So successful was the oyster farming venture that, three years later, a second farm was started in Luderitz. As a result oysters have now become common on the menus of Namibian restaurants.

The manufacturing sector contributes just under five percent of the

GDP. Although this percentage is dwarfed by mining and agriculture, the manufacturing sector provides work opportunities for ten percent of the labor force.

Almost two-thirds of the manufacturing firms are located in Windhoek, with some in the towns adjacent to mines, such as Oranjemund, Swakopmund and Tsumeb as well as towns such as Luderitz, Okahandja and Grootfontein.

The most important of the manufacturing efforts are focused on meat processing, supplying specialized equipment to the mining industry, assembly of goods from imported materials and the manufacture of metal products and construction materials.

Most of the industries are privately owned, some two-thirds of them individually owned. There are a number of German-family owned concerns while others are subsidiaries of South African groups.

The manufacturing industry has grown over the past ten years. Various types of industries have contributed to this from small home industries; labor intensive textile mills, to those involved in the production of leather and steel goods.

Several factors at present restrict manufacturing activity in Namibia, the more important ones being: a small and widely scattered market; narrow range of raw materials; high cost of the infrastructure (roads, water, railways, power, etc.); shortage of sufficient capital and lack of skilled labor and expertise in many fields. Add to this the political uncertainty surrounding the country's future and the inhibiting effect upon manufacturing in Namibia is understandable.

Namibia has a relatively active and well-developed network of wholesale and retail businesses. They supply commercial items wherever there is sufficient demand.

In addition to this normal trade sector, there is a developing flourishing informal trade industry that provides employment and learning business skills for many people. These are the small flea markets and other street market enterprises that have become a source of income for many people

This type of activity has spread to the primitive rural bush areas in the communal areas of Namibia. Here tiny shops have been catering to and supplying the needs of the local inhabitants. These so-called *cuca* shops and bush butcher shops in Owamboland are well-known examples of this kind of trade. The *cuca* shops fullfil most of the needs of the people and are often becoming the social center of the local community.

The value of this type of enterprise should not be ridiculed. It exposes that section of the population still involved in a subsistence economy to the workings of a market economy. It encourages the people to become entrepreneurs and engage in productive work. By following this new path many have raised their standard of living to a considerable degree. (There are now millionaires in Owamboland who started out with a small *cuca* shop and built their fortunes on that.)

A Marxist program would be a disaster for these emerging fledgling enterpises in Namibia.

Although commerce contributed almost twelve percent of Namibia's GDP in 1986, there are obstacles to its growth. They are due to the country's low population density and South Africa's overwhelming influence on the economy.

South Africa's contribution to Namibia's economy is considerable. It provides skilled manpower and technology, has funded the establishment and operation of critical infrastructual services such as railroads, tarred roads, road transport, power, water and telecommunications. South Africa has also spent large amounts of money developing education, health, research, finance, trade and public administration facilities in the country.

Because of this close relationship with South Africa, Namibia is a member of the Southern African Customs Union, which benefits Namibian goods exported to member states.

The country's membership in the Customs Union means that its industries are subject to unrestricted competition with those of other member states. However, Namibian goods enjoy tariff protection against goods from non-member countries. Excise revenue makes a substantial contribution to the revenues of Namibia. For example, in the 1988/89 budget, excise revenues exceeded the direct subsidy contribution of South Africa by R84 million (about $40 million). It contributed some twenty percent of the revenue raised by the Namibian government.[8]

Yet there are those in Namibia who claim that South Africa's leading role in the country's economy is detrimental to the development of commerce inside the country.[9]

This is not true claims Professor Wolfgang Thomas. He points out that whereas SWA/Namibia is dependent on its southern neighbor, its economic importance to South Africa is only marginal. He cautions against the false

---

[8] *Ibid.*

[9] *SWA/Namibia Today,* Section Liaison Services of the Department of Governmental Affairs, Windhoek, March, 1987, p.122.

issue of "the extent, nature and implications of both the potential and the alleged exploitation" of Namibia by South Africa.[10]

The fact of the size, importance and closeness of South Africa's economy can't be wished away by Namibians no matter how they may try to stress their independence from their neighbor.

It is clear as day, from experience elsewhere in the world, that economic development can be stimulated by closer economic cooperation between countries on a regional basis. Closer economic union creates greater opportunity for utilizing a country's resources than a policy of trying to maintain maximum self-sufficiency especially in a country having Namibia's economic problems. Namibia stands to gain more by striving for strengthened ties with the regional economies in southern Africa. Breaking economic ties with South Africa would be "suicidal for any future government of Namibia, including a SWAPO government . . ., said Professor Thomas.[11]

Namibia has tremendous potential for tourism. It is well endowed with tourist attractions, abundant sunshine, scenery, game parks, private game farms, flora, places of historical and archeological interests. More than a quarter of a million tourists visit the country each year.

Since the country has a well-developed infrastructure, which is a prerequisite for the tourist industry, the lack of hotels and accommodations is the major obstacle to an expansion of the tourist industry in Namibia.

Namibia faces the future with many economic pluses. These, however, are held hostage to political forces that will determine her future for good or ill. The resolution of the political will determine the direction the economy will go—towards prosperity or ruin.

---

[10] Thomas, Wolfgang H., *Economic Development in Namibia: Towards Acceptable Development Strategies for Independent Namibia*, Munchen, Kaiser, 1978, p.286.
[11]*Ibid.*, p.88.

5
Winds of Change

Four interrelated factors have affected the political situation in Namibia: international interference; SWAPO's war of terror; the desire of Namibians to be independent; and, South Africa's desire to be relieved of the financial burden caused by its administration of the territory.

Prior to World War II, the League of Nations had awarded the former German colony to the Union of South Africa as a class C mandate. Under the terms of such a mandate South Africa could administer the territory as an integral part of the Union.

Although the mandate gave South Africa the right to administer South West Africa under its own legislation, the Union Parliament passed an act in 1926 granting limited powers of self-government to the territory. In April 1926, a Legislative Assembly was set up in SWA consisting of twelve elected and six appointed members to assist the South African government in running the territory.

From the beginning there was a difference of opinion between the Union and the League on the interpretation of the South West African mandate. The Union government saw no real differences between the mandate and outright annexation to the Union as a fifth province and granted it representation in the Union Parliament.

The League disagreed with this view, but the outbreak of World War II put the question aside.

After the War the controversy stirred anew between the Union and the new-fledged United Nations, the successor to the now defunct League of Nations.

The United Nation's Charter made no provisions for continuing the mandate system under the supervision of the new world body. However, the new organization did create a trusteeship system which could also apply to mandated territories. These territories would be placed under UN control, but only with the explicit consent and agreement of the mandate holders.

South Africa, from the beginning, was cool to the idea.

The United Nations felt that South West Africa should become a trustee territory of the United Nations, coming under the supervision of the UN Trusteeship Council.

South Africa rejected that view on the grounds that the mandate over South West Africa had expired with the League of Nations and South Africa did not recognize the UN as the League's legal successor.

In 1946, South West Africa's legislative assembly requested the South African government to incorporate the territory into South Africa. South Africa formally requested UN approval for this move but its application was rejected. The UN, instead, insisted that SWA now be placed under the UN trusteeship system.

South Africa replied that it would not incorporate SWA, but neither would it place the territory under UN control.

The 1948 elections in South Africa brought to power the Nationalist Party. It began to implement its policy of apartheid in both South Africa and South West Africa.

The National Party also took a hard line view towards the United Nations in regard to South West Africa. They totally rejected any supervisory power the UN claimed it had over SWA. Furthermore, to emphasize the point, South Africa refused to even submit any further reports to it or pass on petitions from the inhabitants of the territory, as they were required to do under the terms of the old League mandate.

The UN in 1949 turned to the International Court of Justice for an advisory opinion on the status of South West Africa. The court gave little comfort to the UN as it ruled unanimously that South Africa was under no obligation to enter into a trusteeship agreement with the United Nations. However, the court did rule that South Africa could not alter the status of the territory unilaterally. This meant that South Africa couldn't grant the territory independence. South Africa rejected the opinion and the impasse continued.

It continued through the fifties with South Africa ignoring the appeals of the UN and continued to administer the territory according to the terms of the 1920 mandate.

During this impasse, the South African government implemented its apartheid policies in South West Africa. Politically, it envisioned that the indigenous ethnic groups in South West Africa would be guided towards South African-style self governing homelands. It was as a result of an incident relating to the implementation of apartheid that the UN again went before the International Court at the Hague.

Rioting had broken out in Windhoek in 1959 when blacks were forcibly removed to their new township of Katatura on the outskirts of the city. Several blacks lost their lives in the rioting and outrage flared in several black African states. These states began flexing their new-found political muscle in the UN and, at their urging, the UN began legal proceedings against South Africa in the World Court.

This time the UN tried a new tack. The plaintiffs used were Ethiopia and Liberia. Why these two? They were the only independent African states in the United Nations that had been members of the old League of Nations.

Their official charge was that South Africa was breaching its obligation under the mandate by implementing apartheid, because the mandate required South Africa to promote the material and moral well-being of the inhabitants of the country.

Furthermore, the UN declared that the findings of the court would not be advisory, but would be binding and would be enforced by the Security Council of the United Nations.

The trial began on November 4, 1960, in the Hague. Almost six years later, on July 18, 1966, the Court dismissed the Ethiopian and Liberian suit on the grounds the countries were not competent to bring charges against South Africa.

A frustrated United Nations reacted by voting to end South Africa's mandate.

Mounting opposition to South Africa's homeland policies in South West Africa increased the hostility of the United Nations. Finally, on August 12, 1969, the Security Council asked member states not to recognize the authority of the South African government over Namibia, as the UN had renamed the country in 1966.

A 1971 ruling by the International Court of Justice that South Africa end its "illegal" administration of the country gave added force to the UN line of attack.

In 1972, the UN Security Council took a new direction toward solving the UN-South Africa impasse when it directed UN Secretary General Dr. Kurt Waldheim "to initiate contacts with all the parties concerned to establish conditions under which the inhabitants of Namibia could exercise their right to self-determination and independence."[1]

During the visits of Dr. Waldheim to South Africa during 1972, the government gave him assurances that the South African policy for Namibia

---

[1] United Nations Security Council, Resolution 309, 1972.

was to prepare them for, and lead them to, independence and self-determination. The next year South African Prime Minister John Vorster said the inhabitants of South West Africa/Namibia should themselves decide on the political future of their country.

Following up on Vorster's statement, the South West African territorial Legislative Assembly passed a resolution in August 1974 calling for constitutional talks among representatives of the various ethnic groups to decide upon the future of an independent South West Africa/Namibia.

This conference took place in the fall of 1975 just prior to the start of the Angolan Civil War to the north. Representatives of all eleven ethnic groups convened on September 1, 1975, in Windhoek in the Turnhalle (an old gymnasium relic from the days of the German colonial occupation that had been remodeled as the conference center for the historic meeting) to deliberate on independence for the country.

This conference, known as the Turnhalle Constitutional Conference, marked the start by the citizens of SWA/Namibia on the course of deciding their own future.

On August 19, 1976, the Conference produced a Declaration of Intent. This envisioned a territory-wide new constitution and set a target date for independence—December 31, 1978. South Africa accepted this date without hesitation.

On March 18, 1977, the Conference reached a consensus on the principles of an interim government. On April 1st they petitioned the South African government for the establishment of an interim government which would lead SWA/Namibia to independence on the basis of a constitution to be drawn up by the representatives of the citizens of the territory.

However, while all this internal activity had been going on, the United Nations had not been idle. In fact they stuck their noses deeper into the affairs of the country. The Security Council, on January 30, 1976, had adopted a measure, Security Council Resolution 385, which spelled out a number of demands on South Africa regarding SWA/Namibia. It also set forth certain conditions for independence for the territory. These included:
- an early exercise by all the inhabitants of SWA/Namibia of their right to self-determination through a fully democratic process;
- UN supervision of this process;
- the peaceful participation of all political parties, including SWAPO;
- termination of South Africa's administration of SWA/Namibia;
- release of political prisoners;
- the return to Namibia of exiles; and
- removal of racially discriminatory laws and practices.

Meanwhile five Western powers—Canada, France, West Germany, Great Britain and the United States—at the time also members of the Security Council (Great Britain, France and the United States are permanent members), sent a message to South Africa urging a settlement of the SWA/Namibia question. Stressing that "international negotiations under the UN auspices continue to be the best way to bring the parties to an agreement on how the process to independence should proceed," the Five began a series of contacts with South Africa.

This arrangement offered potential advantages. Since the Five were members of the Security Council, any agreement they made with South Africa could carry a lot of weight, or even be binding (with the exception of the Soviet Union's veto) on the rest of the Security Council. By acting as middlemen or honest power brokers between the world organization and South Africa, they created a promising diplomatic climate. It was based on the recognition of the advantages for all parties of the seal of international approval on any proposed settlement they might achieve.

As middlemen, the Five could also get in touch with other interested parties that for one reason or another would not have any contact with South Africa. The Five maintained that their sole interest was to find common ground on which a solid agreement could be reached.

Reality turned out to be a different kettle of fish. It is worth going into in some detail, because it exposes the gross hypocrisy of the United Nations in their dealings with South Africa over the question of Namibian independence. As the facts show, it was the United Nations, not the Republic of South Africa, that torpedoed the Namibian independence talks. They were aided in this unsavory act by the Western Five who, instead of being honest power brokers, were actually partners in crime with the United Nations. The whole sordid affair was ably assisted by the media which used the occasion to indulge in what has become a favorite media sport—bash South Africa.

Although the Western Five attempted to create a climate of cooperation and negotiation in their dealings with South Africa over the future of Namibia, there was a big obstacle they couldn't overcome or explain away. The United Nations, of which the Five were important members, had an overwhelmingly biased close identification with SWAPO.

South Africa was apprehensive of this bias towards SWAPO and, as events transpired, their fears were justified.

In 1973, the UN General Assembly had declared SWAPO the "authentic representative of the people of Namibia."[2] That wasn't all, for in the same

---

[2] Leistner, E., Esterhuyien, P., & Malan, T. *Namibia/SWA Prospectus,* Africa Institute of South Africa, Pretoria, 1980, p.11.

resolution the General Assembly supported SWAPO "in their struggle, by all means, including armed struggle, to achieve self-determination, freedom and national independence."[3]

The General Assembly also invited SWAPO to participate as an observer, in the sessions and activities of the General Assembly and in all conferences held under the auspices of the General Assembly. In essence, a terrorist group, SWAPO, was being treated like a full-fledged member of the General Assembly, and by inference of the United Nations, except that it couldn't vote in the organization's proceedings.

Not only did the UN extend observer status to SWAPO, they also helped finance their activities in the UN. Since 1974 the General Assembly has used funds from the regular UN budget to assist SWAPO in financing its offices in New York.

In addition, the UN gave SWAPO $3,351,000 under the UN's World Food Program during the two-year period 1977-79.

SWAPO has also benefited from the annual UN budget of an allocation to the Trust Fund for Namibia (amounting to $500,000 for 1980).[4]

SWAPO, along with the other southern African terrorist groups the African National Congress (ANC) and the Pan African Congress (PAC), benefits from annual grants made by UNESCO and UNDP (United Nations Development Program). An indication of the scope of this aid is that UNESCO allocated $465,000 to terrorist groups in 1979-80 while the UNDP gave a whopping $15,200,000 in 1978 alone.

The UN, through various organs, allocated at least $40 million in aid to SWAPO between 1977-81. This was during the time when the Western Five was touting "international negotiations under U.N. auspices" as being the best way to bring about a SWA/Namibian settlement. The U.S., one of the Five, with taxpayers dollars, has contributed about thirty percent of this total. SWAPO has used these funds to feed, clothe, educate and train its terrorists. UN funds have also been used by SWAPO to train its cadres as government functionaries for the future, if and when SWAPO "liberates" Namibia.

UN Resolution 34/92F (1979), guarantees free publicity to SWAPO provided by the UN Department of Public Information of the Secretariat "to intensify the wide-spread and continuous dissemination of information on the struggle for liberation being waged by the people of Namibia, guided by the liberation movement, the SWAPO."[5]

[3] *Ibid.*

[4] *Ibid.*

[5] "How the U.N. Aids Marxist Guerrilla Groups," The Heritage Foundation, Washington, DC, April 8, 1982, p.11.

The representatives of other political groupings in Namibia are not only denied such UN aid, but have great difficulty in even gaining access to the Secretary General's office.

Unlike Caesar's wife, the UN has been far from being above reproach in its dealings on the Namibian question. Events have revealed just how sleazy a tramp the UN really was.

Negotiations continued between the Western Five and the South African government. The clock was running on the South African envisioned date for implementing independence in Namibia. A little over eighteen months remained for that date when a series of talks were held in early June 1977 at Cape Town.

In the interests of adhering to the independence timetable and the target date, December 31, 1978, South Africa and the Five agreed to a possible scenario to reach that goal.

The South Africans and the Western Five proposed the following:
1. Territory-wide elections by secret ballot on the basis of universal adult suffrage; the purpose of the election to elect:
2. A constituent assembly to draft a constitution for an independent SWA/Namibia;
3. All persons and political parties would be allowed to peaceably take part in the election process;
4. Freedom of speech, press, assembly and the territorial integrity of SWA/Namibia would be respected.

On the basis of this understanding South Africa, after consulting with the Turnhalle Assembly in Namibia, decided against submitting the Turnhalle constitutional draft to the South African Parliament.

The problem to solve, in view of this action, was what or who would govern Namibia in this interim period?

South Africa proposed an administrative authority of seventeen members, representing the eleven ethnic groups in Namibia selected on the basis of the population of each group.

The Western Five was opposed to the idea of basing the selection upon ethnic considerations.

A round-robin discussion among the Western Five, South Africa and representatives of the Turnhalle Assembly led to the agreement to appoint a single Administrator General by South Africa. He would be the interim authority in Namibia until elections could be held and a new government installed on the basis of the Namibian constitution adopted by the elected Constituent Assembly.

At this point it is important to reiterate these salient facts: (1) South

Africa, the elected representatives of the Turnhalle Assembly in Namibia, and the Western Five members of the UN Security Council agreed to a process leading to an independent Namibia by December 31, 1978; (2) the free elections would be for an elected assembly which would draw up a constitution for an independent Namibia; and, (3) until the new government in Namibia took over as per their new constitution, an Administrator General, appointed by South Africa, was to be the central iterim administrative authority. A Special Representative of the Secretary General of the UN would also be installed in Namibia as soon as possible after the appointment of the Administrator General to coordinate the transition process with the Administrator General. Representatives of the primary interested parties—the inhabitants of Namibia, the South Africans and the United Nations—agreed to all these key points.

Keep these points in mind because they have been either ignored or buried by an avalanche of self-serving political rhetoric ever since.

South Africa had demonstrated its good faith by the fact that, within two months of the start of negotiations, it had agreed to a range of requirements that the Western Five had insisted upon for achieving independence for Namibia.

Not only that, but South Africa insisted upon a timetable of events that would result in Namibian indpendance by the 31st of December 1978.

Now the UN duplicity began in earnest, as it started dragging its feet by making new demands upon South Africa, largely concerning the security of Namibia during the transition period to independence.

These demands had all the earmarks of a typical nit-picking stalling campaign: haggling over the number, disposition, composition and function of South African and UN forces.

All this was eating up precious time and caused a delay of nine months before the Five were ready to present their Proposal to all concerned.

Behind all the UN's foot-dragging was the fact that SWAPO didn't favor the Western Five's diplomatic endeavors. SWAPO didn't like the idea of South Africa maintaining security and law and order during the election process in Namibia. Their presence would put a serious dent in SWAPO's terror and intimidation tactics during the election campaign.

SWAPO's proposed solution was to remove South Africa from the security duty during the process and turn security over to a United Nations military force.

How did the UN react to this SWAPO proposal? The UN General Assembly endorsed it as their own. After all, since the UN had embraced

SWAPO to its bosom, one would have been surprised if the UN would have done otherwise.

Nevertheless, such things take time and while SWAPO and the UN General Assembly were working to incorporate SWAPO's idea into the UN's proposal, time was rapidly slipping by.

This haggling and procrastination, resulting from SWAPO and UN initiated action, brought a crisis to the Five's proposal for holding the elections in Namibia in time to grant independence by December 31, 1978.

On March 30, 1978, the Western Five presented their final, definitive and non-negotiable terms to the parties: SWAPO, South Africa and the representatives of the Turnhalle Assembly.

Without waiting for a reply, the Five sent a letter on April 10, 1978, to the Security Council requesting that their proposal be circulated as a document of the UN Security Council.

This new proposal did not have the prior agreement of any of the parties —SWAPO, South Africa or the representatives of the Turnhalle Assembly. It was an arrogant unilateral action by the Western Five.

Nevertheless in spite of serious reservations, the South African government informed the Five that they would accept their proposals.

Again stressing the security aspects inside Namibia, South African Prime Minister John Vorster said, "My government in coming to its decision has also been influenced decisively by the provision that there should be a complete cessation of hostilities (including, *inter alia*, minelaying, killings, abductions, etc.) before any reductions in the South African Forces takes place, that primary responsibility for maintaining law and order during the transitional period shall rest with the existing police forces and that the issue of Walvis Bay is not included in the proposals . . . ."[6]

The day before the Ninth Special Session of the UN General Assembly had met to discuss SWA/Namibia. After their usual bombastic rhetorical excesses, the Assembly passed a pro-SWAPO resolution, in spite of South Africa's acceptance of the Western Proposal. In point of fact, SWAPO had not responded to the West's Proposal by May 4, 1978, the date of the General Assembly's action.

The General Assembly Resolution S9/2 blasted South Africa for being uncooperative while praising SWAPO for their "far-reaching and substantive concessions," which have yet to be revealed, even to this day. To make sure that no one could misunderstand where their sentiments lay, the resolution

---

[6] Text of Reply Concerning SWA Conveyed to the Ambassadors of the Five Western Powers in South Africa by the Foreign Minister, The Hon. R.F. Botha, on April 25, 1978.

referred to all the other political parties in Namibia as "puppets and quislings" of South Africa.

Is it any wonder that both South Africa and those opposed to SWAPO inside Namibia lacked confidence in the UN's impartiality?

While all this diplomatic activity was going on, SWAPO was increasing its terror activity inside Namibia. From its bases in now friendly communist Angola, SWAPO terrorists were launching more frequent and larger terror raids into the country.

On May 4, 1978, the SADF launched retaliatory raids on two SWAPO bases in Angola. South Africa was routinely condemned by the Security Council, but no mention was made of the SWAPO terrorist actions that had precipitated the South African response.

A month later, after getting its nose bloodied by the South African retaliatory strike, SWAPO gave its belated response to the Western Five's proposal. On June 12, 1978, SWAPO said the proposal should be submitted to the Security Council. The Western Five construed this belated grudging statement by SWAPO as an acceptance.

However, by this time the clock had been ticking away relentlessly and it was no longer possible to implement the Proposal in time to achieve Namibian independence on the agreed upon date, December 31, 1978.

Nevertheless, the United Nations carried on with their hypocrisy. On July 21, 1978, the UN Security Council adopted Resolution S/431, 1978 which appointed Mr.Martti Ahtisaari of Finland to be the UN Secretary General's Special Representative for Namibia. The Special Representative was to cooperate with the Administrator General to insure that the terms of the accord were carried out during Namibia's transition period. This meant in effect that the Administrator General had better do what the UN wanted. However, as another example of the UN's delaying tactics, this action by the world body in appointing the Special Representative came some fourteen months after it had been agreed upon by the Western Five and South Africa at a previous 1977 meeting in Cape Town.

This wasn't the only duplicitous aspect of the UN's action that day. The Security Council immediately adopted another resolution, S/432 (1978), on Walvis Bay which: (1) "Declares that the territorial integrity and unity of Namibia must be assured by the reintegration of Walvis Bay within its territory;" (2) "Decides to lend its full support to the initiatives of steps necessary to insure early reintegration of Walvis Bay into Namibia."

This new development was sure to elicit a strong response from South Africa and further muddy the waters over the proposed Namibian settlement.

Winds of Change 51

The South African government quickly responded to the Security Council resolution. Citing international law and the fact that the Organization of African Unity, in 1969, had stressed that the present boundaries of existing states in southern Africa will continue to be the same in the future, the South African Foreign Minister pointed out that the UN General Assembly had also endorsed the OAU's action in Resolution 2505 (XXIV) of November 20, 1969.

Foreign Minister Botha stressed to the UN that Walvis Bay was just as much a part of South Africa as Alaska was a part of the United States. He also pointed out that the final proposal agreed to between the Western Five and South Africa had made no reference at all to Walvis Bay: ". . . while on 25 April 1978 South Africa accepted the Proposal on South West Africa in its final and definitive form, we categorically reject the resolution on Walvis Bay . . . It clearly seeks to prejudge the whole issue. It never formed part of the negotiations leading to South Africa's acceptance of the Proposal . . . ."[7]

He added: "I want to be very frank with the Council. We were shocked by reports that the five Western powers were going to support a resolution of the nature now before the Council. We were shocked and dismayed. My Government concluded that support for such a resolution would raise grave doubts as to the spirit and manner in which the Five would stand behind their own Proposal. We feared that it would so destroy confidence as to make it impossible to cooperate in the implementation of the Proposal. The South African government had at the time come to the conclusion that, were the Five to vote unreservedly for such a resolution, South Africa could no longer cooperate in the implementation of the proposal."[8]

Shortly after this incident, the newly-appointed Special Representative visited Namibia for a fifteen-day visit (August 6-22, 1978). Upon his return to New York, he submitted his recommendations to the Secretary General on the implementation of the Western Five's Proposal.

The Secretary General circulated his report (document S/12827 of August 29, 1978) to the UN membership and informed them it was to form the basis of further Security Council action on the Namibian settlement.

Once again the UN pulled another trick from their overflowing bag with respect to their conduct in the negotiation process. The Security Council now decided that the United Nations contingent of military and police was not large enough and unilaterally increased it. To add insult to injury, they also

[7] SA Foreign Minister's Statement to UNSC, July 27, 1978 (document S/PV2082), quoted in *African Insight*, p.16.
[8] *Ibid.*

came up with a novel idea of granting their police force executive, as well as, normal police powers. There had been no consultation between the UN's Special Representative and the Administrator General, which had been agreed to as a normal necessity as per the terms of the Proposal.

This decision was totally unacceptable to South Africa. Foreign Minister Botha dispatched a letter to the UN Secretary General setting out the South African response. The South African government also circulated this letter to the members of the Security Council (document S/12836 of 6 September 1978). The South African letter deserves looking into at some length, as it graphically exposes the deceitful actions of the United Nations.

This letter stated that, "During our discussions with the Five on this very issue of troop numbers, the South African Government intimated that it was concerned about the danger of insufficient protection of the northern border areas once a reduction of South African troops had started. The Five repeatedly disagreed with our assessment, indicating that once a comprehensive and visible peace had been established there could be no justification for a substantial number of South African troops being stationed in the area . . . .

"The Five persisted in claiming that an atmosphere of peace would be brought into being once a cessation of hostilities took place. They said our concerns were not justified . . . . They urged us to accept that there would be peace, visible peace. If peace were not obtained and did not prevail and last, the implementation of the Proposal would be frustrated and woulds become impossible to achieve . . . . We stressed that in that event, South Africa would be entitled to increase its troop strength to levels sufficient to meet any increase in violence.

". . . Now we find ourselves in the incredible situation where we are told that 7,500 United Nations troops would be needed to undertake tasks which under conditions of total peace we were previously assured could be administered by a few hundred . . . .

"Either peace is to be established or not. If it is established, there is no need for large numbers of United Nations troops. If it is not established, then it remains the responsibility of the South African security forces to insure safety and security . . . ."[9]

The Foreign Minister's letter also pointed out that the parties had been assured that United Nations' precedents would be followed in all respects during the transition period in Namibia. What was the past history of UN participation in prior plebiscites granting independence to former colonies and/or mandated territories?

[9] *Namibia/SWA Prospectus, op. cit.,* pp.16-17.

Winds of Change 53

"In 1956, a team of 23 [UN observers—ed.] was sufficient to monitor a plebiscite in British Togoland in which 159,080 voters participated. 575,267 voted in the 1961 plebiscite in the British Cameroons which was monitored by 34 United Nations observers, despite the difficult terrain and poor communications in the Territory. . . .

"It should be recalled that the terms of reference of most United Nations plebiscite teams were comprehensive and included responsibility for observing and reporting on polling arrangements, voting, counting of ballots and declaration of results. The plebiscites were conducted in territories where communications were often less adequate than in South West Africa."[10]

Indeed, one can legitimately question the UN's reasoning for needing so many troops. But the answer isn't hard to figure out.

SWAPO had been named by the UN as "the sole authentic representative of the Namibian people."[11] SWAPO had also been the beneficiary of generous UN funding. In fact, SWAPO had been treated as if it were a United Nations member. SWAPO's effectiveness in Namibia at this stage, however, depended solely on the success of its coercion and intimidation tactics. But since the vast majority of the UN members are one-party states where coercion and intimidation are the rule, this wouldn't particularly worry them. (They have seldom expressed any concern over the activities of any of the left-wing terrorist groups such as the PLO, IRA, ANC, the Red Guards, or others.)

It would be a terrible blow to the UN's pride and its investment if its favored group, SWAPO were rejected by the voters of Namibia.

There is an unwritten rule of politics in the Third World—he who has the force gets the votes. The massing of a 7,500 man UN force in Namibia, while the UN still recognized SWAPO as its sole Namibian representatives, would send a not so subtle message to all Namibians—SWAPO is our horse.

This force could also be expected to turn a blind eye to SWAPO intimidation tactics to "persuade" their fellow Owambos to cast their vote for SWAPO. It would be the same shameful situation that the British would be party to in the 1980 Zimbabwean elections.

The reality of politics in Namibia, with its numerous political parties, means who wins Owamboland wins the election.

The psychological effect of a supportive UN force plus SWAPO intimidation would insure a SWAPO victory.

[10] *Ibid.*, p.17.
[11] UN Resolution 31/146, para. 2.

This was the underlying reason for the UN force in Namibia. It was its reason in 1978, and it is still the same reason eleven years later. It was not to protect the people, in a time of absolute peace, to use the Western Five's term.

Further evidence to support this contention is also found in the UN Secretary General's second report of February 26, 1979, on the implementation of the Western Proposal. It stated in paragraph eleven: "Any SWAPO armed forces in Namibia at the time of the cease-fire will likewise be restricted to base at designated locations inside Namibia to be specified by the Special Representative . . . ."[12] In essence, the Secretary General's report amounted to giving SWAPO the advantage of establishing bases inside Namibia, something that it had been unable to achieve by military means.

The plot thickens further when one realizes that during the same period of time SWAPO had been telling the people in Owamboland that it would be assisted by the UN to introduce its "troops" in SWA/Namibia.[13]

The South African Foreign Minister also pointed out that "there is no provision for a United Nation police contingent."[14] On the contrary, the Proposal is quite clear in its definition of the responsibility of the police function of maintaining law and order. It rests primarily with the existing police forces. Furthermore, special provision is incorporated in the Five's Proposal for United Nations personnel to accompany the police, when appropriate, in the performance of their duties.

To put the icing on the cake, the United Nations would not monitor SWAPO bases in Angola and Zambia. Of course the UN would at all times monitor the bases inside Namibia where the South African security forces would be restricted as per the terms of the settlement. This was a clear blatant example of UN bias in favor of SWAPO.

All in all, this was a totally new ingredient added to the proposal and the South African government rejected it out of hand.

The Western Five realized that perhaps they had gone a bit too far and that their seventeen-month effort was in danger of collapsing on their heads. They resumed their contact with the South African government to try and patch up their differences.

South Africa replied on the 20th of September 1978, rightfully blaming the Five for all the trouble and concluded that the latest Secretary General's

---

[12] *Namibia/SWA Prospectus, op. cit.*, p.24.

[13] *Ibid.*

[14] *Namibia/SWA Prospectus, op. cit.*, p18.

Winds of Change   55

report breached the agreement between the South African government and the Five.

South Africa also pointed out that it was becoming more obvious every day that the UN was determined to impose its view on South Africa. Thus, South Africa considered herself released from the agreement she had earlier concluded with the Five.

On the same day both the South African government and the Administrator General in Windhoek announced that elections would be held in Namibia for the people to elect their own representatives. The elections were scheduled during the period of December 4 to 8, 1978.

While all this diplomatic double-dealing had been going on, voters were being registered in preparation for the elections envisioned by all parties under the Five's proposal. During the period from June 26, 1978, when the registration period started until October 20, 1978, the end of the registration period, some ninety-one percent of the eligible voters had been registered. The stage was set for the up-coming elections.

The UN's answer was to push ahead and on September 29, 1978, it passed Security Council Resolution 435, which encompassed the Secretary General's report and made no mention of the South African objections. The UN was determined to have its way whether South Africa or the people of Namibia liked it or not.

The resolution also called on South Africa to cooperate with the UN and declared null and void all unilateral measures in relation to the electoral process or transfer of power taken by, as the UN now termed it, the "illegal administration in Namibia."

By this action the UN showed its true colors as it had been their group of Five which had suggested the type of interim administration in Namibia. By passing Resolution 435 they, in fact, broke their own earlier agreement—but then logic or integrity have seldom been strong points in the unreal world of the United Nations.

The UN action shouldn't surprise many. By the 1970's the UN seemed to exist in a world of its own making. As described by the historian Paul Johnson, it "was a corrupt and demoralized body, and its ill-considered interventions were more inclined to promote violence than to prevent it."[15]

The majority of the charter members of the UN had been democracies, by 1975 the membership had increased some two and a half times, with all but twenty-five being totalitarian one-party dictatorships.

[15] Johnson, *op. cit.*, p.689.

To grasp the depths of corruption and cynicism the UN had fallen to, consider the case of Uganda's brutal cannibal dictator Idi Amin. In 1975, Amin was the chairman of the OAU, and on October 1, 1975 he made a rabid speech to the UN General Assembly. He denounced the "Zionist-US" conspiracy and called not only for the expulsion of Israel but for its "extinction" (i.e.-genocide). The assembly gave him a standing ovation when he arrived, applauded him throughout, and again rose to its feet when he left.[16] To add an odious finish to this sorry spectacle, the Secretary General of the UN, who took such a devious and sanctimonious attitude towards South Africa over the Namibian question, gave a public dinner in Amin's honor the day after his rabid speech.[17]

Is it any wonder that South Africa and the people of Namibia didn't trust the UN?

Although diplomatic efforts continued between South Africa and the Western Five representing the UN, the damage had been done. South Africa, continuing to insist that she was willing to grant independence to SWA/Namibia, had lost all confidence in the UN as a vehicle for granting the territory its independence.

Nevertheless, South Africa carried on with the electoral process and held the nationwide elections even though the UN had condemned them in advance as being null and void.

The elections were duly held from December 4 to 8, on the basis of one man one vote to choose fifty members of a Constituent Assembly.

SWAPO not only did not recognize the election but tried to wreck it by a campaign of sabotage, terror and intimidation. Their efforts went for naught as 412,448 of the 443,441 registered eligible voters voted in the election.

The almost seventy-eight percent turnout of the registered voters, clearly showed the inhabitants of Namibia were anxious to get on with the task of working out their own future. The people of Namibia had a tough road to follow as the rest of the world, personified by the United Nations, seemed determined to prevent them from so doing. This was not one of the United Nations' finest moments.

---

[16] Johnson, *op. cit.*, p.536.
[17] *Ibid.*

6
SWAPO: A Marxist-Leninist Organization

The South West Africa People's Organization (SWAPO) evolved out of an organization founded in Cape Town in 1957 by a former railway policeman, Herman Toivo. It was called the Owamboland People's Congress (OPC) and underwent several metamorphosis—the Owamboland People's Organization (OPO) and then, finally, the South West Africa People's Organization. The main reason for the various name changes was twofold: to disguise the organization's tribal base of support in dealing with overseas supporters, and to try and attract members from other ethnic groups in Namibia.

In 1959, protests broke out in the capital of Windhoek over the forced removal of blacks into the new township of Katutura located northwest of the city. The protests eventually escalated into rioting and violence.

Leaders of the protests, among them Sam Nujoma, the future leader of SWAPO, called for a city-wide boycott of municipal services. During the boycott, while the police were arresting some pickets, the crowds around the scene turned ugly and menacing. Unfortunately, the police panicked and the scene erupted into violence. The police, later claiming they feared for their lives, fired into the crowd, killing eleven and wounding fifty-four.

Hoping to prevent an ugly situation from escalating any further, the authorities ordered the protest leaders back to their homes. Instead, Nujoma chose exile. Crossing the border into Botswana, he made his way to Tanzania. There he was welcomed with open arms by Julius Nyerere, the socialist leader of Tanzania.

On April 9, 1960, the name Owamboland People's Organization passed into history and the movement became SWAPO.

Among those who helped Toivo found the original OPC were names that would reappear in Namibia's turbulent political history—Andreas

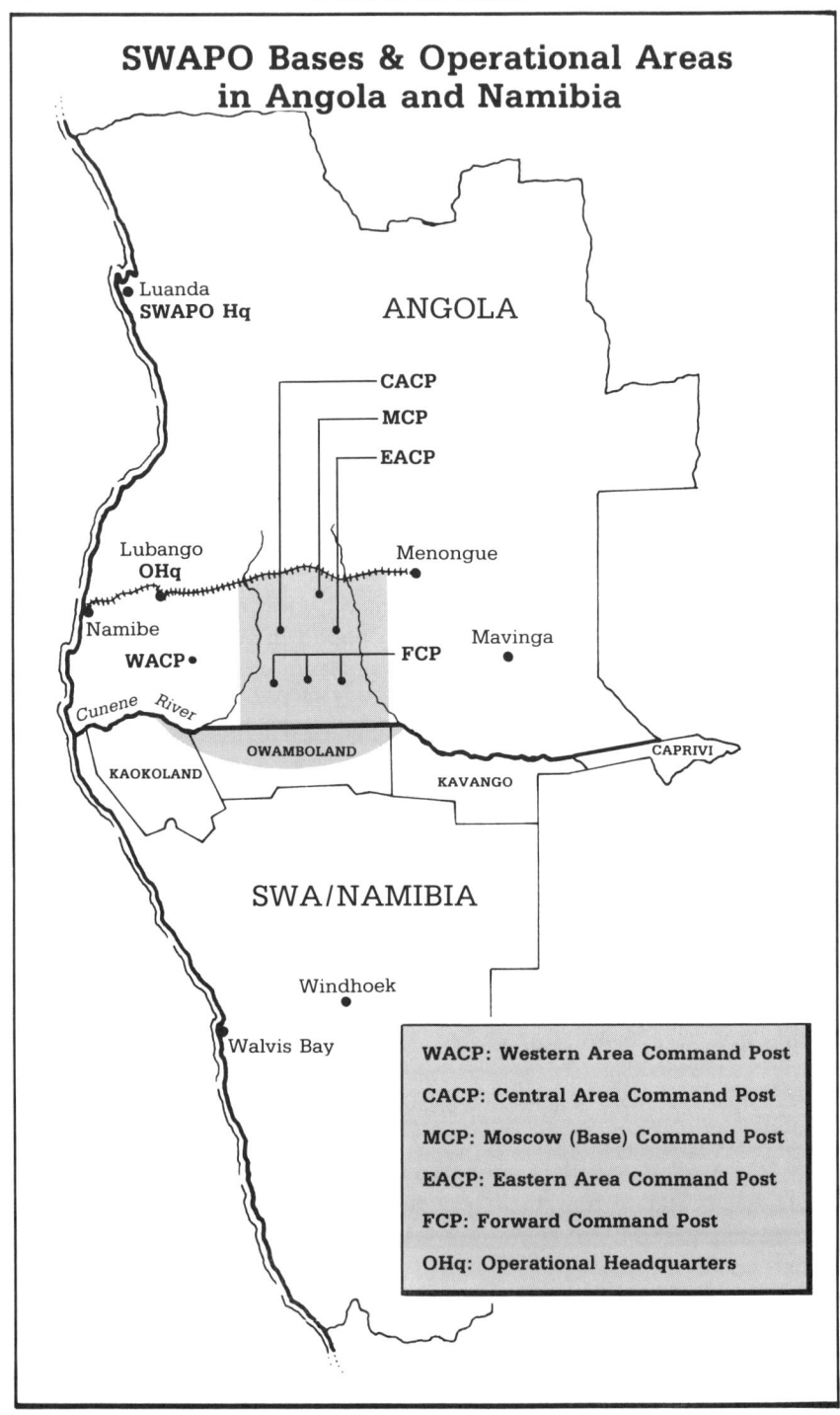

Shipanga, Soloman Mifinawe, Emil Appolus and Jariretundo Kozonguizi. The Congress's main support came from the Owambos. Almost ninety percent of its membership were Owambos although some of its leaders were Herero.

When Toivo changed the name of the Congress to the Owamboland People's Organization his two main lieutenants were Sam Nujoma and Mburumba Kerina, who is half-Herero and half-Owambo.

Personal, philosophical, and tribal differences began to cause tension and schisms within the organization and before the year was over the Hereros left to form the South West African National Union (SWANU).

SWAPO's initial goals were focused on exploiting grievances among the Owambos over migrant labor policies, changing the tribal headman system, and seeking independence for South West Africa/Namibia. But the key issue as far as SWAPO was concerned was majority rule. Given the demographics of Namibia this would amount to Owambo rule. Since SWAPO was essentially an Owambo-based movement this would translate into SWAPO rule.

By 1962, SWAPO, disappointed by its lack of political success, decided upon more radical measures to impose their will on Namibia. Armed insurgency was their answer to the failed less violent political policies of their immediate past. To accomplish this SWAPO created a military wing, the People's Liberation Army of Namibia (PLAN).

Armed force was now going to be SWAPO's vehicle to grab power in any future independent Namibia. To this end, two hundred SWAPO cadres were dispatched to Nasser's Egypt for military training.

In 1963, two events occurred elsewhere in Africa that would give SWAPO's fortunes a boost. Algeria gained independence from France and the Organization of African Unity (OAU) was formed. Both pledged their aid to SWAPO. The Algerians provided military training and the OAU took up their cause as part of its agenda in the international political arena.

In 1964, SWAPO began to infiltrate its newly trained guerrilla-terrorists into the remote northern parts of Namibia to set up rural bases.

SWAPO's terror campaign was launched in February 1966 at Ondumbashe in Owamboland near the Angolan border. Two shops were plundered and the shopkeepers, a Portuguese and an Owambo, were murdered. Other incidents of a similar nature followed: an attack on the village of Oshikango in September; the beating up of two Owambo chiefs in November; a raid on another chief's office in December which resulted in the murder of one of the chief's bodyguards and an attack upon a farm in the Grootfontein area.

It wasn't all SWAPO's game, however, as the security forces struck back and attacked a SWAPO base at Omgulumbashe in Owamboland. The attack was successful in destroying the camp and capturing twenty-seven guerrillas. SWAPO's military wing inside Namibia had gotten its nose bloodied. Of a more serious nature to SWAPO's efforts inside Namibia, the debacle at Omgulumbashe resulted in the round-up, trial and detention of SWAPO leaders throughout Namibia.

The attacks had the classic stamp of a Marxist-style terror campaign. The targets were not those that could fight back such as soldiers or policemen, but tribal leaders, the headmen and their families, as well as shopkeepers and other unarmed civilians. The brunt of the suffering at the hands of the self-proclaimed "liberators" has been borne by the ordinary Owambo citizen who risks being murdered, kidnapped or blown up by landmines whenever venturing out on the roads.

This shouldn't surprise anyone because by embarking upon a strategy of terror and intimidation, SWAPO sought out and obtained the support and sponsorship of the Soviet Bloc states. They responded in their usual manner by lavishing huge quantities of arms and equipment on their new comrades in arms. SWAPO cadres also were taught the fine arts of murder, terror and intimidation by scores of Soviet Bloc trainers and advisors.

Soviet support is still continuing to SWAPO in spite of the phony atmosphere of *glasnost* being used by the Gorbachev regime to hoodwink the West.

The Omgulumbashe disaster also caused further turmoil within the organization. Nujoma's flight from the country he was supposed to be "liberating," gave SWAPO in essence, a schizophrenic twist by creating two groupings within the organization—an internal and external wing.

The internal wing consisted of those who worked through peaceful political activities to bring change to Namibia. Perhaps a better classification of the internal wing would be to consider them as supporters or strong sympathizers of the SWAPO program of radical social reform. Church members, intellectuals and others who saw the organization as anti-white made up the bulk of this faction.

The external wing was committed to a "war of national liberation" and seizure of power in South West Africa/Namibia by force. The external wing was not a cohesive body either. There were divisions within it that caused problems for the organization.

The leadership of the external wing was composed of those who had left Namibia in the 1960's and had never been back. As time passed, they became more and more out of touch with what was going on back inside the country.

With its offices in Luanda, Lusaka, London, New York and elsewhere, the external wing gained worldwide attention, and collected the funds for their guerrilla struggle.

Through their ability to control the flow of money, the external wing had the ultimate say in how the struggle was going to be waged. The ability to give or withhold funds prevented potential rifts between those inside Namibia and their comrades who were globetrotting around the world drumming up support for the movement.

However, all was not well within "SWAPO external." A growing rift was developing between the moderates and the hardliners. The hardliners, led by Nujoma, were insistent upon following the path of a war of liberation. They looked with disdain on those seeking a political solution to the independence question in Namibia.

For example, speaking to the United Nation's General Assembly in May 1973, Nujoma said: "I pledge here and now that we will continue to talk to South Africa in the only language they understand and that is intensification of armed liberation struggle . . . . SWAPO will continue to mobilize the masses and intensify and expand military operations until all the objectives of the struggle are realized."[1]

Disillusioned by the intransigence of their leaders, many exiles returned to Namibia to work within the system and seek a political solution. Among those were such leaders as Jackson Kambode, formerly secretary of SWAPO's trade union organization, Silas Shikongo, a former SWAPO guerrilla commander, and Mburuma Kerina, one of the cofounders of SWAPO.

"I broke with SWAPO on the issues of tribalism, Soviet sponsorship, and increasing violence against their own people," said Kerina, over his break with SWAPO.[2]

The return of the exiles didn't end the problems of SWAPO. A number of those remaining outside the country were still unhappy with Nujoma's leadership.

This growing split finally broke out into the open in March 1976 when the disillusioned members, under the leadership of Andreas Shipanga, held a conference in Zambia to air their grievances. They drew up a list of their complaints against the leadership of Nujoma and his henchmen charging them with nepotism, corruption, waste, inefficiency and the most heinous

---

[1] "How the U.N. Aids Marxist Guerrilla Groups," *op. cit.*, p.8.

[2] Kerina, M., *A Letter to American Friends,* Namibia Democratic Coalition, Manassas, VA 1987, p.1.

crime in their eyes, a failure to exhibit sufficient zeal for Namibian independence.

They demanded the convening of a new SWAPO party congress to discuss their grievances, submit them to the congress for their approval and to decide firmly the course of action SWAPO would follow in the future.

Shipanga's action was a direct challenge to Nujoma's leadership. He responded quickly, and rejected their propsal. His rejection prompted Shipanga and his followers to march on the Lusaka headquarters of SWAPO in protest. Nujoma asked President Kaunda of Zambia for his help in bailing him out of this sticky situation.

Kaunda came to his rescue and ordered the Zambian Army into action to help Nujoma. The army moved in and surrounded Shipanga and his followers. They were rounded up and tossed into a prison camp at Baroma.

Using the Shipanga incident as an excuse, Nujoma had Zambian officials thoroughly purge all those who weren't totally supportive of Nujoma's leadership.

In addition to the problems of violence to advance the SWAPO position and the question of Soviet sponsorship, tribalism—the curse of Africa—infected its poison into SWAPO's body politic. The premier power group within SWAPO is the Kwanyama, the most numerous subgroup of the Owambos. The next most important subgroup in the terrorist organization is the Ndonga. So dominant is Kwanyama power that Sam Nujoma, a non-Kwanyama, knows well that his survival depends on his role of legitimizing Kwanyama control.

The leading SWAPO power brokers make and proclaim policy as they see fit. (Chief among the Kwanyama power brokers are Hidipo Hamutenya— SWAPO's Minister of Information, Peter Mueshihange—SWAPO's Minister of Defense, Finance Minister Lucas Pohamba, and, the People's Liberation Army of Namibia [PLAN] chief of staff, Dimo Amambo.) SWAPO's Central Committee does nothing more than rubber-stamp their decisions and there has never been a formal congress of SWAPO cadres, something Shipanga was trying to organize. Such an internal despotic environment was bound to produce friction within the organization.

The imprisoned dissidents didn't fare too well. According to the Report of the Chairman of the Subcommittee on Security and Terrorism, on Soviet, East German and Cuban Involvement in Fomenting Terrorism in Southern Africa: "Mr. Shipanga and 18 other SWAPO dissidents were eventually released by Tanzania in May 1978. The subcommittee has been unable to develop any information about the fate of the other dissidents arrested at the same time. In his testimony, Mr. Shipanga stated that 2,000 SWAPO members were arrested in April 1976 in Zambia. Other than the 600 who were released in April 1977 and the 18 who were released in May 1978, among them Shipanga, he does not know the fate of the remainder, who he last heard had been taken to Angola."[3]

Shipanga's and his followers' harsh treatment can possibly be explained by other events that were going on inside SWAPO during the same period of time.

In 1976, SWAPO was taking action that would align it more closely with the Soviet Bloc. SWAPO's central committee approved two documents that not only spelled out the organization's programs and goals, but did it in Marxist terminology. These documents, The Political Program, and SWAPO's Constitution, set out the doctrine and program which have been reaffirmed since in books, magazines, pamphlets and all other writings of an ideological nature published by them. In addition, the statements by its leaders have all followed the ideological hue developed in The Political Program or the Constitution.

A reading of these documents leaves no doubt of their Marxist moorings.

". . . The real ideology, objectives, methods, internal structure, and very mentality of SWAPO are absolutely the same in all respects with those of the Soviet Union. SWAPO is nothing but an auxiliary force of Russian aggression in southern Africa working in a context of Soviet revolutionary psychological and disinformation warfare," said co-founder Kerina of his former comrades.[4]

SWAPO has spelled out in its constitution that it is a "national liberation movement" with a messianic mission of "rallying together" the people of SWA/Namibia with two goals; "the struggle for total independence and social liberation."[5]

These buzz-words reflect pure Leninist jargon: "The social revolution can come only in the form of an epoch in which are combined civil war by the proletariat against the bourgeoisie in the advanced countries and a whole series of democratic and revolutionary movements, including the national-

---

[3] Report of the Chairman of the Subcommittee on Security and Terrorism, Senate Judiciary Committee, "Soviet, East German and Cuban Involvement In Fomenting Terrorism In Southern Africa," 92nd Congress, 2nd Session, US Government Printing Office, Nov. 1982, p.9.

[4] Kerina, *op. cit.*, p.7.

[5] Constitution, Art. II, p.3 and Art. III, p.4cf; also Political Program, pp.5-6; see also Appendix F.

liberation movement in the underdeveloped, backward and oppressed nations."[6]

What is social liberation? It is traveling the road to socialism until all vestiges of capitalism are destroyed and the socialist utopia has been reached.

Leonid Breshnev told The International Meeting of Communist amd Workers Parties held in Moscow in 1969, that: "Experience shows that the road of different countries to socialism is marked by such common milestones as the socialist revolution in one form or another, including the smashing and replacement of the state machine of the exploiters; the establishment of one or another form of the dictatorship of the proletariat in alliance with other strata of the working people, and the abolition of the exploiting classes; the socialization of the means of production and the consolidation of socialist relations of production and other social relations in town and countryside; the bringing of cultural values within the reaches of the masses of working people, ie., the cultural revolution in Lenin's meaning of the word."[7]

How does SWAPO's program jibe with Brezhnev's statement? SWAPO's program, bizarrely termed "economic reconstruction," will consist of the "complete elimination of all forms of imperialist domination and the transformation of capitalist exploitation into genuine socialist democracy."[8]

How will this be done? SWAPO's constitution gives the answer: "the people's government exercise control over the means of production and distribution, and pursues a policy which facilitates the way to social ownership of all the resources of the country."[9]

This message is reinforced in their Political Manual. It explains that SWAPO will "use the political supremacy of the people's power to wrest State power from the colonial bourgeoisie, for the purpose of centralizing all the means of production in the hands of the worker and peasant masses."[10]

Who and what are the "people's power" and the "people's government"? Again, SWAPO's own writings spell it out for us: "SWAPO is the people: the people are SWAPO."[11]

---

[6] Lenin, *loc. cit.*

[7] International Meeting of Communist and Workers' Parties, Moscow, 1969, p.11.

[8] *To Be Born a Nation*, ZED Press, London, 1981, p.296.

[9] Constitution, III, B, 7; see also Appendix F.

[10] *Namibia: The Struggle for Final Liberation*, Political Manual of the Namibian Institute of Revolutionary Studies, Office of the SWAPO Organizing Secretary, 1977.

[11] *SWAPO Information on SWAPO*, Interlink Longraph Ltd., London, 1978, p.26.

SWAPO is reminding one and all that it is the only authentic representation of the "people" of South West Africa/Namibia.

SWAPO isn't the only group that makes that claim either. The world's bastion of unreality, the United Nations, also delared SWAPO in 1976 to be the sole "authentic representation of the Namibian people."[12] Incidentally, in the same resolution, the General Assembly gave its approval of terrorism when it supported SWAPO "in their struggle, by all means, including armed struggle, to achieve self-determination, freedom and national independence."

Another key element in a Leninist revolution is that it must be led by a small elite who form and control a socialist vanguard party. It is the communist parties, and only they, who will lead the revolutions.

What does SWAPO consider itself? In announcing its new constitution in 1976, SWAPO said it was going "to unite all Namibian people, particularly the working class, the peasantry, and progressive intellectuals into a vanguard party capable of safeguarding and the building of a classless, non-exploitive society based on scientific socialism ideals and principles."[13]

Even the United Nations has referred to SWAPO as a vanguard organization. The United Nations Institute for Namibia, in its report: Namibia: Perspectives for National Reconstruction and Development, referred to SWAPO in the following: "The tradition of resistance and struggle, and the lessons learnt in the process have made it possible for Namibians to create a national vanguard organization (SWAPO) and to wage an armed struggle under its banner with total independence as the immediate goal before it."[14]

Nujoma has tied his fortunes to those of the Soviet Bloc: "SWAPO will establish political connections with all the countries who wish to do so, but above all with friendly countries such as the Soviet Union and the German Democratic Republic."[15]

He also extolled the virtues of his Russian masters during remarks made to the 26th Congress of the Communist Party of the Soviet Union in March 1981. During his remarks, Nujoma acknowledged Soviet assistance to SWAPO to the point that without the support of the Soviet Union, SWAPO

---

[12] UN Resolution 31/146, para. 2.

[13] Report of the Chairman of the Subcommittee on Security and Terrorism, *op. cit.*, p.10; see: Appendix F.

[14] *Namibia: Perspectives for National Reconstruction and Development,* United Nations Institute for Namibia, Lusaka, 1986, p.44.

[15] Babing, Alfred and Brauer, Hans-Deter, *Namibia,* 2nd Edition, Berlin (DGR), 1981, p.347.

would not have been where it was in 1981. "We address ourselves to the Soviet Union which is giving comprehensive support to the people of Namibia."[16]

It is not the custom of the Soviet Union to allow its communist party Congress to be used as a forum by non-communists. The conclusion is inescapable that Nujoma and SWAPO are part and parcel of the communist movement.

It is also interesting to note that Lenin's birthday is a day of celebration at SWAPO camps. For example, on Lenin's 112th birthday, grafitti on the wall at a SWAPO center read: "Long Live V.I. Lenin."[17]

In fact SWAPO's adulation of Lenin goes well beyond celebrating his birthday. SWAPO uses Lenin as a role model in their terrorist war in Namibia. A SWAPO youth magazine tells why: "To cite Lenin, the revolutionary struggle educates the exploited people, imparts them with the realization of the greatness of their power, widens their horizon, promotes their capabilities, sharpens them in their desire to achieve the self-appointed goal of liberation. That lets us look into the future with confidence."[18]

If many in the West are confused over the question of whether or not SWAPO is a Marxist group, there is no confusion in the Soviet Bloc: "SWAPO at all times confirmed its determination to consolidate and deepen close cooperation on the basis of a joint struggle against imperialism and racism, for independence, democracy and socialism," said an East German publication.[19]

It is hard, therefore, for any person to escape the obvious conclusion that SWAPO is a Marxist-Leninist organization. By thrusting itself violently into the political arena surrounding the question of Namibian independence it poses a threat to the well-being of all the citizens of that troubled land.

---

[16] Report of the Chairman, Subcommittee on Security and Terrorism, *op. cit.*, p.14.

[17] *Namibia Youth*, March-April 1982, back cover. *Namibia Youth* is the bimonthly SWAPO magazine published in East Germany.

[18] "Towards National Democratic Revolution: Perspective on Stages of the Namibian Revolution, *Namibia Today*, Luanda, 6 (1986), p.25.

[19] *Socialism and International Relations,* published by Institute for International Relations of the Academy for State and Legal Science of the DGR, Berlin, 1981, p.158f.

7
Winds of War

In 1962 SWAPO decided to use the bullet instead of the ballot to gain power in Namibia and created a military wing for that purpose. This was the birth of the People's Liberation Army of Namibia (PLAN). To the surprise of no one PLAN has been lavishly supported by the Soviet Bloc in terms of arms, equipment, military training advisors and with vast amounts of political and propaganda support.

How would SWAPO conduct its "war of national liberation?" Given the total backing by the Soviet Union and its surrogates, one could assume that SWAPO would base their insurgency on the Leninist model.

Lenin, however, predicated his theory of power-seizure upon a small elite secret conspiratorial political organization, called the vanguard party. In this aspect SWAPO follows the Leninst model and, in fact, refers to itself as a vanguard party.[1] In Lenin's view, the revolutionary conditions were to be found in the urban centers with their concentrations of political and economic power. For it is here that Lenin's main actors in his revolutionary scene, the bourgeoisie and the proletariat, would interact according to his revolutionary script. Lenin's theory further assumes that the country ripe for his revolutionary forces would be ruled by a government that is alienated from its population. This government is so bad and weak that it will topple when confronted by low-level violence, terrorism and subversion. Lenin's vanguard party would then seize power in a manner more characteristic of a coup d'etat than a revolutionary war: subversion of the police and military and subsequent seizure of radio stations and mass communications outlets, government offices and other state installations. In short, Lenin's theory is predicated upon taking place in advanced industrial societies, not backward Third World countries.[2]

---

[1] SWAPO Information Bulletin, Luanda, No. 4/1981, p.4; see Appendix F.

[2] For a better overview see: *Insurgency in the Modern World,* Bard O'Neil, Wm. R. Heaton & Donald J. Alberts, eds., Westview Press, Boulder, CO, 1980, pp.26-28; see also: Lenin, *loc. cit.*

SWAPO's battlefield in Namibia is Owamboland. There are no large cities in that flat bush terrain. Nor are there even the main actors in Lenin's drama —the bourgeoisie and the proletariat—just subsistance farmers. Therefore, even though SWAPO may think of itself as a Leninist organization and plan a Leninist-style insurgency, Lenin's conditions for carrying out his type of revolution simply do not exist in Namibia.

Such deviations from the purity of the Leninist model, however, have not detered SWAPO or their Soviet masters in the least. SWAPO intended to seize power by means of guerrilla war in Namibia and once they succeeded they could sort out the semantics and theory later. After all, it is the winners that write the history.

This is not to say that revolutionary conditions in Namibia were non-existent at the time. There was unrest and dissatisfaction in Namibia and SWAPO was able to exploit them. But, their strategy better fitted the model of Moscow's principle communist heretic—Mao Tse-tung.

Mao's revolutionary model rests upon a rural-based peasant insurgency. Such an insurgency would grow and eventually evolve into a civil war whereby the revolutionary forces would seize power.

Mao's revolution would pass through several stages, each of which would build upon the success of the preceding stage until ultimate victory.[3] These stages are: the organizational period of building cells, organizing cadres, recruiting and subversion; the period of terrorism; period of guerrilla war; and, the period of mobile or civil war.

SWAPO, as noted elsewhere, had a political organization in Namibia as a result of its activities prior to establishing PLAN. Upon the formation of PLAN the old SWAPO, at least those who didn't go into external exile, became the organization's internal political wing. Their duty was in conformity with classic revolutionary theory: politicizing, organizing and mobilizing the masses of Namibia in favor of SWAPO's new revolutionary order. Due to its inherent handicap of being almost solely an Owambo-based movement, the internal wing has had little success.

Successful revolutionary organizations also routinely use their military wing to promote the achievement of the group's political objectives, by using force as a persuader. The common task of all revolutionary organizations is organizing, politicizing and mobilizing the masses, whether by means of their political or military wing or using both.

[3] Mao Tse-tung, "On Protracted War," *Selected Military Writings*, Foreign Language Press, Peking, 1983, pp.210-219; see also: O'Neil, *Insurgency in the Modern World, op. cit.*, pp.28-31.

It is not surprising then that the primary function of the military wing is similar, but obviously subordinate to that of its political wing.

PLAN was no different. It was given the task of embarking on the political activation of the population in the northern border areas of Namibia. Since two-thirds of the population of the country is located here, the success or failure of PLAN would greatly affect the outcome of their "war of liberation."

Each PLAN terrorist would function as an armed political activist. His military weapon gave him not only status but granted him authority to add emphasis to the revolutionary message he was preaching. His terrorist activities, ideally, were to be restricted to activities which would have a high propaganda value, but which were not too hazardous, as his personal survival was of prime importance.

As a general rule in a revolutionary situation, a terrorist only engages in actions that have a propaganda value. From this it is not difficult to conclude that all revolutionary terrorist activities of an offensive nature can be regarded as armed propaganda.

It is obvious that a military organization, with such a fundamental approach, does not willingly seek combat with the security forces wherever they can find them. The only actions they take are those they are sure they can prevail militarily such as ambush or attacks on small isolated police posts, or those with a guaranteed psychological result: stand-off bombardments with mortars or rockets of bases in densely populated areas, or planting mines to inflict casualties.

Their efforts are directed at converting the neutral section of the population to their side of the cause. PLAN regards the traditional tribal leaders, all respected persons with influence and those sympathetic to the existing state of affairs as their natural enemies. Selective acts of terror and intimidation against them are used as political weapons with the aim of creating a leaderless, defenseless, frightened mass which can be manipulated to do the bidding of SWAPO.

The obvious task of the security forces, which we will go in to more detail elsewhere, was to prevent PLAN from carrying out its program.

In 1965, PLAN launched its military terrorist assault on Namibia when six armed terrorists entered Owamboland. For several months they moved about Owamboland seeking recruits. Their efforts netted them thirty recruits. They gave them a rudimentary course in the terror tactics of guerrilla war and then sent them back to their homes to await the call to action.

Continuing their recruiting efforts, the six set up a temporary camp near Ongulumbashe in the northwestern part of Owamboland. Here they began to train their latest contingent of recruits. Unfortunately for them, their security was bad and word of their camp and its activity reached the authorities. On August 26, 1966, a small police unit raided the camp, killing two and arresting nine, and scattering the rest of the insurgent trainees, many of whom were arrested during the next few weeks.

While the original six were busy in their recruiting efforts, other PLAN members launched the terror campaign in earnest in February 1966 at Omdumbashe in Owamboland near the Namibian/Angolan border.

In October 1968, SWAPO sent two large groups of PLAN terrorists over the border where they began operations in Owamboland. However, within a week fifty-six of them had been captured. As a result, SWAPO changed its tactics and reverted to using smaller groups of terrorists.

In January 1972, a widespread strike by over 13,000 migrant workers which, true or not, SWAPO claimed credit for instigating,[4] led to a state of emergency in the northern areas of Namibia. South African Defense Force (SADF) units were sent there to restore and maintain order.

A year later in January 1973, SWAPO launched a new terrorist offensive in Owamboland. The increased terrorist activity resulted in the South African army assuming overall direction of the counterinsurgency effort in Namibia.

What type of a counterinsurgency campaign would they undertake? Would it be successful or would it fail?

The South African's counterinsurgency thinking was influenced by an American writer, Lt. Col. John J. McCuen. McCuen had written a book, *The Art of Counter-Revolutionary War* (Stackpole Books, Harrisburg, PA., 1966) that analyzed revolutionary war and provided a theoretical framework for successfully fighting it. McCuen's book became the bible for the South African counterinsurgency campaign in Namibia.

To win a revolutionary war, McCuen said, quoting Mao, ". . . the revolutionaries must try to reverse the power relationship (1) by wearing down the enemy's strength with the 'cumulative effect of many campaigns and battles'[5] (2) by building their own strength through mobilizing the support of the people, establishing bases, and capturing equipment, and, (3) by gaining outside political and, if possible, military support."[6]

---

[4] *Namibia: Perspectives for National Reconstruction and Development, op. cit.,* p.44

[5] Mao Tse-tung, "Strategic Problems in the Anti-Japanese Guerrilla War," *Selected Works,* Vol. II, International Publishers, New York, 1954, p.125.

[6] McCuen, J.J., *The Art of Counter-Revolutionary War,* Stackpole Books, Harrisburg, PA, 1966, p.30.

The revolutionaries would do this by following Mao's classic four phases of a guerrilla war: organization, terrorism, guerrilla war and mobile or civil war.

How does a society resist and successfully counter such a revolutionary war? McCuen's strategy was simple in concept but complex in application: use the guerrilla's methods against him. "To protect oneself against the methodical, crushing body blows of the revolutionaries and to be able to strike them in their most vital parts, it is necessary to fight them on their own battlefields—in their own media. It is necessary to parry the revolutionary weapons, adopt them, and then turn them against the revolutionaries."[7]

However, events were taking place in neighboring Angola that would have far-reaching effects on both sides in the terrorist war in Namibia. At first they effected SWAPO adversely.

With the beginning of the Portuguese collapse in Angola in 1974 came large-scale deployment of South African troops in the northern part of Namibia. Many of these troops later took part in "Operation SAVANNAH," in 1975-76. This operation involved sending about 2,000 troops—at the instigation, so it is said, of the American Secretary of State, Dr. Henry Kissinger[8]—to bolster Western-backed factions in the Angolan civil war. The South Africans were to counter the Cuban troops rushed in by the Soviets to prop up the communist backed Popular Movement for the Liberation of Angola (MPLA) faction. Hypocritical international furor over the presence of South African troops in Angola caused their withdrawal from Angola, but their presence in northern Namibia severely restricted SWAPO's activity and forced it underground.

The Portuguese collapse and the outcome of the ensuing civil war in Angola soon became a major blessing for SWAPO and revived its activities. Instead of former Portuguese pressure and hostility, SWAPO was given what every successful insurgency needs—safe bases and sanctuaries in a neighboring state. The new Marxist regime in Luanda permitted, indeed encouraged, SWAPO to set up bases in southern Angola just north of their target area —the Owambo tribal lands in Namibia.

With the withdrawal of South African forces engaged in "Operation SAVANNAH" from Angola in early 1976, SWAPO was able to extend its network of training camps and bases in southern Angola. This facilitated their ability to infiltrate PLAN terrorists over the border into Namibia.

---

[7] *Ibid.,* p.50.

[8] Steenkamp, W., *Borderstrike: South Africa Into Angola,* Butterworth, Wobern, MA, 1983, p.3; "Destabilizing Southern Africa," *The Economist,* July 16, 1983, p.19.

The long open border, flat terrain and heavy bush made insurgent movement in and out of Owamboland very easy either on foot, by bicycle or vehicle.

The introduction of the South African forces and their subsequent movement into southern Angola had caused SWAPO to revert to the organizational phase of their insurgency. SWAPO activity in Owamboland was rather quiet during this period.

The change in power in Angola quickly reversed that situation. SWAPO was soon able to not only move from the organizational to the terrorist stage but as more training bases were established in southern Angola they were able to launch small-scale guerrilla war in northern Namibia. Even though most of the activity involved raids across the border at soft targets and then return to their sanctuaries inside Angola, they were having a discernible psychological impact in Namibia. SWAPO, as a result, was able to recruit many more members than they were losing to the security forces.

The South Africans had their work cut-out for them if they were going to stop SWAPO. They needed not only military and political strength, but also a sound counterinsurgency doctrine to achieve success.

The South African's counter-revolutionary manual would be vital in mounting a successful campaign.

McCuen said, ". . . the counter-revolutionary objectives should be to exploit any advantage gained by maintaining contact, retaining the initiative, and rolling back the revolutionary organization. That is, the counter-revolutionaries must follow the rebels from base to base and from phase to phase with operations designed to keep defeating them in their own media until the revolutionary organization has been destroyed and the counter-revolutionary organization has been firmly established."[9]

Such a process will be long and difficult and one should not pursue it unless one is willing to follow its path to the end. This will take a long and protracted period of time. It will require that ". . . the governing power first stop the revolutionaries in whatever phase they have reached and then drive them back through the proceeding phases: mobile warfare to guerrilla warfare to terrorism to organization."[10]

The South Africans did not succumb to any illusions about the chances of achieving a "quick fix" in solving the situation in Namibia. As early as 1976 senior military officials were making it quite clear that there would be no

---

[9] McCuen, *op. cit.*, p.78.
[10] *Ibid.*

quick, easy solution to the Namibian struggle.[11] As a result, they chose to apply the tried and true counterinsurgency techniques, such as constant patrolling and "hearts and minds" civic action schemes. The South Africans set out to wage their counterinsurgency war in Namibia in the right way.

The most critical analytical decision is the first one—to determine what phase the revolutionary war is actually in. The governing power must be certain it is considering the real critical factors of the type of war they are facing. They must avoid the trap of using conventional military estimates as they are not always valid in a revolutionary war. For example when considering geographical areas one should beware of ". . . the fatefully delusive effects on the leaders—both civil as well as military—of the wall maps which reproduce the situation thanks to the employment of 'coloured thumb-tacks'! It is in the vision of such documents that the responsible officials are inclined, sometimes, to base their reasons for hope . . . But the maps are only statistical documents . . . a map does not indicate the gangrene which works on the mind of the inhabitants. It does not portray the real state of the country, the atmosphere in which the friendly or enemy units live and the population, sympathetic or hostile."[12]

Adding problems to the estimate will be the fact that the insurgents will often be in different stages of their strategy in different parts of the country. For example, although SWAPO was primarily in the organizational phase within Owamboland in the 1976-77 period, they were able to conduct guerrilla war, albeit from bases in Angola, in the more remote areas of northern Namibia.

All these factors must be considered in deciding what stage the enemy is in as they carry out their insurgency against your efforts.

Once past that hurdle, the governing power must develop a proper strategy that will: (1) secure the government's own strategic bases against revolutionary infiltration by SWAPO, and, (2) prevent or delay the development of revolutionary base areas in Namibia. This posed a special problem in Namibia in that most of the population was located near the northern border of the country.

The successful counterinsurgency campaign strategy next required that a long-term plan be developed which would allow the South Africans to not only stop SWAPO but to take the initiative and drive them back through the

---

[11] Steenkamp, W., "Politics of Power—The Border War," in: Venter, Al J., *Challenge: Southern Africa within the African Revolutionary Context*, Ashanti Publishing Limited, Gibraltar, 1989, p.186.

[12] McCuen, *op. cit.*, pp.78-79ff.

various stages of their revolutionary war activity until they had been neutralized.

It was a daunting task. It required the South Africans to not only mobilize, organize, and apply the massive resources necessary to carry out their plan, but to continue on as long as it took to win the war. They also had to do it in a manner that would avoid the most common mistake in pursuing counter-revolutionary war—to do too little too late.

In McCuen's words, ". . . As we will see, counter-revolutionary warfare will require an institution of large-scale civic action in the organization phase, police action in the terrorism phase, low-level military action in the guerrilla warfare phase, and conventional military action in the mobile warfare phase."[13]

The events, both of a political and military nature narrated in this book, all had their effect on or were the result of the counter-revolutionary action taken by the South Africans. It cannot be stressed too often that both revolutionaries, and counter-revolutionaries, if they are to be successful, will use political, economic, educational, psychological and organizational concepts as much, or even more than purely military action.

There is also a fundamental rule of revolutionary war that the prime objective for the revolutionary force is self-preservation.[14] On the other side of the coin, Mao's dictum applies equally to the counter-revolutionary war practitioner. Even though the overall counterinsurgency objective is to destroy the revolutionaries, the immediate objective must be the preservation of the counter-revolutionaries' bases, population and forces. If these go it renders any proposed counterinsurgency plan moot.

The South African security forces accepted McCuen's thesis that the government, ". . . must first establish those populations and areas still under its control into firm strategic bases or base areas on which it can rely 'for carrying out its strategic tasks as well as for achieving the goals of preserving and expanding oneself and annihilating or expelling the enemy.' "[15]

The South Africans built an extensive network of bases not only throughout the northern Namibian border areas, but in areas likely to be prime targets in an expanded SWAPO guerrilla war and along the security forces principal logistic network.

---

[13] *Ibid.*, pp.43-44.

[14] See: Mao Tse-tung, "On Protracted War," *Selected Works*, International Publications, Lawrence & Wishart, London, 1954-56, pp.206-207.

[15] McCuen, *op. cit.*, p.53.

Geography favored the South Africans as the northern border operational area was over four hundred kilometers from the largest city—Windhoek, the capital of Namibia.

The South African bases were strong enough to resist direct assault by PLAN terrorists and also discouraged infiltration in their vicinity. Moreover, by conducting continuous patrols, and sweeps, collecting intelligence and setting up ambushes, the security forces were able to prevent any permanent establishment of SWAPO bases inside Namibia.

Despite all of this, the situation along the border was still giving the security forces nightmares. On the one hand, the bulk of the Owambo population was concentrated close to the border easily accessible and exceptionally vulnerable to hit and run terrorist attacks from the SWAPO bases just across the border. On the other hand, the geography and the nature of the terrain made sealing the border a virtual impossibility.

The South Africans had essentially two options. The first was to concentrate the population in defensible locations, as had proved to be so effective in Malaysia.[16] The other option was to strike at the terrorists where they were concentrated in their bases before they entered Namibia.

Moving the Owambo population into protected villages was not an acceptable for two reasons: it would have alienated the Owambos and destroyed the support of those who were in sympathy with the South African's anti- SWAPO policy; and, given the population's close proximity to the Angolan border, it would not really have offered much protection from SWAPO's activity.

That left the other option; pre-emptive cross-border strikes and follow-up operations against SWAPO sanctuaries in Angola. It was not an easy decision for the South African government to take. At the time the South African Prime Minister was John Vorster. He was not enthusiastic about such operations as the recent Operation SAVANNAH had wrecked his detente policy efforts in southern Africa.

On the other hand, he had to face the hard facts of the rapidly escalating SWAPO activities in Namibia. On October 25, 1977, SADF spokesman Maj. Gen. Walter Black said there were at least 300 terrorists in Owamboland and that contacts between the security forces and SWAPO averaged at least 100 a month.[17] He estimated that a further 3,400 PLAN terrorists were active in Angola and Zambia could rapidly move into Namibia.

---

[16] See: Sir Robert Thompson, *Defeating Communist Insurgency*, Praeger, New York, 1970.

[17] Steenkamp, *op. cit.*, p.6.

Black's warning proved prophetic, as just two days later a large group of terrorists—at least eighty—crossed the border into the operational area where they encountered a small security force patrol. Although vastly outnumbered, the patrol decided survival meant taking the offensive. They attacked the terrorists, and they also had the presence of mind to radio for help. Reinforcements rushed to the scene of the contact and a see-saw battle lasting three days ensued, flowing back and forth over the border. When the shooting finally stopped, SWAPO had suffered a tremendous loss, losing sixty-one confirmed dead to the loss of five security force personnel.[18]

There was little cause or time for jubilation on the part of the security forces, as the battle portended a troubling ominous future. If SWAPO continued to send large units of terrorists across the border it would increase PLAN's ability to escalate the war in Namibia. If enough PLAN terrorists poured across the border they would soon be able to advance their revolutionary war from the guerrilla to the mobile war phase. That would put the counterinsurgency forces in Namibia at a decided operational disadvantage. There simply were not enough security force personnel available to cope with an escalating SWAPO "invasion" from their safe havens in southern Angola.

It is well to recall that while this increased SWAPO infiltration was underway South Africa, the West and the United Nations were deeply involved in negotiations over future independence for Namibia. SWAPO knew this and obviously wanted as many as possible of its terrorists inside Namibia, if and when a ceasefire were to go into effect as part of any international peace and independence plan for the country.

The more SWAPO terrorists that were inside Namibia during a ceasefire, the more they could coerce and intimidate Namibians to support their Marxist political agenda.

As the year 1978 dawned, SWAPO terrorist activities continued to escalate. On February 7, 1978, a prominent Owambo tribal leader, Toivo Shujaga, was assassinated by SWAPO. Exactly two weeks later, a PLAN terrorist gang abducted a teacher and 119 children from the St. Mary's Mission school in central Owamboland close to the Angolan border. Three of the children later escaped and said they had been forced across the border and taken to a SWAPO training camp.[19]

During March 1978, SWAPO's activity seemed to quiet down a bit as the

---

[18] *Ibid.*

[19] *Ibid.*, p.9; confirmed by statement to author by a number of SADF and Namibian civilian authorities.

Winds of War 77

diplomatic efforts over the Namibian independence question were becoming bogged down.

It was just the calm before the storm and it broke dramatically on March 27th when a SWAPO hit-team gunned down one of the original founders of SWAPO and one of the most respected man in Namibia—Clemens Kapuuo. He was chief of the Herero tribe and a long time political foe of the South African government. At the time of his assassination he was also chairman of the Democratic Turnhalle Alliance. SWAPO was obviously trying to remove potential political opponents before they could take part in any UN-supervised elections as part of the process of Namibian independence.

Kapuuo's assassination also signaled the start of more SWAPO terrorist activities in Namibia.

On April 28th, one of the most serious PLAN infiltrations ever, took place when a group of 100 terrorists clashed with a security force patrol in western Owamboland. This incident confirmed South African fears that SWAPO was escalating its infiltrations of larger groups into the operational area of Owamboland.

It was against this background of the deteriorating security situation inside Namibia that the South Africans government decided to launch Operation REINDEER, its first major cross-border operation.

This decision required a lot of courage on the part of South Africa, as it was taken even while they were formally accepting the Western proposal for a Namibian settlement.

The South African government was not being duplicitous, as its critics have claimed. Even before accepting the Western proposal, it had constantly stressed that it would not allow SWA/Namibia to be taken at the point of a gun. The Western diplomats involved in the negotiations were well aware of the South African position on that item. Perhaps they thought South Africa was bluffing. If so, events quickly showed the West's diplomats just how wrong they were.

Perceiving the gravity of the politico-military situation, the South African government decided to launch REINDEER. The South Africans considered REINDEER and subsequent pre-emptive operations to be essential steps in fighting the SWAPO terrorist insurgency in Namibia. They were deemed so important, in fact, that on many occasions the South African government approved them knowing that they would be mercilessly crucified by international political anger and protests from both enemies and friends. Governments do not lightly or often undertake military operations knowing beforehand that they will be subjected to universal condemnation, unless they deem them absolutely necessary. The decisions to undertake "REINDEER" and other cross-border incursions have not been left to the discretion of the military. Such operations cannot be launched without approval at the highest level of the South African government.

The military does not have carte blanche to operate as it sees fit. Each cross-border operation, barring spontaneous "hot pursuit" by security forces chasing a fleeing band of terrorists over the border into southern Angola, has to be specifically authorized, and indeed, is in constant danger of being canceled at the last moment if the political leaders feel the political conditions are too unfavorable.

One of the most important political considerations weighed by the South African government, outside of the international situation, has been the domestic support of the war. Since the South African Defense Force is mostly a conscript force, in which every white male must do two years National Service, use of military power is susceptible to the whims of the white electorate. That electorate, generally speaking, accepts the necessity of the war against SWAPO. Nevertheless, a failure or even a particularly difficult operation involving heavy casualties, could quickly turn into a political disaster for the South African government. Unlike the majority of African governments, the South African government is responsible to an electorate.

The decision to adopt the strategy of cross-border operations, and the separate approval of each of them as they arose, called for much thought, debate and anguish at the highest levels of the South African government.

Given the political and diplomatic situation in the late spring of 1978, the South Africa government obviously thought the security situation in Namibia warranted the launching of cross-border operations.

We will cover some of these, including the first of these, Operation REINDEER, which was launched on May 4, 1978, later in this work. Before doing that, however, let us turn our attention to the political situation that was developing inside Namibia.

8
First Steps Toward Self-Government

The people of Namibia went to the polls in December 1978 to elect their own representatives to a newly-created Constituent Assembly. This was done despite vigorous attempts by SWAPO to disrupt the voting and the prior refusal of the international community to recognize the results.

Shortly before Christmas the South African Prime Minister and his Foreign Minister traveled to Windhoek to confer with the newly elected representatives. Discussions centered on plans to achieve an internationally acceptable solution for the independence of the territory.

Obviously bowing to international pressure the Constituent Assembly adopted a resolution which stated that SWA/Namibia would cooperate in the expeditious implementation of UN Security Council Resolution 435.

The result was a tacit agreement between South Africa, who as the Namibian spokesman, represented the internal parties, and the Western Five that the December elections were viewed as a process to identify legitimate representatives for all the population groups of Namibia.

An exchange of letters ensued between the South African government and the UN Secretary General concerning elections in Namibia. The South African proposed that new elections be held as soon as possible in Namibia, but no later than September 30, 1979. The South African position also stressed that an essential prerequisite for such elections was a cessation of all hostile acts in the country.

The Secretary General agreed, for the most part, with the South African proposal. He said all parties had agreed to a cease-fire and that the sooner elections were held the better and that, "the date of not later than 30 September 1979 is consistent with the Proposal."[1]

---

[1] *Namibia/SWA Prospectus, op. cit.,* p.21.

80   *Death in the Desert*

This led to meetings between the UN Special Representative on Namibia, the Administrator-General and the South African government on the details to begin the implementation process.

As a result of these discussions, the Western Five gave their stamp of approval. Things were looking up for finally resolving the Namibian problem.

In this spirit of optimism, the South African Foreign Minister urged the UN Secretary General to set a date for the cease-fire and suggested it be no later than February 20, 1979.

In the meantime, the newly elected Constituent Assembly was sitting in limbo. The diplomatic activity swirling around them, which they could not affect in the slightest, raised doubts as to the Assembly's legitimacy and purpose. If there were to be new elections in 1979 under the formula being discussed, any work they did on a constitution would clearly be wasted effort. Thus they could only sit as spectators to the events in the international arena that were deciding their fate and that of Namibia. It was simply out of their hands.

However, the UN, in particular the Security Council and the General Assembly, had been making new demands or setting new conditions as the talks had proceeded with the South African government. One of the UN's new conditions that was of particular concern to the various political parties in Namibia provided for the establishment of SWAPO bases inside Namibian territory where none had existed before.

In April 1979 the South African government asked the Constituent Assembly for their reaction to the UN's new proposal. The parties represented in the Constituent Assembly had differing opinions regarding specific aspects of the UN's overall proposal. However, all parties unanimously rejected the idea of SWAPO bases inside Namibia. They knew all too well that they and their supporters would be prime targets for SWAPO intimidators operating from those bases.

Nor were the internal parties optimistic over any guarantees given by countries such as Angola and Zambia that they would or could effectively monitor the SWAPO bases in their countries. These hollow assurances were soon rendered irrelevant when SWAPO rejected the concept of monitoring any of their activities in any of their bases. Nor would SWAPO even agree to prevent any illegal intervention by armed SWAPO forces during the transitional period or during the election process itself.

With good reason the internal political parties were all suspicious of SWAPO and the UN's intentions. They reacted as might be expected under the circumstances.

For example, the Democratic Turnhalle Alliance (DTA), a multi-racial party holding forty-one seats in the Assembly, favored outright rejection of the United Nation's proposals. Furthermore, they favored going ahead and establishing an interim government, so as not to halt the momentum towards independence.

The Action Front for the Retention of the Turnhalle Principles (Aktur) also rejected the United Nation's proposal. They, however, favored calling an all-party conference to decide on what action to take which would lead to independence without shutting the door on an internationally acceptable solution.

The National Namibian Front, though also opposed to SWAPO bases in the country, was opposed to any unilateral solution.

South Africa conveyed the concerns of the internal political parties to the United Nations, but it was obvious that those concerns fell on deaf ears.

"We've had enough," was the prevailing mood in Namibia and action that epitomized the feelings of the people in the country was not long in coming.

On May 2, 1979, the DTA introduced a motion in the Constituent Assembly that would establish a National Assembly made up of the fifty members of the Constituent Assembly and provided for the expansion of the membership to sixty-five, to accommodate the democratic parties not then represented. The new National Assembly would be the supreme legislative authority in Namibia.

The motion also held out an olive branch to the United Nations by expressing willingness to implement independence on the basis of the original Western proposal. But it also stressed that such negotiations should not hinder or delay the internal political, social and economic development of Namibia.

The DTA's motion carried by over a four to one margin.

The Constituent Assembly, even as they were rejecting the UN's plan, asked the South African government to give it full legislative powers. The aim of this request was to develop a legitimate interim government. Such powers would give teeth to its efforts to steer the political destiny of the people of Namibia by performing the normal legislative functions of an independent state. The interim government would carry on in the manner of an independent state until the external interests and others got their act together and worked out agreeable procedures that would lead to an independent Namibia.

The South African government, abiding by the wishes of the Constituent Assembly, informed the UN on May 7, 1979, that it had agreed to the formation of the National Assembly in Namibia. However, the South Africans emphasized to the UN that the new Assembly would not have the right to change the international status of the territory.

One week later the Administrator General's proclamation announcing the establishment of the National Assembly was published in the government's Gazette. On the 21st of May the Assembly held its first session in Windhoek.

For the first time in the history of Namibia there existed an elected body which on its own accord, was able to address and attempt to resolve the problems of the nation and its people. However, it was obvious that the National Assembly did not have full state sovereignty. Before the decisions taken by the National Assembly could become final, they still had to be approved by the Administrator General, as the representative of the South African government. The South African government retained this power because it felt that since it still exercised the mandatory control over the territory, it should have the final say. Nevertheless, a significant start had been made on the road to self-determination by the people of Namibia.

The UN was quick to respond. On May 31, 1979, the General Assembly adopted Resolution (33/206) that expressed unequivocal support for SWAPO, including military support, and totally rejected the formation of the new SWA/Namibian National Assembly. SWAPO interpreted this action as requiring all entities of the UN—its committees, non-governmental bodies, etc.—to cooperate and support the terrorist groups cause.

Thus it seemed that the only style democracy that the UN had any intention of supporting was a long way from Western-style representative democracy.

It was ironic, but not surprising to those who try to follow the convoluted logic of the UN, that the political parties who took part in the elections in SWA/Namibia, claimed to do so under the "Right of self-determination of the people," which is fundamental to the UN Charter. The irony is that this same world body has for years, and is continuing to do so to this day, to act in favor of a power-obsessed clique, SWAPO, which is nothing more than a puppet organization run by Moscow. By bestowing its official blessings on SWAPO, the UN was indeed ignoring and betraying its own Charter!

The Namibians, however, were undaunted and proceeded with the business of beginning to run their own political affairs. One of the first steps the National Assembly took was to set about dismantling apartheid in the territory. During June, the DTA introduced an extremely important piece of

First Steps Toward Self-Government 83

legislation, the "Abolishment of Racial Discrimination (Urban Residential and Public Amenities) Bill." The bill which was designed to outlaw racial discrimination in Namibia, passed easily and became law on July 21, 1979.

The Assembly also enacted other legislation that provided for equal pay for equal work, irrespective of race, and opened membership in trade unions to all races. In addition, education was not only made free, but mandatory for all children between the ages of six and sixteen.

In a very short time, the National Assembly had enacted a program of far-reaching social, economic and educational rights and benefits. In fact it exceeded that which most of the member states of the United Nations provided their subjects.

The growth of self-government continued to gain momentum in Namibia. An executive body, a twelve-man Council of Ministers, was inaugurated on July 1, 1980. While the legislative power was to remain in the hands of the National Assembly, a political body was needed to run the day by day operations of government. The Council of Ministers was designed to fill that need.

Additionally, the South African government transferred to the new government administrative authority and responsibility for all aspects of governing the territory, with the exception of decisions affecting its own constitutional status, foreign affairs and the South African Defense Force. A governmental civil service under control of the Namibian authorities was also established.

Thus the people of Namibia were now exercising, with the three exceptions above, the duties and functions of a sovereign state. Even though the UN and the international community would not recognize their efforts, they were, nevertheless, laying the foundation for the functioning machinery of government when the day of total independence finally arrived. In this process they could well profit from the mistakes of others going from colonial to independent status.

Practice as they might, the functions of self-government, their hands were tied because of one major factor—their ultimate fate was in the hands of others who even denied their right to declare themselves independent. The UN was determined to have its way and even the South Africans, sympathetic as they were, could be a stumbling block to real self-government because of their veto power over the Assembly.

Yet the new government made the best it could out of an intolerable situation. Tension was, however, inevitable and the South African function of oversight was grating to the new government.

Matters came to a head early in 1983 over a seemingly innocuous draft bill changing public holidays in Namibia. The Administrator General took offense to the removal of some holidays celebrated in South Africa and remitted the draft legislation back to the National Assembly. That was too much for Dirk Mudge, the chairman of the Council of Ministers. He submitted his resignation on January 10, 1983. Shortly thereafter, the remaining members of the Council also resigned and sent a joint letter of resignation to the Administrator General.

This irritated the South African government and they promptly dissolved the National Assembly by means of a proclamation (Proclamation AG3 of 1983). The Administrator General again assumed the legislative and executive powers of the central government in SWA/Namibia, thus ending the first attempt at self-government in Namibia. It would not be the last.

9
Multi Party Conference

Although the Administrator General had assumed the reins of government on January 18, 1983, it did not mean the end of efforts inside Namibia to work out an internal political agenda leading to independence.

On September 13, 1983, these efforts were given a boost when members of many of the numerous political parties in Namibia decided to hold a multi-party conference on the political future of the country.

The parties extended an invitation to SWAPO to attend the conference, but they contemptuously declined.

On September 29th Namibia's major political parties met to establish the Multi Party Conference (MPC). This occasion marked the lifting of the political doldrums that had fallen on the country's political scene after the dissolving of the National Assembly in January.

The internal political forces were now back on the difficult road hopefully leading to independence and international recognition.

The first formal session of the MPC was on November 12, 1983. Eight political groups and alliances, which consisted of nineteen parties, attended the historical meeting in Windhoek. The Damara Council, the eleven constituent parties of the Democratic Turnhalle Alliance (DTA), the Namibian Christian Democratic Party (NCDP), the South West African National Union (SWANU) and the SWAPO-Democrats (SWAPO-D) were present.

The National Party of South West Africa (NPSWA) attended the first meeting as an observer but soon became a full member of the Conference. The Labour Party of Namibia (LPN) joined some few months later, while the Namibian Christian Democratic Party and, later, the Damara Council withdrew.

Although the organizers of the conference, namely Moses Katjiuongua of SWANU, Andreas Shipanga of SWAPO-D, Dirk Mudge of the DTA and Justus Garoeb of the Damara Council, did not succeed in involving all Namibian political parties, as they had hoped, it was still the largest and most comprehensive gathering of Namibian political parties ever assembled in the country's history.

The MPC was in a position, UN rhetoric notwithstanding, to discuss, debate and recommend action on the needs, goals and values of Namibian society, representing as it did almost the entire spectrum of cultures, ideologies, religions and races with which the country is blessed—or cursed, as some would no doubt say.

The fact that such a diverse gathering was assembled reflected the growing interest, sophistication and maturity of Namibian society. Such a gathering would have been impossible in 1977 or 1978.

It also showed a very hopeful sign: possible emergent national consciousness, a willingness to subordinate certain narrow and selfish ambitions in favor of broader national concerns.

Although there was a feeling of hope, promise and drawing together to build a nation another equally high emotion was involved—frustration.

This frustration came from the fact that it was outsiders, not the people of Namibia, that were trying to force their solutions on Namibia. It was clear the MPC was fed-up with this seemingly endless situation.

"The spectacle of one group of foreigners who on the basis of their interests objected to the plans of another group of strangers about our independence without either of the two groups having properly conferred with us, became intolerable,"[1] was the consensus of the MPC leaders.

Such a situation "made a farce out of the principle of self-determination." Instead the people of Namibia were treated as a political football to be kicked back and forth among the foreign interests.

The MPC decided to grab the bull by the horns and claim the right to state their own case. Recognizing they had to live in the country and suffer the consequences of any solution, whether theirs or one imposed from abroad, they resolved to do everything in their power that, whatever the outcome would be in the struggle for independence, it would be for the benefit of all Namibians.

They resolved to confer among themselves, representing the various peoples of Namibia, and reach a consensus on how to travel the rocky road to independence.

---

[1] *Namibia: Towards Nationhood,* SWA/Namibia Information Service, Windhoek, 1987, p.5.

This mood was reflected in the closing statement of that first meeting of the MPC.

"We stand today at the decisive crossroads of our country's future. If we succeed in our aim to achieve peace and reconciliation, we are heading for a free, democratic, stable and prosperous future. If we fail, more suffering, struggle, economic regression and bloodshed lies ahead. We dare not fail and to succeed we need the prayers and assistance of all our people."[2]

The prime task the MPC set out for itself was to find a way to lead the country, as fast as possible, to independence.

SWAPO was again invited to join the MPC to talk about peace and reconciliation and to participate with them in the journey towards independence. SWAPO, for the umpteenth time, refused to talk with their "constituents" for whom the UN had anointed SWAPO as their sole representatives.

In spite of SWAPO's rejection, the MPC, having agreed upon a course of action inside the country, began to plead its case outside its borders in an effort to drum up support.

The first stop was Cape Town. MPC representatives conferred, at the end of January 1984, with Dr.Chester Crocker, the U.S.'s African mandarin at the State Department, who was the main negotiator in international forums on the Namibian question. The MPC told Crocker they still recognized that UN Resolution 435 was the basis of moving towards Namibian independence, and they would cooperate in its implementation. But they also said that they would be less than candid if they weren't quite concerned, as well they should be, over UN bias towards SWAPO and the UN's willingness to allow the establishment of SWAPO bases inside Namibia.

The MPC also took the opportunity to use the meeting with Crocker as a chance for tooting its own horn and gaining some credibility. They held a press conference after the meeting and said: "When Dr. Crocker met the MPC mission, he recognized the status and existence of the MPC . . . No one can ignore the MPC any longer."[3] Unfortunately, Crocker's response to this audacious act was not recorded.

However, the MPC was not just travelling abroad to get foreign support. They were also busy at work in Namibia hammering out their declaration of principles which would set out MPC objectives. The declaration had a short gestation period.

[2] *Ibid.*
[3] *Ibid.*, pp.7-8.

88   *Death in the Desert*

On February 24, 1984, just over three months after its creation, the MPC announced that it had reached agreement on a declaration of basic principles. These were embodied in a statement that became known as the Windhoek Declaration. It was a statement of what the MPC's goal and future energies would be directed towards fulfilling. In addition the Windhoek Declaration: (1) affirmed the right to self-determination; (2) pledged support for UN resolution 435; (3) proclaimed the unity of SWA/Namibia; (4) reaffirmed support of the concept that "All Men are created equal"and shall have equal rights and responsibilities irrespective of their national origin, race, religion or political views; and (5) pledged peaceful cooperation in resolving strife in southern Africa.

The statement also promised to draft a constitution within the framework of the West's proposed settlement plan that would not only be "consistent with the Universal Declaration of Human Rights" but also "in accordance with the International Covenant of Civil and Political Rights."[4]

This new, permanent constitution, said the MPC's statement, would ". . . allay the fears and respect the aspirations, ambitions and desires"[5] of those who would live under the new constitution.

The document also promised "to create an economic order which aims at decreasing our dependence on foreign countries by developing and diversifying our economy mainly through our own efforts and improving the quality of life of our people in all fields . . . A sound healthy and strong economy must be the basis of our economic thinking."[6]

The foreign policy to be pursued would be "based on dignity, independence, peace and friendship and peaceful co-existence with our neighbors and the rest of the world . . . "[7]

All in all, it was a document that any Western liberal democracy could embrace as its own.

The statement reflected a spirit of optimism among the political entities inside Namibia. It also showed the determination of the South Westers not to sit back and let others determine their future.

Nor did the MPC rest on its laurels. A few weeks later, on April 18, this statement was followed by the adoption of a Bill of Fundamental Rights and Objectives. The SWA/Namibia Bill of Rights, the former head of SWANU,

---

[4] See: Appendix B.
[5] *Ibid.*
[6] *Ibid.*
[7] *Ibid.*

Jarietunda Kozonguizi noted, ". . . clearly owes much to the American Declaration of Independence."[8]

The Bill of Rights consists of a preamble containing six sub-headings, eleven articles specifying particular rights, a twelfth article that provides for the protection and enforcement of these rights and a final section recording certain fundamental objectives.[9]

The preamble records the desires of the people for independence, peace and reconciliation, to promote individual rights, but also to maintain the cultural, linguistic and religious diversity of the country, while creating a unity "with common loyalties to a single state,"[10] by promoting self-government.

As Kozonguizi told the London conference: ". . . All persons are seen to have been born free and equal, endowed by their Creator with human dignity and inalienable rights. Respect for the rights of all in the prevailing diversity of Namibian society is seen to be essential for peace and stability, while progress towards unity in that diversity is desired by all. Government, moreover, deriving their powers from the consent of the people, are seen to have been instituted for the purposes of promoting the people's safety and welfare, and thus, by implication, for no other purpose. The preamble thus creates the expectation, fulfilled by the catalogue of rights which follows it, that the primary focus of the document will be to protect the rights of the people, whether individually, or in such groups as they may choose to form, from unreasonable interference by government."[11]

What is SWAPO's attitude towards the shape of government in Namibia? It is certainly not one that would protect groups or individuals from unreasonable interference by government. Government, under their system, would be an all pervasive intruder in the lives of all Namibians.

The fundamental policy of a SWAPO regime would be guided, in SWAPO's own words, in ". . . the establishment of a people's democratic government; . . . uniting all Namibian people, . . . into a vanguard party, capable of safeguarding national independence and of building a non-exploitive society based on the ideals and principles of scientific socialism."[12]

---

[8] "The Protection of Human Rights in Namibia," address by F.J. Kozonguizi, conference on Human Rights and Namibia, Sedgwick Center, London, March 27, 1986.

[9] See: Appendix C.

[10] *Ibid.*

[11] Kozonguizi, *op. cit.*

[12] *Namibia, Perspectives for National Reconstruction and Development, op. cit.*, p.744.

This isn't mere puffery to stir up the people, SWAPO truly means what they say. They seek to run every aspect of Namibia down to the last detail, within "the ideals and principles of scientific socialism " as they proudly boast: "National socio-economic planning, as a management function, is a conscious activity which should assist the state in governing the economic, social and cultural life of society."[13] That doesn't leave much out of their centralized state planning scheme.

What is SWAPO's attitude toward the political realm in Namibia? It squares with their Marxist ideology: "Political stability based on a progressive ideological framework is a prime condition for establishing a system of national planning in independent Namibia. In fact ideology is one of the most important prerequistes for carrying out a meaningful and effective planning system at the national level. Ideology here refers to the dialectical sum total of ideas and beliefs contained in the Political Program of SWAPO."[14] What are the "sum total of ideas and belefs contained in the Political Program of SWAPO"? Why its nothing more than the "ideas and principles of scientific socialism"—Marxist newspeak for the establishment of a one-party totalitarian state.

They certainly are not advocating a Namibian version of Jeffersonian democracy.

Contrast SWAPO's program with the MPC's enumeration in their bill of rights, borrowed without shame from the American Declaration of Independence: "The fundamental rights entrenched include the conventional categories of personal, civil, political, social and procedural rights. They are, specifically, the rights to life, liberty, security of person, privacy and equality before the law; the rights to a fair trial, freedom of expression, peaceful assembly and freedom of association; to participate in political activity and government; to enjoy, practice, profess, maintain, and promote culture, language, tradition and religion; the right to freedom of movement and residence and the right to own property. In the interest of achieving an acceptable balance between liberty and social order, of promoting freedom while inhibiting any tendency to anarchy, the scope of these rights is necessarily limited, usually by the requirement of public order, public health or morals. The rights to participate in political activity and government is, moreover, qualified by a phrase borrowed from article 20 of the International Covenant on Civil and Political Rights, which imposes an obligation not to advocate ethnic, racial or religious hatred or to incite discrimination, hostility

---

[13] UN Institute for Namibia, p.746.
[14] *Ibid.*

Multi Party Conference   91

or violence. This is an essential provision in a multi-ethnic, culturally heterogeneous society like that of Namibia."[15]

Few Americans would find fault with the statements and rights enumerated in the MPC's Bill of Rights. It provides the foundation on which to build a better future for all the people of Namibia. It, unlike SWAPO's Political Program, accords privilege to none and equality of rights and obligations to all.

The Bill of Rights was to become an important vehicle in the efforts towards self-governing independence by the country.

Immediately after its adoption, the MPC began negotiations with the South African government over the release of SWAPO detainees held in South Africa. The negotiations bore fruit. On March 1, 1984, two SWAPO members, the founder, Herman Toivo and Willibald Sagaria were released. Two days later the South African Government announced that an additional fifty-four detainees would be released from the prison located at Mariental, Namibia. Eventually seventy-six more were released and the Mariental facility was closed.

However, an essential factor any internal SWA/Namibian political settlement required was the all-important international acceptance. The MPC now turned its attention to convincing the outside world of its committment to freedom and independence, even if mandated through the dubious process of UN Resolution 435.

The diplomatic climate was more favorable for the effort than it had been in the late 1970's. For one thing the United States had rid itself of President Carter and his Administration's flirtations with pro-soviet supported liberation movements. The Carter Administration attitude was epitomized by its chief UN delegate fatuously referring to the Cuban presence in Africa as a "stabilizing" influence. The Reagan Administration was initially more flexible in its dealings with the South Africans. As a result the diplomatic climate between the two nations was less poisoned than previously.

At the same period of time when the MPC was reaching out for foreign support, South Africa's diplomatic efforts towards her neighbors were also entering a new conciliatory stage.

During February 1984 while South Africa's Foreign Minister signed the Lusaka Agreement with Angola for South African troop withdrawals from Angola, the South African Prime Minister and Mozambique's Marxist leader

---

[15] Kozonguizi, *op. cit.*; see also: Appendix C.

Samora Machel were also discussing a non-aggression pact between the two countries. The discussions were successful and a pact, the Nkomati Accord, was formally signed by the two countries on March 15, 1984.

A seemingly different attitude was beginning to emerge in the diplomatic climate in southern Africa. The peace overtures floating around the area seemed infectious. Even President Kaunda of Zambia expressed the view that P.W. Botha, the South African leader, was a sincere man, and declared himself interested in meeting the MPC leaders.[16]

Although President Kaunda may have been humming the tune of peace, the reason for it was that his own country was rapidly becoming an economic basket case. Since all of the so-called frontline states were economically dependent upon South Africa, it didn't take much imagination for Kaunda to realize the trouble for him if South Africa tightened the economic screws on his country. As a wily politician, he knew a meeting with the MPC, under the circumstances made a lot of sense.

A personal element was also involved as some of the MPC delegates had gotten to know Kaunda while they were living in exile from SWA/Namibia.

The flurry of diplomatic activity climaxed in a conference in Lusaka between SWAPO, the Administrator General and an MPC delegation from May 10th through 13th, 1984.

SWAPO had to be dragged kicking and screaming to the conference only by the arm-twisting of Robert Mugabe and the frontline states' leaders.[17]

The conference, to add insult to injury to SWAPO, took place under the joint chairmanship of the Zambian head of state, President Kenneth Kaunda, and former SWA/Namibian Administrator General, Dr. Willie van Niekirk.

The conference, as usual for such events, drew up a statement summarizing the points of agreement as well as those points requiring further discussion. SWAPO got its revenge by refusing to sign the statement. By their actions SWAPO made it clear that no peace treaty was going to come from this meeting in Lusaka.

The meetings, however, were not a total failure. For one thing, by their pressure on SWAPO to talk to other SWA/Namibian political entities, other African countries had tarnished SWAPO's and the UN's claim that the terrorist group was still the sole and authentic representative of the Namibian people.

It, again, showed that SWAPO was not really interested in a peaceful solution in Namibia.

"It is a tragic irony that the last remaining stumbling blocks in the path of

[16] *Windhoek Advertiser,* February 28, 1984.
[17] *The Times,* May 11, 1984.

the establishment of a political and social order characterized by respect for the rights of all, are kept in place by an organization which claims to be fighting for the liberation of all Namibians. I refer, of course, to SWAPO," said Mr. Kozonguizi.[18]

". . . And still SWAPO, trapped in a time-warp of its own making, repeats the chants of yesteryear and clings to a naive belief in the efficiency of the AK-47, the bayonet, the RPG-7 and the landmine. Increasingly estranged from the people of Namibia, from whose loins it was born, but who now seek peace, not senseless conflict, SWAPO's cadres have to rely on brutal intimidation and repression, even of some of their own members and supporters, in order to continue the 'armed struggle.' How tragically pointless it all is."[19]

Although differences between the MPC and SWAPO seemed irreconcilable, the Lusaka conference seemed to bestow a patina of legitimacy on the MPC. That they were now able to demonstrate an ability to act in their own right gave credence to Prime Minister Botha's assertion that the MPC leaders were to assume direct responsibility for the future, as South Africa wished to solve the Namibian issue "in one way or another as soon as possible."[20]

Encouraged by their diplomatic breakthrough at Lusaka, the MPC went further north in Africa seeking support and recognition.

The results were not as tangible as the high profile conference in Lusaka. Although the MPC had gained the impression that there was considerable understanding and perhaps even a lot of sympathy for their plight, none of the states visited gave any hint it was prepared to go to the wall in support of the MPC.

In any case, one thing was clear: a political delegation from SWA/Namibia had never before received so much diplomatic recognition and interest abroad.

One constant theme emerged from their travels around Africa: African countries were in agreement with the MPC that peace and reconciliation were prerequisites to independence. Many African leaders they met with, especially President Felix Houphouet-Boigny of the Ivory Coast, expressed the opinion that the inhabitants of the country themselves should resolve the independence question and, furthermore, it should be done by peaceful discussion around a conference table.

The MPC's travels were not limited to Africa. They flew to the United States for meetings with officials of both the United Nations and the United

---

[18] Kozonguizi, *op. cit.*

[19] *Ibid.*

[20] *Windhoek Advertiser,* February 2, 1984.

States government. Among those with whom discussions were held were the Secretary General of the United Nations, Dr. Javier Perez de Cuellar and, U.S. Secretary of State George Schultz.

At both meetings the MPC stressed the importance of reconciliation and peace to the Namibian independence process. The MPC also stressed quite strongly that it did not want to circumvent the independence plan for SWA/Namibia, but they wanted to make sure that independence in the country was not followed by chaos, violence and economic decline.

These meetings, like their African counterparts, did not produce any iron-clad promises of support. In fact if pledges of support were the only criteria for judging the success or failure of the post-Lusaka meetings, they were obvious failures.

But there were silver linings in the clouds. The most important being that a legitimate non-SWAPO political entity had emerged which was being talked to by representatives from other states. An exceptional breakthrough, viewed in that light, was the meeting with the Secretary General of the same United Nations which still regarded SWAPO as the "sole authentic representative" of SWA/Namibia.

Unfortunately, getting the UN to change its attitude completely and remove SWAPO's special UN status would be comparable to the labors of Hercules. However, as Confucius observed: "The longest journey in the world begins with the first step." The MPC's meeting in late May 1984 was a giant first step on the long, difficult journey to independence for Namibia.

The MPC had been conducting its own foreign affairs as if it were a government in being, instead of a collection of political parties working as a coalition without formal governing authority, which still remained in the hands of the Administrator General.

On March 25, 1985, a delegation from the MPC traveled to Cape Town for a meeting with the State President P.W. Botha. The purpose of the meeting was simple: would the State President institute a transitional government in SWA/Namibia?

The South African government was not hostile to the idea and gave the MPC assurances that their request would be acted upon within one month.

On the 18th of April, the MPC had its answer: the South African government would accede to their request and institute a transitional government to govern the country until an internationally recognized agreement could be reached on the question of independence for SWA/ Namibia.

The people of Namibia were soon to be back in the business of self-government again, although with the UN Resolution 435, sword of Damocles still hanging over their heads.

10
Transitional Government Of National Unity

Nineteen months after the formation of the Multi-Party Conference (MPC) on June 17, 1985, Namibia's Transitional Government of National Unity (TGNU) was inaugurated in Windhoek. South Africa had duly transferred most of the governing functions to the territory in accordance with terms of the Proclamation of the Establishment and Powers of legislative and executive authority for South West Africa, 1985 (Proclamation R101 of 1985).

The South African government retained the responsibility for foreign affairs and defense. The Administrator General still continued to represent the State President of South Africa. As such he has been responsible for South Africa's obligations and responsibilities in Namibia. He also acted as a mediator between South Africa and the new Transitional Government of National Unity.

At the inauguration of the new government, the South African leader P. W. Botha said that while waiting for an internationally accepted solution leading to independence, the current measures should be considered a transitional phase for the internal administration of the country. Botha stressed, however, that until the independence of the territory became a reality, the South African government would not do anything that might jeopardize the international settlement plan. He further warned that if it was not possible for an international settlement to be reached then all parties concerned should explore other ways to achieve Namibian independence.

The message given by the South African leader to Namibia was—you are on your own. At least this was how the Namibians interpreted it.

It was, perhaps, premature for Namibians to feel that way as they still had the cloud of UN Resolution 435 hanging over their heads. Until that matter was sorted out independence was still an event to be reached "sometime in the future."

As might be expected, the UN reacted to the latest developments by condemning them. In a meeting on June 19, 1985, the Security Council denounced the activity in the territory and adopted Resolution 566 (1985) which condemned South Africa for installing, in the words of the UN, a "puppet" regime in Namibia. The resolution further declared that the action was illegal, null and void and that no recognition would be accorded either by the United Nations, any Member State or any group or organ of the UN. The resolution also demanded that the "illegal" and unilateral action be rescinded.

So much for the MPC's prior efforts to open a dialogue with the United Nations. By this action the UN made it clear that it was putting all its eggs in the SWAPO basket and would defend its evil-tempered prodigy with all the means at its disposal.

The tragic part is that the Reagan and Thatcher administrations went along with this blatant showing of contempt by the UN against a Third World country that was modeling its attempt to gain independence and self-determination along Western, instead of Marxist, lines.

In spite of the UN's condemnation, the Transitional Government of National Unity began to organize itself and function as a representative government.

It may not be charitable to the United Nations, but a possible reason for its implacable hostility to the evolving internal political processes in Namibia was the fear that they might succeed. The longer the internal parties have to lay the foundation for self-government and put in place a workable governmental infrastructure, the harder it would be for UN meddling to undo the efforts and turn the situation in favor of its adopted protege— SWAPO. Therefore, it has been in the interests of the UN to torpedo or strangle at birth any effort that might become an obstacle to the imposition of a UN-blessed SWAPO regime.

Again, it tells us much about the lack of backbone possessed by Western governments that allowed the UN to act in such an arbitrary, high-handed manner in Namibia.

Nevertheless, the new government in Namibia was a democratically elected parliamentary government consisting of six parties: Labour Party, Liberation Front (LF), Democratic Turnhalle Alliance (DTA), National

Party of SWA (NP), South West Africa National Union (SWANU) and SWAPO Democrats (SWAPO-D). The members of these parties are represented in the sixty-two member National Assembly. Of this number only eleven are whites, the rest represent all the ethnic groups in the territory.

In a typical parliamentary government, the executive power is also exercised by the legislative body. A group of members are chosen from the parliamentary body and exercise executive, as well as legislative functions. It was no different in the new Namibian government. The executive power was exercised by a Cabinet composed of eight members who were also sitting members of the National Assembly.

The Cabinet, consisting of eight members called ministers, is assisted by eight deputy ministers. However, the deputy minister cannot be a member of the same party as the minister. Both may attend the Cabinet sessions at all times and they represent their ministers when the latter are absent.

The National Assembly has eight standing committees. The committee activities coincide with the eight ministers' respective portfolios. They are: Transportation; Local Authorities and Civic Affairs; Manpower, National Health and Welfare; Justice, Information and Posts and Telecommunications; Education and Central Personnel Institution; Finance and Governmental Affairs; Nature Conservation, Mining, Commerce and Tourism; and Agriculture, Water Affairs and Sea Fisheries.

Each committee must have at least one member of each of the political parties represented in the National Assembly.

Bills are referred to the appropriate committee by the Speaker of the National Assembly. The Speaker is chosen from the members of the National Assembly, but is not a member of any of the standing committees.

All bills, unless the National Assembly gives specific permission by a vote on the matter, must be referred to the appropriate committee within seven days of being introduced.

The committee then discusses the bill, rejects it, amends it, or sends it unaltered to the floor of the Assembly for final action.

There is also a temporary ninth standing committee. Its task is to examine every law which was in force in the territory before the first meeting of the National Assembly and see which of them do not square with the bill of fundamental rights. Those laws which transgress a fundamental right are to be reported to the National Assembly so corrective action can be taken.

Decisions taken by the Cabinet are by majority vote. However, there is a quasi-judicial method by which a member may forestall or even halt a cabinet proposal. If a member can get a legal opinion on a matter before the Cabinet considers it and so informs the Cabinet that the matter under discussion infringes on the right of any person or groups of persons, the Cabinet is required to refer the matter as a legal problem to the Supreme Court of SWA/Namibia for a decision. Unlike our system, this allows the question of constitutionality to be aired before the proposal becomes a law.

Until the court has returned a decision on the matter, the Cabinet cannot act upon it.

The proposed legislation becomes law by a majority vote in the National Assembly. But, unlike many parliamentary systems, the failure to enact a bill doesn't result in the dissolving of the National Assembly.

The chairmanship of the Cabinet rotates alphabetically every three months.

Five members are required to form a quorum at Cabinet meetings, and every effort is made to reach unanimity on all decisions, even though majority rule is sufficient.

The Cabinet may establish committees within itself from time to time to advise it on particular matters. These committees may be made up of any person, minister or non-minister, and the Cabinet can delegate any of its power, duties or activities to these special committees.

The judicial authority, like most Western democracies, functions independent of the executive and legislative authority.

The legal system in Namibia, due to its historical connections with European powers, is based on Roman Dutch law. It is also independent from the South African system, but appeals against verdicts by the Windhoek Supreme Court may be lodged with the South African appellate division in Bloemfontein.

The Windhoek Supreme Court consists of a presiding judge and four other judges. There are also two lower courts: a Regional Court and a Magistrate's Court with a controlling magistrate as well as four magistrates for criminal cases and one for civil cases.

All cases are heard in public, unless there are good reasons why the proceeding should exclude the public.

On September 30, 1985, the National Assembly voted unanimously to set up a Constitutional Council to draft a constitution for a future independent, sovereign Namibia.

The Council was composed of sixteen members made up of members of the political parties in the National Assembly. However, the door was left open to SWAPO and any other political entity in the territory. The Cabinet can and is encouraged to permit other political parties to join the

Constitutional Council. Each party so allowed can nominate two members to the Council. SWAPO steadfastly refused to take part in the proceedings.

The Council would examine various constitutional models and draft a constitution that would make provisions for the protection of rights and freedoms of individuals and groups.

The Council was given a mandate by the Assembly to report a draft bill within seventeen months from the day of its first meeting, which happened to be the 13th of January, 1986. If the Council were unable to meet this deadline, the Cabinet could give them an extension not to exceed six months. The citizens of Namibia, therefore, could expect to see a draft constitution by December 13, 1987, at the latest. As we will see, a draft constitution was ready well before this deadline.

By the end of 1985, then, the machinery of self-government had been set in motion in Namibian Executive Cabinet, an independent judiciary, a representative National Assembly, and a Council that was drafting a constitution.

This process was a far cry from the usual practice in Africa where law, legislation and judicial processes flowed from the barrel of a gun, to paraphrase the late Chinese Communist tyrant, Mao Tse-tung.

Nor did the Namibians rest on their laurels. The political entities—the Cabinet and National Assembly—began the task of finding and developing a common strategy to lead the territory towards the peaceful goal of independence.

It is a common truism that in non-totalitarian systems of government, disagreements arise over matters of much importance. Namibia was no different. Given the nature of the political parties in the National Assembly, differences sprang up over many issues. But, and this should be of considerable interest to those who look kindly on Western-style liberal democracy, those differences strengthened their internal relationships. As a result, their commitment has increased for the ideals of rights and self-government that are the bedrock of Western-style democracy.

The sense of urgency of their quest for self-determination and their bending over backwards to seek national reconciliation were powerful motivating force for their efforts. It enabled them to reconcile their differences, forge ahead and adopt specific programs that were designed to change the status quo.

In the process the members of the Assembly honed their political skills and statesmanship as they found greater insight into the basic needs

100 *Death in the Desert*

and aspirations of their varied and different constituencies. This growing political maturity and sophistication was not lost on observers beyond their borders, in spite of the open hostility of the United Nations. They were achieving some credibility as a governing entity, but they were a long way from escaping the UN's doghouse.

Nevertheless, they carried on as if they were well on the road to becoming a free and independent state. They did so with a fair measure of success. For example, on April 9, 1986, the National Assembly outlawed racial and ethnic discrimination. The Assembly has also established a National Development Fund to assist in planning and financing of various development projects in the country.

In addition, the Cabinet authorized the release of over seventy political prisoners. All SWA/Namibian citizens who had been incarcerated for political-security offenses were released.

As a result of the loss of revenue from fishing activities within the country's unrecognized 200 nautical mile fishing zones, and the overwhelming foreign ownership in the country's mining industry, a sense of economic nationalism has begun to emerge. A considerable body of opinion inside Namibia has been pressing for the renegotiation of the country's fishing and mining concessions.

All this activity in the economic sphere is contrary to the wishes of the United Nations. It is doing its best, through its Council for Namibia, to kill this effort by Namibia.

The United Nations Council for Namibia came into existence by way of General Assembly Resolution 2248, adopted on May 19, 1967. The Council, at present, consists of thirty-one members. They are: Algeria, Angola, Australia, Bangladesh, Belgium, Botswana, Bulgaria, Burundi, Cameroon, Chile, China, Colombia, Cyprus, Egypt, Finland, Guyana, Haiti, India, Indonesia, Liberia, Mexico, Nigeria, Pakistan, Poland, Romania Senegal, Turkey, U.S.S.R., Venezuela, Yugoslavia and Zambia. Three states (Cuba, Nicaragua and Zimbabwe) have been granted observer status by the Council. The vast majority of the Council are anti-West and all are hostile to the Republic of South Africa. Most are sympathetic to the world-wide socialist movement.[1] In the UN scheme of things, the Council was "entrusted" with the authority to administer South West Africa until independence. To ensure that the Council ran its affairs to the liking of the

---

[1] *United Nations Handbook 1988,* New Zealand Ministry of Foreign Affairs, Wellington, New Zealand, 1988, p.21.

Third World, the vast majority of its thirty-one members are from the Third World or are its sympathizers, and it would be responsible to the General Assembly, which would free it from the vetoes of the permanent members of the Security Council (read that to mean the United States and Great Britain).

On September 27, 1974, the Council for Namibia issued Decree Number 1 for the Protection of Natural Resources of Namibia. What did that decree mean? It provided that no person or corporation may exploit (UN's term) any natural resource situated within the territorial limits of Namibia without the permission of the United Nations Council for Namibia.

It is obvious that members of the Council don't practice what they preach. Five members of the Council, Angola, Bulgaria, Poland, Romania and the Soviet Union have been busy plundering and exploiting Namibian fishing resources from Namibian waters without paying any compensation to the people of Namibia. Of the total amount of fish caught in Namibian waters, 63.5% were caught in 1984, 59% in 1985 and 54% in 1986 by these five countries.[2]

Three years later, during the tenure of Andrew Young, the Carter Administration's Ambassador to the UN, the UN General Assembly passed a resolution requesting all member states to take all appropriate measures to ensure the full application of Decree Number 1.

This isn't the end of the story, as the UN is taking its economic blackmail policies against Namibia one step further—it is borrowing a tactic from American liberals of using the courts to impose its agenda. The Council for Namibia is considering using legal proceedings in the domestic courts of UN Member States against corporations or individuals involved in the utilization of the natural resources of Namibia. Given the huge dependency in Namibia on foreign capital and investment this is a potentially ominous development for the economy of the territory. The only conclusion one can draw from this attitude is that the UN, in its infinite wisdom, is determined to destroy the economy of Namibia. It is contemplating this while five members of the Council for Namibia go about their unhindered business of depleting fish from Namibian waters!

In spite of these difficulties, the Namibian Transitional Government

---

[2] Namibian TGNU/Cabinet press release, November 11, 1988; *Namibia (South West Africa) News,* Washington, DC, December 21, 1988, p.2.

has been working constantly to involve all the people in Namibia in creating and insuring a free Namibia. It is pressing ahead with its program of political reform and socio-economic development as a basis to forge a common society with the ultimate aim of internationally accepted independence.

11
The Deteriorating Situation

After 1976 Namibia, faced an escalating terrorist war. The new Marxist government in Angola had now taken SWAPO under its wing by giving it bases and logistical support. Increased support from the Soviet Union and its surrogates poured into the SWAPO terrorists cause along with military supplies and advisors. SWAPO also began reaping the benefit from all the propaganda and other international support given to them from the numerous Soviet "fraternal"organizations throughout the world. The United Nations also jumped into the arena on the side of SWAPO by giving them money, support and international recognition.

On the ground, in parts of Namibia, SWAPO managed to escalate the war from the terrorism phase into the guerrilla war phase of their revolutionary struggle. Their recruiting efforts were having a reasonable degree of success. They were actually recruiting more cadres to their cause than they were losing to the security forces.

With their major bases—training, logistical and command center—safely over the border in Angola, prospects seemed rosy for SWAPO.

From the Angolan sanctuaries, SWAPO terrorists could easily walk across the border into the operational area of 47,000 square miles, about the size of New York state, though with a population of barely six hundred thousand—carry out their acts of terrorism and walk back across the borders to return to the safety of their bases.

It is well to remember that SWAPO's ultimate goal was to take political power in Namibia by military means. Their revolutionary campaign had a clearly defined political end and in accord with Maoist doctrine it was necessary for the revolutionaries to politicize the masses. As Mao had stressed in his writings, ". . . Without a precise, specific political program we cannot mobilize all the armed forces and all the people . . . Next, it is not enough to mobilize only once; political mobilization for the . . . War must be done regularly. Our job is not merely to recite our political program to the people . . . but we must link it up with the developments in the war and with the life of the soldiers and the people, thereby transforming the political mobilization for the war into a regular movement. This is a matter of the first magnitude on which victory primarily depends."[1]

In short, as SWAPO's military situation improved so should its political fortunes. The two factors are closely related in a revolutionary context.

However, the converse is also true from a counterinsurgency perspective. By reducing the insurgent military threat, the governing authorities can regain the confidence of the masses and by in doing, reduce and, hopefully, eliminate the subversive political influence within the country. As the American counterinsurgency expert, Bard O'Neil said, "Although the insurgent threat is largely a political-administrative one, this does not mean military success is unimportant. Beside inflicting material and personnel losses on the insurgent movement, and in some cases forcing the insurgent movement from familiar terrain, military victories can enhance government morale, undermine the insurgent image and impress the population. It must be remembered the insurgents are trying to establish an image of strength in order to convince the people they will succeed; when most of the victories go to the government side, the insurgents' credibility suffers."[2]

The South African government's overall program was to provide a security umbrella so that the major portion of the counterinsurgency program—civic action, political action and psychological warfare—could operate in an atmosphere conducive to success. The immediate security goal was to inflict losses on SWAPO revolutionaries, undermine SWAPO's image and destroy their organization inside Namibia. A comprehensive campaign had to be planned and conducted in such a way as to minimize civilian losses. As Noel Barber stressed, ". . . In this kind of war, one stray bomb that killed one innocent child could make a thousand enemies . . . it was better to police villages than to destroy them."[3]

Running up an impressive body count of dead SWAPO terrorists wasn't enough. As had been demonstrated by J.K. Cilliers in Rhodesia/Zimbabwe,

---

[1] Mao Tse-tung, "On the Protracted War," *Selected Works, op. cit.,* Vol. II, pp.204-5.

[2] O'Neil, *op. cit.,* p.25.

[3] Barber, Noel, *The War of the Running Dogs,* Weybright & Talley, New York, 1971, p.63.

"What was required was an awareness that the war could not be won only in terms of killing armed combatants, but in gaining the active support and involvement or at least neutrality of increasing numbers of the local black population. This could only have been achieved by first providing the black rural population with permanent protection, or enabling these people to protect themselves."[4]

The South Africans were determined not to repeat Rhodesia's mistake of not protecting the rural population. Not only would they protect them but, combined with their other programs, were determined to win the "hearts and minds" of the people. This would be done by demonstrating their determination to carry through with promised reforms and granting the people of Namibia their political independence. As Thompson had earlier concluded, "What the peasant wants to know is: Does the government mean to win the war? Because if not, he will have to support the insurgent. The government must show it is determined to win."

The South Africans showed their determination to win in many ways. They poured a large number of troops and police into the operational area to provide security against the depredations of SWAPO. They established numerous military and police bases in the operational area. These bases were widely dispersed and put the presence of security force personnel near and among all the population centers in the operational area. The presence of these bases allowed the security forces to conduct a program which McCuen said, ". . . must be apparent, effective, and stable so that the people recognize its existence, can depend upon it, and will be confident of the future."[6]

The South Africans bit the bullet and expanded their security program into two campaigns: an internal and an external campaign which became mutually supportive. The internal campaign was geared to destroying SWAPO's organization and killing or capturing its terrorists inside Namibia. The external campaign focused at first on the task of destroying SWAPO bases in southern Angola. Later on, the external campaign had two purposes. The first purpose was to force the SWAPO infrastructure of training bases and logistical centers further north away from the border. This would require the infiltrating terrorists to travel longer distances to get to the operational area in Namibia. This would, in turn, allow elements of the security forces to intercept them before reaching Namibia. It would also strain the SWAPO

---

[4] Cilliers, J.K., *Counter-Insurgency in Rhodesia,* Croom Helm Ltd., Kent, England, 1985, pp.244-5.

[5] Thompson, R., *Defeating Communist Insurgency,* Praeger, New York, 1966, p.146.

[6] McCuen, *op. cit.,* p.57.

supply chain which would mean that those terrorists that escaped detection and destruction enroute could not spend as much time in the operational area due to lack of logistical support. The second purpose was to increase the problem for SWAPO to carry out its revolutionary action in Namibia by making SWAPO facilities more remote from the operational area. The further apart the terrorists and their commanders were, the more difficult would become their command and control. The reduced efficiency in command and control combined with the reduced time the terrorists could spend in the operational area affected SWAPO's manpower situation. It severely hurt SWAPO's recruitment efforts in Namibia which further reduced SWAPO's effectiveness dramatically.

The security force's internal operations could also develop into external operations in that the security forces often engaged in hot pursuit and chased SWAPO terrorists back over the border into Angola, often engaging in running battles throughout the pursuit.

External operations would have a high political cost. Howls of indignation by Western politicians and media, vituperative speeches and resolutions of condemnation in the United Nations, came as expected. All of this abuse was heaped upon South Africa in spite of the indisputable fact that Angola was being used as a sanctuary and springboard for the war of terrorism in Namibia. (An important lesson for students of counterinsurgency warfare is the significance of cross-border operations against insurgent bases and sanctuaries. Heavy patrolling and civic action may supress insurgent activity within the country, but, with external sancuaries, the initiative would almost always remain in the hands of the insurgents. There is little point in conducting internal operations, no matter how successful, if an inexhaustible stream of reinforcements can enter the country with impunity. It is well to remember an old military axiom that one cannot win a war by fighting defensively. Cross-border operations against insurgent facilities would allow the security forces to take the initiative and use military force in the most advantageous manner.)

The security forces main effort had been directed at internal operations. This, unfortunately but inevitably, gave SWAPO the advantage of the initiative. They were free to decide when and where they would enter Namibia and what they would do once inside the country. As a result the security forces main efforts and operations revolved around finding the terrorists, then either capturing or destroying them. Owamboland's geography was no help either as it is extremely flat and its dense bush offers the terrorists exceptional cross country mobility and good concealment.

Operations—both internal and external—have had several features in

The identity papers of a Soviet advisor to SWAPO in Angola.

Statue commemorating the schutztruppe, the mounted Imperial German soldier who imposed German rule in Namibia while it was a German colony—German South West Africa.

Peaceful Kavango River scene near Bigani in the Western Caprivi.

Motorcycle troops preparing to go after two SWAPO terrorists reported to be hiding out at a local *cuca*.

Motorcycle patrol preparing to investigate a SWAPO terrorist sighting in Owamboland.

A rush across the flat Owamboland terrain in an attempt to surround and trap the terrorists in the school.

Motorcycle troops searching school for two SWAPO terrorists who attempted to hide in the school buildings.

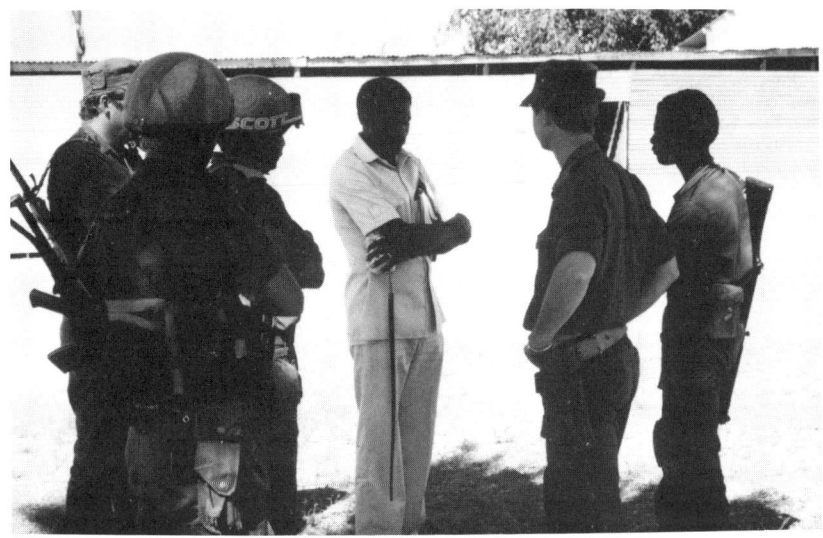

Motorcycle-mounted troops question teacher about hiding two SWAPO terrorists in his school.

After the action is over, the troops take a break.

Namibian diamond mine on the Atlantic Coast near Oranjemund.

Diamond mine workers sweep the rocks clean in their search for diamonds in Namibia.

Rare rain shower in Namibia.

Sunset on the Zambezi River in the Caprivi Strip.

Road to Omega, home of the Bushmen Battalion.

Bushmen trackers follow spoor while rest of the platoon follows in Buffels.

Bushmen from 201 Battalion on SWAPO spoor.

Contact! SWAPO spotted, troops dismount to fight them on the ground.

Squad leader from 201 Battalion keeps in radio contact with his platoon leader while following SWAPO spoor.

Bushmen machine-gunner and his loader fire at cornered SWAPO terrorist.

Another SWAPO terrorist killed by the Bushmen battalion troops.

Bushmen at Omega operating a primitive bush forge, shaping a piece of iron into a knife blade.

The emblem of 201 Battalion's reconnaissance wing says it all.

Mounted patrol in the operational area looking for SWAPO terrorists.

Outdoor john in a tree near Katima Mulilo.

Rossing uranium mine in Namibia. It is the largest open-pit uranium mine in the world.

Early morning fog sweeps inland from the Atlantic Ocean over the dunes of the Namib Desert, bringing life-giving moisture to many creatures that live in the desert.

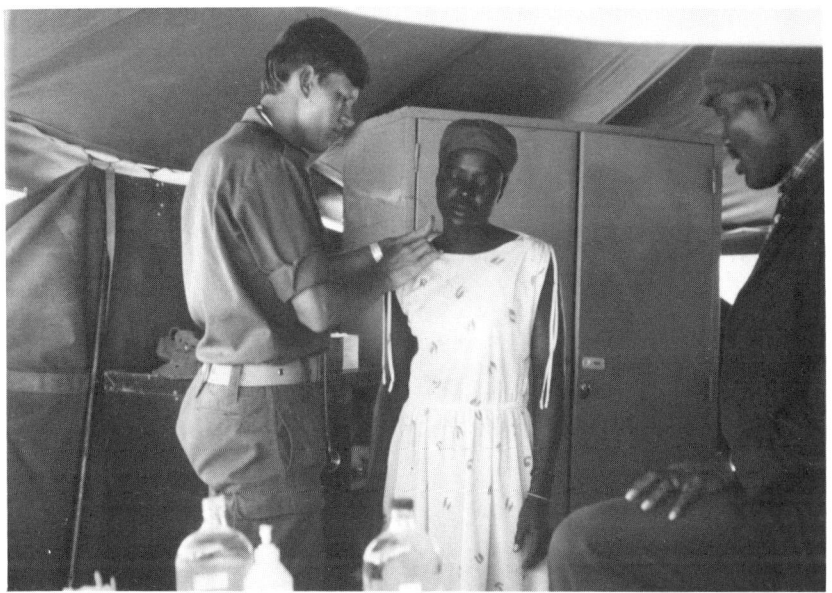

SADF medical doctors treating the local population as part of their humanitarian counterinsurgency effort.

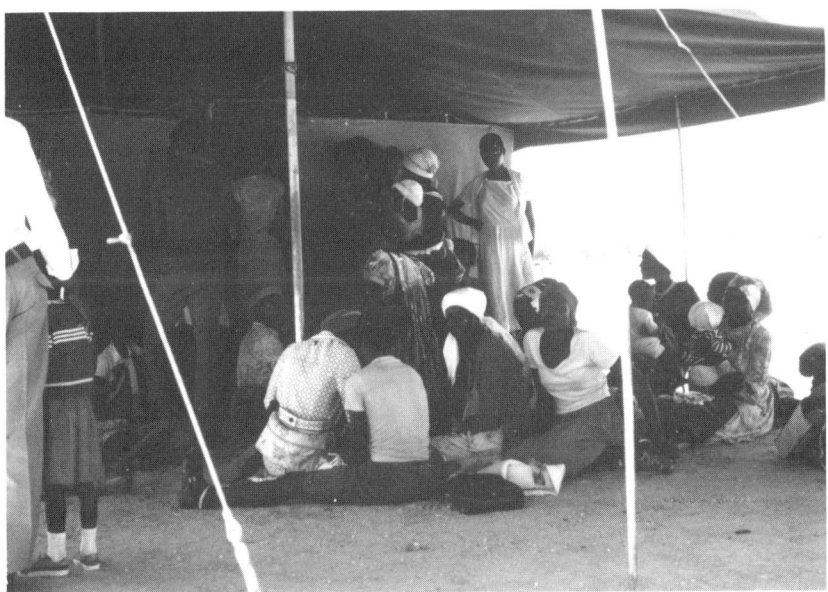

Sick call for civilians at Okatope. SADF doctors provide medical care to locals near their bases.

Portable medical lab. SADF medical technicians preparing culture smears to aid in diagnosing diseases in Namibia.

Winning the "hearts and minds" through the Word of God. SADF soldiers distributing the Bible written in one of the Owambo languages.

Soviet-supplied landmines used by SWAPO in their terror campaign in Namibia.

Sweeping a dirt road in Owamboland for SWAPO landmines.

SWAPO terrorist briefcase bomb, a favorite terrorist weapon in Namibia.

Barclay's Bank in Oshakati destroyed by a SWAPO briefcase bomb in February 1988. The blast killed 28 innocent civilians, most of them black Owambos.

New Soviet anti-tank mine containing a shaped charge capable of destroying any tank in the world.

The inhospitable Namib Desert stretches from Angola to South Africa along the west coast of Namibia. The country is named after this desert.

A lonely palm tree in the Hoarusib River canyon on the Skeleton Coast of Namibia.

Romeo-Mike force of 101 Battalion heads for its operational area.

SWAPO terrorists moving through the bush in southern Angola on their way to infiltrate into Namibia. Shortly after this picture was taken, the terrorists were shot by SWATF security forces.

Author with SADF officer while on operations in the bush with 101 Battalion.

"They're out there." 101 Battalion troops pause momentarily while on a hot SWAPO spoor.

A late lunch in the bush while hunting SWAPO.

Soviet advisors conferring with SWAPO terrorists in Angola.

Soviet advisor instructing SWAPO terrorists in Angola.

Soviet advisor conducting a sandtable military training exercise at a SWAPO terrorist base in Angola.

UN supports terrorism. Supplies found in a SWAPO base. Note the labels: UNHCR—United Nations High Commissioner for Refugees; and, UN's World Food Program.

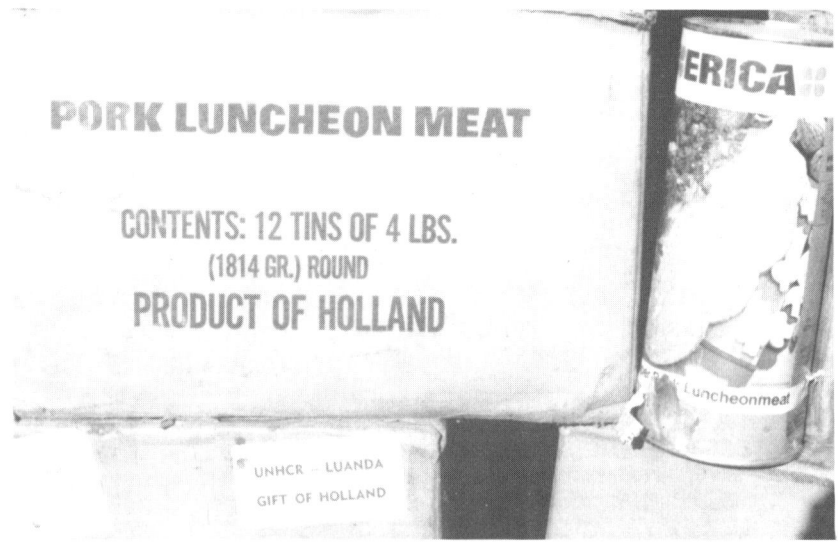

Herero recruits of 202 Battalion undergoing physical fitness training.

Ovahimba male in traditional dress.

Ovahimba hut made of reeds and leather.

Scanning the bush for FAPLA armored units, 61 Mechanized Battalion Ratel with a 90 mm. cannon.

Mounted SWATF soldier dismounts to check out a *kraal* for information on SWAPO terrorists.

Mounted infantry watering their horses during a patrol in the operational area.

Tall termite hills are a common sight in Owamboland.

Loosening saddles, a mounted patrol takes a break from its hunt for SWAPO terrorists.

32 Battalion sign at the entrance to their base in the Caprivi Strip.

Troops from 32 Battalion move through the bush looking for SWAPO spoor.

Early morning convoy preparing to depart Oshivello for the journey to Ondangwa.

SADF base protecting a valuable watertower in Eastern Owamboland.

common: (1) to seek actively to contact and engage SWAPO terrorists; (2) to search and pick up spoor of the terrorists and follow the tracks to a contact; (3) to be seen by the population and by this visible presence encourage a sense of security among the population; (4) to gather intelligence; and, (5) to conduct psychological warfare (or "comops" as the South Africans call it) aimed at both winning the hearts and minds of the people and discrediting SWAPO.

On the Namibian border separating the operational area from Angola, a flat sandy strip 100 meters wide has been cut through the bush by bulldozers. This strip, or cutline as it is called, is the first line of defense and runs the length of the border between the Cunene River on the west and the Kavango River in the east. The border is frequently, but irregularly patrolled. Often spoor found on this sandy strip are the first indication that SWAPO terrorists have crossed the border. These tracks are followed-up as indeed are all such tracks found in the operational area.

Other elements of the security force patrol extensively throughout Owamboland on foot, horseback, or in vehicles, as the situation and terrain dictate. Highly mobile reaction forces are kept on alert throughout the operational area to come to the scene when a group of PLAN terrorists have been located and fixed. Often, however, the contact is fought out at close range by the patrol that first makes contact.

The security forces also employ ambushes as well as listening and observation posts depending upon the situation and nature of the terrain. Search and destroy operations and sweeps are launched in the operational area at irregular intervals.

More passive measures include providing protection for likely targets and officials of the civil administration, sweeping the roads for mines and convoy escort. Other examples include providing special police officers to guard tribal headmen, and protecting road works and water facilities.

Along with the security operations, the South Africans have engaged in a massive civic action program, and have encouraged and assisted in the development of internal political alternatives to SWAPO with the eventual goal of total independence for Namibia.

Neither the security program nor the civic action program have been conducted in a vacuum. There is a symbiotic relationship between them. The failure of one will surely lead to the failure of the other. Keeping this in mind, we will examine some examples of the security measures taken by the South Africans to roll back the revolutionary onslaught of SWAPO.

Though internal and external operations will be examined separately, the reader must remember that often both were occurring at the same time.

One also should not forget that other political and military activities were underway that would affect the success or failure of the counter-revolutionary effort in Namibia. The counter-revolutionary stewpot contained a number of diverse ingredients all simmering together at the same time.

The fact that the South Africans were able to mount a massive counterinsurgency effort in the face of overwhelming international support of SWAPO showed a key element of a successful program the determination to carry it out to the end. Without this will to succeed, their efforts would have foundered early in the game.

Let us now turn our attention to the terrorist war in Namibia.

12
The Bush War Heats Up

Mao Tse-tung, the master practitioner of guerrilla war, stressed the importance of bases for the guerrilla. He said: ". . . as the war is at once protracted and ruthless, it is impossible to sustain guerrilla war in the enemy's rear without base areas . . . What then are the base areas for a guerrilla war? They are the strategic bases on which a guerrilla war relies for carrying out its strategic tasks as well as for achieving the goals of preserving and expanding oneself and annihilating or expelling the enemy . . . There have been in history many peasant wars of the roving insurgent type, but they all failed. In the present age of advanced communications and technology, it is more than ever an entirely groundless illusion to attempt to win victory after the fashion of roving insurgents."[1]

Bases are of critical importance to the success of the guerrilla. They are no less important to the efforts of the government that is fighting the insurgency. Establishing bases by themselves will solve nothing except giving the government control of the precise real estate occupied by the bases. For a successful counterinsurgency effort these bases must be used as stepping stones for the government's efforts in winning back control of the country.

This requires some hard choices for the government. First of all, they have to accept the fact that if successful guerrilla operations are being carried out against them then the guerrillas must have some support among the local population—perhaps even a majority of it.

Tempting as it may be, the government in all likelihood doesn't have the resources to try and do everything at once. They can't run around the countryside trying to stamp out all the little incidents started by the guerrillas.

[1] Mao Tse-tung, "Strategic Problems in the Anti-Japanese Guerrilla War, *Selected Works*, Vol. II, p.135.

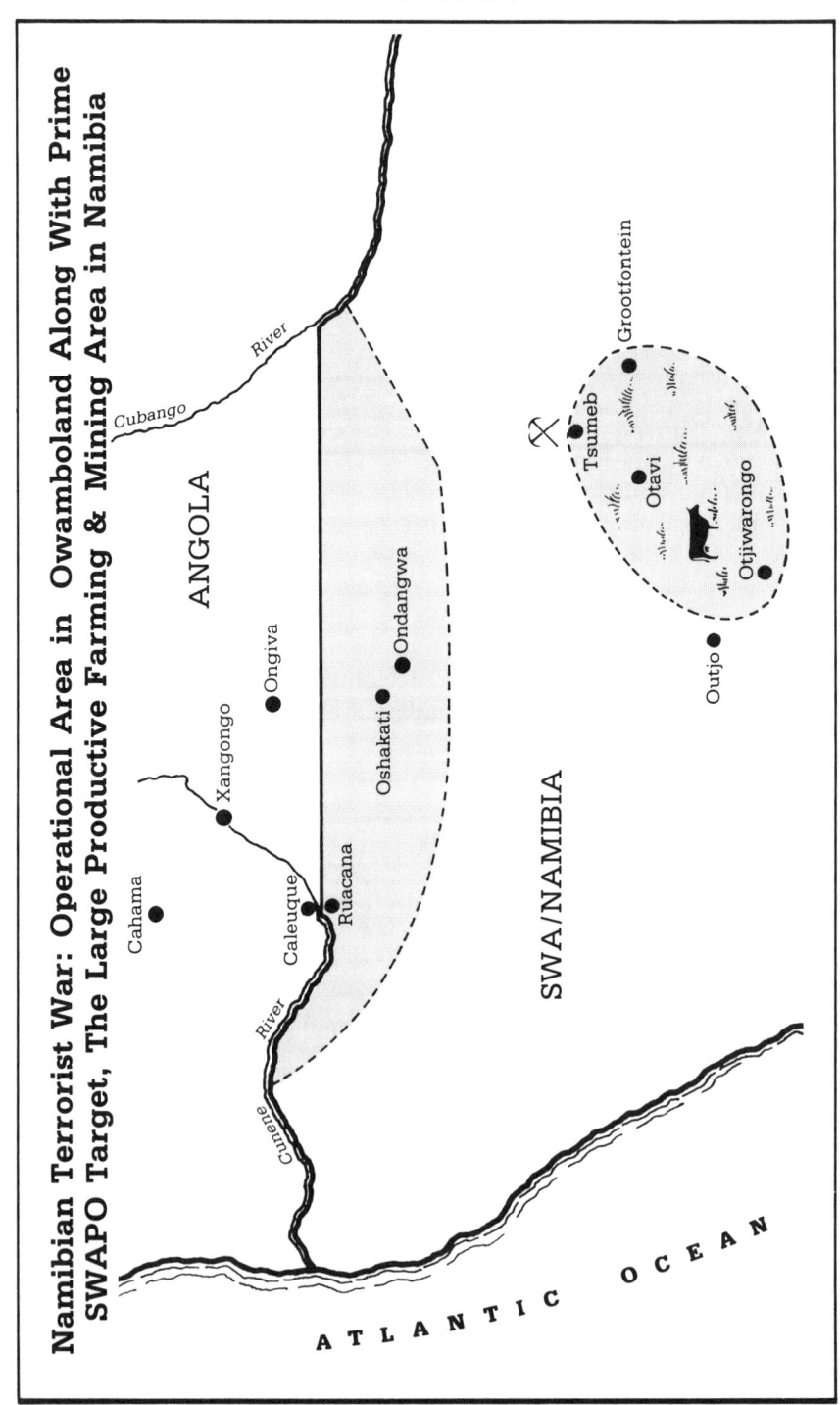

Instead, they must take a cold, hard look at the situation and develop a plan of action based on what that reality is and not on what they wish it to be.

From this hard-nosed appraisal of the actual situation a plan must be drawn up that will accomplish the counterinsurgency goal of winning back the country and defeating the insurgents. This plan, encompassing the realities of the situation, must in a step-by-step manner carry out the government's counterinsurgency program. Probably nothing is more important to the government than the early realization that this effort is going to take a long time—years rather than months—and their plans should reflect that.[2]

McCuen advocates, and the South Africans have agreed, that a successful counterinsurgency program used by the governing authorities be based on the oil spot strategy. They needed to set up bases, designed not only to protect the population from attack, but also to allow the government to carry out political and socio-economic measures which would win the population away from supporting the guerrillas. The government influence would spread out from these bases like an oil stain or *tache d'huile,* as its innovator Joseph Gallieni, termed it, eventually engulfing the population.[3]

This means the establishment of firm bases as centers for launching a counterinsurgency effort. These should be established not merely on the basis of territorial considerations, but also on population considerations. These bases fall into three rough classes: those bases in areas already under government control; those in hostile areas under control of the insurgents; and, those in areas not controlled by either the government or the guerrilla.

Consideration must also be given to controlling, if not initially then by regaining control, the major population and other essential areas such as food producing, mining, oil, industrial, etc..

It should be apparent that the job requires more than simply scattering groups of soldiers or policemen willy-nilly throughout the countryside to show the government's presence and hoping the insurgents will be cowed into submission. Such an effort is doomed to failure as the Nationalist Chinese efforts in China during their long civil war and the French efforts in Indochina demonstrated.

The problem then for the South Africans in Namibia was to undertake a

---

[2] McCuen, *op. cit.,* p.196.

[3] Beckett, Ian, *The Roots of Counter-Insurgency: Armies and Guerrilla Warfare, 1900-1945,* Blandford Press, London, 1985, p.15.

carefully planned, long-range effort, to accept the tremendous costs involved, and not only defeat SWAPO militarily, but remove its socio-political influence.

Having made the decision to travel on the long, lonely, costly and hard path of counterinsurgency, they set out to do the job with a determined effort.

As a result of the South African incursion into Angola in 1975-76, the military already had some base facilities in Namibia to support that effort. Thus, when the decision was made to launch an all out counterinsurgency campaign against SWAPO they did not have to start from scratch.

The presence of South African troops for the Angolan venture also had a detrimental effect on SWAPO's efforts to set up permanent bases inside Namibia. Instead, SWAPO set up their main bases a short distance over the border in Angola. By being close to the border SWAPO terrorists could walk across and remain in Namibia until detected and chased out by the security forces.

In the early stages of the counterinsurgency effort SWAPO cadres were seemingly crossing the border back and forth at will.

Nevertheless, the South Africans, heeding McCuen's dictum, began adding to their military infrastructure in Namibia. They built a series of strategic bases, especially in the northern border area where the bulk of SWAPO's activities were concentrated.

Bases were built or enlarged at Katima Mulilo, Bagani, Rundu, Tsumeb, Eenhana, Grootfontein, Ondangwa, Otjiwarango, Oshakati and Ruacana. These bases were located not only for their military value, but with other criteria in mind as well: near areas of large population groups, near sources of water and electrical power, sources of mining, farming areas or important logistical facilities such as paved roads and railway lines.

Katima Mulilo, near the eastern end of the Caprivi Strip, was turned into a fortress to cope with SWAPO infiltration from neighboring Zambia. An important nearby airstrip, Mapacha, was enlarged to provide air support for the operations in the Caprivi Strip.

Rundu, the administrative capital of Kavongoland, became the focus of counterinsurgency operations in the Kavongo. Located on the banks of the Kavongo River, which in this area forms the border with Angola, it was also the terminus of a hardtop road running in a northeastern direction from Grootfontein.

Grootfontein was an important location for many reasons. It was near the large commercial farming areas; it sat astride an important road junction; it was an important rail terminal linking northern Namibia; and a large air base was located near the town. Grootfontein soon evolved into one of the most important logistical centers serving the operational area in northern Namibia. From it supplies move northeasterly to Rundu and the Caprivi Strip or northwesterly to Ondangwa and Owamboland.

Otjiwarango was important in that it protected the large cattle farming areas in its vicinity; linked by a paved road and rail line, it sat astride the line of communications from Windhoek north to the operational area.

Ruacana, located on the Cunene River, which forms part of the border with Angola, had strategic as well as economic significance. It anchored the western end of the security forces operations in Owamboland and, equally important, it provided protection for the hydroelectric and water facilities built at the Ruacana Falls. The electricity and water were vital to the economic well-being of Namibians, especially those in northern Namibia.

Ondangwa was a key logistical, air and personnel base for operations in Owamboland. Supplies, moving up from the south were stored here for further distribution throughout Owamboland. Many of the SADF fighting units involved in the counterinsurgency effort were located in small bases surrounding the town. From these bases smaller units were established in company-sized camps throughout Owamboland. These camps, in turn, became the focal points of security force activity in the area surrounding them.

The huge airbase at Ondangwa was the center of air operations throughout the operational area.

Ondangwa became the jumping off center for most of the future cross-border operations the South Africans were to conduct as they drove the SWAPO infrastructure further away from the operational area in Namibia.

These, then, were the key strategic bases set up by the South Africans as they faced the difficult challenge posed by SWAPO's insurgency.

From these strategic base areas and the company-sized bases located in areas undergoing heavy SWAPO guerrilla activity, the security forces carried out the war against SWAPO. Operating from these bases, the security forces were constantly seeking to engage any SWAPO guerrillas operating in their assigned areas. They were constantly on the move, patrolling the area, setting up ambushes and whenever possible attacking the SWAPO guerrillas. All the while, they were establishing an intelligence system in their area, collecting information that could help them in their future efforts against their elusive enemy. Perhaps most important of all, they were contacting the people and assisting them in many ways, from treating their sick to digging water wells and teaching their children.

The security forces constant presence in the areas around these bases had the eventual effect of altering SWAPO's cock-sure practice of strutting around the operational area as they pleased. Contacts with the security forces resulted in heavy casualties for the terrorists and soon they were forced to switch most of their activity to night.

Since the majority of the population of Namibia was located in its northern border areas, so too were the majority of the strategic bases and their affiliated scattered company posts. The bulk of the population was, therefore, within access of the government's counterinsurgency effort. On the other hand, this population concentration was still accessible and vulnerable to the politicizing and terrorizing of SWAPO who could sally forth from their nearby sanctuaries in Angola.

Having decided to follow McCuen's "oil spot" strategy, the South Africans quickly moved to make life as miserable as possible for SWAPO inside Namibia. By carrying the fight to the enemy with small well-armed mobile units operating from both the strategic bases and the numerous satellite company-sized bases, the security forces concentrated on seeking out the SWAPO insurgents; destroying them; preventing them from establishing permanent bases in Namibia; disrupting their organization and hindering their plan for revolutionary action; finding and destroying arms and supply depots and disrupting SWAPO's logistics and communications systems inside Namibia. All this was done not only to destroy SWAPO personnel, but to keep the survivors more worried about their own security than to think about carrying out the organization's revolutionary program.

As a result, SWAPO was forced to change its tactics. Instead of being able to wander freely, day or night, terrorizing the locals, terrorist groups now crossed the border from their bases in southern Angola, mostly at night. Once in Owamboland, they hid during the day in some isolated *kraal* and ventured out at night laying their mines, intimidating the local population and trying to spread their gospel of Marxist dogma.

Often the first indication of their presence was when some vehicle, often a civilian, set off a landmine. When such mine incidents have occurred, security force units with trackers have been called in to find and destroy those responsible. Arriving at the scene of the incident the unit's trackers search for the tracks, or spoor, of the terrorists who had laid the mine. Often no tracks would be found as they had either been obliterated by the terrorists or by the wind. If tracks were found they were often days old and the terrorists were long-gone from the area. (A mine can sit for months before its victim happens to trigger its deadly mechanism.) Tracks, however, are followed to determine where the terrorists were heading next and other security force units are notified that the terrorists may be operating in their area.

If the mine was set off shortly after it was laid, there was a good chance the security forces would find the terrorist spoor and be able to track it. Often their tracking accomplished nothing more than chasing the terrorists back over the border to their sanctuaries in Angola. But sometimes the unit caught up with the terrorists and a short, sharp little battle ensued. Usually the security forces, because of better training and fire discipline, decimated the SWAPO unit that had made the mistaken decision to stand and fight. Even in the rare occasions when a well-laid SWAPO ambush caught the security forces and inflicted casualties on them, SWAPO knew that reinforcements were nearby. As a result, SWAPO seldom exploited any temporary tactical advantage they had, but quickly broke off contact and headed for the safety of their bases in Angola.

At times the security force reinforcements caught them before they made it back to the border and inflicted numerous casualties on the fleeing terrorists. This had the result of forcing the terrorists not only to move during the night, but to split up their forces into smaller units.

Soon a pattern evolved in the security force operations in Owamboland. Small units, normally no larger than a platoon, would sweep through the bush, looking for terrorist spoor, or gathering intelligence on the whereabouts of SWAPO. The most common form of intelligence gathering was questioning the local population encountered during their sweeps. The units also would stop at *kraals* periodically to seek intelligence from the natives living there.

The vehicles, or the horses carrying the security force personnel, would stop in battle formation (Most patrols and sweeps were mounted either on vehicles, horses or both.) and either an Owambo soldier, or one who could speak Owambo, would approach with the unit's leader and talk to the headman of the *kraal*. These chats would take some time as the process followed a somewhat rigid informal ritual, all done according to local Owambo custom and in one of the Owambo tongues.

"Good morning, or afternoon . . . nice weather . . . how is your family . . . how are your crops . . . etc."?

To follow our customary Western practice of getting right down to business is an insult and a good way to alienate the headman. It would then be next to impossible to get any useful information out of him.

After several minutes of protocol and chit-chat, it was possible to get down to business.

"Have you seen any strangers in the area?"
"How many and how long ago?"
"Were they carrying weapons . . . etc?"

This was a slow, time-consuming process that often as not didn't produce much except the fact that the security forces were showing the flag, and keeping SWAPO away from that particular *kraal*.

In addition to being visible to the local population, it also gave the security forces an opportunity to practice some civic action. The unit's medic would dispense vitamins, aspirin, candy for the kids, and other common medicines for simple ailments. They would make arrangements for those with serious ailments to get proper medical treatment by either arranging transport to a nearby medical facility or, depending upon the situation, have the unit's medical doctor visit the *kraal* to treat his new patient.

In this way the security forces were showing the local population that not only were they there to protect them from SWAPO, but were there to help them in other ways and slowly win their trust.

Oftentimes, and with increasing frequency as the government's "oil spots" began spreading together, the security force's patience was rewarded and a local tip would lead to the destruction of a terrorist unit operating in the area.

Many times, especially in a "hot area," a patrol would come across tracks made by the terrorists. When such an event occurred, and the tracks were fresh enough, the patrol would immediately report the find to its headquarters, then set out to track down and capture or kill the terrorists.

If the tracks indicated a large group of terrorists and they were fresh enough, other units might join in to pin-down and destroy the SWAPO group.

The original patrol would still continue in pursuit of the SWAPO unit, following its tracks. The other units would be moved to positions in anticipation of cutting off the terrorists' escape route, or to set up an ambush in the hope that the terrorists will be driven into their killing ground.

Then a deadly game of hide-and-seek would ensue with the hunted usually hoping for one of two things to happen: for darkness to come as the security forces couldn't track them in the dark, or they would reach the safety of Angola.

The thick bush of Owamboland favored the hunted as it was extremely difficult for the security forces to cordon a leak-proof area around the fleeing terrorists. Kill many they did, but others slipped through gaps in the security forces line and, using the thick bush to their advantage, the survivors would make their way back to Angola.

Two personal examples and one made famous by a Bushman tracking and reaction force unit will provide some typical examples of small unit security force operations in the operational area of Owamboland.

Bush War Heats Up

****

In World War I, two weapons apparently spelled doom for the horse cavalry: the machine gun and the tank.

Old traditions, however, die slowly, and the cavalry didn't bow out of modern warfare until the Polish cavalry died in a last futile charge against German tanks in 1939.

Although most of the world's military organizations have relegated the horse cavalry either to the museum or a small ceremonial detachment (like that prancing around Buckingham Palace in London), not everybody has gotten rid of their horses.

The horse cavalry is alive and well in southern Africa. Here in thick bush mounted soldiers have become an important element in the war against SWAPO Marxist terrorists.

There are basically five reasons why the old horse cavalry has been revived, minus the sabres, in the terrorist war in Namibia: visibility, range, speed, the ability to operate in terrain where it is impossible to use mechanized vehicles, and, last but not least, the lack of sufficient numbers of helicopters.

The bush covering most operational areas in Namibia is both high and thick. However, a soldier mounted on a horse, riding tall in the saddle, has a better, often unhampered, view of the situation and can see much further ahead than if he were on foot. (Purists may shudder at my designation of them as horse cavalry, claiming they function more like dragoons—they travel mounted, but fight dismounted. My view is that horse cavalry is a more common term than dragoon.)

A man on foot, carrying his combat load, can track through the bush for about fifteen kilometers before tiring and becoming less attentive and thus less effective. On a horse, that same man can stay on the track for about thirty-five kilometers, much farther than a chased SWAPO terrorist can run.

A horse is also faster than a man on foot, so mounted soldiers can, and often have, run down pursued SWAPO cadres, many of whom have died from being trampled by the pursuing mounts.

If caught in an ambush, the mounted troops can spur their mounts and get away more quickly from the killing zone to cover.

Motorized bush bashing (chasing SWAPO through the bush where roads are non-existent) is normally done in the mine-proofed Buffel and Casspir vehicles. These are able, widely used, and effective transport which carry the infantry through the bush into battle. But chasing SWAPO by knocking the scrub bush flat with your vehicle is obviously no way to sneak up on your enemy. Horses can do it much more quietly, and a horse can go places a Buffel or Casspir can't, especially places that are often terrorist hideouts.

One motorcycle and horse mounted unit operated out of a small company-sized base called Okatope in central Owamboland. Okatope is located just off the main paved road from Oshivelo to Ondangwa, the main convoy route for supplies running from Grootfontein north to the operational area. It is also a few short kilometers west of a powerline that runs from the Ruacana power complex on the Cunene River down to the agriculture and mining areas around Grootfontein and Tsumeb.

The powerline, in addition to being an inviting sabotage target, also happens to be an infiltration route for SWAPO terrorists coming from their bases in Angola. They slip across the border and follow the line south to their target area.

The security forces know this and take countermeasures to foil their efforts. Part of this effort is to use the mounted troops at Okatope, which consist of three platoons of horse-mounted infantry, or cavalry if you wish, and one platoon of motorcycle-mounted infantry.

The 500cc Honda motorbikes patrol the roads and the powerline, and can be used for high-speed, cross-country sweeps and searches.

The chief assets of the motorbikes are speed and operating range. The bikes can roar through the flat bush at speeds, depending on the terrain, well in excess of horses or other motorized ground transport vehicles. Their operating range is over eighty-five kilometers per day.

Motorbike tires are their most vulnerable point: long, tough spines of the thorn bush can easily puncture a motorbike tire. The motorbike troops are so well trained, however, that they can change and fix a flat in a mere twelve to fifteen minutes.

One incident in the routine at Okatope typifies the small unit conduct of the counterinsurgency war against SWAPO from the viewpoint of a company of mounted-infantry.

One night in April 1984, SWAPO had blown down five telephone poles in a futile attempt to cut the phone lines from Ondangwa to the south. In this case SWAPO's attempt failed because, although they blew down five poles, they didn't bother to cut the phone wires held up by the poles.

The first troops on the scene, at dawn, picked up the spoor, now several hours old, of five terrorists who had been involved in the incident.

A platoon of Captain Bariss Barnard's (the CO of Okatope) mounted infantry was going to sweep the bush in the vicinity of the incident. They were hoping to find more evidence of and perhaps even flush out the terrorists.

Captain Barnard's cavalry would sweep from the site of the incident eastward, following the tracks of the five, towards the powerline and infiltration route. The tracks soon disappeared as the terrorists had either persuaded or forced some locals to drive their cattle through the area obliterating their tracks.

Nevertheless, it was apparent the terrorists were heading towards the powerline when their spoor was destroyed and Captain Barnard decided to continue a general sweep towards the line. Other elements of 53 Battalion, to which Captain Barnard's unit was attached, would set up ambushes and stopper groups on the flanks of the sweep. A force of 53 Battalion's motorized infantry in Buffels would sweep down the powerline, wait, occupy a blocking position and, hopefully, scoop up anything fleeing from the approaching calvary.

Due to the size of the forces involved (about a company of troops) and the area being swept (several square kilometers), it was impossible to blanket the entire area. The pursuit force hoped that if the terrorists had gone to ground in the area, the movement of the troops would stir them up and force them to move. Then their spoor could be picked up and they'd be hunted down.

An infantry section (a squad in American terminology) mounted in a Buffel follows the mounted infantry platoons sweeping the area. The noise of the Buffel, in which the section is riding as a backup force, is not a factor, as the cavalry, depending upon the terrain and thickness of the bush, is normally moving anywhere from 500 meters to a kilometer ahead. Any terrorist lurking in the bush would be stirred up by the horses long before the sound of the Buffel would carry to any terrorist hidden in front of the sweep.

A word about the South African developed Buffel. It is a mine-resistant armored personnel carrier which sits on a truck chassis. This chassis is its main weakness. While the vehicle gives an amazing amount of protection to its human passengers, the blast of a mine usually ends up bending the vehicle's truck frame. This puts it out of action until extensive repairs are carried out.

The newer anti-mine vehicle, the Casspir, is an improvement on the Buffel, because its chassis is part of the main body of the vehicle. When it strikes a mine, a wheel assembly is often blown off. This can be replaced in the bush in a matter of a few hours. But the Casspir is new and expensive, so the Buffel is still being widely used in the counterinsurgency effort in Namibia.[4]

[4] For more information on mine proof vehicles, see: Stiff, P., *Taming the Landmine*, Galagos, Alberton, RSA, 1985.

Both vehicles have one thing in common: riding in them is a bouncing, jolting experience. Half of the time is spent hanging on for dear life to prevent body and gear from bouncing out into the dirt. This in spite of being strapped in via a shoulder harness. The rest of the time is spent dodging branches that tend to sweep back into the passengers' faces while bashing through the bush.

Once the sweep got underway a routine quickly developed. The mounted infantry would move ahead in a skirmish line looking for signs of the terrorists, and the Buffel would follow.

The route would weave around as the *kraals* in the sweep area where checked out. *Kraals* in the bush are not laid out in a suburban developer's neat geometric patterns, so the skirmish line would move back and forth to check them all out in the course of the sweep. When *kraals* were close to one another two riders would split off and check them out.

It was routine and sometimes boring work, especially when the sun beat down unmercifully as you toiled through the seemingly endless bush, breathing dust from the ever-present fine sand stirred into the air by your passage. Boredom was resisted by the realization that contact could come at any moment, especially for the horsemen. They resisted boredom more easily —their necks were on the line.

Back and forth the patrol continued its sweep, although steadily pressing eastward towards the power line, looking for signs of the pole-blasting SWAPO terrorists. Periodic stops were made to rest the horses and troops, and to maintain a slow and as thorough and consistent search of the area as possible.

As part of their design, the Buffel and Casspir carry an enormous quantity of drinking water (which helps absorb some of the force of a mine explosion) for resupplying the troops and horses. This water is available through a tap on the vehicle to replenish canteens or water cans. This mobile source of potable water also gives the security forces an edge over the terrorist he is pursuing as the SWAPO terrorist must either carry his water supply with him or get it from the local population. When running for his life from the security forces, he is likely to feel the effects of thirst long before his pursuers who carry a large supply in their vehicles.

Finally, the patrol reached the power line. The company commander and some of the mounted troops with him were sitting on the edge of the powerline clearing in the meager shade waiting for the patrol. It had reached the end of its sweep and had turned up nothing.

That's the way it often is on operations in Owamboland. You cover miles and miles of hot, dusty bush, often to find no signs of the terrorists. But such seemingly endless, unsuccessful sweeps still were important facets in the overall counterinsurgency effort. They not only established and continued security force contact with the people letting them know that protection was at hand from the SWAPO terror tactics, but also prevented the infiltrating SWAPO cadres from settling in and establishing permanent bases in Owamboland.

The security forces can't relax their vigilance. If they do, that's when the infiltrating terrorists will plant their mines or murder innocents, all to the detriment of the overall counterinsurgency effort in Namibia.

****

Another incident, again from Okatope, brought home the usefulness of the motorbikes in the counterinsurgency effort. It was touched off by a report from two of Captain Barnard's Owambo soldiers who had just returned from a little off-duty relaxation at a local *cuca* shop. (These are small, privately-owned shops operated by local Owambos that dispense goods, including the local home-brewed beer. These shops are named after an award-winning beer that was brewed in southern Angola while it was still a Portuguese colony.) It seems that a couple of terrorists were patrons of this particular *cuca* and were bragging about their SWAPO affiliation to the assembled customers. Since the terrorists were armed and the two Owambo soldiers, who were dressed in civilian clothes, weren't, they decided to slip out, return to Okatope and get help.

Captain Barnard decided upon immediate action and assembled the motorcycle platoon. Off they went followed by two sections of infantry accompanying them in the Buffels, toward the *cuca* hoping to bag the two boastful terrorists.

The reaction force sped north up the hardtop road towards Ondangwa for about eight kilometers, then turned off the road and plunged into the bush. The *cuca* was located a few kilometers west of the road, across table-flat sandy bush country, near an old mission and a school run by a teacher suspected of being a SWAPO sympathizer.

The motorbike force with the Buffels behind them roared up to the *cuca,* riders peeling of to the right and left, encircling the *cuca* to cutoff anyone trying to flee. Captain Barnard and a dozen of his men searched the *cuca,* safeties off their weapons and ready for action.

But the troops had been seen as they rode across the flat terrain, and the two SWAPO terrorists had fled toward the school. Barnard ordered a remount and the force headed for the school, a short distance away.

The school was a different matter than the *cuca.* Bigger, and with about

400 students from the fourth grade through high school, the school buildings proved more difficult to surround. The line of troops stretched a little thinner.

Captain Barnard talked to the headmaster-teacher of the school, the suspected SWAPO sympathizer, and told him it was necessary to search the school and he must clear all the classrooms. That proved to be easy because most of the students had already poured from the classrooms to stare curiously at the armed men.

The remaining youngsters trooped out and joined their classmates. As they did so, they were scrutinized by Captain Barnard and the two Owambos who could identify the terrorists if they tried to sneak out with the kids.

The students enjoyed the spectacle because it gave them an unexpected break, but their teachers didn't like it one bit. Many of them didn't even try to keep looks of hostility off their faces as they sullenly watched the troops search the classrooms.

One by one the classrooms were searched. Then, as the troops were preparing to move to another building of the school complex, one soldier noticed a small trapdoor in the corner of a classroom.

"Check that out!" ordered Captain Barnard. A soldier was given a boost up by two others and pounded open the trapdoor.

A loud crash was heard at the other end of the building, and a great shout went up from the milling school kids outside as two frightened terrorists burst out through a door and ran through the crowd.

Apparently panicking when the trapdoor was raised, the terrorists evacuated their hideout by simply crashing through the ceiling and bolted out of the classroom door.

No fusillade of shots followed them, as the security forces didn't want to risk hitting any of the kids, many of whom had wandered from the immediate vicinity of the school to goof off and play. Thus they were scattered out all over the area and the terrorists used them as a buffer to get away.

Off went the troops in hot pursuit, following the fresh spoor. But the terrorists, running literally for their lives, didn't lose their wits. They hit a couple of the many scattered *kraals* in the area and played hide-and-seek among them with the security forces. The security forces were forced to slow down as they had to search each *kraal* along the path of the fleeing terrorists. At one *kraal* the terrorists delayed the biker patrol many precious minutes by forcing the *kraal* occupants to drive their herd of cows over their tracks, obliterating them.

By using such tactics, they slipped away from Captain Barnard's men, and managed to hitch a ride in a truck before a police anti-terrorist unit that had taken over the pursuit from the army tracked and trapped them. Both terrorists were killed trying to shoot it out with the police not far from the *cuca* and the school.

****

A more typical anti-terrorist operation was carried out in late 1982 by elements of 201 Battalion, composed entirely of Bushmen from Namibia. The battalion's primary area of operation is Owamboland, but occasionally they operate in Kavangoland and Kaokoland as well. The battalion is composed of four rifle companies, A, B, C, and D. Of these two are always in the bush for six-week long operations while the other two rest and retrain at their primary base—Omega—located in the Caprivi Strip.

The Bushmen rifle companies are organized into seven teams of twenty to twenty-three men each. The weapons used by the Bushmen are the principal infantry assault weapons used by the South African army. Captured weapons, such as the Soviet RPG-7 antitank grenade launcher are widely used by the Bushmen, and other security force elements as well. They are plentiful as huge quantities have been taken from captured SWAPO bases and caches. The RPG-7 is an extremely versatile attack and support weapon in the bush war.

Most of the teams in the Bushmen company are reaction force teams. They are held in reserve until any security force unit makes a contact with SWAPO terrorists or fresh SWAPO spoor is discovered. Since the modus operandi of the terrorists is to break contact and flee, the usual action of the security forces is to track and chase them. The Bushmen reaction force teams are well-suited for this task.

Each team is further divided into two or three smaller groups, each with a motorized fighting vehicle—the Buffel anti-land mine troop carrier.

Upon picking up the SWAPO spoor and following it, half of the group will run on the track while the other half rides in the Buffels as a mobile reserve. After an hour or so, they switch roles, giving their buddies on the ground a chance to rest. It is therefore possible to keep fresh trackers running on the track—and run they do!

In late 1982, elements of 201 Battalion picked up the spoor of seven SWAPO terrorists in eastern Owamboland which led to a 238 kilometer marathon tracking operation. Of that distance, the Bushmen actually ran on the spoor for 190 kilometers. They followed the terrorists for three days before making contact. It took two more days and two more contacts to stop the fleeing terrorists. All seven were killed during the course of this operation, while the Bushmen suffered no losses.

The seven dead terrorists were part of SWAPO's so-called "special forces" detachment. SWAPO recruits, whether volunteers or shanghaied civilians, are sent to Lubango, SWAPO's military headquarters in Angola for training. After six months of basic military training, the better recruits are selected and sent to other SWAPO bases for specialized training as SWAPO's "special forces."

They take advanced courses in such terrorist tactics as sabotage, ambush, assassination and anti-tracking techniques to prepare them for small-group infiltrations into their target areas inside Namibia. However, they have not been very effective and they have been largely neutralized by the counterinsurgency efforts of the security forces.

The South African security forces were slowly but surely expanding their areas of control. They were seriously disrupting SWAPO's timetable for a violent Marxist revolutionary takeover in Namibia.

Yet a vexing problem remained that caused the South African counterinsurgency program enormous difficulties—the presence of SWAPO bases and sanctuaries over the border in nearby Angola. As long as SWAPO could cross the border with ease, the South African effort to successfully counter the guerrilla was seriously flawed. The enemy was still too close to the population and could slip with ease in to Namibia to kill, maim, and intimidate the local population.

The presence of these bases hung like an ominous cloud over Owamboland, creating a climate of fear in the local population that kept them aloof from the security forces. Those bases had to be sorted-out or else the counterinsurgency effort would soon be spinning its wheels.

Punitive cross-border strikes on these bases were the solution, but it was not an easy course of action to take, as we shall see in the next chapter.

13
Into Angola—Operation REINDEER

Operation REINDEER, the first crossborder operation launched under the new South African policy of hitting SWAPO sanctuaries in neighboring Angola, was really three separate attacks linked only by timing and overall purpose.

They were: an airborne assault on Cassinga, some 250 kilometers inside Angola; an overland assault on a series of SWAPO bases near Chetequera, twenty-five kilometers north of the Angolan border; and a helicopter-borne sweep through a series of small SWAPO bases seventeen to twenty-one kilometers east of Chetequera.

Overall command of REINDEER was under Maj. Gen. Ian Gleeson (now Lt. General and Deputy, SADF). The operation was unique not only because it marked the first under the new South African policy, but because it also featured the first true airborne assault ever carried out by the SADF. It also marked South Africa's entry into modern mobile warfare. The operation became the testing ground for new equipment and tactics from which valuable lessons were learned and put to use in the future.

The small Angolan mining town of Cassinga was a tempting target. It had become SWAPO's main operational headquarters in southern Angola. There was also a large training complex that could hold up to 1,000 terrorists. The guerrilla base had a large motor pool, headquarters buildings, shops, parade ground and an extensive defensive system of trenches.

Even though SWAPO claimed the complex was a refugee camp, the large amount of war materiel captured and destroyed, the documentary proof seized proving its military nature, and aerial photographs of the network of defensive trenches and fortifications, showed that SWAPO's claim was an outright lie.

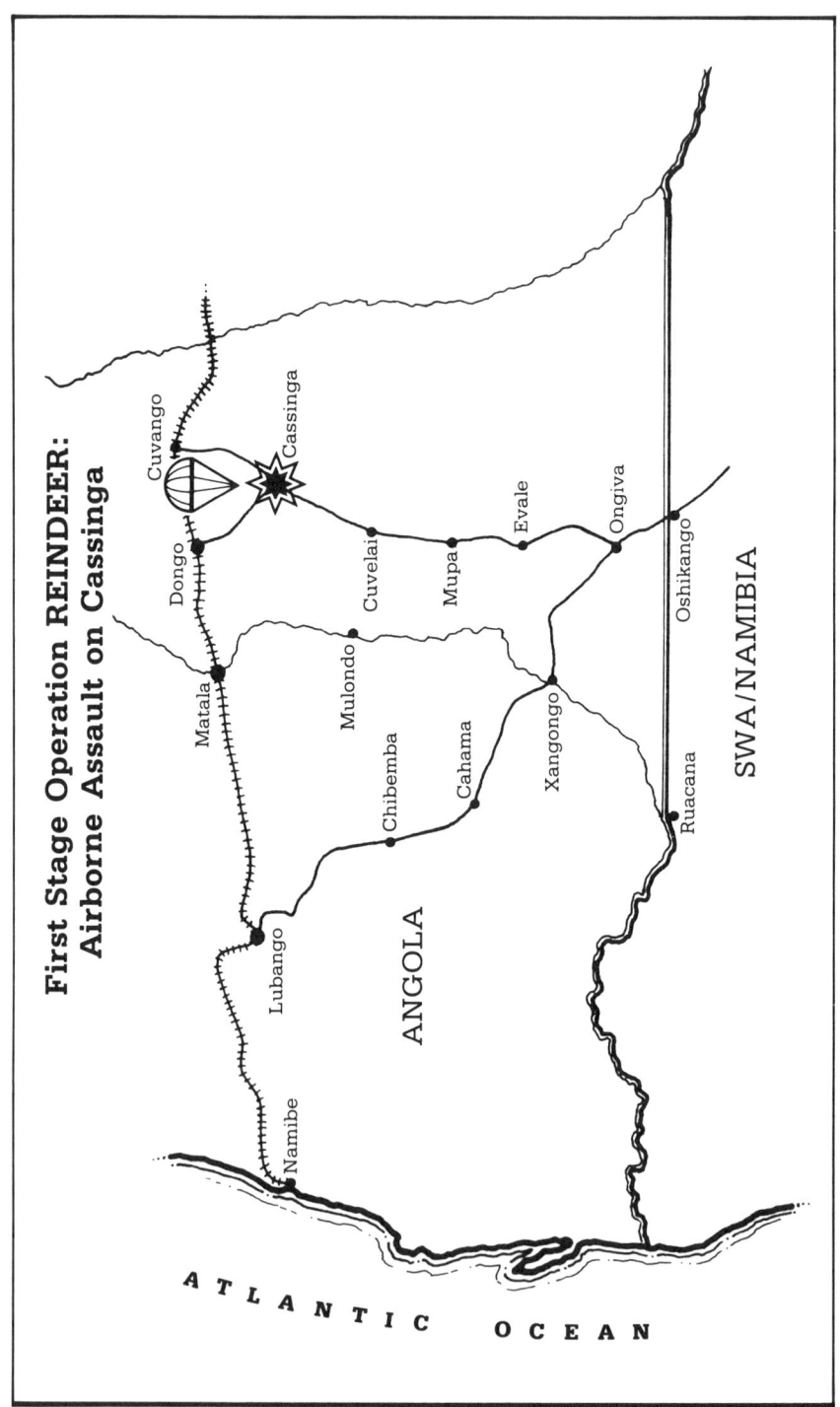

The destruction of the complex at Cassinga would not only damage SWAPO's operational ability, but would give the organization's image a severe jolt as well.

Tempting a target as it was, there was a major tactical problem—it was located deep inside hostile territory. A conventional attack would have been infeasible. The attackers would have to fight their way some 250 kilometers through hostile territory which would give SWAPO time to evacuate the base and move out of harm's way. The only way to attain surprise and catch the enemy at the target was to strike with airborne troops.

The obstacles to overcome were daunting and required a high degree of calculated risk: if the attack were successful, it would be virtually impossible for the lightly-armed paratroopers to fight their way south to Namibia; they would have to be withdrawn by helicopters.

The South African Air Force helicopter fleet is small both in size and numbers of aircraft. The bulk of the job would have to be done by Pumas, which could carry only ten troops at a time. The helicopters would also be vulnerable to both ground fire and air attack and in Angola there were plenty of Cuban-piloted MIG-21's which would be around to prey on the choppers.

Another danger to be considered was the fact the Angolan Army (FAPLA) had a force, equipped with tanks and armored personnel carriers, based at Techamutete only sixteen kilometers south of Cassinga. The lightly-armed paratroopers would face a formidable problem if this FAPLA force were to come to the rescue of its Marxist comrades in Cassinga.

In spite of all this, the overall plan of REINDEER included an airborne attack. The plan included Cassinga because the SADF considered the gains to be worth the considerable risks involved. Destroying the main SWAPO operational base would hamper terrorist operations in Namibia for a long time; it would deal a blow to SWAPO's image and morale; and it would yield an invaluable harvest of intelligence material.

Since Cassinga was so far north of the border, the SADF planners reasoned that SWAPO would consider it to be almost immune from attack, especially an airborne assault. Thus, the attacking force would enjoy and be able to capitalize on the benefits of complete surprise.

The planners presented the pros and cons of the Cassinga attack to General Magnus Malan (then Chief, SADF), who thought long and hard on the matter before giving his okay.

The principal aims of the attack were to kill or capture the SWAPO commander at Cassinga, Dimo Himambe and as many of his staff as possible; to kill as many SWAPO terrorists as possible; to capture some terrorists for interrogation; destroy all ammunition dumps, equipment and weapons; and to capture important documents, especially those showing Soviet links to SWAPO.

Speed was the criterion—a rapid attack followed by a swift withdrawal.

The man chosen to lead the attack was one of South Africa's most illustrious soldiers, Colonel Jan Breytenbach, who would retire from the Army in 1988 as South Africa's most decorated soldier.

In a twist of irony, Breytenbach's younger brother, Breyten, living in exile in Paris, is a Marxist supporter of the Marxist anti-South African terrorist group, the African National Congress (ANC).

The plan called for the attack to be carried out in several phases starting with an extensive aerial bombardment. After this, the paratroopers would launch their airborne assault. Part of the group would land west of the town and attack from the west. Other elements would land outside of and around the town to seal it off and block any reinforcement attempts or by SWAPO to escape the fate planned for them.

After completing their mission the troopers would be lifted-off by helicopters operating from a nearby temporary forward base set up twenty-two kilometers east of Cassinga.

To cope with any unexpected problems and to provide cover for his troops and the withdrawal helicopters, Breytenbach had at his call jet fighters and close air support bombers of the South African Air Force.

The whole operation from attack to withdrawal was optimistically estimated to take two hours. Estimates and plans were one thing, reality turned out to be something entirely different. The venture started out almost disastrously for the South Africans.

At exactly two minutes after eight in the morning of May 4, 1978, the South African Air Force commenced its pre-assault aerial bombardment on Cassinga. With accurate bombing and strafing of the terrorist camp with 30mm cannon, the opening salvo of the attack went off according to plan.

Explosions rocked both the town and the terrorist camp. Large parts of the terrorist camp were engulfed in flames, sending dense billowing clouds of smoke and dust into the air. The aerial bombardment had come as a complete surprise and the way was open for the paratroopers to begin their assault.

The paratroopers were all hooked up and ready to jump from their C130 Hercules aircraft as they approached their drop zones. So far everything was on schedule for the 8:06 a.m. jump.

Finally the green lights flashed in the planes, signalling the troopers it was time to go. They shuffled to the doors of their aircraft and launched themselves out into the air. Strings of billowing khaki-colored parachutes formed behind each departing aircraft. The airborne attack was under way.

At this moment, fate reared its ugly head and things began to go wrong.

The dense smoke pouring from Cassinga had caused some of the pilots to miscalculate their release-point and the paratroopers were sent out the door three seconds late. Three seconds may not sound like much, but it can be a long time in an airborne assault. It was especially critical at Cassinga where the drop zone was only 450 meters wide and restricted in length by a bend in the winding tributary of the Cubango River that flowed by the town.

To add to the problem, the paratroopers had jumped into a strong, gusting wind of over thirteen knots. It was pushing them even farther away from their drop zone. Few of the paratroopers landed anywhere near their designated targets. Some landed across or even in the river and those who managed to land on the right side of the river were much further south than they should have been.

It looked as though a first class disaster were in the making for the airborne assault force deep inside enemy territory. A determined counter-attack by SWAPO at this point could have rolled-up the South African force. Such an attack, however, required bold, decisive leadership and SWAPO's commander, Dimo Himambo, had fled the town after the initial aerial bombardment. Without this leadership, SWAPO missed a golden opportunity. Instead they ran to their defensive positions and waited there for the South Africans.

It was obvious to Breytenbach that the original plan was coming unhinged. He regrouped those men he had with him, modified his assault plan and waited for the men who had landed on the wrong side of the river to cross over and rejoin his force. One thing was certain, it was going to take longer than the two hours the original plan called for to take Cassinga.

Reorganizing his forces, Breytenbach and his men began the nasty job of clearing the town of its SWAPO terrorists.

Much bitter fighting followed, especially in the elaborate SWAPO defensive trench system, before the town was cleared and secured at a little past noon.

Now it was time to call in the helicopters and withdraw, some three hours behind schedule. SWAPO had other plans, however, and asked for the armored column to come from Techamutete to counterattack the South African forces.

An armored column led by five T34 Russian tanks and BTR152 armored personnel carriers, all manned by Cubans, the Angolan government's Praetorian Guard, rushed towards Cassinga.

Part of the South African paratroopers had been sent south of Cassinga as a blocking force astride the Techamutete road to prevent enemy reinforcements from coming to the aid of Cassinga. This force was just a small anti-tank platoon. Fortunately for them, while their buddies were busy in Cassinga with SWAPO, they had time to prepare their hasty anti-tank defenses as best they could, laying mines and siting their anti-tank rockets. It was fortunate they took these measures, even though they were under-equipped to stop the armored column.

As the column approached, the BTR152s spread out on either side of the road in attack formation. Moving north towards Cassinga, they ran into the mine field. This slowed the column down and the South Africans blasted away at them with anti-tank rockets. The combination of the rockets and anti-tank mines destroyed five BTR-152s and one T-34 tank. More importantly, it temporarily halted the advance of the armored column. But not for long, as the T-34s resumed their steady although slower advance north.

The anti-tank platoon was ordered to withdraw as help was on its way from the South African Air Force. The Mirages and Buccaneer aircraft of the air force pounced on the column wreaking havoc on it as it had no anti-aircraft defense. The air attack stopped the armored column dead in its tracks on the outskirts of Cassinga just in the nick of time.

At 5:45 a.m., two Puma helicopters had departed from Omauni base in Namibia and flew towards the location some twenty-two kilometers east of Cassinga where the forward helicopter base would be established. From there they would carry out the withdrawal of the paratroopers from Cassinga. Having made sure the area was clear, the leader of the group radioed the Ondangwa headquarters, giving the all clear signal. At 7:00 a.m., fifteen helicopters left Omauni for the forward base carrying a forty-two-man security element for the temporary base, a medical team and drums of extra fuel. After they arrived and set up a defensive perimeter, all they could do was wait until the call came to extract the troops from Cassinga.

The first call came, three hours late, about noon. It was for a medevac to bring the wounded back to the forward base. There they would be sent to Eenhana in five helicopters.

The helicopter's second mission was rougher. Under heavy fire, it snatched the anti-tank platoon from the face of the armored column and carried them safely back to the forward base.

With air cover provided by the air force's Mirage jets, the rest of the evacuation proceeded smoothly. Troops were already being ferried from the forward base back to the Eenhana base in eastern Owamboland and safety.

Finally, at 7:00 p.m., the last elements left the forward base to return to Namibia.

The battle at Cassinga was over and an almost disastrous start had been turned into a daring major victory for South African arms. Cassinga cost the South Africans three known dead, one missing and presumed dead, and eleven wounded. According to SADF sources at least 600 SWAPO terrorists were killed, and another 340 wounded, while the armored column's losses were sixteen dead and sixty-three wounded.

The first phase of REINDEER was over.

Chetequera was not in Cassinga's class as targets go for it consisted of little more than a collection of bush huts surrounded by trenches. Its garrison was a lot smaller than Cassinga, but it was, nevertheless, an important target. In spite of its unimpressive appearance, it was one of SWAPO's main supply depots and the headquarters for terrorist operations in Western Owamboland.

Just south of Chetequera were a series of SWAPO bases known as the "Dombondola Complex." They were located only six to ten kilometers north of the Angolan border. SADF intelligence estimated that these bases had about 570 well-armed SWAPO terrorists.

After a pre-assault aerial bombardment, a battle group made up of mechanized infantry and armored cars would assault Chetequera. The base would be attacked from the rear, captured and destroyed. After destroying the bases in the "Dombondala Complex," the battle group would then head back towards Namibia.

The battle group, code-named "Juliet," was made up of officers and men from 2 South Africa Infantry Battalion group based at Walvis Bay. It was under the command of Commandant (now Brigadier) Frank Bestbier, another wily exerienced South African infantry officer.

Chetequera was to be the debut for the Ratel, the South African-developed infantry fighting vehicle. This new weapons system could carry a squad of men into battle protected by its armor from enemy small arms fire. It could do more than ferry troops into battle. It had a turret-mounted 20mm cannon that could give direct fire support to the troops on the ground. (Later models of the Ratel would carry a 90mm gun or an 81mm mortar, but the first model used in REINDEER carried only the 20mm cannon.)

Other vehicles were the mine-proof infantry carrying Buffel and the Eland-90 armored cars. The Elands were a version of the French Panhard AML-90, were built in South Africa and adapted to function in the bush wars of the region.

Juliet's task was to cross the Angolan border south of Chiambo, advance north while keeping to the east of the "Dombondala Complex," until it reached the road linking Chetequera to Cuamato. Here the battle group would assemble in battle formation, wait for the softening-up aerial bombardment and then attack Chetequera.

The target was almost completely surrounded by a system of trenches. However, the trenches were more extensive to the south of the target, indicating SWAPO expected any attack to come from that direction. Juliet's attack would be from the north at the rear—the weakest point.

While Bestbier's group was taking care of the primary target, Chetequera, two completely separate units were to attack directly north over the border and take care of SWAPO bases south of the object of Juliet's attention. These two groups, originally called Combat Team 1 and 2, eventually became known by the names of their respective commanders—Serfontein and Joubert.

On paper the plan seemed simple. The Angolan terrain, with its thick bush, soft sand, flat, featureless and devoid of recognizable landmarks, plus the resistance by SWAPO, all would combine to make Juliet's task anything but a cake-walk.

Although neat lines drawn on maps indicated the presence of "roads," all too often they were nothing more than rutted paths through the bush. Leaving these vehicle-bashing "roads" and traveling cross-country was of no help. It subjected both vehicles and occupants to punishing jolts and jars. It was over this type of terrain Juliet had to pass in order to successfully carry out its mission. The operation would be a test of both human and mechanical durability.

At 10:00 a.m. on the morning of May 4, 1978, Juliet crossed the Angolan border. Almost immediately Angolan terrain started taking its toll on the column as the paved road in Namibia ended and the rutted dirt tracks of Angola began.

The dirt track over which the group was traveling was taking a terrific pounding from the heavy vehicles. Every so often a vehicle would bog down in the sand. In some places the sand became so soft that only by towing could a stranded vehicle get free. Adding to the difficulty was the fact that most often it had to be done by sheer muscle power.

Because of the delays the group was falling well behind schedule. Nevertheless, Juliet pressed on through the thick bush, arriving at the assembly area only ninety minutes late.

This delay caused the opening air attack to be moved back from noon until 1:15 p.m.

However, the SAAF Canberras and Buccaneer bombers were a further fifteen minutes late and their attack didn't get started until 1:30 p.m.

The planes made their bombing runs and clouds of smoke rolled up and, as one participant said, ". . . it looked as if the whole base was on fire . . . ."[1]

---

[1] Steenkamp, *op. cit.,* p.109.

Operation REINDEER

The air force spectacular pyrotechnics, notwithstanding, Bestbier had a problem which further delayed Juliet's assault. His forward air controller could not contact the aircraft because of problems with his radio. Juliet could not press home the attack until Bestbier was certain the air bombardment was over. The resulting five minute delay gave the SWAPO defenders time to recover their wits and man their defenses. This, no doubt, was a factor in stiffening their resistance when the attack finally began.

At last, the attack began, and the leading element ran into another problem. The "open" ground over which they were supposed to be attacking was actually a maize field of flourishing growth some two meters high. Faulty visual reconnaissance had failed to spot the field. It obstructed their view of the target at Chetequera. The attack was slowed up and couldn't be carried out as planned.

Other elements in the group ran into the same problem. The tall thick bush and high maize fields severely restricted the Ratel's and the armored car's observation and fields of fire. In addition, the attack was coming under heavy fire from the SWAPO defensive positions who were wildly shooting at any movement in the bush and maize fields caused by the passage of the South Africans.

The situation, although not developing according to plan, was not out of hand and Juliet stormed into Chetequera pressing home its infantry assault. The assault was not the rapid movement one would normally expect from a mechanized force. The dense bush had not only slowed the vehicles down but forced the assault troops to attack in an improvised on-the-spot manner that caused much confusion among the attackers. To add to the muddle, numerous vehicles got bogged down in the trench complex around the base.

Command and control became increasingly difficult and the fighting quickly evolved into a series of separate vehicles fighting their own individual battles at close quarters as part of a general melee in the thick bush.

In spite of the stiff enemy resistance, and the obstacles—both manmade, the trench and bunker complex, and natural, the thick bush, maize fields, soft sand and tall anthills—the assault took only eleven minutes.

Meanwhile, other elements of Juliet also moved through the objective area, clearing the trenches of SWAPO in short, sharp firefights using grenades and small arms fire.

While the trenches were being cleared, the assault unit regrouped and commenced mopping up operations. They soon realized there were still a lot of terrorists who had survived both the initial bombardment and the ground assault.

Some sharp fighting remained to pry out and destroy the SWAPO

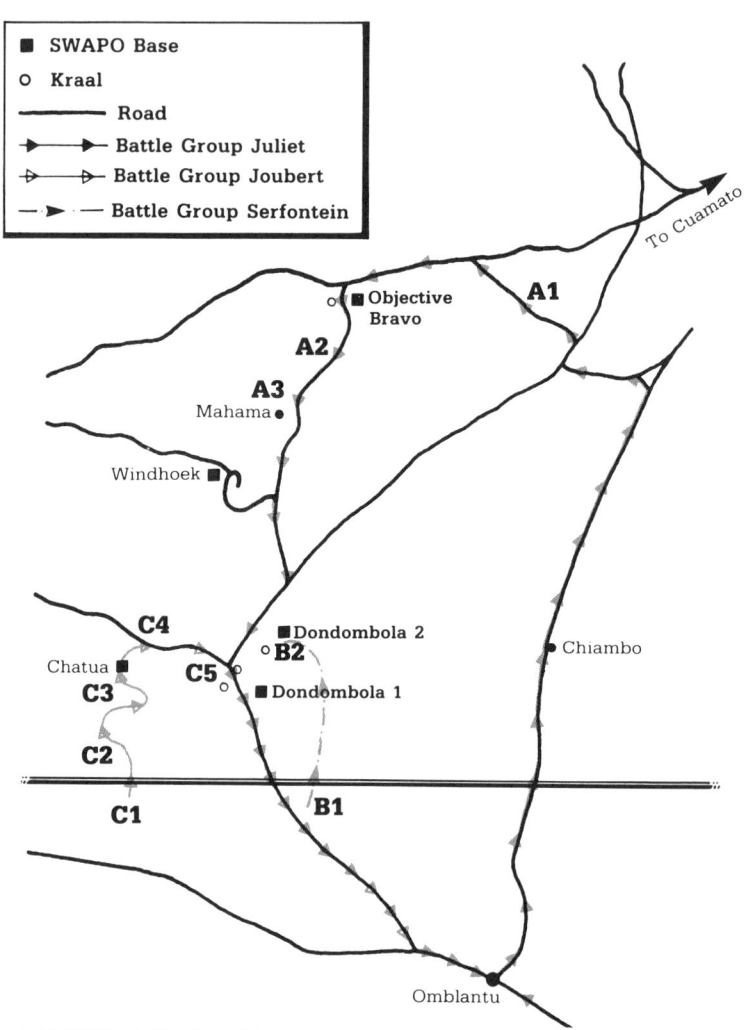

Operation REINDEER

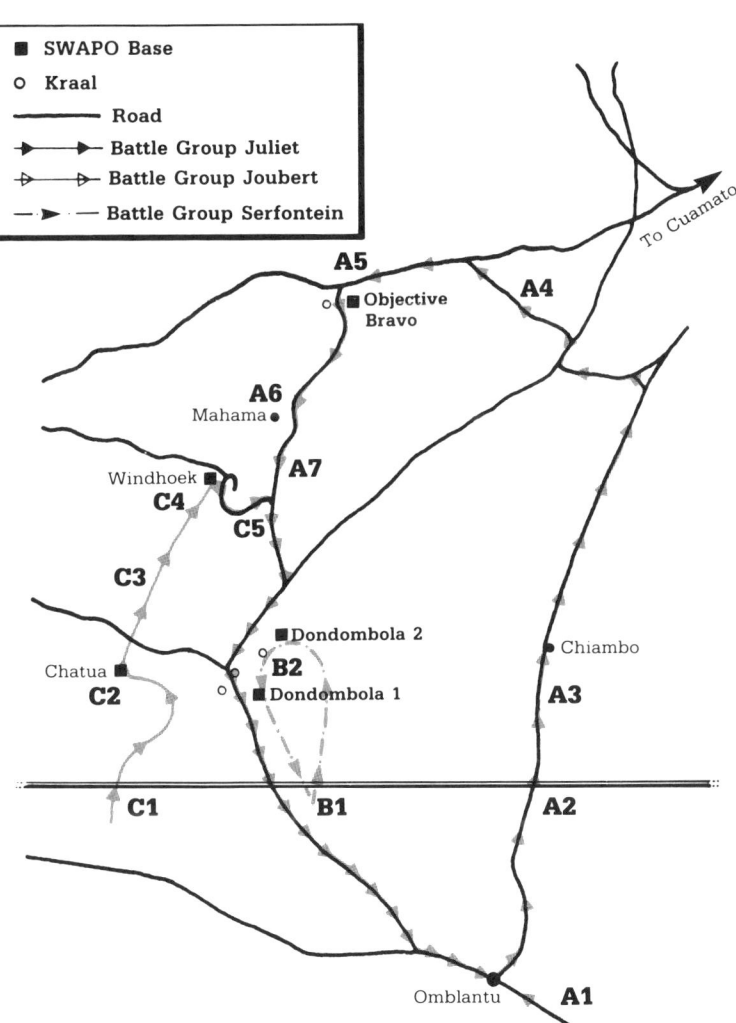

Second Stage of Operation REINDEER— How It Was Supposed To Happen

- ■ SWAPO Base
- ○ Kraal
- ——— Road
- ▶——▶— Battle Group Juliet
- ▷——▷— Battle Group Joubert
- —▶—·— Battle Group Serfontein

(A1) Bestbier takes Battle Group Juliet northward on D-1
(A2) crosses the Cutline
(A3) and assembles for D-Day advance to Cuamato
(A4) Battle Group Juliet forms up and waits for SAAF to hit Bravo

(A5) Battle Group Juliet attacks Bravo
(A6) deals with Mahama
(A7) and heads home

(B1) Combat Team Serfontein crosses Cutline
(B2) and attacks Dombondola complex

(C1) Combat Team Joubert crosses Cutline
(C2) attacks Chatua
(C3) advances on Windhoek
(C4) captures it
(C5) and joins Battle Group Juliet

fighters from their defensive positions.

At last the shooting died down as almost all the terrorists were either killed or surrendered. Some lucky few managed to slip away in the thick bush and hide. By 3:30 p.m. all resistance had ended. Juliet forces then quickly cleaned up the camp to collect enemy weapons, documents and equipment. A significant haul was taken back to Namibia with the column, while the rest were destroyed in place.

As soon as Bestbier got the reports from all the units in his command, it became clear that Juliet had won a big victory. A total of 248 SWAPO terrorists had been killed and 200 were taken prisoner. Juliet's losses had been two killed and ten wounded.

By 4:00 p.m., Juliet had completed mopping up of SWAPO and reconsolidation of the battle group forces. The original operation plan called for Juliet to head back towards the border and attack a SWAPO base at Mahama before setting up defensive positions for the night, still in enemy territory.

The operation was now so far behind schedule that Maj. Gen. Gleeson ordered Juliet to forego the attack on Mahama and set up its night defensive positions. Juliet was to proceed towards the border the next day, linking up with Combat Team Joubert on the way.

After leaving Chetequera, Juliet moved south down the road towards the border before pulling off and setting up defensive positions for the night. Perimeters were set up, sentries positioned, weapons cleaned, rations were opened to feed the hungry troops; then the battle-weary, grime-covered troops got some well-needed rest.

Combat Group Joubert's operational plan called for the Group to cross the border and advance due north and attack the SWAPO base at Chatua. If necessary, Joubert could call on support from Combat Group Serfontein, if Chatua proved to be too tough a nut for Joubert to take out on its own.

Combat Group Serfontein's operational plan required it to cross the border and advance due north for four kilometers. Depending upon the situation, it would either assault the SWAPO base Dombondala 2 or support Combat Group Joubert's assault on Chatua. If Joubert's group didn't require their services, Serfontein's group would attack Dombondala 2, destroy it then and attack SWAPO bases at Dombondala 1 and Haimona.

Due to the unexpected heavy resistance encountered by Juliet at Chetequera, Maj. Gen. Gleeson's headquarters at Ondangwa considerably modified both groups' plans.

On D-day, South African artillery shelled the SWAPO bases at Chatua and Dombondala 1 and 2. As soon as the bombardment stopped the two combat groups crossed the border and headed for their objectives.

Serfontein reached its first objective, Dombondala 2 and found the base deserted, with a large amount of weapons and equipment left abandoned by the terrorists. It was obvious SWAPO had pulled out in a hurry. Serfontein's men collected the arms and ammunition, then burned the base to the ground.

This done, Serfontein was ready to carry out the rest of its mission when headquarters canceled it. This ended the group's participation in the operation.

Combat Group Joubert's operation got off on the wrong foot. First of all, for unknown reasons, it crossed the border two and a half hours late and then proceeded to get lost. It found itself approaching the target from the wrong direction. To correct this error and still carry out the mission, would require swinging the group around as they passed close by the target. To reduce the risks involved in this manuever, Joubert intended to call for an artillery barrage on the SWAPO base. Joubert hoped this would keep the terrorists pinned down while his group executed the swing around the base.

Unfortunately, the barrage never materialized, due to a communication's breakdown. The manuever had to be executed without the artillery support. Lady Luck smiled on the group as SWAPO neglected to take any action against it.

Once in position the group attacked the SWAPO complex. An infantry assault, supported by armored cars, rolled over the base. A short, but fierce, fire-fight in which eight terrorists were killed, broke the SWAPO resistance. Within thirty minutes Joubert secured the base and seized large amounts of arms and ammunition.

As night was approaching, headquarters ordered Joubert's group to dig in for the night in positions northeast of Chatua. After an uneventful night, Joubert left for its rendezvous with Juliet, which was working its way south towards the Angolan-Namibian border.

At 10:00 a.m. both forces reached the border and the second phase of REINDEER had come to a successful conclusion.

The unique South African 32 Battalion would carry out the third phase of REINDEER, a series of heliborne attacks on the SWAPO base complex, the Omepepa-Namuidi-Henhombe group, located seventeen to twenty-one kilometers east of Chatequera.

An aura of mystery and intrigue surrounds this elite SADF unit which grew out of the chaos of the Angolan Civil War of 1974-76, when remnants of Holden Roberto's National Front for the Liberation of Angola (FNLA) lost out in a three-cornered struggle after the Portuguese pulled out.

The arrival of Cuban troops and Russian advisors coupled with the curtailment of US aid to pro-Western factions in Angola allowed the Marxist Popular Movement for the Liberation of Angola (MPLA) to seize power in Angola.

Fearing retribution from their enemies the MPLA, hundreds of FNLA members fled southward to escape the firing squads they rightly believed awaited them.

As the South Africans were withdrawing from Angola because of the political fallout resulting from Operation SAVANNAH, a problem arose: what to do with the FNLA refugees? There was no place of refuge left for them in Angola, and they had no hope of mingling with the southern Angolan tribes since they were all Bakongo from the extreme north near the border with Zaire.

The South Africans, recognizing the determination and fighting spirit of these refugees, retrained, re-equipped and formed them into a battalion led by SADF officers and a sprinkling of regular SADF NCO's. The battalion's first commanding officer was none other than Col. Jan Breytenbach, the leader of the airborne assault on Cassinga during REINDEER.[2]

The South Africans kept the unit's existence secret until 1981, and then the public was only told that it existed. This was certainly no news to anyone who had served in the operational area fighting SWAPO terrorists. Even today, 32 Battalion still shrouds most of its operations in secrecy. It is considered to be one of the best counterinsurgency units in the world.

Even at its inception in 1978, 32 Battalion was an outstanding unit. Under its second commanding officer, Commandant (now Brigadier) Gert Nel, months of continuous counterinsurgency operations in the vast, trackless bush in the operational area had bloodied and tempered the unit.

Now it was 32 Battalion's turn to do its part in REINDEER.

D-day for Nel's troops was May 6, 1978, by which time all the troops involved in the other two phases of REINDEER had returned to Namibia. Nel would have five rifle companies, an 81mm mortar platoon, and a troop of 140mm artillery guns to carry out his mission. Helicopter gunships would provide his air support.

His operational plan was simple: between D-day and May 10th, four of his rifle companies would cross the border and supported by the artillery and helicopters, attack and destroy one SWAPO base after another.

At 4:15 a.m. on D-day, 32 Battalion crossed the border and headed

---

[2] For a more detailed history of 32 Battalion, see: Breytenbach, J., *Forged in Battle*, Saaymen & Weber, Cape Town, 1986.

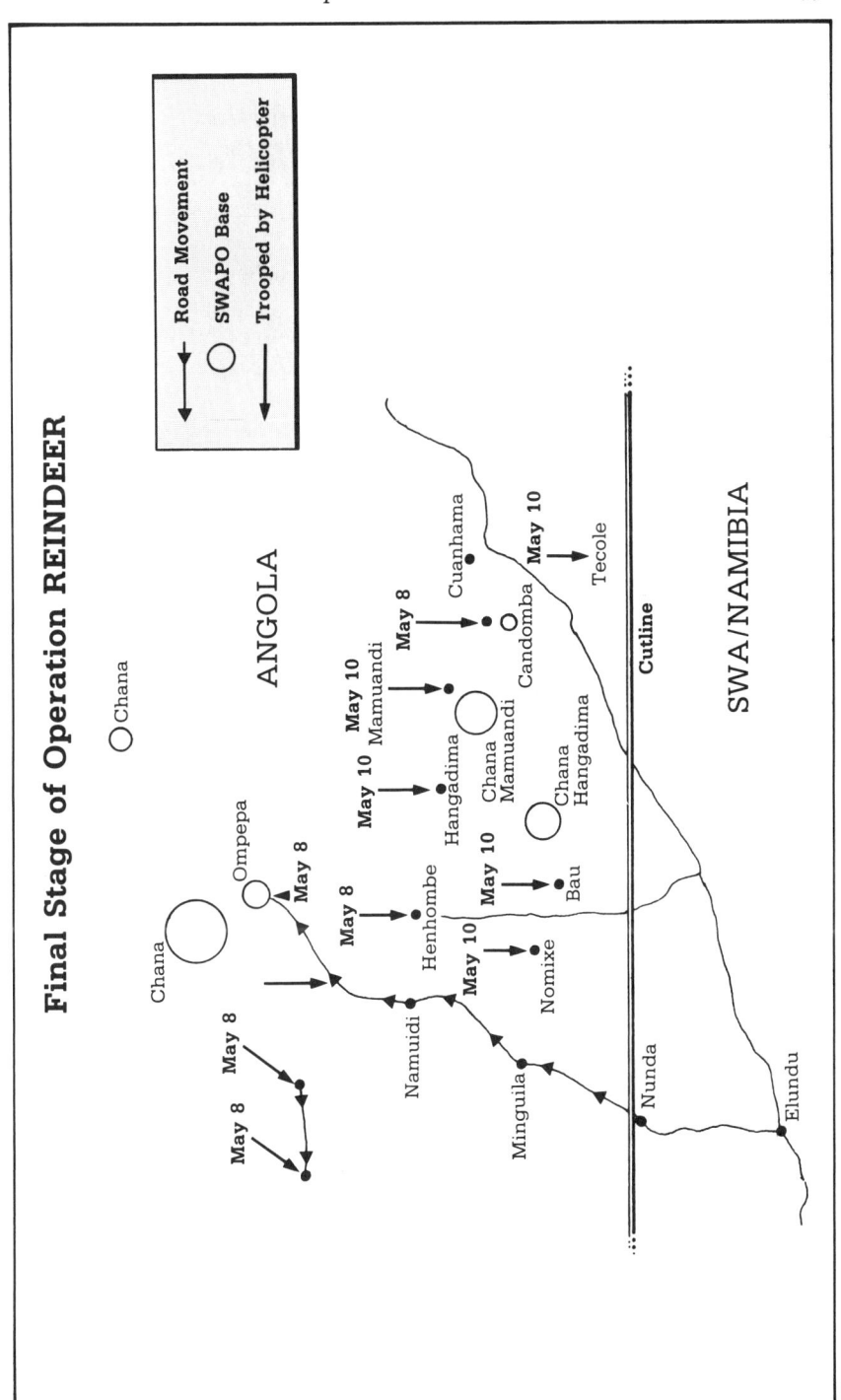

towards the first target, Minguita. At 8:30 a.m., the force made contact with SWAPO at Minguita. The troops attacked and SWAPO abandoned the base and fell back to Namuidi, about four kilometers to the west.

The battalion pressed on but was forced to spend the night in the bush before taking on Namuidi. By noon the next day, the battalion had taken and destroyed Naumuidi. The force advanced towards its next target—Omepepa. Night again came before they could assault the SWAPO camp.

The next day (May 8), Nel's men launched a heliborne assault on the camp and in short order not only was it destroyed, but two others in the vicinity of Onelumona were sacked. They then advanced on Henhombe, but discovered no SWAPO presence there. However, at nearby Ohaipeto they discovered and quickly destroyed two SWAPO camps.

On May 10th, Nel's forces quickly rolled up a series of SWAPO camps among them Hangadima, Mamuandi, Bau, Namine and Tecole. By early afternoon, 32 Battalion had finished their mission and were enroute back to Namibia. By 4:00 p.m. all of its elements were back across the border. Operation REINDEER was over.

What had REINDEER accomplished? The South Africans had destroyed SWAPO's main operational planning base, and numerous other SWAPO facilities in southern Angola. The loss of these facilities seriously disrupted SWAPO's forward staging capabilities and made their job of supporting terrorist operations in Namibia much more difficult.

Some 1,000 trained SWAPO terrorists were killed and a further 200 captured compared with the loss of six South Africans killed and thirty wounded. Of equal importance to the loss of SWAPO's manpower and equipment was the intelligence gained on the organization. It would be of great help in carrying out future counterinsurgency efforts against the terrorist organization.

The loss of large numbers of trained personnel was a brutal blow to SWAPO. In fact SWAPO has never been able to fully recover from this even to this day. This has forced SWAPO, while deploying its terrorists, to mix their surviving trained personnel with larger numbers of raw recruits. This led to an overall rapid decrease in efficiency. At the end of 1979, SWAPO losses, averaging ninety a month, were higher than their recruiting rate. This was causing an overall net loss of manpower for SWAPO. Fewer terrorists meant fewer incidents which hindered SWAPO's revolutionary program and enabled the South African counterinsurgency program to pick up steam.

REINDEER showed that not only were the South Africans capable of conducting deep incursions into enemy territory, but more importantly, they were willing to do so. This forced SWAPO to move its main planning and operational headquarters much deeper inside Angola. That had further adverse effects on their command and control capabilities.

SWAPO learned some bitter lessons from REINDEER. They discovered their bases, modeled on those of their East Bloc instructors, with barracks, parade grounds and elaborate trench systems were like dinosaurs in the bush, easily spotted and vulnerable to mobile assault. SWAPO soon tried to hide their bases by putting them underground and attempting elaborate methods of camouflaging their presence.

SWAPO also moved their bases closer to those of the Angolan Army, hoping that the FAPLA presence nearby would act as a deterrent to future South African attacks.

As far as the South Africans were concerned, REINDEER was a success and had given invaluable battle experience to the SADF. It was the first of many cross-border operations which would take the war to SWAPO in its own backyard.

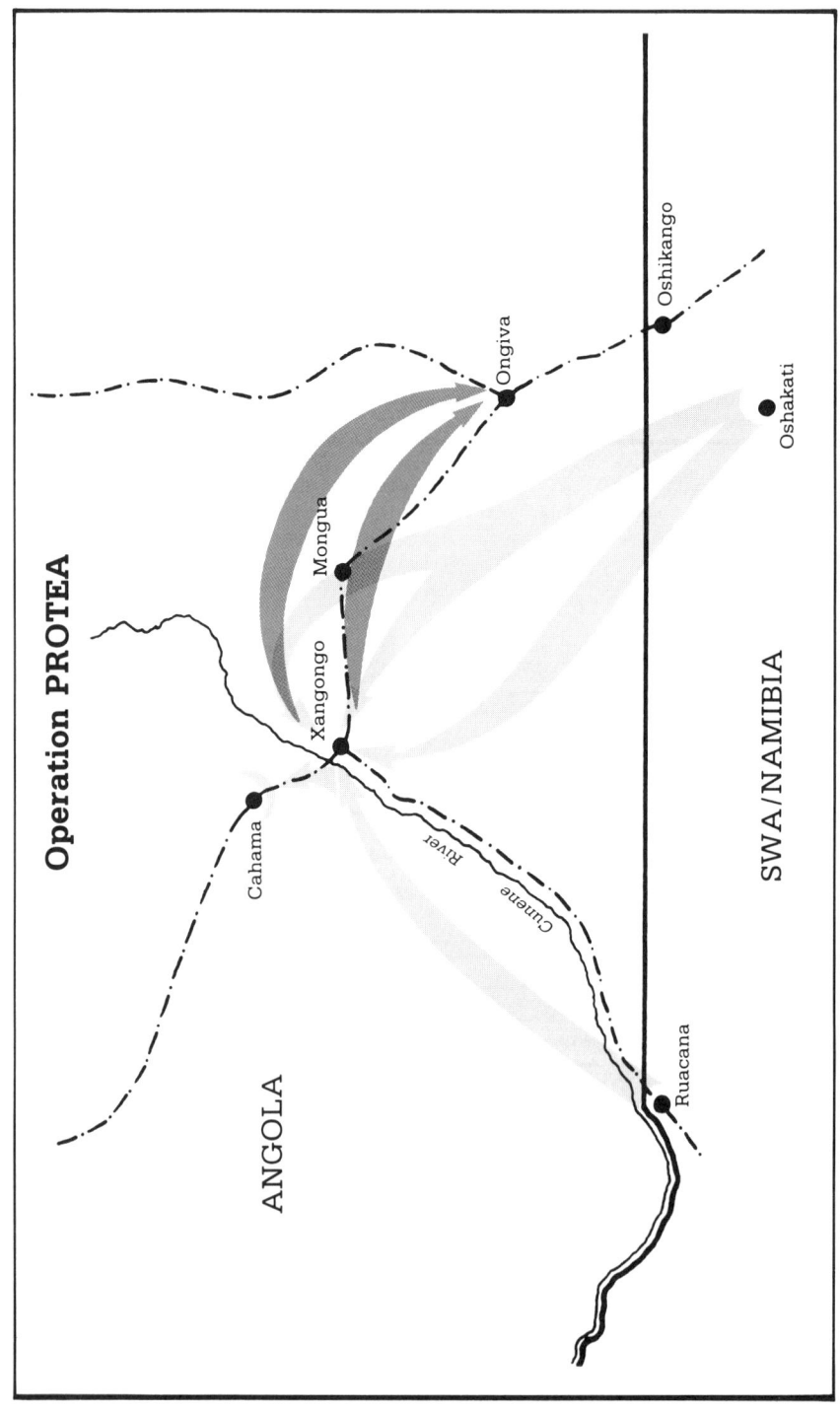

14

Into Angola— Operation PROTEA

Operation PROTEA was launched on August 23, 1981. Its objectives were to destroy SWAPO's command and training center at Xangongo and to destroy SWAPO's logistic bases at Xangongo and Ongiva.

Xangongo was the headquarters of SWAPO's "northwestern front." The headquarters planned and directed SWAPO terrorist elements whose area of operations were primarily in the Kaokoland, and western and central Owamboland. There were other SWAPO bases located to the south and southeast of the town. These bases were supply depots and training bases for SWAPO recruits.

The destruction of this SWAPO complex would have a detrimental effect on SWAPO's operations in their so-called northwestern front.

Ongiva, under fifty kilometers from the Angolan-Namibian border, was an important SWAPO logistical and personnel center which supported operations in central and eastern Owamboland, and terrorist activities in the Kavangoland.

Both Xangongo and Ongiva, because of their proximity to the operational area in Namibia, were key base complexes in supporting SWAPO's revolutionary war effort in Namibia.

Their destruction would, at the minimum, delay the SWAPO infiltration timetable, inflict casualties on SWAPO personnel, and disrupt their logistical system and training cycle.

In addition, PROTEA would have a tremendous psychological impact on both the enemy and the people of Namibia. It would reinforce the message Operation REINDEER delivered to SWAPO that they no longer had the luxury of sanctuaries in southern Angola. As long as SWAPO continued its terrorist activities in Namibia it could expect to be on the receiving end of further security force operations in Angola.

PROTEA also showed the people of Namibia the security forces were serious about countering SWAPO's terror campaign in Namibia. By so doing, they gave added proof that they were serious in their efforts to provide a security blanket so the people of Namibia would have a comparatively peaceful situation in which to build their future.

SWAPO, as a result of REINDEER, had adopted a strategy of moving its bases closer to FAPLA bases in an effort to discourage attacks by the South Africans. By the time of PROTEA, the SWAPO logistical system had become entwined with that of FAPLA, especially in the area of Angola west of Ongiva. SWAPO's new base strategy of hugging FAPLA's did not stop South African attacks although the South Africans went out of their way not to involve FAPLA in the fight.

Prior to the attacks on Xangongo and Ongiva, the South African Air Force dropped pamphlets stating their quarrel was with SWAPO and SWAPO alone. But at the same time, they warned the inhabitants not to assist SWAPO. The leaflets, however, took away the element of surprise and gave the defenders the warning they were about to be attacked.

Orders were also issued to the security force personnel involved in the operation to avoid contact with the locals and the Angolan forces, as much as possible, but not to the point of endangering their own lives. If protecting their own lives meant fighting with the Angolan forces, then so be it.

A three-pronged mechanized force of Ratels, Buffels and Eland armored cars advanced on Xangongo from Ruacana, Oshakati and Ondangwa. Part of their mission was to isolate the town to prevent possible Cuban and FAPLA reinforcements in Humbe and PeuPeu from coming to the aid of their soon to be beleaguered comrades in Xangongo.

The rest of the force attacked the SWAPO complex in and around the town.

The mixed SWAPO-FAPLA force was in well-prepared defensive systems consisting of trenches, bunkers and even dug-in tanks.

"We had to attack them in their bunkers and in their trenches with their defensive weapons geared for defensive fire," said the chief of the South African Army, Lt. Gen. Jannie Geldenhuys. Several fierce battles were fought out between integrated SWAPO and FAPLA forces, which at the time, rendered the action more like a conventional war rather than normal small-unit counterinsurgency operations.

The presence of trenches and bunkers and satellite bases characteristic of the SWAPO complex at Xangongo and Ongiva indicated the terrorists were trying to apply some lessons learned from their disastrous shellacking during REINDEER.

They had obviously changed their concept of base defense. Done away with were such things as permanent buildings, parade grounds, clear perimeters and visible lines of fortified trenches.

Instead, SWAPO bases were located, as much as possible in close proximity to a FAPLA unit, hoping to no avail, to come under the umbrella of their protection.

The physical layout of the bases had also changed. The bases expanded in size—at least in the area they covered. Large undefined patches of the Angolan bush now became the new lair of the terrorists. These were dug into the ground and were camouflaged to keep their presence hidden from the prying eyes of the South Africans. SWAPO went to great lengths to avoid such tell-tale signs of a military facility's presence as parade grounds, defensive works, perimeter trenches and barbed-wire entanglements.

Concealment was now the by-word in SWAPO base complexes. That, plus the nearby presence of FAPLA units, would render the new bases less vulnerable to South African attacks—at least that was what SWAPO hoped.

SWAPO's efforts, while not successful, did place more demands on the security forces. Intelligence became even more crucial to the success of future cross-border operations. It was imperative that it be precise and up to date and collected in such a manner that it didn't alert the enemy as to his becoming a future target.

The new base setup also affected the tactics of both sides. SWAPO figured the major threat to their base security would come from the South Africans attacking north from Namibia. Thus, they established their defensive strongholds to face that threat from the south.

An attacking force always risks severe losses or defeat when attacking straight into the strength of the enemy's defense. Thus an attack from the rear or a flank would lower both the risks and possible casualties, especially if the attacking forces achieved surprise. But in order successfully to carry out such maneuvers, the attacking force had to be aware of the nature and extent of the defenders positions and forces—hence the requirement for accurate, up to date intelligence.

Fortunately for the South Africans, not only was their intelligence superb, but their superior discipline, tactical and operational abilities enabled them to carry the day successfully against the heavily defended SWAPO targets.

Surprise was achieved at the Xangongo complex as neither the Soviets nor SWAPO ever dreamed the South Africans would attack such a heavily defended area. (In addition to the normal FAPLA elements in Xangongo, the security forces estimated that there were 23,000 FAPLA and 7,500 Cuban soldiers at Lubango capable of moving south and come to the aid of the defenders at Xangongo.)

Attacking from the flanks and rear while feinting a frontal assault, the South Africans quickly rolled up the SWAPO/FAPLA defenders at Xangongo.

Ongiva was spared the surprise element due to the attack on the SWAPO complex at Xangongo. Nevertheless, even though SWAPO knew they might be attacked, they figured their defenses could stop them. However, the South Africans swept in from the rear and only the size of the complex made its capture take longer than Xangongo.

The South African assault on Xangongo was successful and the surviving communist forces beat a hasty retreat into the thick bush just outside the town.

Fleeing in haste with the SWAPO and FAPLA survivors were a group of thirty Soviet advisors—along with seven women and a number of children.

In their scramble to avoid the South Africans, the Russians left behind their personal possessions and a huge quantity of documents, which incontrovertibly confirmed the growing Soviet involvement with SWAPO's terrorist war in southern Africa.

At the Soviet headquarters in Xangongo, the assault forces found charts and maps still on the wall which detailed command structures and strategy for SWAPO, all written in Russian.

The married Soviet advisors lived in a huge house next to the headquarters, with their wives and children. They obviously never expected the South Africans to attack otherwise their families would have been left behind in Luanda or the Soviet Union.

They seemed to live a squalid existence. The residence was full of empty wine and vodka bottles which were scattered throughout the house. The kitchen table was covered with unwashed dishes, utensils and moldy, stale food. Apparently, hygiene was not a priority item with the Soviets in Angola.

The Soviets were clearly involved in the affairs of both SWAPO and the Angolan army. The documents captured at Xangongo showed Soviet involvement down to the brigade and battalion level in FAPLA. Their duties were not restricted to providing military training. The Soviets were also responsible for the administrative and political life of the brigades or battalions to which they were attached.

The Soviets at Xangongo were attached to the FAPLA 19th Brigade and had been since April 1978 when the first party of Soviet military advisors, fourteen commissioned and non-commissioned officers, arrived in Xangongo.

After securing their first objective, with Xangongo cleared of SWAPO and FAPLA forces, the main body of the South African force moved southeast towards their second target Ongiva.

Brushing aside feeble FAPLA attempts to stop the South African advance at Mongua, they reached Ongiva on August 26, 1981 and attacked the SWAPO/FAPLA force dug in around the town. After two days of fighting, Ongiva fell to the South Africans.

Soviet military advisors were also at Ongiva, but were not as lucky as their compatriots at Xangongo who had fled out of harm's way. Several Soviet officers were killed and a warrant officer was captured. Warrant Officer Second Class Nikolai Feodorovich Pestretsov was one of the military advisors attached to FAPLA's 11th Brigade at Ongiva when he was captured.

Pestretsov was a mechanic whose job was to train his FAPLA counterparts in the proper maintenance of their Soviet-supplied vehicles.

In late 1979, he was working at a motor plant in Kaliningrad in the Soviet Union when he and four other plant workers were offered the opportunity to come to Angola. Pestretsov was the only one to accept the offer.

He and fifteen other Soviet personnel who had been chosen from all over the Soviet Union were given a briefing on their new duties in Angola by the Main Cadre Directorate in Moscow. He and his comrades then left for Angola in December 1979.

After his arrival in Luanda his passport and other documents were taken away. He was issued two certificates; one identifying him as a Soviet citizen and an advisor on vehicle repair; and the other serving as a drivers license.

His career in Angola was varied. He stayed in Luanda for three months and worked on maintaining Angolan government civilian vehicles. He was then transferred to Lubango and was attached to the base repair battalion, where he functioned as an advisor, supervising FAPLA technical personnel.

After a month he was sent to Xangongo where he stayed six months, attached to the repair company of FAPLA's 19th Brigade.

He then went on a two-month vacation back to the Soviet Union and when he returned he brought his wife with him.

Pestretsov was transferred to Ongiva in December 1980 where he remained until his capture. He was attached to the repair company of FAPLA's 11th Brigade, supervising and training FAPLA technical personnel and was in charge of maintenance of the brigade's wheeled vehicles.

If any proof were needed of direct Soviet involvement with SWAPO, it was obtained during PROTEA.

The South African Defense Minister, Magnus Malan, commenting on the Soviet presence during PROTEA, said it was without doubt proof that Russia not only supplies SWAPO with armament, but shows them how to use them.

"Apart from these incidents, an enormous amount of Russian propaganda material was found in the immediate vicinity of SWAPO HQ. This is a clear indication of Russia's plans for South Africa," said Malan in a press conference after PROTEA.[1]

Propaganda material wasn't the only stuff found in the SWAPO bases. The South Africans seized about 4,000 tons of military hardware, valued at over $200 million. This included, in addition to enormous quantities of small arms and ammunition, such major military items as tanks and armored vehicles, anti-aircraft guns and numerous trucks and other logistical vehicles.

The presence of tanks and armored personnel carriers in the insurgent's arsenal proved conclusively that SWAPO intended to progress soon from the guerrilla to the mobile warfare stage in its war of national liberation in Namibia. Tanks and armored personnel carriers are useless weapons for guerrillas fighting a guerrilla war in the African bush. South African concern over SWAPO's increasing capability to escalate its revolutionary war to the mobile warfare stage, which was the reason behind cross-border operations turned out to be fully justified. SWAPO's military hardware seized just north of the Namibian border provided irrefutable proof of SWAPO's military plans and the correctness of the South African estimate and response.

As to be expected, South Africa was roundly condemned in the usual quarters—the international press, the UN, the OAU, and other diplomatic circles in Europe and the Third World, for its action in southern Angola during Operation PROTEA. Although, for once, an American Secretary of State showed some common sense concerning the situation. Secretary of State Alexander Haig pointed out that the South African operations should be seen against the background of repeated attacks by Soviet-backed guerrilla terrorists. Unfortunately, this slight breath of realism in American diplomacy toward events in southern Africa soon blew over, replaced by the usual anti-South African cliches that seem to characterize the State Department's everyday attitude on southern Africa.

Operation PROTEA was yet another stinging defeat to the Soviet clients in southern Africa. At least 1,000 members of SWAPO and FAPLA

---

[1] Sector 10, Op Protea, 1 Military Printing Unit, 1982, p.17.

were killed during the operation and almost a quarter of a billion dollars worth of Soviet-supplied war materiel were seized or destroyed by the South Africans.

Thirty-eight prisoners were captured, including ten SWAPO terrorists. One captured SWAPO terrorist admitted getting part of his military training in the Soviet Union. He also confirmed that SWAPO was also getting military training in Angola from Soviet military trainers.

Many people in southern Angola took advantage of the confusion caused by the South African attacks in southern Angola, to flee across the border to Namibia and freedom from Marxist Angola's reign of terror. The refugee's stories of horror and depredation under the dismal rule of Marxism-Leninism in Angola, hopefully, will help inoculate Namibians who heard about the gruesome course of that fatal political disease. Here was living proof that, if given the chance, people will consistently vote with their feet and flee the type of system that SWAPO wishes to impose on Namibia. The arrival of refugees from Angola was a psychological debacle for SWAPO's revolutionary cause.

SWAPO's timetable was severely set back by Operation PROTEA. The resounding defeats had driven the organization even further north away from its operational area in Namibia and with a heavy loss of life to its trained personnel. In contrast to the heavy losses suffered by SWAPO, the South Africans lost only ten men.

SWAPO's losses were not restricted to manpower alone, as they suffered a tremendous loss of material either destroyed or captured by the South Africans.

Several major SWAPO bases had also been destroyed. And, as Lt. Gen. Geldenhuys said, "Their command structure, for the time being, has been disrupted and their logistic system is damaged, and at the moment, ineffective."[2] The general felt that it would take at least a year for SWAPO to recover from the crippling effects inflicted upon it by PROTEA. The operation had caused SWAPO terrorists to be scattered in confusion all over southern Angola. Their cross-border infiltration capability into Angola had been severely hampered and their morale had plummeted to a new low.

The end of PROTEA didn't end the South African activity against SWAPO in southern Angola. While the terrorists were still reeling from their beating during PROTEA, the South Africans struck again.

A SWAPO regional headquarters, in southeastern Angola at Chitequeta, was trying to regroup the scattered and demoralized terrorists. Located some

---

[2] *Ibid.*, p.22.

240 kilometers north of the Angolan border, Chitequeta was to be the main objective of the new South African cross-border operation, code named DAISY. This operation would put the finishing touches on the work of PROTEA.

On November 1, 1981, a South African mechanized force of Ratels and Buffels, attacked the SWAPO base complex killing seventy-one SWAPO terrorists. The immense size of the SWAPO complex, some thirty-five square kilometers, allowed the bulk of the 1,200 terrorists reported to be assembled there, to escape into the bush. Otherwise the casualties would have been far greater. Nevertheless, the South Africans had destroyed another SWAPO command and logistic base and captured a huge quantity of arms and ammunition. The SWAPO logistical system had suffered another big loss within three months of PROTEA. SWAPO terrorists were further demoralized, as they scattered into the bush and fled further north into Angola.

The South African forces attack on Chitequeta represented their deepest penetration into Angola since the civil war some six years before.

Operation PROTEA, and its appendage DAISY, were not isolated incidents in the South African counterinsurgency campaign. They were part and parcel of the strategic decision to carry the war to SWAPO, be it in Namibia or southern Angola.

15
Namibianizing The War

Local self-defense has been a significant component of virtually every successful counterinsurgency campaign. As McCuen said, "One thing is absolutely certain. Self-defense by the population is a necessary element of the counter-insurgency organization. Without auxiliary police and militia to protect it, the population is likely to pass under revolutionary control, irrespective of how satisfied and indoctrinated the people may be. Personal security is one of the strongest of all drives."[1]

The South Africans paid a lot of attention to McCuen's dictum by organizing local self-defense units in Namibia. It made sense in a lot of ways.

No one likes to be at the constant mercy and whim of a bully. Yet bullying tactics were the centerpiece of SWAPO's revolutionary program for Namibia. The only thing a bully understands and respects is force. Reason won't deter the bully, only force will. However, it is almost impossible to protect everyone from the bullying depredations of revolutionary terrorists —the security forces simply lack the manpower and resources.

Organizing local self-defense units among the population frees up elements of the armed forces to concentrate on destroying the terrorists instead of tying them down guarding villages and installations. Involving the population in their own defense also commits them firmly on the side of the government.

This automatically puts the person joining the local militia or self-defense unit at odds with SWAPO and makes him a target of SWAPO's

---

[1] McCuen, *op. cit.*, p.113.

reprisal attacks. But now he isn't such a "soft target" as he has received arms, military training and, initially supervision by professional South African officers and NCO's. By joining others collectively they could and often did successfully resist SWAPO attacks.

It should be self-evident that joining the self-defense effort in Namibia against SWAPO, gave the individual a stake in the outcome of the counterinsurgency effort in which he was now personally involved.

Losers in most guerrilla wars throughout the world, and especially so in Africa, are not merely disarmed, given amnesty and told to be good citizens of the new regime. They are normally punished rather severely for being on the losing side. The best they can hope for is to be allowed to hold on to their lives, albeit in fear and misery. Their normal lot is liquidation as class enemies.

Thus, joining a self-defense group in a revolutionary situation can place one in a precarious situation—it commits him, for better or worse, to the government's counterinsurgency effort. This has a ripple effect in that it normally brings along the individual's family and some of their relatives into the pro-government circle. For example, it is estimated that by 1987, as a result of the formation of 101 Battalion in Owamboland, 10,000 Owambos were brought solidly on the government's side in the war against SWAPO.[2]

The presence of these self-defense units and their success in countering acts of terrorism serve as a constant on-going counter to SWAPO's attempt to coerce other Namibians to following the terrorist group.

As long as Namibians, not just the "boers from South Africa," are joining together, pursuing and killing SWAPO terrorists, it tarnishes the credibility of SWAPO and its supporters, such as the United Nations. If SWAPO were, as the UN proclaims, the sole representative of the Namibian people, then why are Namibians taking up arms to fight SWAPO?

In the eyes of the uncommitted, especially in Owamboland the scene of the revolutionary battle, the sight of armed Namibians protecting themselves and their neighbors from SWAPO "liberators" was becoming a commonplace occurrence. This action was in vivid contrast to SWAPO's method of sneaking across the border, like thieves in the night, and hiding out in the daytime from armed Namibian security elements hunting for them. The SWAPO terrorists emerged only at night to plant mines, most of which killed or maimed civilians, and to murder or intimidate before scurrying back across the Angolan border before their fellow Namibians caught up with them and ended abruptly their careers.

---

[2] Author's conversations with Namibian officials in Windhoek, Ondangwa and Oshakati.

One of the most critical problems in organizing any counterinsurgency self-defense force is the process of screening its recruits for loyalty to the government. Any revolutionary organization worth its salt would attempt to infiltrate the self-defense force and try to subvert it.

The situation in Namibia, however, helped the screening process as the self-defense units were set up on ethnic or tribal basis. Since SWAPO was an Owambo-centered organization, the non-Owambo units were neutral or even hostile to SWAPO's revolutionary program. They were susceptible to SWAPO's gun-point intimidation tactics, but the opportunity to participate with their fellow tribesmen in their own defense provided them with a way to resist their long-standing tribal enemy.

The security forces could thus devote the bulk of their screening efforts to Owambo recruits. Here events in Owamboland came to their assistance. There has been chronic unemployment in Owamboland and a career in an Owambo ethnic military unit provided one with a stable, steady source of income. (The self-defense force in Namibia was being paid the same pay as the South African soldier.) It also gave the individual a legally sanctioned method of retaliation against the SWAPO terrorists who had ravaged and murdered his kith and kin throughout Owamboland.

The South African efforts of establishing effective self-defense units in Namibia had an added advantage in that the organizational basis already existed.

During World War I, South African troops, under the command of General Louis Botha, invaded the then German protectorate of South West Africa to secure the territory for the Allied Forces. On July 9, 1915, the German forces surrendered and ever since the defense of the territory has been the responsibility of the South African Defense Force.

Not surprising, the defense of the territory was set up along South African lines. Up until 1975 only white citizens of Namibia were called upon to undergo military training. This training was done in South Africa not Namibia. Those white Namibians wishing to pursue a military career had to join the South African Defense Force and hope they could get assignments back in Namibia.

Those who didn't want to be professional soldiers but still wanted to be part of the defense of the territory could join either the Citizen Force or a local Commando.

Citizen Force units are comparable to the active reserve in the United States. They are trained as conventional soldiers and the units they belong to are part of the conventional military establishment—infantry, artillery, armor, etc. Like our active reserve, these units undergo a regular training schedule in order to be familiar with current military weapons, tactics and techniques.

Commandos have no American counterpart. Commandos in Namibia also form part of the reserve force, but are specially trained in counterinsurgency warfare. They are organized on a regional basis and are trained to react quickly against any terrorist infiltration.

Since they operate in their own locale they have an excellent knowledge of the local terrain. This knowledge is important in successful counterinsurgency operations and the Commandos are trained and capable of putting it to good use.

With this system in being in Namibia, all that was really needed was to expand it to the non-white areas of Namibia.

It is well to recall that the military effort was not being carried out in a vacuum. There were important political decisions both inside Namibia and in the international arena that had great influence on military matters.

One of the major political processes taking place in the country was the effort to secure independence for the country. As these political moves were gaining momentum, it became obvious to the South Africans that an independent defense force for the territory had to be established. Because of the small population of Namibia it was also obvious that military training could not be limited to whites only and the government decided to recruit from all population groups. An integrated Namibian defense force would give all Namibians—blacks, browns and whites—a stake in the future of their own country. It was a decision that not only provided adequate manpower for future armed forces in Namibia, but, more importantly, it provided a big counter to SWAPO propaganda. It demonstrated that thousands of non-white Namibians not only opposed SWAPO but were willing to bear arms to prevent the terrorists from seizing power.

The fact that UN Resolution 435 has insisted upon the disbandment of these newly established territorial forces shows how much SWAPO and its UN friends feared them. This shouldn't surprise anyone. SWAPO has been committed to seizing power in Namibia by force and it could not tolerate the presence of an effective counter to its goal. Therefore, any armed opposition must be abolished. Since SWAPO couldn't prevail by force of arms, it had to get rid of its opponents by other means—using the efforts of its host and protector, the United Nations.

But in 1975, the evil machinations of UN Resolution 435 had not been committed to paper and the South Africans were concerned with setting up an embryonic South West Africa Territorial Force (SWATF), as they termed it.

Their first organizational efforts involved the Bushmen. They were trained as trackers in the Caprivi Strip. This unit proved so successful that it quickly mushroomed into an independent Bushmen battalion, designated 31 Battalion.

Based on the success of the Bushmen battalion, other battalions were raised in the populous northern region of Namibia: 33 Battalion in the Eastern Caprivi; 34 Battalion in Kavangoland; and, 35 Battalion in Owamboland.

Applications to enlist in these units far exceeded the requirements of the units. This allowed the authorities to be very selective and they chose only the most fit and reliable.

Subsequently, two more battalions were set up, one in Bushmanland —36 Battalion; the other in Kaokoland—37 Battalion.

The organizational and training effort didn't stop in northern Namibia, it continued in central and southern Namibia as well.

Because of the diversity of the population in the central and southern parts of the country, it wasn't feasible to establish ethnic battalions. Multi-ethnic battalions would have to be formed. Since tribalism is the curse of Africa, putting members of different and often hostile tribes together in a military unit was a venture not entered into lightly. Nevertheless, the authorities decided to form one and recruitment started in 1977. 41 Battalion was formed with its headquarters in the capital city of Windhoek.

The government took another important far reaching step on August 1, 1980, at the same time as the establishment of the SWATF, when it removed the color restriction and allowed non-whites to join the Commandos.

Non-white Commandos (non-white in that no whites lived in the area) were formed in Damaraland, Hereroland, Khomasdal, Katatura, Rietfontein, Aminuis and Namaland. This added further strength and national effort to the existing unconventional reserve force.

Successful counterinsurgency operations in Namibia depended upon security force tracking ability and upon their mobility. Obviously, the territorial units would have to be proficient in these skills in order to be able to prevail over SWAPO terrorists.

On June 1, 1977, a Namibian specialist unit was formed to train the infantry in tracking, the use of dogs as trackers, as well as using horses and dirt-bike motorcycles for rapid deployment and patrol work in the bush. The training base was set up at Otavi while the headquarters of the unit, 1 SWA Specialist Unit as it became known, was at Oshivello.

Towards the end of 1979 the SWA Military School was established at Okahandja. Here is where the future officers and non-commissioned officers of all races would be trained for the independent Namibian armed forces.

A major step towards the creation of this independent force occurred on August 1, 1980, when a Department of Defense was formed for SWA/Namibia under the Administrator General of SWA. For the first time in the history of the territory, control over an independent Namibian defense force became the responsibility of Namibians.

As of that same date all the units created in the territory became known as the South West Africa Territorial Force (SWATF). Overall planning, liaison and cooperation between the SWATF and the SADF is carried out by a joint committee. One of the joint committee's most important initial tasks was to establish an independent headquarters organization for the SWATF. The changes also affected the designation of the battalions that had been raised during the past five years:

Prior unit Designation	New SWATF Designation
31 Battalion in Western Caprivi	201 Battalion
33 Battalion in Eastern Caprivi	701 Battalion
34 Battalion in Kavangoland	202 Battalion
35 Battalion in Owamboland	101 Battalion
36 Battalion in Bushmanland	203 Battalion
37 Battalion in Kaokoland	102 Battalion
41 Battalion in Windhoek	911 Battalion

From the inception of the program to form military units composed of Namibians until they became an independent national defense force had only taken five years. The units were conceived and tested in battle. They proved their mettle and could compare favorably with other military forces on the African continent. On the day it came into existence in August 1980, the SWATF was larger than eight other defense forces in Africa. By 1984, its growth rate made it larger than thirteen other African armies.

Although manpower is one criterion for comparing armies, it is the fighting capability of the army that really counts. The SWATF can hold its head up proudly as it has been tested in battle and passed with flying colors, suffering no defeats at the hands of its enemy—SWAPO. The new defense force has even taken part in some of the cross border operations to destroy SWAPO bases in PROTEA and ASKARI. SWATF units were present along with SADF units to help Jonas Savimbi's UNITA halt the Soviet-directed 1985 and 1987-88 offensives against their stronghold in southeastern Angola.

How effective is SWATF? By the middle of 1987 it was very effective.

According to the Institute for Strategic Studies, University of Pretoria: ". . . At present the counterinsurgency function is mainly undertaken by units of the SWA Territory Force, while elements of the SA Army in SWA/N are mainly responsible for providing for the conventional defense of the country and undertaking the specialist supporting functions. At present 72% of the combat personnel in the northern border areas is made up of Black and Coloured soldiers and policemen of SWA/N and this ratio could be further increased if the country had the required financial and material capabilities to cater for further growth in their security forces."[3]

We will take a closer look at two units of the SWATF, 101 Battalion composed of Owambo soldiers and 201 Battalion composed of Bushmen. The author has spent a considerable amount of time with both units during numerous visits to the operational area in Namibia, and has been with them while they were conducting counterinsurgency operations against SWAPO terrorists.

****

The Bushman battalion actually had its genesis in Angola. During the SADF's withdrawal from Angola during Operation SAVANNAH in 1975-76, they came across groups of Bushmen abandoned by the Portuguese in southeastern Angola when they gave up their former colony.

These Bushmen were in bad shape. They had been worn out by MPLA troops who had hunted them down and tried to exterminate them whenever they could. Those who had so far survived were too sick and weak to secure even the barest necessities of food and shelter in the land ravaged by the on-going civil war. The South Africans gave the Bushmen food and medical treatment and brought them back to Namibia with them to keep them from the tender mercies of SWAPO's genocidal squads.

The Bushmen come from two tribes—the Mbarakwengo and the Vasquela. Although both were traditional mutual enemies in the past, the continuous warfare in the region has caused both groups to settle in the Western Caprivi Strip of Namibia.

There are close to 5,000 Bushmen living at Omega base, the headquarters of 201 Battalion. The Bushmen and their families live in a full-service community which is part of, and not separate from, the military compound at Omega. Here they receive food, clothing, medical and dental treatment and all the rest of the services and conveniences of a modern military base. The military also provides social services to help the Bushmen bridge the gap

---

[3] "The War in SWA/N," ISSUP bulletin, 4/87, Pretoria, p.9.

between his stone age hunter-gatherer culture and the modern twentieth century technological society he is now caught up in.

Bushmen soldiers get the same pay as white soldiers, although it took a bit of time for them to get used to it as the concept of "money" did not exist in their primitive culture.

Unmarried Bushmen soldiers live in typical military-style barracks, while the married live in family housing. A married Bushman gets one house for each of his wives—some have as many as three—and constructs his own dwellings with wood furnished by the government.

The Portuguese had used the Bushmen as local militia (like the Montagnards in Vietnam). The South Africans decided to capitalize on their exceptional natural tracking and bushcraft abilities and organized them into a specialized counterinsurgency unit.

The South African Defense Force has seconded five officers to the battalion. The rest of the white element, both officers and NCO's, are from Namibia.

The key operational elements of the battalion are its four rifle companies and a reconnaissance wing. Two of the companies are in the bush for a six-week tour while the remaining companies rest and retrain at Omega. After the bush tour the companies return to Omega and their place is taken by the other half of the battalion. At least half of the battalion is on operations at all times and the rotational schedule insures that fresh troops are in the bush hunting SWAPO.

Although a Bushman soldier can leave the unit whenever he wants, few do. The reason is simple: the Bushman is at the bottom of the social scale in black Africa. He is surrounded by ancient enemies who would like nothing better than to kill him. In the battalion he is not only safe from the depredations of his ancient enemies, but is able to use the skills his culture has honed to a keen edge over the centuries. He can use these skills to great effect to get back at his enemies. So why leave such a situation?

War, however, results in casualties and the fortunes of war extract a toll on friend and foe alike. But the Bushmen battalion, and most of the Namibian units, do not invalid out their wounded and crippled. They stay with their comrades and are given jobs such as base guard duty and other garrison duties that take up a soldier's time. This frees the regular Bushman soldier for rest and retraining so that he is able to concentrate on the job at hand—polishing up his skills as a soldier instead of doing necessary, but tactically useless housekeeping jobs that are the bane of garrison soldiering—so that he is well prepared when it's time to return to the bush.

Many would think that after thirteen years of fighting these warriors wouldn't need further training. But the Bushmen come from a society drastically different from our own. They have been hunters and gatherers for centuries and now they have been thrust squarely in the middle of a twentieth century counterinsurgency war. Their training periods at Omega are geared to help them rapidly adapt to the benefits and evils of the eighties. They are, to use an understatement, "widening the scope of their experiences."

For example, to attain a very basic military skill— shooting a rifle, they had to overcome centuries of acculturation. Bushmen from time immemorial have killed their game with a bow and arrow. They instinctively aimed their arrow above their target to compensate for the drop it takes on its flight to the target. When first shooting his rifle the Bushman recruit always aimed high to compensate for his assumed drop of the bullet. It took him months of patient practice before he could aim and shoot his rifle like other soldiers. After overcoming this cultural block, however, most have developed into excellent shots.

After individual training the Bushmen undergo extensive unit training, especially at the company level, in order to operate more efficiently in cohesive large-scale units. The units develop and incorporate new tactics into their bag of tricks for successfully countering the tactics of SWAPO.

This is a constant on-going process as SWAPO quickly adapts counter-measures to the tactics they face. One of the commanding officers of the battalion hit the tactical nail squarely on the head when he said, "If we want to win this war, we have to be one step ahead of SWAPO."[4]

After their initial difficulties with adjusting to military life, the Bushmen have caught on quickly to the complexities of modern warfare, and have adapted their innate excellence in bushcraft to it. Able to survive long periods on minimal food and water, the Bushmen have an instinctive, highly developed sense of danger. They can run on a track, while figuring out where an enemy would go or should go to either escape detection, set up an ambush or booby trap, or any number of situations that might arise in bush warfare.

The Bushmen look for the unnatural—a missing spot of dew on a blade of grass that should be, but is no longer there. This is one small example of things they notice that indicate the passage of human feet that have upset the natural setting. They are plain as day to the Bushmen, and this skill has made life miserable for SWAPO.

Their ancient cultural skill also help them with some of the infantry-man's weapons. They are deadly, for example, with the 60mm patrol mortar.

---

[4] Conversation with Cmdt. Brian Adams, OIC, 201 BN. July, 1983.

It is a weapon of simple but rugged design—a 60mm tube with the standard baseplate, legs and aiming assembly removed. A small interchangeable breechpiece replaces the base plate and a couple of hooks are welded on the tube so it can be carried over the shoulder by a sling attached to the hooks.

To fire the mortar, the Bushmen place it on the ground, use the hand holding the tube to adjust for trajectory and windage, drop a round down the tube with the other hand and fire. One man can effectively fire this weapon. The Bushmen are very good at determining projectile trajectory because of their proficiency with their age-old weapon—the bow and arrow. In their hands the patrol mortar has become a highly mobile and deadly weapon.

The reconnaissance wing, or "recce wing" as they're known in southern Africa, has a different tactical organization and mission than the rest of the battalion. It is made up of five operational teams of six people per team. Each team has two whites and four Bushmen. This gives it great flexibility as it allows the team to break into two units of three men each.

The battalion uses the recce wing primarily for surveillance or clandestine missions in its operational area. This involves dangerous behind-the-line incursions—such as sneaking around in the bush looking for SWAPO bases or arms caches, and gathering information and intelligence on SWAPO units moving in the area. More often than not these missions are done in Marxist Angola.

These operations require stealth, steady nerves, and well-trained, disciplined troops. To be successful, their presence must not be detected by SWAPO or by SWAPO sympathizers who may tip off the terrorists.

There is a true story told at Omega base about a recce team that was concealed in the bush about fifteen meters from a combined SWAPO/FAPLA camp in southern Angola. A FAPLA sentry was suspicious of a shadow behind a particular bush which was in fact a Bushman recce team member. But the sentry was either too scared or too lazy to walk over and check it out. Instead, he walked back and forth, staring at the bush. The team members were sure they were on the verge of being engaged in a firefight with over a hundred enemies.

Finally the sentry whipped out a wrist-rocket-type slingshot, picked up a small stone and fired it at the shadow. It struck the Bushman squarely on the thigh and at that range it struck with considerable force. But the Bushman stopped his involuntary impulse to cry out in spite of the excruciating pain. He didn't utter a peep, nor did he move even though his leg was throbbing with pain. Not getting any reaction, the sentry convinced himself that there was no danger and settled down. After a while he became complacent and drowsy and this allowed the recce team to slip away undetected from the dangerous situation.

The struck Bushman, although walking with a limp for a couple of days, still was able to carry on and wasn't a hindrance at all to his teammates or their mission.

The Bushmen's tracking and bushcraft skills enable the recce teams to survive alone in the bush for long periods of time without outside support. Staying in the bush without need of constant resupply makes detection harder and allows them to keep on their mission.

Usually, the only inkling SWAPO has that the security forces are on to their presence, because the recce team has discovered and tracked them, comes when a reaction force of Bushmen suddenly attacks them.

Such tactics, in addition to the obvious one of killing the terrorists, also disrupts their lines of communication and supply and instills a sense of fear in the terrorists that it's not safe anywhere in southern Angola or Namibia. In short, SWAPO's program of revolutionary action gets a far distant second-place priority to the increasingly prime duty of mere personal survival.

****

The origin of the Owambo unit, 101 Battalion, can be traced back to 1974, when it was designated 1 Owambo Battalion under the command of Captain McChlachlan. In point of fact, it was a battalion in name only for it was nothing more than a home guard unit of around 150 men.

In 1977, it was changed from a home guard unit and renamed 35 Battalion. Its primary function was training and support although it did have one company that was actively engaged in counterinsurgency combat operations against SWAPO.

It trained and provided Owambo trackers and other support elements such as interpreters and drivers for various SADF elements operating in Owamboland.

At this time all the soldiers were Owambos while all the NCO's and officers were white. This situation has changed dramatically. By 1988, eighty percent of the NCO's were Owambos and one of the companies was under the command of an Owambo commissioned officer. Owambos were moving up in the battalion's rank structure as fast as they could be trained and qualified. All this was due to the far-reaching changes that occurred as a result of the establishment of an independent Namibian defense force.

In 1980, the unit was redesignated 101 Battalion and its mission was changed from an operational training unit to a support unit for other SADF elements. This mission didn't last long. In 1981, the battalion got a new commanding officer whose influence changed and molded the unit into what its supporters claim is the best counterinsurgency unit in the world.

Col. Willie Welgemoed (then a commandant) assumed command of 101 BN in 1981 and changed the unit's emphasis from support to operational duties.

Welgemoed did not, however, jettison the battalion's prior emphasis on training and support. The battle with SWAPO over power in Namibia would be decided on who won the hearts and minds of the Owambo people. It was crystal clear to Welgemoed that his all-Owambo unit would play a crucial part in that campaign. In his mind, not only should the Owambo soldier be in the forefront fighting SWAPO, the battalion should and could become the leading institution in the Owambo's fight against SWAPO.

As there has been far more volunteers to join the battalion than available positions, the unit can be selective and take only the best possible recruits. To be chosen they must first pass a selection course that is basically a series of physical fitness tests including a ten kilometer forced march. Potential recruits must also have a basic knowledge of tracking and bushcraft.

Once selected they go through a rigorous basic military training course which turns them into tough, competent soldiers of the battalion. As a result of the training, the Owambo soldier in the battalion possesses characteristics that are sought in any army: loyalty to both the unit and his fellow soldiers; a strong sense of patriotism to his fellow Owambo tribesmen; and an aggressiveness that makes him a good soldier in conducting war against SWAPO terrorists.

Welgemoed's program for the battalion used these characteristics and emphasized five factors in the battalion's modus operandi:

1. The unit would deploy as a reaction force throughout Owamboland.
2. It would support SADF units by supplying them with trackers, interpreters, intelligence, and civic action personnel. In addition, the battalion would also supply two mounted platoons on either horses or motorbikes to work in conjunction with SADF units.
3. It would carry on with its old training function by providing basic and advanced training for Owambo recruits. The battalion would also provide other training through its civic action schools at Miershoop and Otavi along with advanced courses at Okayanga.
4. The battalion would provide schools and other social and medical services for the Owambo soldier's families.
5. The battalion would work closely with the local population through

its civic action company and assist the local Owambo government in its efforts to provide protection and services for the Owambo people.

Welgemoed intended that 101 Battalion would play a major role in the counterinsurgency effort in Owamboland and that it would be local Owambo's doing it. "The war is actually in Owamboland, not in the south. So it makes sense to use them: they know the area, the customs, and they can talk the language," summed up Welgemoed.[5]

He envisioned not only the local tribesmen taking over control of the war on the ground, but through their civic action programs, negating and destroying SWAPO's organizational infrastructure as well. The key to winning the hearts and minds of the Owambo people lay with using their fellow tribesmen to carry out the counterinsurgency mission.

The military centerpiece of 101's counterinsurgency program was their company-size mobile Romeo-Mike force. These highly mobile forces operated not only throughout Owamboland but often went north of the border to intercept SWAPO terrorists enroute to Namibia. This practice became more widespread after Operation PROTEA, but was temporarily halted during the period of the Joint Monitoring Commission (JMC), and was only discontinued after the Tripartite peace agreements signed by Cuba, Angola and South Africa.

The Romeo-Mike force had an enormous impact on SWAPO as now they were not even safe in their would-be sanctuaries in southern Angola. Since the Owambo tribal boundaries spilled over into southern Angola, 101's presence there served to remind their fellow Owambos that SWAPO wasn't the only game in town.

Each Romeo-Mike force company consisted of a headquarters unit and four reaction force platoons. Each platoon had three sections, or squads in US military terminology. Each reaction force platoon also had five vehicles—four Casspir mine-proof fighting vehicles and one logistical truck to carry the platoon's extra ammunition, fuel, spare parts, and rations. The platoon commander and his platoon sergeant had one fighting vehicle while each of the three sections had its own separate Casspir.

The Casspirs were designed and built in South Africa for the South African Police (the name is an acronym derived from CSIR—Council for Scientific and Industrial Research—and SAP—South African Police), and are used by both 101 Battalion and *Koevoet*. They are constructed with small-arms bullet-resistant steel and are designed to deflect and minimize the

---

[5] Interview with Cmdt. Welgemoed, April, 1984.

effects of exploding anti-tank mines—a favorite weapon of SWAPO. They are extremely well-built. They have a maximum road speed of sixty miles per hour. It is the ideal vehicle for 101 Battalion's wide-ranging operations. There was an actual incident in the Kaokoland that proves the Casspir's effectiveness. A battalion commander was traveling in a Casspir when it detonated four SWAPO land mines stacked one on top of the other; he and his RSM (regimental sergeant major, the equivalent to our battalion sergeant major), the only occupants of the vehicle, both survived the blast. The RSM had the wind knocked out of him as he was thrown out of the vehicle. The battalion commander, who was driving, suffered a compression fracture of the spine as he was strapped in the driver's seat via a shoulder-harness seatbelt.

Romeo-Mike force's tactical operations all flow from their constant patrolling, looking for signs of the enemy or collecting intelligence about his movements, bases, arms caches, anything that could provide a clue as to SWAPO's whereabouts. The platoon sections scour the bush looking for SWAPO spoor. While the Casspir inches along at a speed of five to six miles per hour, several Owambo soldiers are fanned out in front of it on foot looking for tracks. The soldiers remaining in the vehicles are not just resting, they are also searching the ground and the area looking for signs of the enemy.

If fresh SWAPO spoor is picked up the whole team will begin to follow it. Back and forth, cutting across the spoor, the team will sweep not only to follow the original spoor, but to see if the terrorists have split up. Over the radio the other teams are notified and they will leapfrog the tracking team to try and cut off SWAPO's escape and force the terrorists into a fatal confrontation with 101's soldiers.

Unlike the Bushmen, who dismount and engage the enemy on foot, 101's Romeo-Mike forces fight on wheels using the mobility and protection of the Casspirs. A typical contact would entail a charge by the Casspirs towards the cornered terrorists with all guns blazing. This can be an awesome amount of firepower as each soldier has an automatic assault rifle, and the Casspirs carry mounted machine guns and some even 20mm automatic cannons. The charge is usually sufficient to crumble any SWAPO resistance, but the action doesn't stop there.

After the initial charge the Casspirs will circle the contact at top speeds, constantly enlarging the circumference of their circling movement. This is done for two reasons: by moving at high speeds while circling, they can avoid hits by surviving SWAPO terrorists using the RPG-7 anti-tank rocket; and they can catch and destroy the SWAPO terrorists trying to flee from the contact.

The mobile tactics of 101 Battalion are extremely effective and the unit consistently leads all military organization in Namibia in the number of SWAPO terrorists killed in contacts with the security forces.

****

Successfully combatting an insurgency requires good thorough police work. The campaign against SWAPO was no different.

The authorities involved the local population through the use of special police constables. These were volunteers, recruited locally in Owamboland, the Kaokoland, Kavongoland and the Caprivi. Their duties were local protection. They guarded the local government and tribal officials and also protected installations, *kraals* and villages from SWAPO terrorists.

Special constable guard detachments varied in size depending on the terrorist threat in their area and the type of targets they were protecting. If the threat was large or the target critical the detachments could be bigger than a platoon. Normally, they were made up of just a few men.

All volunteers attended basic eight weeks training at a special police constables school in Ondangwa before being sent out to their local guard detachments.

One of the most successful police counterinsurgency units in Namibia was the mobile unit called *koevoets* (pronounced "koofoos"). *Koevoet* is an Afrikaans word meaning "crowbar." Like a crowbar, the unit has pried the SWAPO terrorist out from the midst of Owamboland better than any other Namibian or South African security force unit. (*Koevoets* produce eighty percent of the terrorist kills in the operational area.) From its inception until the end of 1988 the unit had killed at least 3,000 SWAPO insurgents.[6]

The unit was the brain child of Col. (now Maj. Gen.) Hans Dreyer, who had some opinionated and forceful views on a special police unit to conduct counterinsurgency operations. The unit was originally set up in 1978 to develop and exploit intelligence that was gathered by the police. Their original task was to collate and pass this intelligence along so the security forces could react quickly and exploit the information. In addition, the unit provided trackers for other units.

Relying on other units for a reaction force, however, caused problems and often by the time the intelligence was collated, passed on to the reaction force and then acted upon, it was too late.

Dreyer continued to press his view that a special police unit should combine both tracking ability and reaction force capability. Finally, the

[6] *The New York Times International,* January 15, 1989, p.3.

authorities bowed to Dreyer's arguments, and in 1980, the unit formed its own reaction force to cut through the red tape and eliminate all the delays. The new reaction force was a tremendous success, engaging in thirty-six contacts in its first ninety days of operation. It didn't take long for the *koevoets* to become well-known throughout the operational area. During its first year of operation, the unit had killed 511 SWAPO terrorists while losing only twelve of its own men.

Koevoets are a mobile counterinsurgency platoon-sized group made up of locally recruited special constables and NCO's. They were led by regular police officers of the South African Police (SAP) seconded to the unit or by officers of the South West African Police (SWAPOL). The unit headquarters exercises overall control of operations from its command center located at Oshakati. Upon the analysis of intelligence throughout the operational area, headquarters will concentrate *koevoet* units where needed. Thus, the units are not bound to any specific area, but can go wherever they are needed.

Each group has four Casspir anti-mine personnel carrying vehicles and a mine-protected logistical truck. Each Casspir carries a section of ten men, commanded by a sergeant or a senior special constable. The overall group (platoon) commander is either an officer or a warrant officer.

The arms carried are the R-5, a short version of the SADF standard R-4 assault rifle, the FN MAG, 7.62mm machine gun, the 60mm patrol mortar, and one Casspir in each group has a mounted 20mm cannon.

Koevoets are highly mobile and have an awesome amount of firepower at their disposal.

A *koevoet* group's normal operating procedure is to alternate one week in the bush and one week back at their base for rest, repair and maintenance.

The secret of *koevoet's* success is working with and relying on timely information from the local population in the operational area. The information they get is up to date and obtained through normal police work. Their approach to counterinsurgency is that it is essentially normal police work involving a lot of combat and that it is not warfare in the normal military sense.

Koevoets, like 101 Battalion, also use the principle of setting a thief to catch a thief by employing former terrorists to catch SWAPO. In fact, about a quarter of *koevoets* are ex-SWAPO terrorists. Not only do they pursue their former comrades with the zeal of the converted, but their knowledge and use is invaluable due to their uncanny insight into the likely movements and reactions of the hunted SWAPO groups. They have been there and know what goes on in the mind of a SWAPO terrorist. They will follow a trail to a conclusion no matter where it may take them. They are not restricted by battalion, company or military sector boundaries. It is not unusual for *koevoet* groups to chase their target back and forth through Owamboland, over the border into Angola and to catch them near their bases some distance into Angola.

Contacts with single terrorists or small groups of SWAPO are handled by the tracker pursuing them on the ground. Larger contacts are normally carried out mounted, taking advantage of the vehicles' firepower, maneuverability, protection and fields of vision. Being mounted lessens confusion in that all one's men are mounted while those running on the ground are the bad guys. This procedure eliminates most of the confusion as to friend or foe, common to a major contact.

In general, *koevoet* personnel come from the ethnic group in whose area they will be operating. Owambos work in Owamboland, Kavangos in Kavangoland, etc.... However, the groups are not made up exclusively of sub-tribes within the main tribal area. They are usually mixed so that each group will have at least one or two men from each area who will be familiar with its terrain, people, dialect and customs. This procedure is similar to having policemen patrol the neighborhoods they grew up in—they know it and the people living in it.

Koevoets have been so successful that SWAPO and its disinformation network of leftist friends have mounted a world-wide campaign to discredit them. They use the usual tactic of the left: when all else fails accuse your opponent of committing atrocities. This is the tack SWAPO and its leftist supporters have taken against *koevoet*. They have charged them with alleged barbarous acts against the people of Owamboland.

The propaganda conveniently ignores the fact that the success of *koevoet* operations depends upon the friendship and cooperation of the people of Owamboland. This fact puts the lie to such SWAPO-inspired accusations. It is the local Owambos who point out the hidden terrorist in their midst, show the policemen which tracks are the terrorists' and not the locals'. SWAPO terrorists may be misinformed, but they are not brain dead. They have learned the hard way not to wear military boots with their characteristic treads. Instead they wear civilan shoes or even go barefoot. Their tracks then are picked up through intelligence which almost always comes from the local population. If the policemen brutalized and alienated the local population, they would not volunteer such information. On the contrary, they would keep their mouth shut and avoid the police like the plague. But they don't. Instead they give them the information that has led to the failure of SWAPO's revolutionary action in Owamboland.

Has the South African counterinsurgency effort paid off? Did it affect the attitude of the population and win their hearts and minds? The following show that indeed it did:

1. The flow of tactical information from the people to the security forces increased (see graph);

2. After 1984, the ability of SWAPO to voluntarily recruit terrorists inside Namibia ceased;

3. SWAPO terrorists were unable to survive among the people, especially in Central Owamboland, the most densely populated part of the country, where approximately twenty-five percent of the people of the country live;

4. SWAPO clearly contracted possible areas of operation due to the inability of the terrorists to survive among the people of Kaokoland, Kavongoland and the Caprivi Strip;

5. The size and efficiency of the local security forces grew as a result of their voluntary recruitment and training in the northern areas. This has evolved to the situation, prior to the implementation of UN Resolution 435, where over seventy-two percent of the combat soldiers in the northern operational area were Namibian black and colored soldiers and policemen.

(See chart on facing page.)

Numbers of incidents where the people have voluntarily supplied information to SWATF:

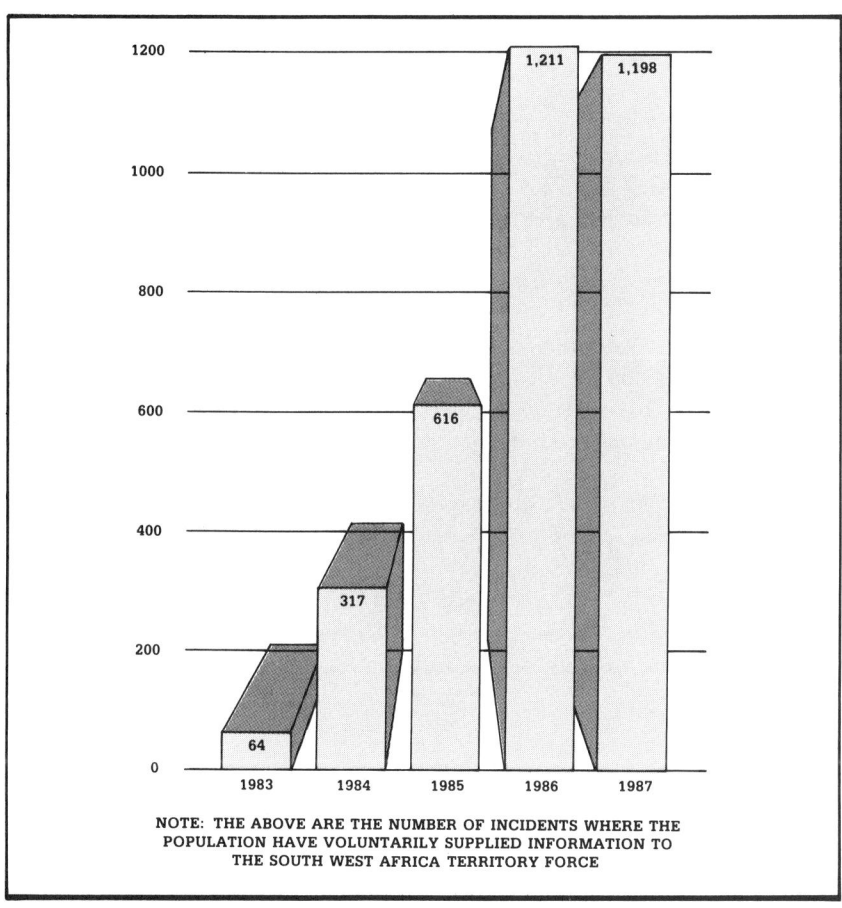

NOTE: THE ABOVE ARE THE NUMBER OF INCIDENTS WHERE THE POPULATION HAVE VOLUNTARILY SUPPLIED INFORMATION TO THE SOUTH WEST AFRICA TERRITORY FORCE

A prime purpose of any counterinsurgency effort is to provide a stable situation for the government to carry out needed reforms. This was done in Namibia. As result of these reforms, the emotional wave generated years ago by SWAPO has been neutralized to a great extent.

The security forces, by ensuring protection of the people of Namibia, played a major role in giving the government the time and the ability to carry out the political, social and economic reforms that blunted SWAPO's revolutionary efforts in Namibia.

The counterinsurgency effort also aimed at bringing about a division between the population and the terrorists—in effect isolating the terrorists. The inability of SWAPO terrorists to survive in Owamboland shows the success of the security forces in isolating them from the population.

The success was not due to blind luck, but because the security forces used the right counterinsurgency tactics. Perhaps, nothing better illustrates the success of the SADF and SWATF counterinsurgency efforts in Namibia than the words of Sir Robert Thompson. His prescription for achieving success against guerrillas shows why there was success in Namibia:

"Getting government forces into the same element as the insurgent is rather like trying to deal with a tomcat in an alley. It is no good inserting a large, fierce dog (conventional forces with tanks, artillery and bombers—ed). The dog may not find the tomcat [SWAPO insurgents—ed]—if he does, the tomcat will escape up a tree [fade into the bush and hide, or high-tail it back to sanctuaries in Angola—ed]; the dog will then chase the female cats in the alley [alienate the population, destroy their crops, homes, etc., as it wanders around the area; or they do it out of spite and frustration because they couldn't find the terrorists—ed]. The answer is to put in a fiercer tomcat [tough, well-trained small counterinsurgency units such as the Bushmen, 101 Battalion, and the Police Counterinsurgency Units, to name a few—ed]. The two cannot fail to meet because they are both in exactly the same element and have exactly the same purpose in life. The weaker will be eliminated."[7]

The SADF and SWATF were not the weaker tomcats.

---

[7] Thompson, *op. cit.*, pp.119-120.

16

Operation ASKARI—December 1983 to January 1984

According to Maj. Gen. George Meiring, the Military Commander of South West Africa, the primary aim of Operation ASKARI, "was to disrupt the planned infiltration of SWAPO's special units into South West Africa."[1]

ASKARI intended to stop almost 1,000 SWAPO terrorists from infiltrating from Angolan sanctuaries into areas of operations in Namibia. The terrorists normally would wait until the onset of the rainy season, January through March, before attempting such large-scale movement across the border into Namibia. During the rainy season, the heavy rains wash out their tracks making it extremely difficult for the security forces to hunt down the infiltrators.

However, the rains came early in December 1983 and this precipitated the South African preemptive strike against the SWAPO military staging bases in southern Angola.

By striking at SWAPO's military bases in southern Angola the South Africans were attempting to deny sanctuary, as much as possible, to SWAPO close to the terrorist area of operations.

The results of prior large-scale South African cross-border preemptive strikes, REINDEER and PROTEA to name just two, had been major setbacks to SWAPO. Not only had the terrorist organization suffered enormous losses of trained personnel and supplies, but the operations forced SWAPO to move their bases farther north in Angola.

---

[1] Press conference, Maj. Gen. George Meiring, Windhoek, January, 1984.

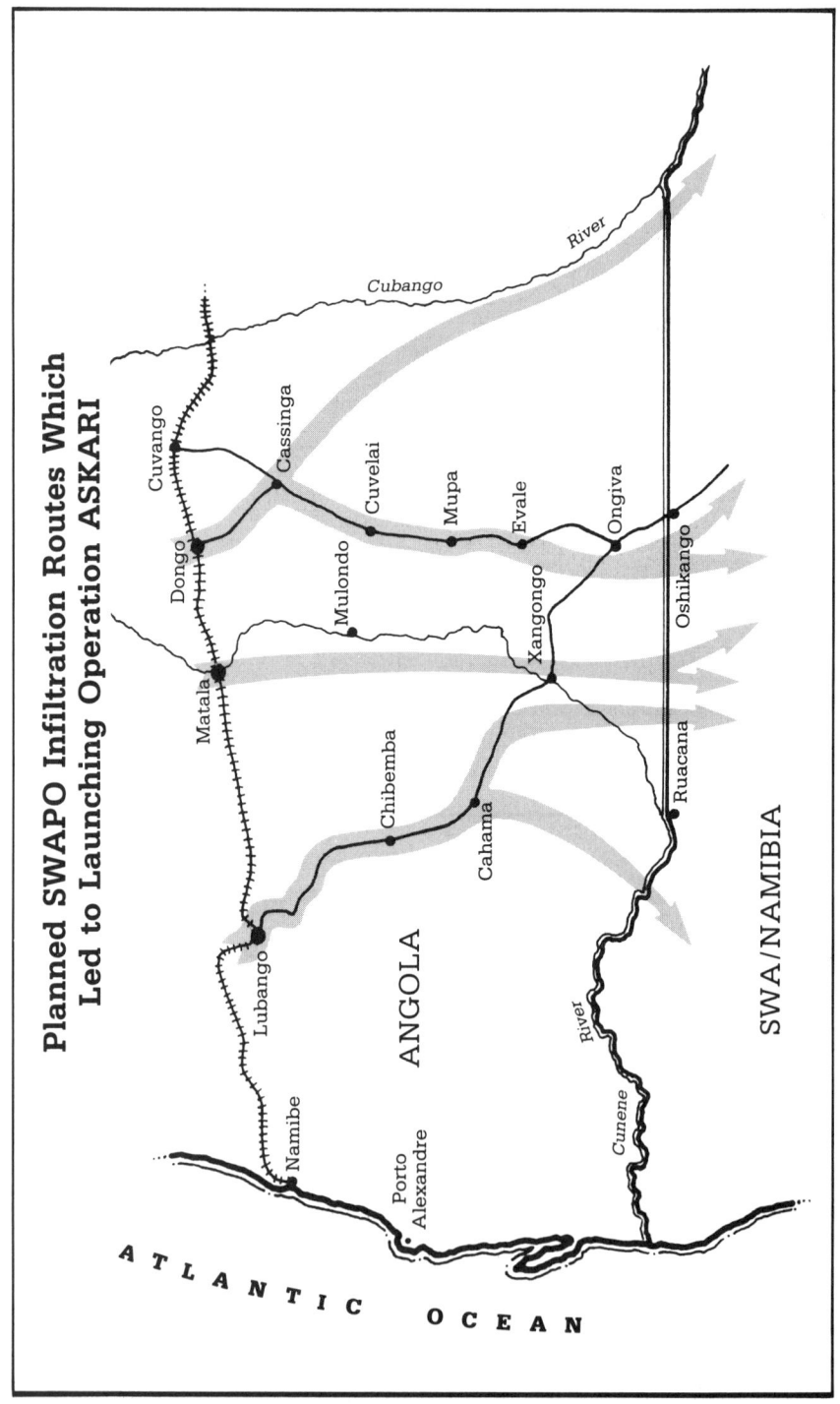

This relocation had detrimental effects on SWAPO in three ways. The terrorist bands now had to expend a good deal of their effort just to get from their bases in Angola down to the Angolan-Namibian border. South African security force units made the terrorists' journey more dangerous now by extending their patrols over the border looking for infiltrators. These patrols forced SWAPO to break their infiltrating groups into even smaller units to avoid detection. The down side of this was that the smaller the group the fewer supplies and weapons they could carry with them. Since SWAPO had no bases in Namibia, they had to bring everything necessary for their war of terror with them on their own backs. By the time the terrorists, who had eluded and survived the security force patrols, reached their target area, they were low on supplies, often exhausted and faced a population that was growing more hostile to their terror tactics.

The further away the SWAPO bases were from the populous northern Namibia border areas the less of a psychological threat they were to the people of Namibia.

Command, control and communications problems increased and intensified for SWAPO the further away they were from their revolutionary battlefield.

The difficulties created by South Africa's cross-border operations had a cumulative effect on SWAPO. REINDEER severely reduced SWAPO's trained manpower and disrupted their communications and logistical system. PROTEA forced the terrorist organization to move its training and logistic bases further north in an effort to escape the long arm of the South Africans. The operations placed enormous strains on SWAPO communications and their logistical system, further reducing the efficiency of the revolutionary effort.

Ultimately, the cumulative difficulties forced SWAPO to send a large number of insufficiently trained terrorists on a harrowing and tiring journey in the rain and mud south to Namibia in the hope that some of them might succeed in reaching their destination and be able to carry out their mission of terror. And it seemed that nowhere could they afford to relax on their journey, as units of the South African security forces were hunting them like sharks ready to devour their prey.

"It is our duty to protect the people of South West Africa and to prevent the enemy from crossing into the area where they can commit their murderous deeds against unarmed civilians," Meiring told reporters at his Windhoek press conference.[2]

---

[2] *Ibid.*

ASKARI started out as a search and destroy operation against these small bands of SWAPO terrorists working their way south towards Namibia and the bases from which they were coming.

South African intelligence had pieced together most of SWAPO's operational plan for the impending rainy season infiltration. The SWAPO plan called for a seven-prong movement into Namibia by specialist units composed of terrorists trained to infiltrate and operate in small groups.

After leaving their main bases at Lubongo, Matala and Dongo in Angola, the SWAPO groups would follow one of the seven prongs aimed for either Kaokoland, Western Owamboland, Central Owamboland, the so-called triangle of death (area of intense counterinsurgency operations by the security forces) which is the Otavi-Tsumeb-Grootfontein area, or one of the two prongs heading for Eastern Owamboland and the Kavango region of Namibia.

Based on this intelligence, the South Africans decided to meet this proposed major infiltration effort of SWAPO by attacking and interdicting it. This preemptive strike was given the code name ASKARI.

The South African force used in ASKARI included four major combat groups, plus a fifth which was involved far to the east of the major activity during the operation.

The combat groups were: Task Force Echo-Victor, Task Force Delta-Fox, Task Force Victor and Task Force X-Ray. The fifth component was Combat Team Tango.

Task Force X-Ray was made up of 61 Mechanized Battalion and attached units: three motorized infantry companies, one armored car squadron, two troops of mobile rocket launchers, one artillery battery, two anti-aircraft batteries, a recconnaisance element and a troop of engineers.

X-Ray's mission included sending an element west of the Cunene River to capture Quiteve and to pin the enemy down in Cahama. With these two objectives secured, the element would be in a position to protect the western flank of X-Ray from attacks by FAPLA/SWAPO reinforcements that might try to prevent the Task Force from carrying out its main mission. With their western flank secured, X-Ray could move on to the next phase of the mission. That was to link up with Task Force Delta, to attack and capture Cuvelai.

Quiteve was quickly captured without much resistance, but Cahama was a different matter. The enemy was defending Cahama in strength—a brigade as opposed to the combat team. But since the plan was to pin the enemy forces down and prevent them from to reinforcing their comrades to the east, the capture of Cahama was not essential to the operation. Nevertheless, the FAPLA/SWAPO defenders had to be given a bloody nose to convince them to

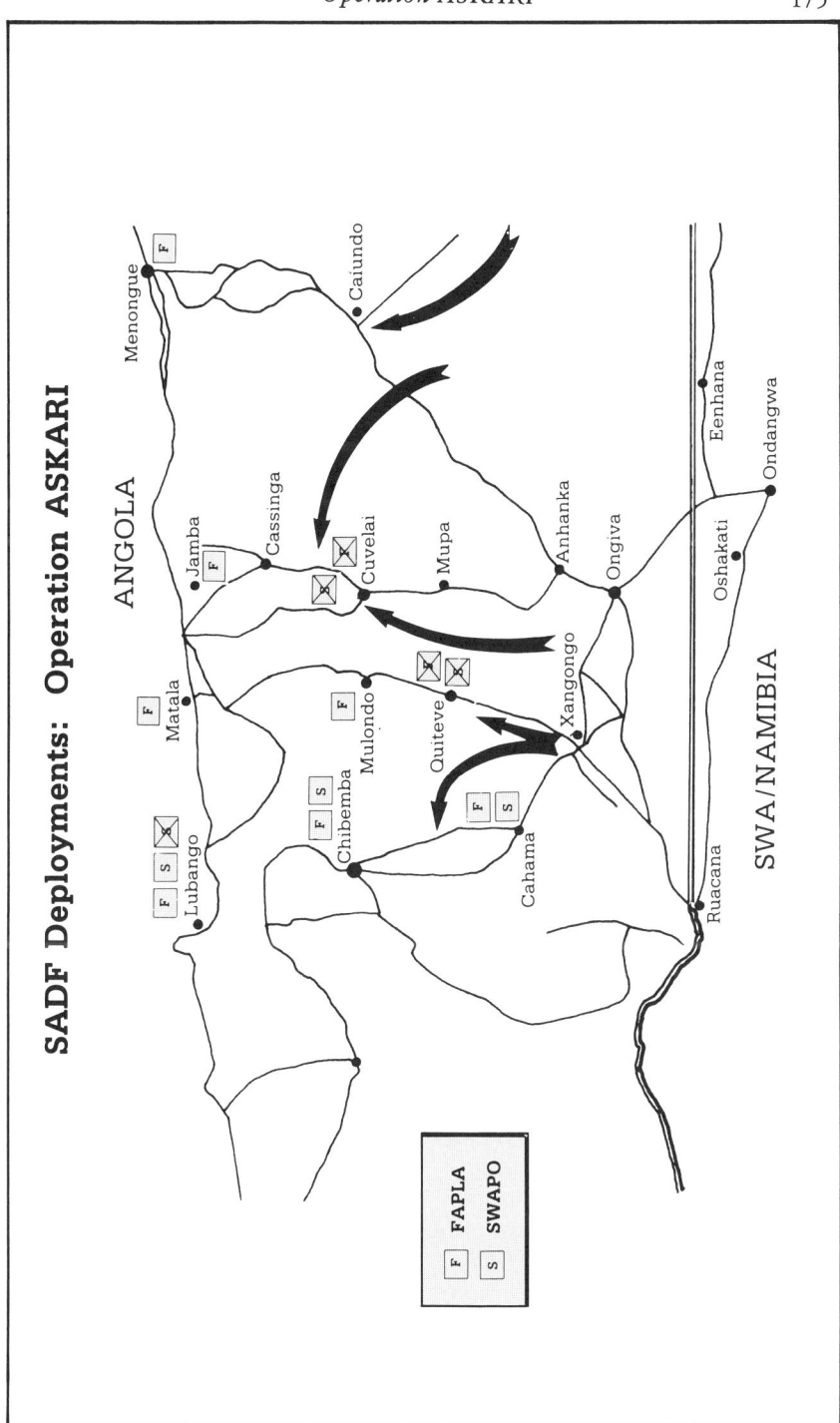

sit tight and stay out of the rest of the developing fight.

On December 20, 1983, a combat team bypassed Cahama to the east and executed a feint toward Chimbemba to test the enemy's reaction. Since Chimbemba, in the eyes of SWAPO, was the stepping stone for an attack upon their operational headquarters at Lubango, they reacted strongly to the South African feint. They launched an armored column consisting of T-54 tanks and armored personnel carriers to deal with the threat.

A fierce fire-fight broke out which resulted in both the FAPLA/SWAPO column and the South African "advance" grinding down to a protracted stalemate.

Meanwhile other elements of X-Ray attacked Cahama from the south. Just to the west of Cahama, there was an advanced SWAPO headquarters manned by approximately 200 terrorists. Its function was to direct the terrorist infiltration efforts from this advanced position.

Heeding the old saying "the better part of valor is discretion," the terrorists abandoned their headquarters and fled into Cahama, where they would enjoy the protection of FAPLA and Cuban forces stationed there.

During previous incursions into Angola, the fighting was over and done within a short period of time because there was little interference by the Angolans or Cubans. South African security forces had gone to great lengths in dropping leaflets and making radio appeals stating their quarrel was with SWAPO and not the Angolans or Cubans.

"We don't like becoming involved with FAPLA and Cuban forces, and would rather respect them in their areas and expect them to respect our fight against SWAPO," said General Constand Viljoen, chief of the SADF.[3]

This time, however, the Angolans and Cuban forces got heavily involved in the fighting.

The defenders were well prepared and there was little cover for the combat group just outside the enemy's defensive perimeter.

Heavy fighting raged back and forth with both sides suffering casualties. However, the fire discipline and ferocity of the attack convinced the defenders to stay in their positions and leave their comrades to the east to their own fate. They didn't venture out of Cahama until after the South African operation concluded.

Task Force X-Ray had successfully completed the first part of its mission.

The task force celebrated New Year's Day 1984 by taking a short, well-deserved rest (4:00 a.m. to 2:00 p.m.). That afternoon they moved off to

---

[3] Norval, M. *Gung Ho*, February 1985, p.45.

carry out their second task—to link up with Task Force Delta and capture Cuvelai.

While X-Ray was getting its brief rest before moving northeast to link up with Delta, elements of Delta were fighting for their lives.

A combined FAPLA and Cuban force, with their Soviet advisors, had ambushed a unit of Delta on New Years Eve near the town of Cuvelai.

Delta, made up predominantly of Citizen Force (comparable to our Active Reserve or National Guard) called up for duty in ASKARI, had sent out a battle group of about 600 men to probe and test the enemy's defenses. The South Africans were probing towards a SWAPO base near Cuvelai when they ran into two battalions of Cuban troops, soon reinforced by SWAPO terrorists and FAPLA forces of the 11th Mechanized Brigade. This enemy force was backed by a company of Soviet-supplied T-54 tanks. The combined communist force attacked the probing unit from Delta.

The situation looked bleak for the South Africans. Outnumbered better than six to one, they faced more than 4,000 troops with superior firepower provided by the tank company.

All of a sudden, a counterinsurgency operation had quickly developed into a conventional battle. Assessing the situation later, General Meiring said, "The security forces did not have heavy caliber arms with them and had to fight against much more powerful firepower."[4]

In spite of the odds, the Delta group hunkered down and slugged it out with the SWAPO, FAPLA and Cuban forces in a three-day battle.

After three days of fighting, the 11th Brigade suddenly withdrew from the battlefield. One of the battle casualties was the communist tank company. It no longer existed. The South Africans had knocked out all twelve of the T-54 tanks. Using the Ratel armored personnel carriers mounting 90mm guns and anti-tank rocket launchers, the tank unit was destroyed.

Superior training, better discipline, and the Ratel's ability to find targets in the thick bush due to its higher silhouette and better manueverability, saved the day for the South Africans. All these factors paid off in the battle for Cuvelai as the SADF suffered only seven killed while communist deaths exceeded 324.

But the outcome had been a close thing and the nature of the battle pointed out that future incursions into Angola might have a more conventional than counterinsurgency nature. Cmdt. Faan Greyling, commander of Delta, pointed out that in view of the type of weaponry deployed against the security forces, it would force the SADF, in the future, to have

---

[4] Meiring press conference, *op. cit.*

similar weaponry available when operations are launched against SWAPO.[5]

The communists broke off contact and fled in spite of having superiority in manpower, firepower and being directed by Russian military officers while fighting from well-prepared positions.

Captured documents clearly proved Soviet involvement. Some documents contained comprehensive detailed sketches and instructions fashioned by Soviet army officers that were so meticulous in their design that they left open spaces between the Russian lines, in order to permit instructions in any language to facilitate comprehension.

Maps with battle instructions written in Russian were also captured. Other maps containing both Russian and Portuguese writing, that the FAPLA commanders had utilized the Russian instructions and translated them into Portuguese—the lingua franca of Angola.

Some captured documents showed that Soviet officers were operating and directing SWAPO, FAPLA, and Cuban forces down to the company level. In one instance, the Soviets urged their clients to hold a position "at all costs" and "down to the last man." Fortunately for the beleaguered unit of Delta, the communist troops didn't follow the Soviet advice. Perhaps, this was because the Soviet advisors dispensing such advice to their SWAPO and FAPLA comrades were among the first to flee when the communist forces broke off the fight.

Why did the enemy suddenly break off contact and retreat? Nobody knows for sure except the commander of FAPLA's 11th Brigade and, if still alive, he isn't talking.

By the third of January 1984, 61 Mechanized group had linked up with Delta.

At 8:00 a.m. the next morning both launched the final attack on the SWAPO-FAPLA defensive complex at Cuvelai. By 6:00 p.m. the last communist forces had fled the town. All that remained was the mopping up of a few scattered disorganized bands in the vicinity. On the 5th of January, Cuvelai was firmly in the hands of South African forces and the battle of Cuvelai was over.

Five days later Task Force Delta withdrew leaving 61 Mechanized Battalion battle group holding Cuvelai.

Combat Team Tango's job was to disrupt the planned SWAPO infiltration into Eastern Owamboland and Kavangoland. Operating west of the Cubango River, Tango moved north towards the town of Caiundo

---

[5] Sector 10, Op Askari, "Burgermag Dra Sy Deel By," 1 Military Printing Unit, 1985, p.19.

engaging in a series of small firefights with groups of SWAPO terrorist working their way south towards Namibia.

The presence of Tango quickly had a negative effect upon SWAPO's infiltration plan. After a few isolated clashes the SWAPO terrorists either broke up into small groups of five or six terrorists who continued to try and run the gauntlet to Namibia, often with disastrous results, or they scattered into the bush and worked their way back north to regroup and lick their wounds.

Task Force Echo-Victor's job was to disrupt the SWAPO infiltration as the Task Force worked its way north to its primary area of operations between Cuvelai and Cassinga.

The task force was made up of units from the famous South African Army unit 32 Battalion.

The "Buffalo Battalion," nicknamed after its cap badge, the head of the ferocious African Cape Buffalo, has a well-earned outstanding reputation within the South African Army. On August 27, 1985, the unit was officially presented with its Unit Colour—the first time that had ever been done in the operational area. (The ceremony usually takes place at the unit's home base in the Republic of South Africa.) A highlight of the parade was the commissioning of nine black officers. A year later *Paratus*, the official magazine of the SADF, said 32 Battalion had "the best fighting record in the SA Army since World War II."

Although 32 Battalion has been involved in all major South African incursions into Angola, most of its missions were covert small-unit search and destroy operations above the "cutline" border with Angola.

Search for SWAPO terrorists and destroy them when found is the battalion order of the day. 32 Battalion uses stealth, surprise and speed to carry out its missions. But the search is nearly always long and difficult. It demands skill in bushcraft, the ability to live off the land and not require constant resupply. It requires tracking ability approaching that of the Bushman, to travel swiftly and silently at night and during the heat of the day across some of the toughest terrain in Africa. The troops must be constantly on the alert and poised for sudden, quick and deadly contact with SWAPO.

Soviet Bloc weapons are normally used during operations. This simplifies the resupply problem as the SWAPO guerrillas have well-stocked supply sites ready for the taking by the men of 32 Battalion and the SADF has thousands of tons of captured Soviet equipment, readily available for use by its forces. Use of captured Russian-supplied weapons also adds an element of confusion for the enemy. A group of armed blacks encountered in the bush carrying SWAPO weapons can more readily pass as fellow comrades than if they were carrying normal-issue SADF weapons. Since SWAPO and FAPLA also wear the same uniforms and use the same Soviet weapons, the confusion also extends to FAPLA as the following incident during ASKARI points out.

During Operation ASKARI the South African forces moved north toward the SWAPO stronghold at Cassinga, spearheaded by 32 Battalion.

Rapidly moving north, 32 Battalion occupied the small town of Techamutete, south of Cassinga. The FAPLA forces had fled before them, but a few of the FAPLA troops were a little tardy in their retreat and, as darkness approached, got mixed in with 32 Battalion.

Three of these FAPLA stragglers arrived at the FAPLA command post in Techamutete, which had been taken over by Col. Eddie Viljoen, the officer in charge of 32 Battalion.

In Portuguese, they asked to speak to the officer in charge. They were escorted into the presence of Viljoen, a bearded scruffy-looking individual, dressed in camouflage fatigues. (32 Battalion wears camouflage fatigues of a pattern similar to the old Portuguese Angolan pattern worn by both SWAPO and FAPLA.)

The three FAPLA soldiers, one of them a lieutenant, put down their rifles, made themselves at home, and were given coffee and food.

While eating, Viljoen asked them:

"Who do you wish to speak to?"

"The Cubans," replied the FAPLA officer.

"Who do you think we are?" asked Viljoen.

"Cubans?"

"Wrong. Guess again," said the South African.

"East German?" was the quizzical reply.

"Wrong. Guess again."

"Russians then?" asked the FAPLA officer apprehensively.

"No, guess again," replied the patiently amused South African.

"We don't know, who are you?" said the now thoroughly alarmed Angolan.

"We are the South Africans," came Viljoen's reply.

Upon hearing that, one of the FAPLA soldiers was so startled he dropped his food.

All three of them were momentarily paralyzed. Then they looked at each other and started shouting at each other, trying to pin the blame on one another for falling into the hands of the South Africans.

The South Africans waited until their outbursts subsided and then made them prisoners of war.⁶

Tango's mission was a huge success which threw a big monkey-wrench into the SWAPO rainy season infiltration attempt into Namibia by causing them to flee further north into Angola.

Millions of dollars worth of Soviet-provided equipment was destroyed by the South African security forces during ASKARI, but weapons worth millions more were captured. Among them were an intact AGS-17 automatic grenade launcher and a complete SAM-9 surface-to-air missile defense system.

The AGS-17 was captured from SWAPO at Cuvelai. It is a 30mm, air-cooled automatic grenade launcher, described by General Meiring as, "one of the most sophisticated weapons of its kind in the world." A circular drum magazine holding twenty-nine rounds is simply inserted into position, and machine gun-like, the grenades are hurled for distances of up to 1750 meters.⁷

The complete Soviet mobile SAM-9 (NATO code name "Gaskin") ground to air missile defense system captured during ASKARI was the first such complete system to fall into the hands of the West. It was part of the comprehensive anti-aircraft defense network in Angola, that far exceeds that country's defensive requirements. The SAM-9 is bigger, faster and far more maneuverable than the SAM-7. The SAM-9 will explode near a target and doesn't have to make contact with an aircraft to bring it down.

The missile launching tubes of the captured SAM were mounted on an adapted Soviet BRM2 amphibious armored vehicle. The system is easily deployable and it only takes about 90 seconds to reload the missile tubes.⁸

In executing Operation ASKARI, the South African forces had successfully disrupted the logistical base for the planned SWAPO rainy season infiltration and had forced the terrorists to withdraw north deeper into Angola.

Having accomplished their purpose, the South Africans withdrew their forces. The direction of events in the troubled region now passed once again into the hands of the diplomats.

---

⁶ Author's conversations with SADF officials during numerous trips to the operational area in Namibia.

⁷ Section 10, Op Askari, *op. cit.*, p.23.

⁸ *Ibid.*, p.22.

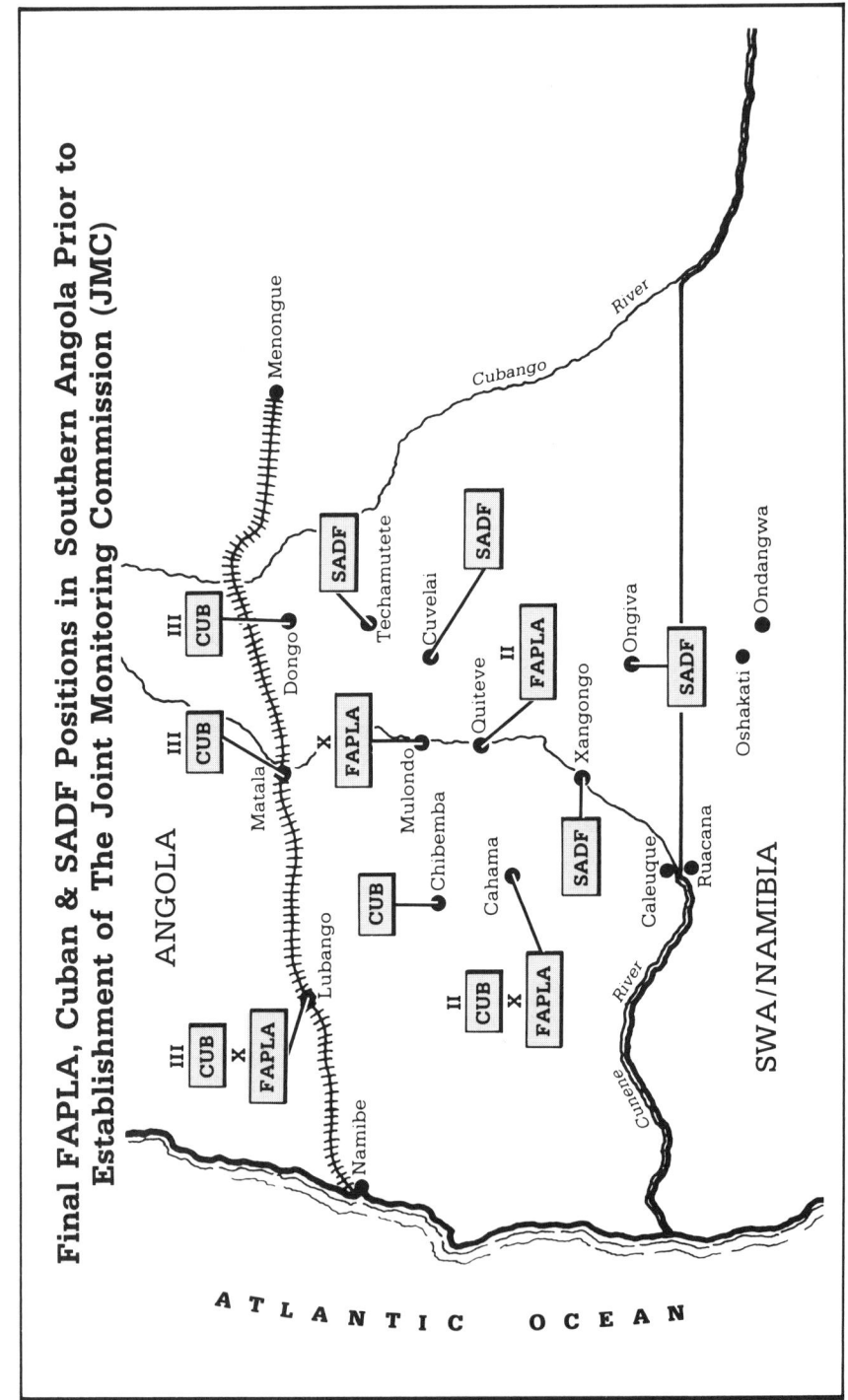

17

The Joint Monitoring Commission

Operation ASKARI had given SWAPO and its allies the Cubans and FAPLA a good beating on the battlefield.

As is common with communist regimes, when facing a military setback they resort to a well-orchestrated propaganda campaign to recoup their losses by means of diplomacy.

The gist of the propaganda was to pin the aggressor label on South Africa and accuse it of the "occupation" of parts of southern Angola.

The UN Security Council duly passed a resolution (on December 20, 1984) condemning the military strike against the terrorist bases in Angola and demanded the "immediate, unconditional withdrawal" of all South African forces from Angola.

Responding reflexively like Pavlov's dogs, the West took up the same refrain. France termed the action "totally unjustified" and also called for the withdrawal of South African troops.

Demonstrating the hypocritical unreal world of UN international politics, the French government added: "Arguments that these attacks were essentially an act of self-defense against SWAPO fighters are not acceptable."[1]

Britain termed the action "a flagrant violation of international law" and urged withdrawal of all foreign troops from Angola.

The United States declared: "Once again we call on South Africa to desist from these attacks."[2]

[1] *The Citizen,* January 7, 1984, p.2.
[2] *Ibid.*

West Germany expressed "deep concern" over the South African incursion into Angola.

Reported the West German foreign ministry, "the government notes with deep concern that Pretoria in recent days has not only continued its military action, but intensified them.

"These attacks, which have caused further loss of life and widened the threat to peace in the region, are all the more to be condemned because they interfere with efforts to promote confidence building measures in Angola that will further the United Nation's peace plan for Namibia."[3]

From the safety of Algiers, SWAPO head, Sam Nujoma, added his voice to the chorus of those condemning South Africa. He called the attack into Angola "a prolongation of the aggressive policy applied by the Pretoria regime since 1981."[4]

In a perverse way Nujoma was right. Pretoria had been pursuing an aggressive policy against his cadres since 1981. But he neglected to state that Pretoria's policy was in response to the terror and intimidation tactics of his SWAPO cadres.

South Africa's Foreign Minister, Roelf "Pik" Botha, had no trouble placing the blame squarely where it belonged—on SWAPO.

"South Africa cannot sit with folded hands while hundreds of SWAPO terrorists infiltrate South West Africa to commit murder," Mr. Botha said.[5]

The chief of the South African Defense Force, General Constand Viljoen, also pointed out that just as the United States could not afford a Grenada on its doorstep, South Africa could not afford to have enemies at its front door.[6]

All the rhetoric in the world couldn't alter the situation on the ground—a portion of southern Angola was effectively occupied by units of the South African Defense Force. Furthermore, in the process, the South African forces had given the tripartite—Cuban-Angolan-SWAPO—forces a good licking, which considerably tarnished the war-fighting image of the these forces.

Since military steps were out of the question, SWAPO and its supporters launched a diplomatic onslaught in the UN and the West to inflict the maximum political damage on South Africa. By casting itself in the position of the aggrieved victim, Angola hoped to achieve what she could not do with

---

[3] *Ibid.*, December 31, 1983.

[4] *Ibid.*, December 28, 1983.

[5] *Rand Daily Mail*, December 30, 1983.

[6] *Ibid.*

her army—remove the embarrassing presence of the South Africans from her territory.

The West, including the U.S. State Department, ably assisted Angola in this effort. The sword of Damocles which the U.S. government held over the head of the South African government was its veto over repeated attempts in the UN Security Council to impose total world-wide economic sanctions against South Africa. The U.S. message to Pretoria was pull your troops out of Angola or else we won't veto the next UN sanction measure."

Bowing to this threat the South African government tried to salvage as good a deal as possible by offering to withdraw its forces from Angola, if Angola would end her support of SWAPO.

Originally, the South African government had planned to make this offer on New Years Eve. However, the UN Security Council had scheduled a debate on the Angolan situation for the 16th of December, so the planned date for offering the initiative was moved up in an attempt to take some of the sting out of the UN debate.

The South African government delivered a letter outlining its proposal to the UN the day before the scheduled debate.

The heart of the proposal was an offer to withdraw South African forces from Angola by January 31, 1984, if Angola would guarantee that Cuba and SWAPO would take no action that would threaten the security of South West Africa.

South Africa also promised to keep her forces out of Angola for another thirty days, which would be extended if Angola kept her side of the bargain. This was a crucial point, for it is during this time of year—the rainy season in southern Angola and northern Namibia—that SWAPO makes its biggest attempt to infiltrate its terrorists into Namibia.

"Show us your good intentions by preventing SWAPO infiltration and we won't have to send our troops into your country to stop them" was the crux of South Africa's position.

After much bluster and weaseling, the Angolans decided to play the diplomatic game. On January 3, 1984, the Angolans indicated to the Secretary General of the UN that they would be amenable to a thirty-day truce starting on January 31st, provided certain conditions were met.

The Angolan conditions were: that SWAPO agreed to a truce; that South Africa would withdraw all of her forces from Angola; and, that within fifteen days of the end of the thirty-day truce, South Africa would implement Resolution 435 leading to independence for Namibia "without extraneous considerations in that context." In other words, no linkage of a Cuban withdrawal from Angola to the question of Namibian independence.

Although they were clearly rejecting the U.S. and South African desire for linkage of a Cuban withdrawal to a settlement of the Namibian independence question, Angolan willingness to accept a truce provided the opening the diplomats needed.

A negotiated settlement now offered benefits to both parties. Angola saw a face-saving way of ridding themselves of the embarassing situation of South African military operations on her territory.

For South Africa the settlement provided not only the possibility of getting her critics off her back, but also the possiblity of improving the security situation in Namibia and halting the terror acts of SWAPO.

Five days later the South African Minister of Defense, Magnus Malan, announced that all South African forces involved in Operation ASKARI would be out of Angola within a week.[7] This announcement, however, was tempered with a warning to SWAPO that South African forces would, if necessary, strike again "regardless of the consequences."[8]

The United States, led by Assistant Secretary of State for African Affairs, Dr. Chester Crocker, set about the task of organizing meetings between the South Africans and the Angolans.

While getting the two southern African countries together, Crocker also embarked on the difficult task of trying to convince SWAPO not to upset the fragile truce by sending its terrorists into Namibia after the South African forces were out of Angola.

Washington was basing its hopes on the fact that SWAPO had requested the UN to arrange a ceasefire and a meeting between SWAPO and South Africa.[9]

Looming ominously over these efforts was the South African warning that, if SWAPO sent its terrorists into Namibia, South Africa reserved the right to send its troops back into Angola to deal with them.

Crocker's efforts began to bear fruit as the Angolan government announced on January 17th that a thirty-day truce was a distinct possibility. Exploratory talks between Crocker and representatives of the Angolan government in Cape Verde Islands from January 18 to 20, 1984 followed this announcement. During these talks, the Angolan representatives gave assurances to Dr. Crocker that they would prevent SWAPO and the Cubans from entering the area being vacated by the South African forces. Crocker

---

[7] *Ibid.,* January 9, 1984.

[8] *Ibid.*

[9] *Johannesburg Star,* January 9, 1984.

duly passed these assurance on to the South African government. As a result, South African Prime Minister P. W. Botha announced on January 31st that South African forces were pulling out of Angola as of that day.

However, while the South African forces were pulling out of Angola, there were growing indications of a large scale SWAPO infiltration into the area being vacated, contrary to the Angolan government assurances.

So serious was this infiltration threat that the South Africans halted their troop withdrawal until the Angolans removed the problem posed by the SWAPO threat.

It had become clear that "actions spoke louder than words" and something more than Angolan assurances was needed to keep SWAPO and the Cubans from fomenting mischief in the wake of a South African withdrawal.

Taking the initiative, Prime Minister Botha proposed tripartite discussions among South Africa, Angola and the United States to "establish a proper framework for the disengagement of South African forces." To show good faith, the South Africans ordered the withdrawal to proceed and be completed by the 15th of February except for some 300 troops who remained to monitor SWAPO movements.

Both the Angolan and United States governments agreed to the South African proposal for tripartite talks.

Angola suggested the talks should be held at the Mulungushi conference center in Lusaka, Zambia and President Kaunda readily agreed to host the meeting. Both South Africa and the United States quickly accepted the Angolan suggestion and Kaunda's invitation to host the talks in Lusaka.

The initial meeting took place on the evening of February 13th. Dave Steward, Deputy Director of the Department of Foreign Affairs and Chief of the South African Army, Lt. Gen. J.J. Geldenhuys represented South Africa. The Angolan delegation consisted of Lt. Col. Ngongo Monteiro, FAPLA Deputy Chief of Staff and Lt. Col. Sabriaho Sequeira, commander of FAPLA's 5th Military Region, in whose area the South Africans had been operating. Nick Platt of the State Department represented the United States.

At the outset the Angolans were truculent, demanding a total unilateral withdrawal of South African forces.

South Africa, on the other hand, proposed establishing a joint commission composed of Angolan and South African personnel to monitor the situation in order that neither SWAPO nor the Cubans would exploit it.

After much argument and discussion, mediated by the American delegation, the South African view prevailed.

Once over that hurdle, all sides agreed that the sooner a joint South African/Angolan commission were set up the quicker the situation on the ground could be monitored.

Having agreed on a general course of action to follow, the participants quickly got down to business to work out the details. The conferees agreed upon and put into writing nine specific points. This paper, known as the "Mulungushi Minute", effectively set up the Joint Monitoring Commission (JMC). The paper's nine points were:

(1) Both sides agree to the establishment of a joint South African/Angolan Commission as soon as possible.
(2) The first meeting of the Commission will take place in Lusaka on February 16, 1984.
(3) The Commission, with equal representation of forces from both sides will be located at Ongiva in Angola.
(4) The Commission will be free to travel throughout the area in question as required at the request of either or both parties.
(5) The purpose of the Commission is to monitor the disengagement and to detect, investigate and report any alleged violations.
(6) The withdrawal will be completed during a 30-day period.
(7) Both sides agreed to the symbolic presence of an American observer of the Commission's activities.
(8) Angola promises to keep SWAPO and the Cubans out of the area in question.
(9) Both sides agree that the process would be an important step in establishing conditions leading to peace in the region including the SWA/Namibian question through the implementation of UN Resolution 435.

Both sides left the talks satisfied. South Africa had succeeded in getting accepted the concept of a monitoring commission. Angola had succeeded in getting South African forces out of her territory by diplomatic means, thus covering up the military failure of her forces to evict them.

The scene quickly shifted back to the political arena. On the morning of February 16th, talks took place between the Foreign and Defense ministers of South Africa, "Pik" Botha and Magnus Malan, and the Angolan Minister of the Interior, Lt. Col. Alexandre Rodriques, and the United States representative, Dr. Chester Crocker. President Kenneth Kaunda of Zambia chaired the meeting.

The meeting quickly reached a consensus and the agreement, now known as the Lusaka Agreement:

(1) Authorized the establishment of the JMC as outlined in the "Mulungushi Minute;"
(2) Provided that the JMC headquarters would move south in steps culminating with the withdrawal of South African troops from Angola;
(3) Provided details for the first initial meeting of the JMC;
(4) Named the members of the JMC;
(5) Set out as one of the first acts of the JMC: to clear the Cassinga-Cuvelai road of landmines;
(6) Provided for terms of the withdrawal and specified the length of each phase;
(7) Established the function of the JMC-to monitor the withdrawal and to see that there would be no South African, SWAPO or Cuban forces in the area vacated;
(8) Defined the area in question;
(9) Stressed, again, the importance of clearing the Cassinga-Cuvelai road of mines;
(10) Assigned patrol responsibilities to the JMC—the Angolans would patrol the area north of the JMC headquarters, the South Africans would patrol the area south—and established procedures to investigate alleged violations.
(11) Restricted U.S. paricipation to meetings on or near the SWA/Angolan border, and only at the request of both sides;
(12) Gave the JMC the authority to carry out any additional duties which the Angolan and South African governments might assign it.

A joint statement was released at the end of the conference announcing the adoption of the Lusaka Agreement: "On February 16, 1984, delegations of the People's Republic of Angola, the Republic of South Africa and the United States of America met in Lusaka to discuss steps to further the process of peace in southern Africa."[10]

[10] Heitman, H-R, & Dorning, W.A., *Militaria*, 18/1, 1988, p.5.

Responding to President Kaunda's assessment that a historic opportunity now existed to make progress, the conference achieved the following results:

* Creation of a joint South African/Angolan commission to monitor the disengagement process in southern Angola and to detect, investigate and report any alleged violations of the commitments of the parties.
* The first meeting of the Joint Monitoring Commission took place in Lusaka on February 16, 1984. Further meetings will be held in other mutually agreed locations at the convenience of the parties.
* It was agreed that a small number of American representatives could participate in the activities of the Joint Commission at the request of the parties.

The delegates had agreed that the task of the JMC in the weeks ahead would be to facilitate the successful completion of the disengagement process and to establish an effective cessation of hostilities. The delegations were aware of the numerous complex and unresolved issues standing in the way of a successful resolution of the many problems in the region. This included the question of the Namibian independence under the terms of UN Resolution 435.

All the participants were extremely appreciative of the efforts of President Kaunda, who was instrumental in arranging and conducting the successful conference.

In spite of the sense of accomplishment generated among participants of the Lusaka conference, basic unresolved problems remained.

Angola felt the agreement cleared the way for the implementation of UN Resolution 435, which would effectively cut off UNITA's major supply route.

South Africa, on the other hand, felt that implementing Resolution 435 could only be possible after the Cubans had withdrawn from Angola.

Since the Cubans were propping up the Angolan regime, it should have been evident that they wouldn't leave until their Marxist ally was firmly in control. As long as Jonas Savimbi's forces were a threat to the Angolan government, the Cubans were sure to stay.

In short order, Angola and Cuban actions exposed the Lusaka Agreement as nothing more than a standard Marxist-Leninist stratagem to dupe their adversaries and to buy time to shore up their sinking fortunes. From the first, it was clear the JMC would be plagued by doubt and disagreements which would detrimentally affect its mission.

One of the first doubts was whether FAPLA would be willing to fire upon SWAPO terrorists they ran into who were infiltrating into the area under JMC responsibility. This was obviously a sensitive issue because of the close relationship between FAPLA and SWAPO.

At first FAPLA did perform its JMC duties in the manner envisioned by the Lusaka Agreement, including clashes with infiltrating SWAPO terrorists.

However, the situation rapidly deteriorated, especially as the JMC began its moves south towards the Angola-Namibian border.

On March 21st, the JMC moved to Mupa and the cooperative situation between the two parties began to fall apart.

It soon became clear to the South Africans that the Angolan Army did not have the ability to control SWAPO. Militarily, SWAPO terrorists were better trained and led than the Angolan soldiers and FAPLA didn't really desire to control their Marxist comrades. To make matters worse, it became evident that FAPLA and SWAPO were even working together. FAPLA was either turning its back on the terrorist infiltration or alerting SWAPO to the locations where JMC forces were patrolling, enabling them to avoid clashes.

The Angolans were also using the withdrawal process to build up their conventional forces in the area being vacated by the South Africans. FAPLA was deploying Soviet-supplied SAMs, radar systems, and even tanks into the vacated area.

On May 2, 1984, the JMC moved to Ongiva, the last JMC move before reaching the border. The attitude of the Angolans towards the JMC worsened considerably, and it was fast pushing the process towards disintegration.

FAPLA cooperation with SWAPO was now becoming more blatantly open. The South Africans were killing or capturing PLAN terrorists wearing Angolan army uniforms. They soon discovered more proof of cooperation. For example, the security forces found a document on a terrorist proving that collusion existed between SWAPO and FAPLA: "On 19 June four Cadres of our group have been caught by FAPLA for we did not consult them before, anyhow they did not harm them, only warned them to consult each other when we want to approach the area which they are occupying."[11] Violations, incidents and clashes with infiltrating

---

[11] *Ibid.*, pp.17-18.

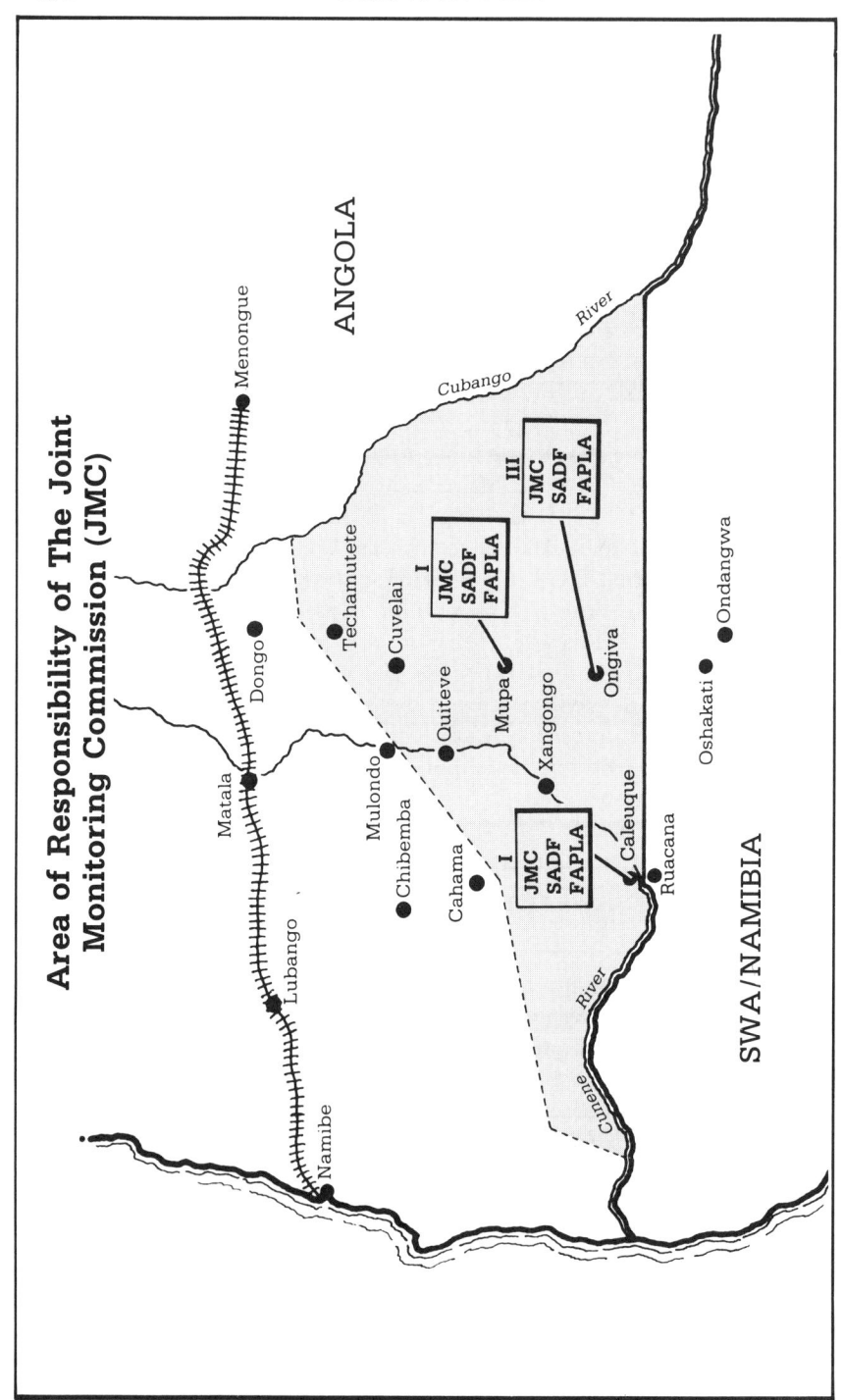

terrorists were reaching new heights—all contrary to the letter and spirit of the Lusaka Agreement.

As the JMC approached its last move to the border, a question loomed large—what, if anything, should be done to replace the JMC?

The South Africans suggested establishing a Joint Peacekeeping Commission. This proposal soon escalated into a major foreign policy issue and led to direct talks between the Administrator General of Namibia and Sam Nujoma, head of SWAPO. This meeting occurred on July 24, 1984 on Cape Verde Island.

The meetings, which had convened on an optimistic note of a possible cessation of hostilities in the Namibian terrorist war, proved to be of little value. Nujoma insisted that SWAPO would be prepared to cease hostilities only if both sides agreed to an immediate implementation of UN Resolution 435. Nothing came of the Cape Verde talks nor of the proposal to set up a Joint Peacekeeping Commission.

All that was left for the now moribund JMC was to make its last move from Ongiva to the border and then fade into history. But nothing happened and it seemed if the JMC might just be going to drift along in limbo. The Angolans seemed in no hurry to get the JMC to make its final move. After all, they had re-occupied most of their territory and, as long as the JMC existed, there was little chance that South Africa would raid Angolan territory. This situation also helped SWAPO for the same reason. In the meantime, both Angola and SWAPO could move their forces and equipment into the area without fear of South African retaliation. Angola really had no incentive to ask for the final move of the JMC to the border.

South Africa was growing increasingly frustrated by the situation. She had to stand quietly and watch the blatant SWAPO and FAPLA violations of the Lusaka Agreement. Yet the South Africans' hands were tied by the same agreement and they had to grit their teeth while SWAPO built up their forces for further future attacks on Namibia.

By mid-April 1985, the South Africans decided that they had tolerated all they could and took the bull by the horns. They suddenly announced they were going to unilaterally withdraw their forces from Angola without consulting the JMC. The move took the Angolans by surprise and made the JMC a useless organization. Bowing to the inevitable, the JMC was formally disbanded on May 16, 1985.

The JMC had been born with bright prospects for bringing peace to the area. It failed because of the unwillingness of the Angolans to live up to their part of the agreement. As a result, three more years of strife and bloodshed would go by before another attempt would be made to bring peace to the region.

18
Civic Action

"Winning the population can tritely be summed up as good government," said guerrilla warfare expert Sir Robert Thompson.[1]

The South African security forces took to heart Thompson's statement and, in partnership with the civil authorities, undertook a widespread active civil and military program to improve the quality of life for all Namibians.

Our focus, however, will be in Owamboland where the vast majority of the South African counterinsurgency effort was centered. Action taken in the operational area that hurt SWAPO had beneficial ramifications throughout Namibia. Since the majority of Namibians were living along the northern border and were potential targets of SWAPO coercion and propaganda, it followed logically the major counterinsurgency efforts would be there.

For an effective counterinsurgency effort to succeed, in Namibia or elsewhere, it must offer the people something better than what the revolutionaries are promising.

SWAPO was promising freedom from South African rule, but was actually offering a one-party Marxist-style society with its oppression and misery after independence. The South Africans were, in spite of UN meddling, offering Namibians a parliamentary-style independent government and a free enterprise market-oriented economy.

The main task was, while providing security from SWAPO violence, to develop political, social and economic infrastructures that would deliver a better life for all Namibians. This was a hard job to accomplish, but inaction would have handed Namibia over to the not so tender mercies of SWAPO.

This immense job had to be done while the security forces stabilized the

---

[1] Thompson, *op. cit.*, p.42.

security situation inside the country. As Thompson had said, ". . . it is a great mistake to imagine that either democracy or economic progress can be forced in unstable conditions. They will achieve a far more dynamic growth when normal conditions are restored and the population's energies, relieved from the strain of war, can be released for constructive purposes."[2] Bearing that in mind, the South Africans decided that a successful counterinsurgency program in Namibia would require sufficient force to break any SWAPO hold on the people by providing adequate security to allow them to choose alternatives other than SWAPO. The authorities also felt they had to create new organizations or strengthen existing organizations to mobilize popular support for their program.

We will leave the security aspects of the counterinsurgency program to other chapters in the book with the caveat that the civic action program required success by the security forces or the civic action program would have been doomed from the start.

Since Namibia is an arid country, any program to better the lives of its citizens had to consider the essential question of water.

Apart from the rugged terrain in the extreme northwest near Ruacana, Owamboland is an exceptionally flat plain. This plain descends gradually in a southerly direction towards the Etosha Pan. Central Owamboland is covered with a network of shallow water courses known as *oshanas*. The inhabitants have situated settlements and crop lands on what little high ground there is, between the *oshanas*.

A large part of Central Owamboland lies above a large subterranean brine lake. This means that people, animals and plants are dependent on surface water. During the rainy season (October to April) there is enough water in the *oshanas* but they dry up during the winter (June through August).

Improving the supply of water on a year-round basis would have a very positive effect on the lives of the inhabitants of Owamboland.

In order to make water more readily available to Owamboland, the South African government made an agreement with Portuguese Angola in the late sixties to provide water from the Caluequque Dam in southern Angola. South Africa also agreed to provide much of the financing for the project.

This project would have established an integrated irrigation scheme for Owamboland, and would also have provided electricity generated at the Ruacana hydroelectric complex, not only for Namibia, but for most of Southern Africa.

---

[2] *Ibid.*, p.113.

However, when the current Marxist regime took over in Angola, it cancelled the agreement. Now water must be pumped from Ruacana which can provide only ten percent of the planned amount of water.

The government built a pipeline and a canal system that carries the water from Ruacana along the main road to Oshakati and Ondangwa in central Owamboland. A secondary pipeline leads north of Ondangwa to serve Oshigambo, Etale and Eenhana.

Though SWAPO views these pipelines as sabotage targets they will normally only inflict minor damage on them as the terrorists know that permanent destruction would totally alienate the Owambo people who depend upon the water.

In spite of the non-cooperation of the Angolans, Namibia has undertaken an extensive program to provide enough water for domestic use, industry, mining, agriculture and recreation. The civil authorities currently administer 126 water schemes to provide water throughout the country. One of the more ambitious schemes is the Eastern National Water Carrier. When completed it will transport water over a distance of 710 kilometers from the year-round Kavango River, on the northern border to the interior as far south as the capital, Windhoek.

The authorities built dams, canals, and pipelines and sank boreholes to bring reliable supplies of water to more and more Namibians. In a semi-arid land water can be as precious as gold. Having a reliable supply of water has gone a long way to better the lives of the people and under-cut SWAPO propaganda.

Another program devoted to bettering the lives of Namibians was in the area of health care.

Namibia's health care service is among the best in Africa with a ratio of one medical doctor to every 4450 inhabitants. Its ratio of 166 people per hospital bed is Africa's third best.

In the operational area of Owamboland alone, there are fourteen hospitals. There is a 700-bed state hospital at Oshakati, three new government-run hospitals at Ogandjera, Tsandi and Ombalantu. In addition to the four government-run hospitals are ten private mission hospitals run by religious missionary societies—two Roman Catholic and eight Finnish. The central government in Windhoek subsidizes the mission hospitals even though most of the mission societies running the missions have been sympathetic to SWAPO. In addition there are thirty-one clinics throughout Owamboland. The Roman Catholic and Finnish mission societies run most of these.

The South African Defense Force (SADF) makes a large contribution to the maintenance of medical services in Owamboland. Regular clinics for the local population are held by the medical officers attached to the numerous military bases located throughout Owamboland.

As part of their "winning the hearts and minds of the people," medical corpsmen treat minor medical problems of people encountered by their units during their patrols in the bush. The medical corpsmen refer major medical problems encountered during these patrols to the nearest facility with a doctor—either a military base or one of the clinics or hospitals in Owamboland. If the problem warrants, the patient may be further transferred to the Windhoek State Hospital Complex, one of the most modern in Africa.

A system of regional hospitals, clinics and bush and mobile clinics, excluding those of the SADF, make health services available to, and within the reach of, virtually all inhabitants of Namibia. All together, Namibia has sixty-eight hospitals and 171 clinics looking out for the medical welfare of its people.

In the past, the health care system placed emphasis on treating and curing diseases. Now, even though these still are a large part of the Namibian health care program, emphasis is shifting to the prevention of disease.

The government has undertaken an extensive immunization program against such diseases as poliomyelitis, diptheria, whooping cough, measles and tuberculosis.

Other public health programs include programs that involve the responsibility for the prevention and control of epidemics and fighting malaria and other infectious diseases.

Health education, family planning, care for the aged, medical and dental services at schools are also part of the civic action program undertaken by the civilian and military authorities in Namibia.

The authorities have launched major civic action programs in the operational areas on the northern border of Namibia to improve the economy of the area. Since most of this area is rural, the economy is based on subsistence agriculture.

Early in the terrorist war, while SWAPO was escalating its pressure on Namibia, both the government and private sector brought new development projects to the area. In 1976 and 1977 these projects included three new national corporations established to involve rural communities in the northern border area in self-help programs designed to provide new sources of jobs and industry.

In 1978, in a move that showed confidence in Namibia's future, the economic planners decided to centralize the efforts of the three corporations and integrate them into a single national development effort. The First National Development Corporation of SWA/Namibia (FNDC) was founded. Its job was to develop trade, manufacturing, mining and agriculture throughout the country. FNDC functions as the central government's conduit to stimulate the development of a market-oriented economy in Namibia via government-backed loans. FNDC operates in the private sector and not only encourages private Namibian initiatives in developing the economy, but actively seeks investments in Namibia by foreign businessmen.

The FNDC also has another important function: it will finance and manage projects where private interests cannot or do not want to get involved. It, however, does not function in the American manner of "throwing money at a problem." Its primary goal has been to encourage and promote private enterprise and not to become a gigantic welfare scheme.

FNDC offers financing, training and expertise. Rural development, especially in the communal subsistence areas found in the operational area, have been an important part of its activities. It has made loans when projects appeared viable, and created or maintained work opportunities, processed local raw materials, manufactured products for the export market or produced commodities to replace items previously imported into Namibia.

Some projects that FNDC has been involved with include a number of crop farming and stock breeding projects, tourist facilities, three bakeries, two meat processing factories, garages, a dairy, soft drink bottling plant, wood-carving industry, agricultural research facilities and providing small industrial/retail units for rent throughout the country.

In Owamboland FNDC activities include: a soft drink bottling plant in Oshakati that produces soft drinks under license from Coca Cola of South Africa; a meat processing plant and a bakery in Oshakati with a capacity of producing 17,000 loaves of bread a day.

A lively trade activity has sprung up in the operational area due to the influx of money from the security force presence in Owamboland. These are the numerous (over 6,000) small retail *cuca* shops that not only provide an income, but are also a status symbol for the owner.

The economic activity generated by the civilian and military authorities has transformed the lives of many Namibians for the better.

As a developing Third World country, Namibia suffers from a shortage of skilled labor. Part of the government's civic action program was to enlarge and use the educational system to provide the expertise needed by the labor force to successfully participate in Namibia's developing economy.

By 1987 these efforts were such that there were 11,945 teachers teaching a total of 364,400 pupils at 1,114 schools. This is a teacher to pupil ratio of about one to thirty.

The following chart portrays the progress made since 1971:

Year	Pupils	Pupils % Population	Teachers	Pupils/teacher
1971	142,000	18.6	4151	34.3
1976	189,000	21.4	5459	34.6
1981	249,000	24.1	8139	30.6
1985	336,000	28.6	10,372	32.4
1986	350,000	30.0	11,121	31.5
1987	364,000	30.0	11,945	30.5

The schools include more than forty secondary institutions, thirty pre-primary schools, three centers for the handicapped and two agricultural schools. The primary schools instruct in the mother-tongue as far as possible.

The educational process encompasses all tribal and ethnic groups in Namibia as the following shows:

Distribution of pupils & teachers per ethnic group, 1987

Ethnic groups	Schools	Pupils	Teachers
Owambo	501	198,533	4786
University	85	38,707	1460
Kavango	221	32,270	1052
Caprivi	65	19,453	729
White	65	16,823	1181
Coloured	37	15,696	652
Nama	46	15,351	625
Rehoboth	39	10,000	456
Damara	23	9,512	391
Tswana	2	1,016	40
	1,122	364,404	11,945

Education in the operational area of Owamboland has grown substantially in spite of intense efforts by SWAPO to destroy the system. As the figures show, there are almost 200,000 pupils going to over 500 schools in Owamboland. When you consider that boys must stay home until the age of nine to twelve to look after cattle, the number of pupils in school is amazing. When you add the security situation in, it clearly demonstrates that raising the educational levels of their children is a prime goal of Owambo parents.

The SADF are assisting in this effort. As the SADF has relied chiefly on conscripts for its manpower, a lot of teachers find their way into the ranks. The SADF assigns these teachers, as their military duties, to teach in the schools near the South African military installations in the operational area. The military, then, is also involved in a hands-on people-to-people educational effort throughout the operational area.

The central government in Windhoek directs education through its Department of National Education. The department is responsible for its far-reaching educational program and has overall supervision of training the teachers throughout Namibia. The schools under the authority of the department are fully integrated and are open to children of all races.

All government schools adhere to the same syllabus and pupils take the identical final school examinations to ensure uniform standards.

Looking forward to the future, the government established a center for higher education in 1980. Called the Academy, it is an institution of higher learning unique in Africa. It is an autonomous educational institute that provides three different kinds of education through three branches: the University of Namibia, a Technical College and the College for Out of School Training. The three branches of the Academy perform three major functions: (1) needs-oriented training to prepare students for the future; (2) research relevant to the country and its people; and, (3) community service.

The Academy has grown more than two-hundred-fold since its first classes in 1981 and has established accredited campuses at Oshakati, Rundu and Katima Mulilo, in northern Namibia.

The University of Namibia offers degrees and post-graduate work in five departments: Science, Arts, Nursing and Medical Science, Economics and Management Science, and Education. Nursing and education courses are offered at the Academy's campuses in norther Namibia.

The Technical College provides career-oriented training in the fields of business, commerce and management. Its courses are thorough requiring a minimum of three years study before graduation.

The College for Out of School Training offers both theoretical and practical training in many of the trades. This training allows students to not only learn a trade, but also to improve their skills in their current one. There is a section, the Distance Training Section, that allows students who live in outlying areas in the country the opportunity of furthering their studies without interrupting their careers.

The government and military are not the only ones involved in education in Namibia. Several private sector organizations are involved in uplifting the lives of the working people in Namibia. Among those involved are: The First National Development Corporation (FNDC), the Institute for Management and Leadership Training (IMLT), the Private Sector Foundation (PSF) and the Rossing Foundation. Subjects covered are numerous and varied, from marketing, bookkeeping, taxation and personal finance to bricklaying, leather-work and needlecraft.

Education represents an investment in the future of a free and independent Namibia. Namibians will be better prepared than most of their neighbors to shoulder that burden.

The governing authorities have placed a high priority on housing as part of its civic action program. Government policy has been developed to support the idea that each inhabitant of Namibia should be able to own property according to his means.

The housing needs of people who have a good steady income are taken care of by the normal workings of the real estate market and the normal finance capital associated with it.

Many employers in Namibia, including the permanent government bureaucracy, have developed housing assistance programs to help their employees purchase their own homes. The banks and two building societies, the SWA Building Society and Namib Building Society, all provide private loans for home purchase.

In 1982, the government instituted a program to lessen the housing shortage for lower income families. It set up the National Building and Investment Corporation (NBIC) which put the government in the home building and real estate business. NBIC designs houses that are within the reach of the low income families and will lend up to 100 percent of the purchase price. The loans are repayable over a thirty-year period, and depending upon the size of the loan, the interest usually won't exceed ten percent.

However, to ensure that a family does not use their entire income to repay the loan, NBIC structures the loan so that a family will not spend more than twenty-five percent of its monthly income on housing. This leaves the rest of the family income for necessities such as food, clothing, transportation, medicines, etc.

"Home ownership can be seen as one of the most stabilizing factors and to a large extent, the backbone of any community," said the Managing Director of the SWA Building Society. In the Namibian context it is very important as it instills a sense of ownership right in property in the individual. It gets him used to owning his house or patch of ground. Such a state of affairs is directly contrary to what SWAPO preaches: socialism with its abolition of private property.

The deeper the roots of private property ownership sink into the consciousness of the Namibian people, most of whom come from tribal areas steeped in the concept of communal ownership traditions, the less attraction SWAPO's socialist program will have for Namibians.

The civic action program carried out by the South African and local Namibian authorities, in general, has followed McCuen's blueprint.

SWAPO intends to force its program of scientific socialism on Namibians, whereas the governing authorities used persuasion to sell their program. They did it by the simple method of showing that the governing powers were offering something better than SWAPO was: a self-governing freedom within a prosperous free-enterprise economy.

Debating SWAPO on the merits of free enterprise versus socialism was not enough. The governing authorities had to show proof of the advantages they advocated through action or implementation at the local level. The civic action program, which was more involved than that briefly described, demonstrated the wisdom of McCuen that "the population will be won or lost depending on whether or not the governing power can solve the direct, day-to-day problems of the people."[3]

Satisfying the day-to-day needs of the people, combined with their growing political maturity convinced the people that, not only was the government operating for the benefit of the people, but that it was carrying out programs of a permanent nature. This gave the people of Namibia a stake in the stability being brought about by the civic action programs and raised hopes for the future of their country.

Was the program a success? At this stage one can say yes, with the caveat that excessive UN meddling in the up-coming independence elections could undo a lot of the achievement of the counterinsurgency effort—much to the detriment of the people of Namibia.

Barring such UN meddling or an unchecked SWAPO intimidation campaign during in the election process, the program will have been successful. A good indication of this success is that the attitude of the people in the operational area has swung in favor of the security forces.

"With greater awareness amongst the local population of the true nature of SWAPO and of essential elements involved in a revolutionary war, coupled with a feeling of greater personal security, a new dimension has emerged. This was mainly brought about when the people started reporting the presence of terrorists and terrorist equipment to the security forces. This

---

[3] McCuen, *op. cit.*, pp.59-60.

voluntary flow of tactical information to the security forces resulted in the present situation where the population is increasingly becoming an environment hostile to the terrorists. As the members of PLAN [Peoples Liberation Army of Namibia] are depending on the people for their survival, it is obvious that PLAN is losing the natural advantages which were previuosly taken for granted. Mao Tse-tung's basic principle governing successful insurgency, namely that the insurgent should be a fish in the sea of people, does not apply to PLAN anymore . . . It has been claimed that the people are supplying security forces with information merely for the financial gain to be had. This may be true. However, it should be borne in mind that the system of financial reward was originally instituted during the previous decade, and that it has only been since 1984 that the people of the affected area have started availing themselves of this. Reprisals are an ever present possibility in an insurgent environment and it therefore appears that the system only became viable once the personal security of the people could be guaranteed to a greater extent than had been the case previously."[4]

McCuen maintains that it is important to "commit the local leadership of all hues to the side of the government."[5] The evolution of the Democratic Turnhalle Alliance (DTA) and the Multi Party Conference (MPC), to a large extent, showed the South Africans had a reasonable degree of success. They were not able to attain large-scale Owambo participation in either the DTA or the MPC (fear, tribal animosities, or both can expain this). But even without Owambo wholesale participation the counterinsurgency efforts obeyed McCuen's dictum: "the legitimate aspirations and rights of all elements must be carefully considered and nurtured."[6] The South Africans did have a program which took away the psychological and political initiative from SWAPO. In fact, SWAPO's sole hope now lies with the United Nations and the implementation of UN Resolution 435.

A primary objective of the South African counterinsurgency strategy was to establish a motivated, informed and politically stable population which is not amenable to the siren song of SWAPO's Marxism.

The Institute of Strategic Studies of the University of Pretoria (ISSUP) pointed out that, "In this process most of the political and social grievances have been done away with. As a result, the emotional wave generated by SWAPO has been neutralized to a great extent, although the organization is

---

[4] *The War in SWA/Namibia,* Institute for Strategic Studies, 4/87, Pretoria, pp.8-9.
[5] McCuen, *op. cit.,* p.86.
[6] *Ibid.*

doing everything in its power to regenerate emotional animosity against the Transitional Government of National Unity. The second purpose of the srategy was aimed at bringing about a division between the population and the terrorists. At present a small number of terrorists are active in only a part of Owambo and as a result of a higher degree of personal security, the people of Owambo are able to hold their own to a greater extent against PLAN."[7]

In Namibia SWAPO, even at the height of its activities between 1976-83, was never able to destroy or infiltrate the civil infrastructure. Therefore, it was not necessary for the South Africans to start from scratch and replace it. Instead, their task was to restore order and tranquility so the existing civil administration could still function and carry out programs and reforms. As the ISSUP report shows, "In the execution of the counterrevolutionary strategy, the security forces are employed in a supportive role as the sharp edge against the armed revolutionary enemy. It is the responsibility of the security forces to create the physical environment in which the policies of the state can be implemented."[8]

This counter-revolutionary strategy requires a long-term process by the government as McCuen stresses, "which will allow him not only to stop the rebels' progress but to seize the initative and drive them back through the successive stages until they have been neutralized."[9]

Under the security umbrella provided by the South Africans, the authorities have not only stopped SWAPO, but have taken away their ability to gain a victory through their own efforts. By the end of 1987, South African counterinsurgency experts were convinced that "in order to ensure its continued existence, SWAPO will ultimately be forced to return to the democratic political system in SWA. As soon as this occurs the revolutionary wheel will have turned full circle, and SWAPO will have to return to the evolutionary process of development which it abandoned on 26 August 1966."[10]

Although Namibia is still a developing country and has a long way to go, by Western standards, the average person lives a lot better today than he did ten to fifteen years ago before the authorities embarked upon their massive civic action program.

As the various parties as the implement the provision of UN Resolution

---

[7] *The War in SWA/Namibia, op. cit.*, pp.10-11.

[8] *Ibid.*, p.11.

[9] McCuen, *op. cit.*, p.79.

[10] *The War in SWA/Namibia, op. cit.*, p.11.

435, SWAPO will return (on the coattails of the UN) to the political process in Namibia. The success of the South African counterinsurgency program will have forced them to do so. The South Africans have proved that a democratic state is capable of successfully waging a successful protracted war against a revolutionary opponent.

Namutoni, a Beau Geste-type fort built during the German colonial period in Namibia. It is now a rest camp in the Etosha National Park in Namibia.

Waterhole in Etosha National Park.

Elements of SWAPOL unit Zulu-Whiskey in Casspir (R.) and Wolf Turbo (L.) vehicles pause on the Namibian-Angolan border during a search for SWAPO terrorists.

On the chase! Zulu-Whiskey policemen follow fleeing SWAPO terrorists' spoor.

Helicopter gunships are called in.

Contact! A white phosphorus grenade explodes, giving off a distinctive white smoke for the gunships to home-in on.

Another SWAPO terrorist, in a fresh new Angolan Army uniform, falls to the guns of SWAPOL's Zulu-Whiskey policemen.

Author with Zulu-Whiskey police constables during a SWAPOL counter-insurgency operation near the Angolan border.

Road sign passed by SADF units during Operation ASKARI.

61 Mechanized Battalion on the march during Operation ASKARI.

Truck loaded with captured Soviet recoiless rifles and mortars seized during Operation ASKARI.

Soviet automatic grenade launcher (AGS-17) captured by SADF during Operation ASKARI.

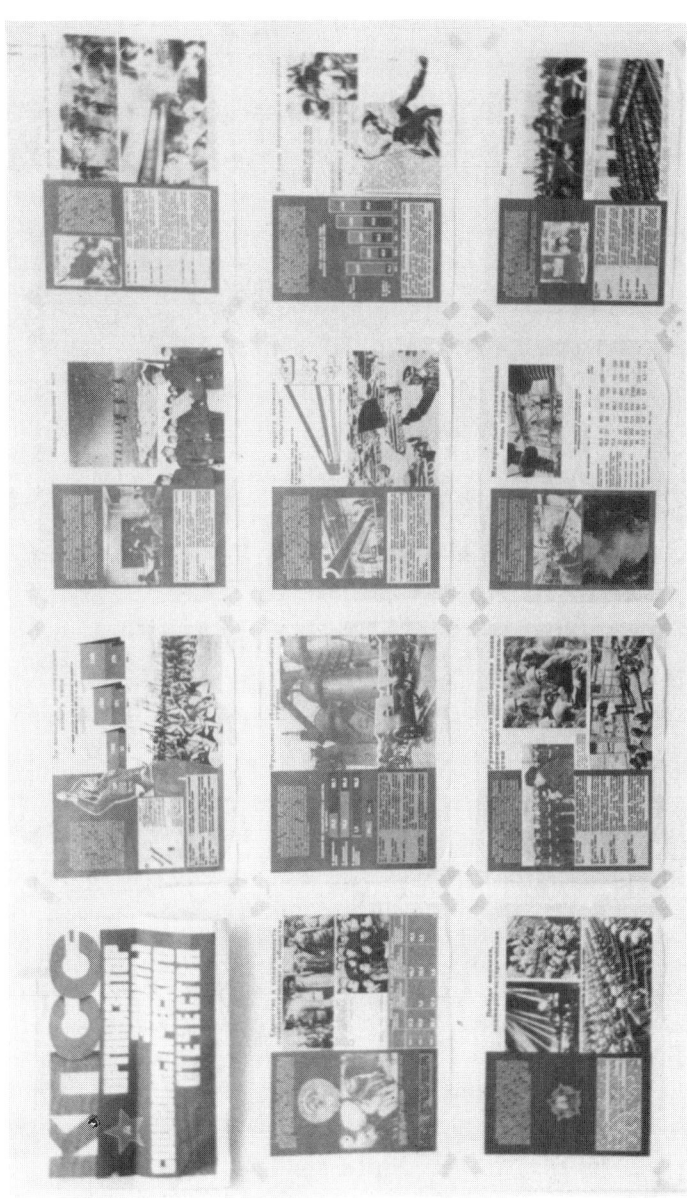

Captured Soviet literature found in SWAPO bases in southern Angola.

SAN submarine Maria von Riebeck leaving Walvis Bay on a patrol.

Stark, desolate Namibian terrain.

Abandoned Angolan-Namibian border post at Oshikango.

Credit: UNITA photo

"Red Admiral" Rosa Coutinho (center, white uniform), shakes hands with Dr. Jonas Savimbi, while the leader of the MPLA, Agostinho Neto (front left) looks on. Coutinho had just completed negotiations with the Angolan liberation movements in which the Portuguese pledged free elections in Angola. The pledge was a sham as Coutinho's goal was to put the Marxist MPLA in power with the help of Cuban troops.

Surf from the Atlantic Ocean crashing on the desolate Skeleton Coast of Namibia.

Giraffes at a waterhole in the Etosha National Park of Namibia.

Sand falls! Wind-blown sand cascades like a waterfall over the edge of the Horisub River canyon on the Skeleton Coast of Namibia.

Ostriches running in the Namibe Desert near the desolate Skeleton Coast.

SADF Impala jets provide close air support for SADF units on cross-border operations in southern Angola.

SA Navy missile-firing Strikecraft patrols the foggy waters off the coast of Namibia.

Soviet fishing trawler/spy ship in fog-shrouded Namibian waters near the port of Walvis Bay.

Lt. Gen. Ian Gleeson, Assistant Chief, SADF, briefs reporters on the military situation in Namibia.

SWAPOL constables on SWAPO's spoor.

A heavily laden SWAPOL constable in the bush on the trail of SWAPO terrorists.

Zulu-Whiskey *koevoets* preparing their evening meal during operations against SWAPO.

Bushmen looking for Angolan and Cuban troops during Operations MODULAR, HOOPER and PACKER.

Bushmen from 201 Battalion firing a RPG-7 rocket during Operations MODULAR, HOOPER and PACKER.

"Clay castles" on the Skeleton Coast of Namibia.

The wind blows sand across the deadly dry Namib Desert.

"Sand dollars," an emergency source of water in the Namib Desert—if you are lucky enough to find them.

Soviet helicopter destroyed by UNITA at Lomba River.

Native *kraal* in Ovamboland.

UNITA forces getting last minute instructions before moving out to attack FAPLA forces near Cuito Cunavale.

UNITA soldier moving through the bush looking for the enemy.

Dr. Jonas Savimbi and his staff direct UNITA forces during fighting north of the Lomba River.

The spoils of war, destroyed Soviet-supplied equipment on the Lomba River battlefield.

Soviet truck destroyed during the battle of the Lomba River.

South African Oliphant tank firing at a Soviet-supplied T-55 tank during Operations MODULAR, HOOPER and PACKER.

Soviet T-55 tank under fire by SADF in Operation MODULAR.

The Soviet tank is destroyed by the Oliphant.

201 Battalion soldier advances during Operations MODULAR, HOOPER and PACKER.

Bushmen machinegunner replenishes his ammunition during Operations MODULAR, HOOPER and PACKER.

Over fifty years old and still reliable—the DC-3, or Dakota as it is known in Africa, is still the workhorse of the SADF.

SADF engineers crossing a river prior to building a pontoon bridge during Operation MODULAR.

South African G-5 howitzer crossing a river during Operations MODULAR, HOOPER and PACKER.

South African Ratel crossing a river during Operations MODULAR, HOOPER and PACKER.

Communist FAPLA bunker destroyed during Operation MODULAR.

Soviet 76 mm. howitzer captured during Operation HOOPER.

Joint Military Monitoring Commission meeting at Rundu monitoring the South African pullout from Angola on August 30, 1988. The Cuban representatives are wearing Angolan Army uniforms. From left to right: Cuban in FAPLA uniform; Cuban in FAPLA uniform; South African in SADF uniform; Angolan in FAPLA unform.

Final South African pullout from Angola, August 30, 1988, as SADF units cross the Kavango River at Rundu into Namibia.

19
Outside Support

An analysis of revolutionary wars has shown that, from the revolutionaries' point of view, getting outside support for their cause is a vital and fundamental principle of revolutionary strategy.

It is also a vital principle of counterinsurgency warfare that the governing power should also seek outside support.[1] In many instances outside support is crucial otherwise the insurgency will topple the government. A poor country faced with a revolutionary force that is receiving massive amounts of outside help may not be able to offer much resistance to the rebels. It takes political will and a massive mobilization of resources by a government to defeat an established revolutionary movement in a long protracted war—requirements that are beyond the reach of most countries. Thus, outside aid is of crucial importance to a successful counterinsurgency program.

This is because, the revolutionaries can concentrate their efforts as they wish, in critical or rural, undefended parts of the country, while the government must try to defend all its people and all of its territory and critical assets. Such an effort is often beyond the means and will of the country involved, especially the developing nations where insurgencies are most likely to occur.

Even if the country can afford its counterinsurgency efforts from an economic standpoint, it will also require political support in the world arena if for no other reason than to counter or neutralize the political efforts of the guerrillas.

It has been no different in the Namibian situation. Outside support has loomed large and, even though the jury is still out as this work goes to print, it may be the determining factor in who will ultimately rule in the new independent Namibia.

[1] McCuen, *op. cit.*, p.69.

SWAPO has had outside support in spades. As mentioned earlier, it has gotten and still continues to receive massive amounts of Soviet Bloc aid. It is also the beneficiary of vast amounts of political and propaganda support from the socialist international community, the Organization of African Unity and the anti-Western Third World in general.

The United Nations has adopted SWAPO like an orphan, given it money (estimated as high as a billion dollars total over the years), facilities and a platform for its propaganda efforts on the world stage.

SWAPO even gets money from the free world in the form of direct subsidies from countries such as Denmark and the other Scandinavian countries. Religious organizations such as the National Council of Churches and the World Council of Churches and many mainstream Protestant and Catholic churches give it direct cash donations. SWAPO uses these donations to help fund its war of terror on innocents inside Namibia.

Angolan assistance in both material, training and base facilities as well as giving actual physical protection to SWAPO in The People's Republic of Angola benefits SWAPO enormously. It has enabled SWAPO to continue its efforts for as long as it has in spite of its declining fortunes in conducting its revolutionary war.

Without this outside help, SWAPO long ago would have been consigned to the dustbin of history. Instead, it stands to gain solely through the efforts of its international friends that which it has utterly failed to attain on the battlefield—political power in Namibia.

South Africa, on the other hand, has suffered severely from its lack of outside support. The total arms embargo against South Africa initiated by the United Nations has deprived the South Africans of the ability to purchase or obtain material that would have eased their counterinsurgency burdens.

The example of helicopters will suffice to show their predicament. The helicopter is a tremendously adaptable combat and logistical support weapon in a counterinsurgency campaign. Helicopters can quickly transport troops and supplies over long distances to carry the fight to the guerrillas; provide supporting fire to ground elements; transport wounded to treatment facilities and provide a high degree of tactical flexibility to counterinsugency efforts, to name just a few of their more obvious capabilities.

The South Africans had a fleet of Alouette and Puma helicopters, purchased before the arms embargo. However, they could not buy replacements nor spare parts and this affected the way in which they could be used. The South Africans simply didn't have the luxury of using helicopters in a vigorous counterinsurgency role as, for example, the French did very effectively in their Algerian War. Inability to get a sufficient fleet of modern helicopters dictated and limited the South African tactical approach to the war against SWAPO.

The oil embargo was also an impediment to their effort in Namibia. The counterinsurgency campaign in the desert environment required vast amounts of petroleum-based fuel and lubricants. In spite of the UN's oil embargo, South Africa could still get some of its oil from conservative anti-communist Arab states, especially Iran under the Shah. After his ouster, Khomeini shut off this major source of oil. South Africa had built two synthetic plants to take advantage of its vast coal deposits by converting that coal into oil. This has not been a cheap process, but it has ensured that South Africa would have its own source of oil. That source, coupled with what it can buy on the world spot oil market, has provided the Republic with its essential oil products. The effort does extract a cost—precious resources that could be used in other ways within South African society are expended to get oil.

The South African's had to fall back on their own devices and they have adapted well. Nevertheless, their inability to tap into the world's modern military arsenals has added costs, in both money, men, material and time, to their counterinsurgency efforts against SWAPO.

South Africa was not able to generate much international political support for its efforts in Namibia. Its pariah status among the nations of the world meant that South Africa had to go the effort alone.

There were many individuals of stature throughout the world that could see the true nature of SWAPO. Many gave vocal support to South Africa's efforts in Namibia. But they were few and far between when compared to the cacophony of support generated by the UN, the Soviets, and the socialist community throughout the world. Their voices were drowned out by this chorus of SWAPO sympathizers.

South Africa was helped more by the political and diplomatic incompetence of SWAPO than it was by its own efforts to generate support on the world stage. SWAPO has been perhaps one of the least sophisticated of the Marxist revolutionary movements and Sam Nujoma is not noted for his charismatic personality. He often proved a liability to his cause. In numerous interviews with journalists, he has come off as an arrogant radical Marxist thug who preferred the uniform of expensive Saville Row suits and the luxury of elegant five-star hotels to the fatigues and bush huts of his People's Liberation Army of Namibia (PLAN) comrades in the war zone of southern Africa.

In spite of these warts, SWAPO had at its beck and call the worldwide propaganda network of the Soviets and their front organizations, the left-liberal religious network of the World Council of Churches and the publicity organs of the United Nations.

South Africa was totally outmatched in the international popularity contest.

The weak link in SWAPO's armor was its true nature as a Marxist Soviet puppet. This became the centerpiece of South Africa's attempt to counter the pro-SWAPO propaganda blitz. As time went on, more knowledgeable people became aware of SWAPO's brutal nature. But, many rational people especially in the Carter Administration, preferred to ignore reality. The South Africans were never able to roll back or neutralize the effects of SWAPO's massive propaganda effort.

The advent of the Reagan Administration did bring a bit of a respite. When Reagan took office the general attitude of the United States changed from the outright hostility of the Carter Administration, to one of guarded neutrality. Ronald Reagan had made a career out of being a vehement anti-communist. At least the new administration would not easily accept the pronouncements of the United Nations about its protege SWAPO as the gospel truth.

The new administration's policy towards South Africa was termed "constructive engagement." This meant that negotiations would replace confrontation in U.S. dealings with South Africa. This new attitude did not mean the outright support of the South African counterinsurgency program in Namibia. In fact the U.S. was, at times, too quick to condemn South African actions in the war. This usually occurred when the South Africans were launching one of their incursions into Angola. Then, like Pavlov's dogs, the U.S. State Department would add its shrill barks to those howling with hypocritical indignation over the latest South African action.

The South Africans, however, did have a unique source of outside support. That source was the National Union for the Total Independence of Angola (UNITA).

UNITA was the guerrilla movement headed by Dr. Jonas Savimbi. They were trying to liberate Angola from the Marxist government in Luanda, which was giving aid and support to SWAPO.

UNITA's support was not in the form of an alliance nor did it send its forces into Namibia to fight alongside those of the security forces. It was a marriage of convenience: UNITA was fighting the Marxists in Angola and SWAPO was helping the Luanda regime against UNITA. Therefore, there was, in this instance, a mutuality of interests between South Africa and the Savimbi movement.

Savimbi himself had long called for independence in Namibia. The newly emerging internal political, social and economic programs that were evolving in Namibia were not hostile to his long-held views on an independent Namibia. His support, overt or covert of the process towards independence did not represent a change of his political views.

Last, but not least, the South Africans had been helping his guerrilla movement with supplies and other support. South Africa's Operation SAVANNAH, its intervention in the 1974-76 Angolan civil war, was intended to assist UNITA in achieving a military stalemate and to force a negotiated settlement in the internal dispute in Angola.[2] The escalating Cuban and Soviet presence in Angola knocked that scheme into a cocked hat.

Nevertheless, UNITA was valuable to South Africa's counterinsurgency efforts in Namibia. By the end of 1985 at least half of PLAN's terrorists were tied down helping the Angolan Army fight UNITA. Thus some 4,000 terrorists were not available for the SWAPO terror campaign in Namibia.

UNITA guerrillas were operating throughout Angola in areas where the South Africans could not go. Yet the intelligence gathered by the guerrillas was often shared with the South Africans. This was extremely valuable to South Africa because, in addition to SWAPO camps in Angola, the African National Congress (ANC) also had training facilities in Angola. From these camps they infiltrated through Botswana and Zimbabwe into the Republic of South Africa to launch terrorist attacks. South Africa was interested in any information about them, their training and personnel movements. Often, such information came from the observations by UNITA guerrillas.

UNITA was also in a good position to observe the activities of the Soviet Bloc and Cuban advisors who were becoming more and more involved with the affairs of SWAPO.

The intelligence provided by UNITA was extremely valuable to the security forces' counterinsurgency efforts in Namibia.

The area of southern Angola under the total control of UNITA provided a buffer zone between SWAPO and their targets in northern Namibia. It lay north of the Kavangoland and the Caprivi Strip and was a key factor in eliminating SWAPO influence in these areas, especially the Caprivi Strip.

The French counterinsurgency expert, Roger Trinquier, advocated forming guerrilla bands, *maquis* as he termed them, against the enemy. Under his concept, he would have advocated forming guerrilla bands to divert the efforts of the Angolans away from supporting SWAPO to fighting for its own survival.

---

[2] "Cuban Involvement in the Angolan Civil War: Implications For Lasting Peace in Southern Angola," Pretoria, Institute for Strategic Studies, University of Pretoria, *Bulletin,* 4/88, p.4.

Trinquier based his theory largely on his experiences in the French-Indochina War in the early 1950's. As a major, in 1951, he was given command of all behind-the-lines military operations in Indochina (Vietnam). This effort was the idea of the French commander-in-chief in Indochina, Marshal Jean de Lattre de Tassigny. De Lattre had decided to turn the Vietminh's skill in fighting behind the lines (guerrilla warfare) against the Vietminh itself by putting anti-communist guerrillas deep inside Vietminh territory. These units were known as the GCMA *(Groupements de Commandos Mixtes Aeroportes*—composite airborne commando groups).

Within two years Trinquier had over 20,000 men under his command. This figure had risen to 54,000 when the whole Indochina War was brought to a close by the fall of Dien Bien Phu and the GCMA's passed away into history.

Despite the debacle of the battle and the loss of the war, Trinquier did not feel his *maquis* teams were a failure: "The action of French maquis teams did, however, permit the evacuation without loss of the fortified camp of Nacan; the reconquest by Laos of the provinces of Phong-Saly and Sam-Neua without the help of regular troops; the total interdiction of the direct road from Lao-Kay to Dien Bien Phu for the entire duration of the siege, as well as the immobilization of more than fourteen battalions of the Vietminh regular army on Route R.P. 41, the umbilical cord of the besiegers; the recovery of hundreds of prisoners, etc.

"And yet, the establishment of *maquis* in the Tonkinese Upper Region, right in the middle of an area under Vietminh control, seemed a gamble when it was undertaken in 1952. This potential of the maquis command, although scarcely noticed at the time and already forgotten, ought not be lost sight of."[3]

South Africa did not need to follow Trinquier's blueprint and create *maquis* in Angola. UNITA was already in place and had been there prior to the outbreak of hostilities in Namibia. Working with UNITA was a logical step to take in the South African counterinsurgency effort.

One should not get the mistaken impression that the South African-UNITA cooperation was a one-way street in favor of South Africa. The objective of at least three South African incursions into Angola was solely to assist UNITA. They were: Operation SAVANNAH 1974-76; the air and ground support to thwart the Soviet-directed conventional dry season offensive in 1985 against UNITA's capital, Jamba; and the 1987-88

---

[3] Trinquier, Rodger, *Modern Warfare: A French View of Counterinsurgency,* Praeger, New York, 1964, p.110.

Operations MODULAR-HOOPER-PACKER which halted the latest Soviet-directed attempt of FAPLA (Peoples Armed Forces for the Liberation of Angola) to seize Savimbi's capital.

The other South African incursions into Angola had been aimed at SWAPO bases and infrastructure. These sometimes also had a beneficial effect on UNITA. It relieved Angolan and SWAPO pressure against UNITA and huge amounts of Soviet-supplied materiel captured by the South Africans during these incursions found their way into UNITA's arsenals.

Was UNITA helpful to South Africa? It was in many ways. In addition to the obvious military ways—tying down SWAPO, providing a territorial buffer and intelligence gathering—it also showed the South Africans were capable of working with and assisting black African leaders, something that went contrary to the false preconceived image of the stereotypical racist South Africans.

It is in the interests of both UNITA and South Africa that a free and independent Namibia comes into being. A Marxist Namibia would quickly seal its borders with Dr. Savimbi's area of Angola as well as with South Africa. Instead of getting aid and comfort from Namibia, a Marxist regime there would be positioned to stab UNITA in the back, and would no doubt do so with alacrity.

A Marxist Namibia would also open its territory to the African National Congress and help it export its Marxist-Leninist terror campaign across the border to South Africa. South Africa would then face the prospect that all of her northern borders, with the exception of Botswana, would be manned by hostile Marxist, or Marxist-leaning regimes, committed to the utter destruction of its government and society. Anything that could help stave off that frightening scenario would be of extreme value to the Republic of South Africa.

Major FPLA-UNITA-SA Battles During 1987 Communist Offensive

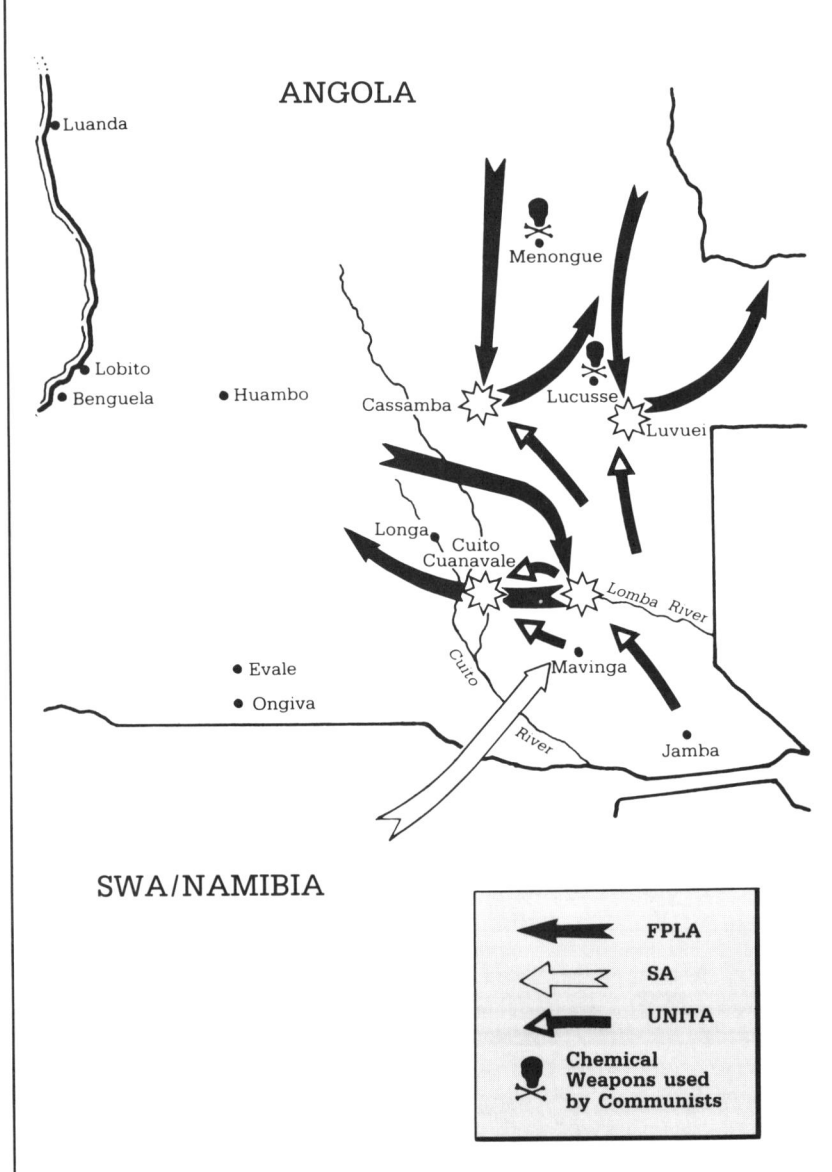

20
Aid to UNITA—Operations MODULAR, HOOPER & PACKER

During August 1985, the Angolan communist government launched a major dry season offensive against UNITA using massive airpower, tanks and 20,000 troops under the control of Russian General Konstantin Chaknovich. Nor was Soviet involvement limited to him alone. The Soviets were in this offensive up to their eyeballs, exercising tactical control of the communist forces all the way down to the battalion level. The ultimate objective of the offensive was the capture of Jamba, UNITA's capital and the destruction of Savimbi and his movement.

The Soviets knew UNITA lacked air defense and anti-tank weapons and they thought their armor and air power would carry the day. But they miscalculated the fighting abilities of the UNITA forces and the military skill of Savimbi and his officers. UNITA skillfully withdrew their forces in the face of the massive armored thrust, luring the armored columns deep into the bush where Savimbi's forces could attack their flanks.

The battle plan of the Soviets called for launching a two-front offensive on August 15—the first from the towns of Luena and Moxico. The Soviet-directed column from these towns, using Russian T-34, T-55 and newer model T-62 tanks, would move east into the Cazombo salient that juts into neighboring Zambia, capture the town of Cazombo, then turn south and link up with a second offensive column. This thrust was a feint. The true mission of the offensive was given to the second column, which was to move

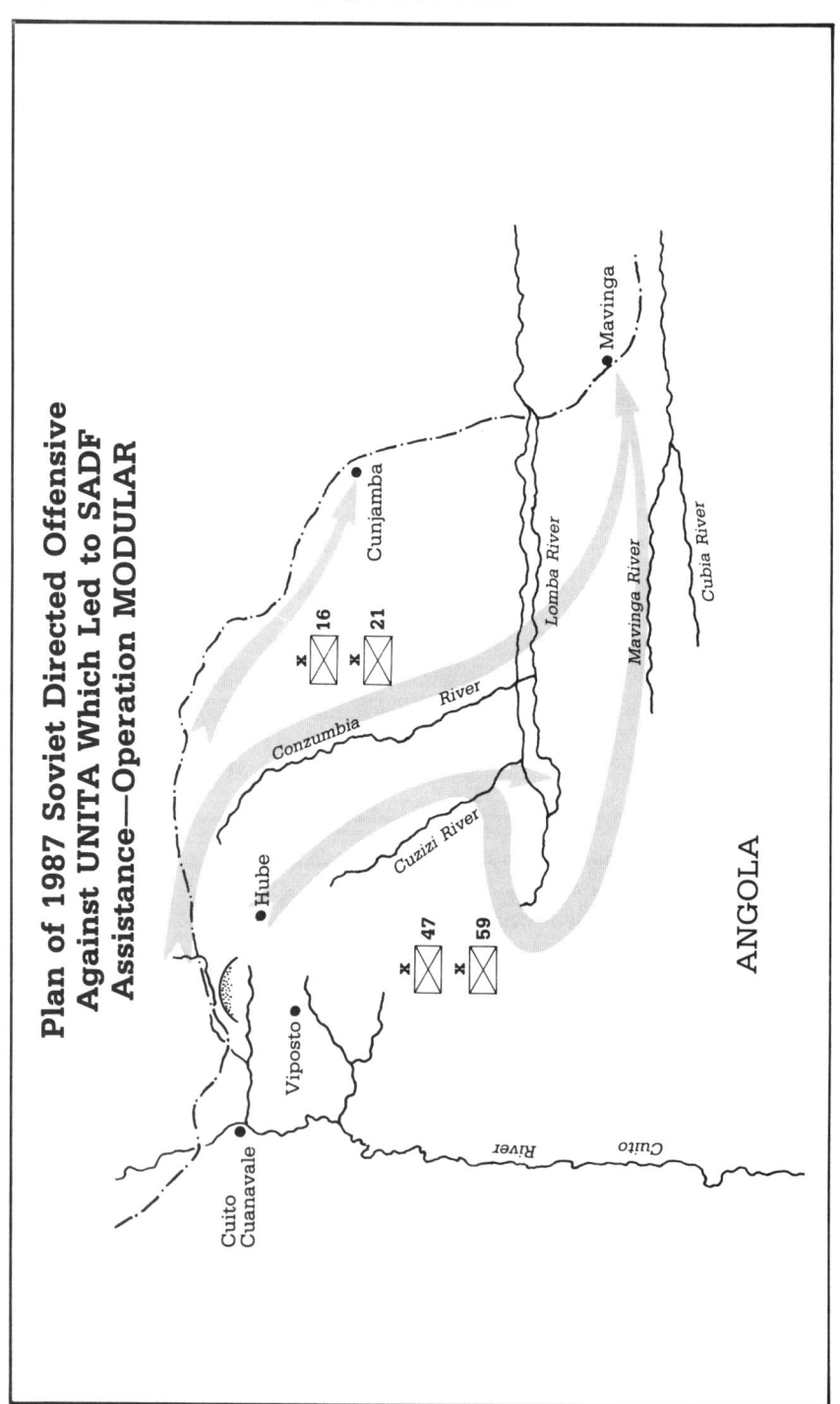

southeast from Menongue to Cuito Cuanavale. There it would split into two prongs and initiate a pincer movement attack upon its objective—Mavinga. The town was important for two reasons: its airfield could be used as a forward air support base and it could become the logistical base for operations against UNITA in eastern Angola. This would shorten the main supply route for FAPLA operations in southeastern Angola. From Mavinga the communist forces would pose a direct threat to Savimbi's headquarters and stronghold in Jamba.

That was the plan. Executing the plan proved to be another matter, as UNITA was determined to stop the attack. "If we don't survive, we die," Savimbi said. "I am bound to survive."

Both arms of the pincers ran into serious difficulties. The right arm slowed in the soft sandy soil, was attacked by several UNITA brigades. The right element quickly called on the left arm for assistance. As the left arm moved to help, UNITA mortar and artillery fire and air attacks by planes of the South African Air Force raked the rescuers. The huge heavy armored vehicles and trucks of the column couldn't maneuver in the soft, sandy tracks and were destroyed en masse. Savimbi, seeing the plight of the FAPLA columns, showed his brilliant generalship: He ordered most of his soldiers defending Cazombo from the northern column to reinforce the defenders of Mavinga. These troops moved rapidly over 200 kilometers and enabled Savimbi to concentrate his forces while the FAPLA forces were still divided. UNITA launched a counterattack on September 26 and after three days of heavy fighting, the Soviet-directed troops withdrew.

The 1985 Soviet-directed offensive by the FAPLA was the strongest challenge to UNITA since the Marxist-Leninist MPLA had seized power. It clearly indicated that the MPLA wasn't about to be "weaned" away from the Soviets by the soothing words of naive diplomats at the State Department.

Instead, the Soviets poured in $3.5 billion worth of military equipment to replace and upgrade that lost during the ill-fated 1985 offensive.[1] Meanwhile, the FAPLA replaced its casualties by a press-gang style of conscription that was scooping up 16-year-olds into the Angolan Army.

Retraining and re-equiping the Angolan military required almost two years before FAPLA was ready to try another major offensive against UNITA. The Soviets again poured weapons and ammunition into Angola to back yet another frontal assault launched from Cuito Cuanavale to capture the UNITA stronghold at Mavinga—the gateway to Savimbi's capital at Jamba.

[1] *The Economist,* November 27, 1987, p.16.

Although the 1987 Soviet-directed offensive was similar in nature to their ill-fated fiasco two years earlier, there were some differences. In 1985, the plan called for a river crossing of the Lomba River prior to the final attack on Mavinga. UNITA successfully repulsed this crossing attempt and its failure precipitated the destruction of the FAPLA force shortly thereafter.

The 1987 communist offensive hoped to profit from the bitter experience of the Lomba River debacle.

In August four brigades of Soviet and Cuban-led FAPLA forces (47th, 59th, 16th and 21st Brigades) moved again from Cuito Cuanavale in a slow methodical advance to the southeast towards Mavinga. The advance was proceeding along the road—actually it was nothing more than a dirt track cut through the bush—from Cuito Cuanavale southeastward to Cunjamba; between the Conzumbia River and Cunjamba the advance would turn south, cross the Lomba River and capture Mavinga. From there the advance would proceed south, capture Jamba and destroy the UNITA movement once and for all. That was the Soviets' plan.

The communists added a new twist, showing they had learned something from their whipping two years earlier. The 47th Brigade was to split off from the main thrust and either work its way south of the source of the Lomba or cross the Lomba much further west near the junction of the Lomba and Cuzizi Rivers. The 47th would then move along and secure the southern bank of the Lomba near the junction of the Lomba and Cuzizi Rivers. This would enable the 59th Brigade and the bulk of the force to cross the river unimpeded to link up with the 47th and march on Mavinga.

The 16th and 21st Brigades were to move into the area between the town of Cunjamba and the Lombo River. Their purpose was to prevent an expected South African/UNITA attack on the flanks of the Cuban/FAPLA forces crossing the Lomba River.

The communist forces advanced slowly and methodically, preceded by a screen of infantry to clear the area of UNITA ambushes. The bulk of the armored vehicles and armored personnel carriers would slowly follow behind the dismounted infantry sweeping the bush. The whole column would advance in this manner for six to eight kilometers per day. Each evening, they would stop, and set up a fortified, dug-in defensive position before settling in for the night. The next day they would continue in the same manner, reminiscent of the advance of an ancient Roman Legion—march a certain distance, then build a fortified camp before spending the night.

Caution wasn't the only thing causing the advance to proceed at such a snail's pace. The terrain and the dirt track that passed as a road was slowing the movement of armor and vehicles that were designed for combat on the

Aid to UNITA

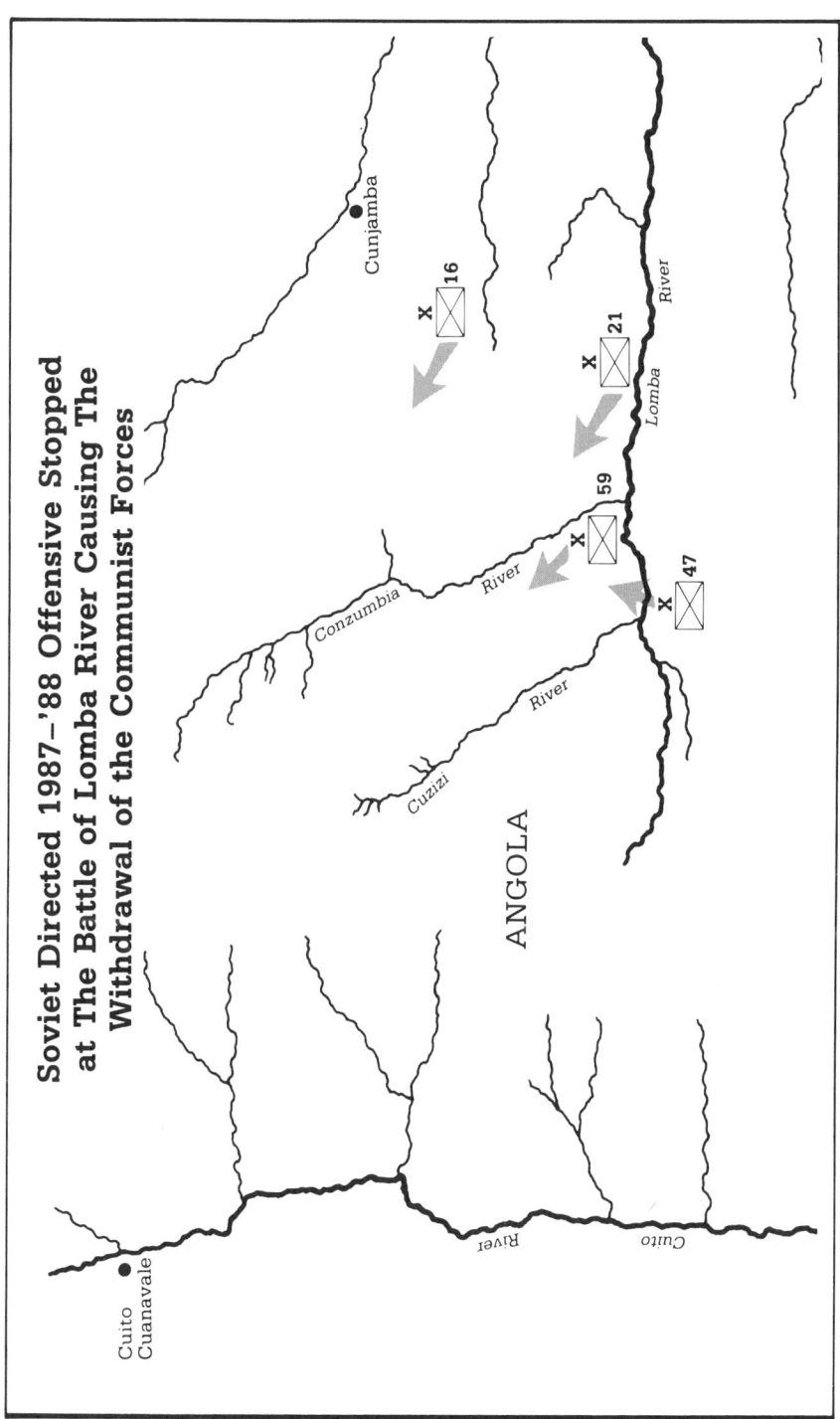

plains of Europe not the African bush. The non-existent roads in southern Angola took their toll on both men and equipment of the communmist forces.

The presence or possibility of FAPLA's 47th Brigade south of the Lomba River was a new and dangerous threat to UNITA's position and Savimbi requested SADF assistance.

The South Africans responded and a mechanized force, led by the veteran of Operation ASKARI—61 Mechanized Battalion—moved over the border from Rundu and headed northwest to intercept FAPLA's 47th Brigade.

The South African force was under the command of Colonel Deon Ferreira. He had received three sets of orders for his force to carry out: (1) to halt and reverse the FAPLA/Cuban advance on the UNITA strongholds of Mavinga and Jamba—Operation MODULAR; (2) to inflict maximum casualties on the retreating enemy—Operation HOOPER; and, (3) to force the enemy to retreat to west of the Cuito River—Operation PACKER.[2]

Near the junction of the Lomba and Cuzizi Rivers the South Africans met and utterly destroyed the 47th Brigade, removing the communist screening force from south of the Lomba River. The South African attack caught the communists by surprise as they were expecting any attack by the South Africans or UNITA to come from the east in the area between Cunjamba and the Lomba River. This was the area they had sent their 16th and 21st Brigades to defend against the expected attacks. Instead the attack had come from an unexpected direction—the south.

Heavy fighting was also going on north of the Lomba River as UNITA forces repulsed an attempt by FAPLA's 16th Brigade to capture Cunjamba.

After mopping up the FAPLA/Cuban survivors in the Lomba-Cuzizi-Conzumbia River area, the South Africans and UNITA went over to the offensive and began pushing the communist forces back towards Cuito Cuanavale—Operation MODULAR.

There were two weapons the South Africans used in Angola—one for the first time—that contributed to crushing the Soviet-directed offensive: the Olifant main battle tank and the G5 and G6 155mm artillery systems.

The presence of Olifant tanks in southern Angola was a first for the SADF while the G5 had been used before in Angola, especially to help UNITA stop the 1985 FAPLA offensive.

The use of the Olifants showed the South Africans had profited from

---

[2] "Cuito Cuanavale: Veil lifted at last," *Paratus*, March, 1989, p.14.

their near disastrous experience with Soviet-supplied armor during Operation ASKARI.

FAPLA armored forces took part in both the 1985 and and the current offensives against UNITA. This made it almost a matter of necessity for the South Africans to use armor to thwart the FAPLA offensive. The best weapon to destroy a tank is another tank and since UNITA had no armored forces, the job fell on the shoulders of the SADF.

As the FAPLA armored thrust came towards the Lomba River it was met by the Olifants and the first full-scale tank-on-tank armored battle yet fought in southern Africa began. The result was an overwhelming triumph for the South Africans. All but ten of the seventy-two Soviet T-55s engaged in the battle were either destroyed or captured within the first thirty-six hours. The remaining ten were captured during mopping up operations by the South Africans over the next few days. These tanks were found scattered about in the bush, intact but abandoned by their crews who had fled into the bush.

In marked contrast, the South Africans had two of their tanks temporarily put out of action. One lost a track when it hit a mine, the other took a hit through its engine. Both were repaired in the field and took part in further operations.

Contributing to the success of the South Africans was their undisputed superiority in artillery. The advantage was not measured in numbers of guns —FAPLA and the Cubans actually had more artillery pieces than both UNITA and the South Africans combined. What carried the day for the South Africans was the tremendous technological superiority of their G5 and G6 155mm howitzers.

Most informed military experts throughout the world consider the G5 to be the best 155mm howitzer in the world. Its performance in southern Angola justified that belief. What made the G5 and the G6—the newer self-propelled upgrade of the G5 system—so effective was their great accuracy at extreme range—approaching 40 kilometers.[3] FAPLA/Cuban counterbattery fire was ineffective because they were outranged by the South African artillery. FAPLA's counterbattery radar could determine the bearing from which the shells were coming, but they could never determine how far away the guns were, making locating them impossible. Nor could the enemy's Soviet MIGs find the guns. The Soviet planes searched in vain often

---

[3] *Janes Defense Weekly,* March 25, 1989, p.525; see also: Heitman, H-R, *South African War Machine,* Presidio, Novato, CA, 1985, p.45.

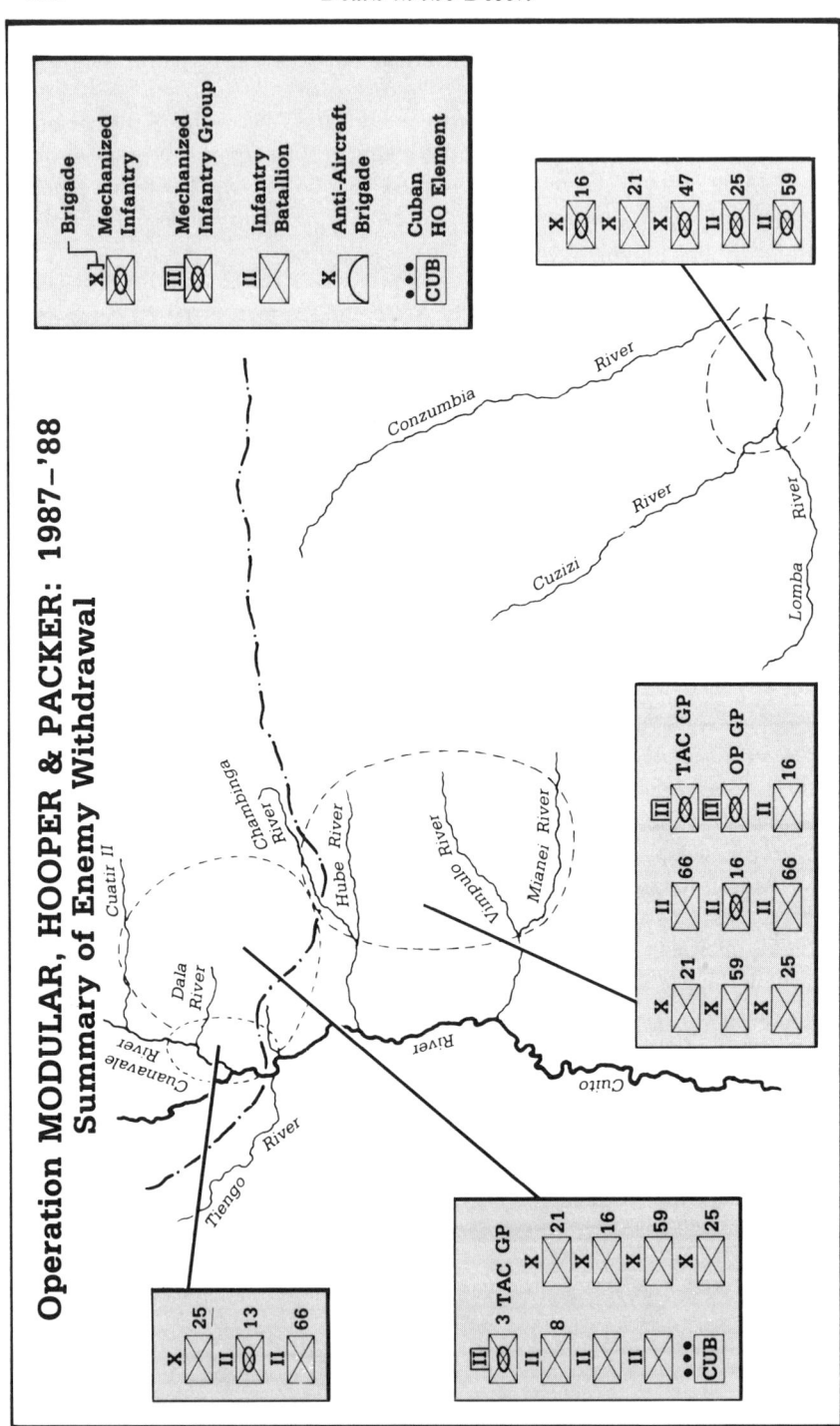

thousands of meters short of the actual gun locations.

As the FAPLA/Cuban offensive was stopped, the South African/ UNITA force went over to the offensive ending MODULAR and beginning Operation HOOPER. HOOPER's task was to inflict as much damage as possible on the retreating communist forces. The long, strung-out columns of retreating FAPLA/Cuban vehicles were hounded from the flanks by UNITA's guerrillas. They were pursued by the mobile UNITA units and the South African mechanized forces and pounded unmercilessly by the deadly G5 and G6 artillery fire.

The bulk of HOOPER's activity was to support UNITA's drive towards Cuito Cuanavale and to clear the area east of the town between the Cautir and Chambinga Rivers of all FAPLA forces. On January 13, 1988, they attacked FAPLA's 21st Brigade and sent them fleeing for safety west of the Cuito River. During this battle over 250 FAPLA soldiers from the 21st Brigade were killed and large quantities of arms were captured or destroyed, including fourteen tanks.

On February 14, 1988, HOOPER forces launched a second attack against FAPLA's 59th Brigade. The brigade withdrew with 230 FAPLA soldiers killed and nine more Soviet tanks destroyed.

On February 25, 1988, South African and UNITA forces attacked positions manned by FAPLA's 25th Brigade south of the Tumpo River, twenty to twenty-five kilometers east of Cuito Cuanavale. The attack ran into an extensive anti-tank mine field, which stopped the tank-supported South African/UNITA attack with the loss of two Olifants. In spite of this, the intense artillery bombardment and infantry assaults inflicted heavy casualties and pinned down the FAPLA survivors.

Even though some FAPLA forces remained on the Tumpo River the South African/UNITA force succeeded in capturing the tactical highground in the area, the so-called "Chambinga heights." This high ground dominates Cuito Cuanavale and its nearby territory. UNITA still holds the Chambinga heights.

At this point HOOPER was effectively over and Operation PACKER was in full swing.

PACKER was on-going with much of HOOPER in that its objective was to drive the FAPLA/Cuban force back across the Cuito River to it west bank. From the South African's last position twenty to twenty-five kilometers east of Cuito Cuanavale, including the Chambinga heights, the G5 and G6 artillery took on the task of chasing the enemy forces west of the Cuito River. They were successful in this mission: "We'd succeeded in dispersing the entire enemy force, save one battalion, to beyond the Cuito River," said Colonel Ferreira.[4]

Foreign observers were quick to comment on the effectiveness of the South African artillery at Cuito Cuanavale. *Janes Defense Weekly* said: "Since 10 January, 170 to 200 shells have hit targets in and around the town (Cuito Cuanavale) daily.

"The vital air base close to the town is thought to have been inoperative for some time, with radar and air defense systems destroyed by shelling, the runway craterized and aircraft movements rendered hazardous in the extreme—several having been destroyed on the ground."[5]

Added *Soldier of Fortune*: ". . . Cuito Cuanavale is reported to be in shambles; its buildings destroyed and its radar network knocked out. The removal of Cuito Cuanavale from the overall Angolan radar network grid creates a serious gap in the aerial defenses of Angola, a situation which the Soviet Union has spent billions of dollars trying to prevent. Aircraft that were left behind at the airstrip also became casualties of the ongoing battle."[6]

Arm-chair strategists may question the success of the South African action at Cuito Cuanavale because the South Africans failed to capture the town. Such chairborne tacticians miss the key point: the capture of Cuito Cuanavale was not part of the operational plan. The main reason being the geographical facts of life. To capture the town would require an assault river crossing of a two mile wide river. The size of the South African force, never more than 3,000 men, would render such an amphibious attack in the face of hostile fire a risky gamble indeed. To attempt to seize and occupy a town in enemy territory with a two mile wide river between one's forces and one's target would be at best, a fool-hardy venture. In addition, capturing the town would require garrisoning troops there to hold it. Cuito Cuanavale was not a SWAPO base so it made no sense for South Africa to keep troops there. Garrisoning the town with UNITA forces would tie down manpower that could better serve UNITA's guerrilla war elsewhere in Angola. By holding the Chambinga heights it is possible to dominate Cuito Cuanavale without having to occupy the town.

The goal had been to drive the Cuban/FAPLA forces back over the Cuito

---

[4] *Paratus,* March, 1989, p.14.

[5] *Janes Defense Weekly, op. cit.,* January 30, 1988.

[6] Venter, A.J., "Seige at Cuito Cuanavale," *Soldier of Fortune,* May, 1988, p.37.

Aid to UNITA

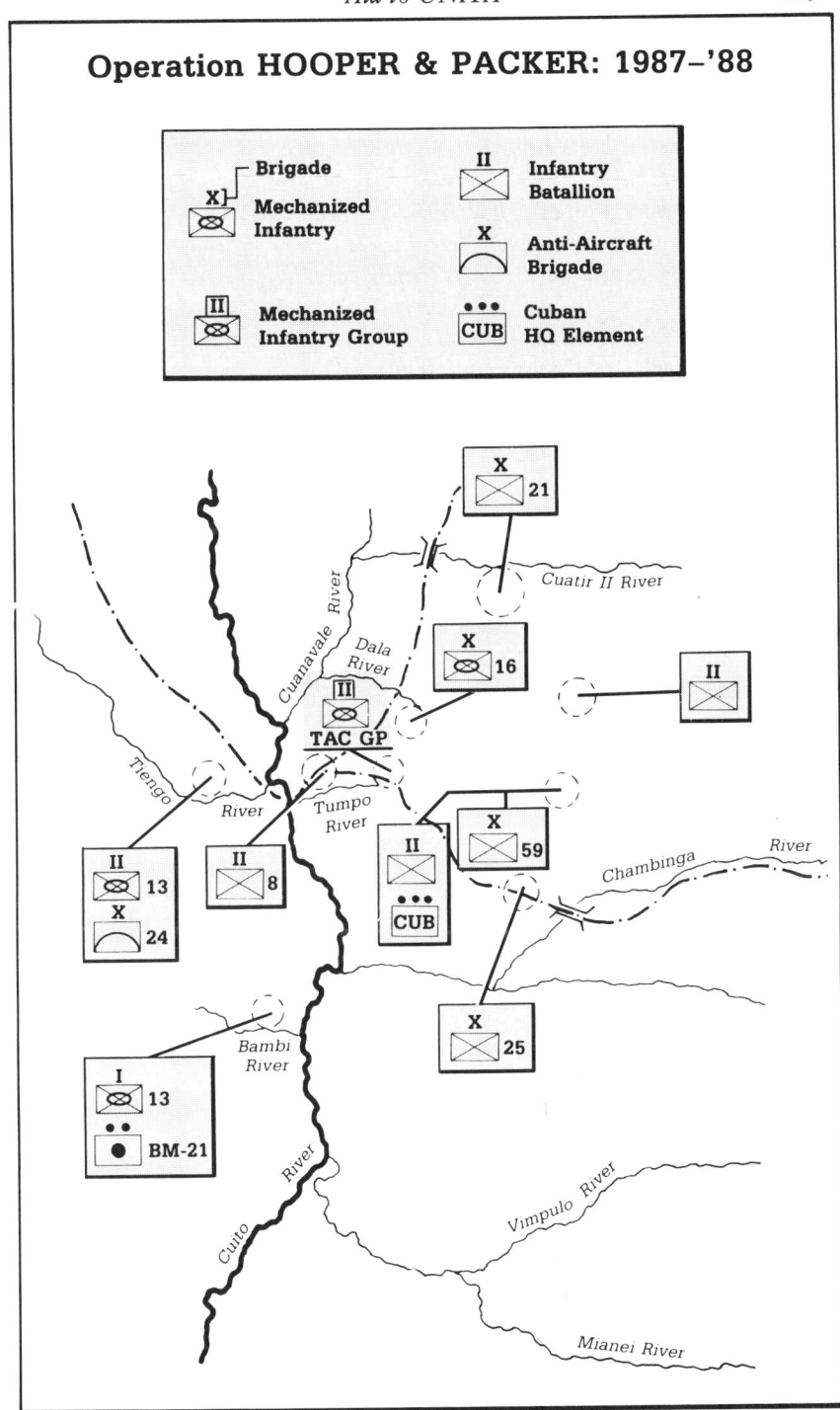

River. That was accomplished with the minimum amount of troops and effort.

Even the Soviet officials conceded that their latest attempt to destroy UNITA and punish its South African ally had not succeeded. M. Ponomorov, writing in *Krasnaya Zvezda*, on May 20, 1988, said: "The people's armed forces for the liberation of Angola have not been able either, even with the help of the Cubans, to decisively defeat the enemy and drive him out of the territory or the country. The result, frankly speaking, was an impasse."

Ponomorov was being circumspect, Colonel Ferreira was a bit more candid: "If defeat for South Africa meant the loss of 31 men, three tanks, five armoured vehicles and three aircraft, then we'd lost. If victory for FAPLA and the Cubans meant the loss of 4600 men, 94 tanks, 100 armoured vehicles, 9 aircraft and other Soviet equipment valued at more than a billion rand, then they'd won."[7]

The latest communist offensive had come to an ignoble failure, and the battle once again shifted to the political and diplomatic arena.

---

[7] *Paratus, op. cit.*, p.14.

21

Cuban Involvement In Southern Africa

There have been several popular misconceptions over the role of the Cubans in southern Africa. The most widely held canard is that they are in Angola to protect the Luanda government from the ravages of the South African Defense Force, which has "repeatedly violated the territorial integrity of the People's Republic of Angola." This version is nothing but solid Marxist propaganda.

So prevalent is this myth that its essence was included in the bilateral protocol signed between Castro's Cuba and Communist Angola for the withdrawal of Cuban forces from Angola. The preamble among other things states: "That the acceptance and strict fulfillment of the preceding provisions eliminate the causes which motivated the request by the Government of the People's Republic of Angola—in legitimate use of its rights envisioned by Article 51 of the United Nations Charter—for the sending into Angolan territory of a Cuban internationalist military contingent to insure, together with the FAPLA [the Angolan Government army], its territorial integrity and sovereignty against the invasion and occupation of a part of its territory."[1]

To have any credibility and to sustain itself over long periods of time, a lie or myth must contain a grain of truth somewhere in its makeup. Such is the case surrounding the myth concerning the Cuban presence in Angola.

The South Africans have over the years made numerous incursions into Angola in either their counterinsurgency role against SWAPO or to help UNITA resist the onslaught of Soviet-directed offensives against its capital.

---

[1] Text of Pacts on Namibian Independence and a Pullout by Cuba," *The New York Times*, December 23, 1988.

For a while, after Operation ASKARI in 1983-84, South Africa had occupied strategic bases in southern Angola from which it monitored and countered SWAPO's infiltration activity directed at Owamboland. Technically, this was an occupation of Angolan territory, but there was no movement by the South Africans to make it permanent. In fact South Africa quickly resorted to diplomacy in an attempt to eradicate the cause of its action—SWAPO activity originating from Angolan territory and directed at Namibian citizens in Namibia.

To put the Cuban presence in Angola in its proper perspective, it is necessary to go back and examine events centered around the Portuguese withdrawal from Angola in 1975.

There were three liberation movements in Angola that were not only trying to kick the Portuguese out of the country, but also seeking to assume power in their place. They were: the *Frente Nacional de Libertacio de Angola* (FNLA), the *Movimento Popular de Libertacio de Angola* (MPLA) and the *Uniao Nacional para a Indepencia de Angola* (UNITA).

Of the three movements, the FNLA was considered to be the strongest militarily. It had concentrated all it efforts to develop its military prowess at the expense of economic, political and cultural considerations. It opened the guerrilla war against the Portuguese with a February 4, 1961 attack in Luanda on the post office and several police and army barracks.

Under the leadership of Holden Roberto and based in Zaire, the FNLA had over the years built up, at least on paper, a formidable military force numbering about 10,000 men. However, FNLA's ability was in theory only. Its leadership was corrupt, its soldiers poorly trained, lacked leadership and zeal for fighting. The Portuguese had largely neutralized it by 1974.

Although the FNLA fired the first shots in the armed confrontation with Portugal, it was not the oldest of the three movements. That distinction belonged to the MPLA. It was founded in Luanda in December 1956 by Dr. Antonio Agostinho Neto and several communist radicals of mulatto origin. Although it claimed to be the "peoples party", the MPLA was a minority party limited to the mixed blood community in and around Luanda and to the Mbunda tribe whose lands were adjacent to Luanda.

The MPLA was not regarded as being as efficient a military force as the FNLA. One reason for this was that the MPLA was based a long way from the scene of the guerrilla war. It was based in the Congo and was separated from Angola by Zaire. It was extremely difficult to infiltrate guerrillas into Angola from Congo-Brazzaville through Zaire. When the MPLA did manage to get insurgents into Angola they tried to avoid clashes with the Portuguese but clash with them they did.

After several skirmishes with the Portuguese, the MPLA in 1963 fled to the Congo, moving to Congo-Brazzaville, where, under a new Marxist regime, its fortunes looked more promising. Yet they still had difficulty infiltrating into Angola and did their best to avoid the Portuguese. Instead they pursued their war against their rivals the FNLA in the north and UNITA political organizers in the east.[2]

So intense was the MPLA's hatred of Roberto's movement that they would often inform the Portuguese where FNLA units were located and let the Portuguese army wipe them out.[3]

The MPLA, however, was no military problem for the Portuguese. It was so beset by internal factions and feuds, the movement had almost ceased to exist as a fighting force in 1972. The MPLA had fallen to such a sorry state that Moscow had withdrawn its support.[4]

In March 1965, Neto traveled to Moscow and returned with Soviet support. Arms and supplies began arriving at the MPLA bases in Brazzaville. Neto's anointment by Moscow pushed him into the top circles of Third World radical chic.

The following year, 1966, Cuba made her entry into the affairs of the MPLA by providing military trainers and an elite bodyguard for MPLA President Neto.[5]

In 1964, FNLA's Foreign Minister, Jonas Savimbi, became uncomfortable with the political future of the movement. It had always been known as a military rather than a political force. Savimbi wanted to change the movement's emphasis.

Two years later, in March 1966, Savimbi broke with the FNLA and founded UNITA at Mwonga in Angola's Moxico province.[6] At first, UNITA operated from bases in Zambia. Its guerrillas were sent into eastern Angola where they conducted their operations. UNITA lost the good will of Zambia when it sabotaged the Benguela railroad, the main route used to ship copper, Zambia's main export, to the outside world. For this transgression, Savimbi was kicked out of Zambia, spent months in exile in the Congo, and finally

---

[2] Venter, A.J., *The Terror Fighter*, Rustica Press, Cape Town, 1969, p.31; Bridgland, F., *Jonas Savimbi: A Key to Africa*, Paragon House, New York, 1987, p.91.

[3] Marcum, J., *The Angolan Revolution*, Vol. II: Exile Politics and Guerrilla Warfare 1962-1976, MIT Press, Cambridge, MA, 1978, p.211.

[4] Marcum, John, "Lessons of Angola," *Foreign Affairs*, Vol. 54, No. 3, April, 1976, p.413; for a description of the internal feuding within the MPLA, see: Bridgland, *op. cit.*, pp.108-110.

[5] Marcum, *The Angolan Revolution, op. cit.*, p.225; Bridgland, *op. cit.*, p.64.

[6] Bridgland, *op. cit.*, pp.68-69.

moved his command inside Angola, establishing a base in a sparsely populated region. This left him no choice but to build his base of support with the local population and in classic guerrilla manner he slowly built up his political organization.

Savimbi was unique among the leaders of the three factions fighting the Portuguese. Whereas Roberto and Neto operated from sanctuaries in Zaire and Brazzaville, Savimbi led UNITA from the Angolan bush. His willingness to take the same risks as his men made them not only loyal and determined fighters, but had the effect of solidifying loyalty to his fledging political organization.

Trouble was brewing in Portugal that was to have far-reaching consequences in Angola. It all grew out of a small book, *Portugal and The Future*, authored by General Antonio De Spinola, Deputy Commander of the Army. The book, published in February 1974, was highly critical of the Portuguese wars in their colonial empire. Spinola maintained that Portugal faced certain defeat it it tried to win the wars against the insurgents by military means alone.

His book appeared at a crucial time in Portuguese history and it became an instant public hit. Portugal, one of the poorest countries in Europe, found the staggering cost of fighting the wars a severe drain on the economy. At the time of the book's publication, Portuguese military expenditures on the colonial wars in Angola, Mozambique and Guinea-Bissau were taking fifty percent of Portugal's budget.

A group of dissident officers formed a secret group, the Movement of the Armed Forces (MFA), to protest the government's policies and the wars in the overseas colonies. "We must end, once and for all, this damned colonial war, which is consuming everything, including the dignity of military professionals of a civilized nation," became the rallying cry of the dissident officers.[7]

On April 25, 1974, the dissident MFA officers staged a coup d'etat and Spinola became the new President of Portugal.

Spinola replaced the Governor-General of Angola with the leftist Vice Admiral Rosa Coutinho. Coutinho, nick-named the "Red Admiral," would play a pivotal role in the seizure of power by the Marxist MPLA in Angola.

The new leaders quickly moved to halt the fighting in Portugal's African territories. In early May, the Portuguese announced in Luanda that the three

[7] *Ibid.*, p.103.

insurgent groups would be treated as legitimate political parties as soon as they stopped fighting.

This was followed up with an announcement on the 19th of May that the 50,000 Portuguese troops would cease all military operations against the insurgents. For all practical purposes Portugal's counterinsurgency war against the rebels in Angola was over.

The three liberation movements were caught off guard and eventually became embroiled in futile arguments and bickering among themselves. They immediately started jockeying for position to take advantage of the changing military situation in Angola.

The FNLA moved forces into northern Angola and by late September 1974 it had established itself over a large area of northwestern Angola. It was centered on the area where the Bakongo tribe, which Roberto was a member of, lived in Angola. Having established his base in northern Angola, Roberto sent a large delegation to open a FNLA headquarters in Luanda where the FNLA began their campaign to gather support for their movement. Roberto hoped to capitalize on the presence of Bokongo tribesmen in the capital as his base of support. Since the Bakongo comprised five to ten percent of Luanda's population, Roberto was counting on his tribal ties to strengthen his political hold on the capital.

While this was going on, the MPLA was going through another of its seemingly endless internal quarrels. There were three factions competing for power and only pressure from Presidents Ngouabi of Congo-Brazzaville, Kaunda of Zambia and Nyerere of Tanzania prevented the movement from flying apart. A temporary truce was agreed to by the three factions which gave Neto the presidency of the MPLA.

The truce didn't last and the other two factions renounced Neto. The faction led by Daniel Chipenda left the movement in disgust and took along 2,000 of the MPLA guerrillas under his command.

Neto, nevertheless, held a conference with his faction. They elected him president of the MPLA and, more importantly, both Portugal and the Soviet Union accepted Neto's faction as the bona fide MPLA. This recognition added a new patina of respectability to the MPLA in the eyes of many throughout the world.

With the leadership of the MPLA secured by foreign recognition, Neto turned his attention to getting the movement into the upcoming race for power in the soon to be independent Angola. The MPLA opened an office in Luanda a month after the FNLA had opened theirs in the capital. Neto had two aces up his sleeve: the MPLA's traditional center of support had always been in Luanda; and Neto had an ally in high places in the capital—the

Portuguese Governor-General Vice Admiral Coutinho. Coutinho was an open leftist and he looked with great favor and sympathy on Neto's leftist socialistic ideas. He turned a blind eye to the weapons that had been pouring in to the MPLA from the Soviet Union since it had resumed military aid to the MPLA in late August 1974. British intelligence estimated the Soviets gave almost $6 million dollars worth of weapons to the MPLA in the last four montha of 1974.[8]

Coutinho's bias was obvious even to the foreign media. Portuguese officials conceded that the MPLA, once thought to be by far the most important of the liberation movements, didn't have the support of the people of Angola. It would in all likelihood require outside support in order to gain power. *The Observer's* Luanda correspondent wrote, "... Admiral Rosa Coutinho and most of the other Portuguese officials here appear to be still backing the MPLA, and this has led to suspicions among the other two movements and most of Angola's whites that the administration plans to prop up the MPLA."[9]

UNITA, however, opted to pursue a political policy of reconciliation and unity among the three movements to deal as unified Angolans with the Portuguese over the question of independence.

Savimbi hosted a conference at Cangumbe from October 26-29, 1974, with delegates of all three movements in attendence. Savimbi's purpose was the formation of a united front among the three movements to deal with the question of independence.

Coutinho arrived at the conference its second day and pushed for a transitional government under terms offered earlier by Portugal in August. The terms were to establish a transitional government in Angola to include not only the representatives of the three movements, but also representatives of the fifty or so groups that had popped up like mushrooms, after the coup in Portugal. The transitional government envisioned by the Portuguese would pave the way for free elections in two years.

The Portuguese proposals were rejected by the three movements. Savimbi stressed that UNITA would not serve in any transitional government unless the MPLA and FNLA were also represented.[10]

Savimbi then left on a tour of black African states in an effort to get their support in promoting unity among the three movements and to speed up the independence process in Angola.

---

[8] *Ibid.*, p.116; Marcum, *The Angolan Revolution, op. cit.*, Vol. II, p.432.

[9] Borrell, J., *The Observer,* December 7, 1974.

[10] Bridgland, *op. cit.,* p.112.

After getting the encouragement and support of African leaders such as Kaunda of Zambia, Nyerere of Tanzania and Kenyatta of Kenya, Savimbi turned to a harder task—getting the leaders of the MPLA and FNLA to agree to a unity proposal.

After a series of meetings and negotiations with Roberto and Neto the three movements signed accords on November 25 and December 18, 1974, agreeing to work together for independence.

As the year drew to a close the Portuguese agreed to hold talks on January 10, 1975 with the three movements to work out a timetable for Angolan independence.

On January 10, 1975, representatives of the three liberation movements met with Portuguese officials in the Portuguese coastal town of Alvor. An agreement and timetable for independence was worked out by the parties and signed on January 15, 1975.

Under the terms of the agreement elections would be held on October 31, 1975, for a national Constituent Assembly and the date set for independence would be on November 11, 1975.

Until independence the governing power would be held by a Portuguese High Commissioner and a transitional government made up of representatives of the three liberation groups. Each movement would have three ministerial posts in the transitional government, and each group would hold the premiership on a rotating basis. The Portuguese would also hold three ministerial posts as well as the High Commissioner's post.[11]

Named as the Portuguese High Commissioner was Vice Admiral Rosa Coutinho, the MPLA's "friend in high places."

The Alvor Agreement could start a process that could lead to independence and a multi-party democracy. Unfortunately, it did not work out that way as months prior to the agreement Chinese and Soviet meddling in Angola assured that Angolan independence would flow from the cartridge box not the ballot box.

During the mid-sixties and seventies there was a serious rivalry between the People's Republic of China (PRC) communist regime and the Soviet Union as to who was the true champion of the Third World liberation movements. The involvement of one would almost by reflex bring the other into the picture. It was no different in Angola.

In June 1974, almost seven months before the Alvor Agreement, the Chinese sent 120 instructors and 450 tons of weapons to the FNLA in Zaire.[12]

---

[11] See: Norval, *Red Star, op. cit.*, pp.204-211.

[12] Marcum, *The Angolan Revolution, op. cit.*, Vol. II, p.246.

Chinese aid to the proclaimed anti-communist Roberto seemed a strange thing to do. But since the Soviet Union was the traditional supporter of the MPLA, the PRC threw its support behind the FNLA.

The Chinese support of the FNLA forced the hand of the Soviets. If they wanted any influence in the soon to be independent Angola they had better deal themselves back into the game and make sure their favorite comes out on top. They dealt themselves back in by resuming military aid to the MPLA in August. At the same time the Soviet Communist Party proclaimed that "the MPLA was the true spokesman of the Angolan people."[13]

In December 1974, while the three liberation movements were agreeing to a united front, the MPLA sent a large contingent of its officers to the Soviet Union for military training.[14]

The U.S. was well aware of the increased military aid going to the MPLA and it decided to back the FNLA with covert aid.

Even though the three superpowers were now involved in the internal affairs of Angola to one degree or another, it was the Soviets' aid that carried the day. The Chinese, in spite of their boasts of being the true champions of the Third World liberation movements, did not have the resources to match the Soviets' capacity for dispensing and delivering aid. Nor did the United States, reeling from the after-effects of both Vietnam and Watergate, have the stomach to match the communist action. The U.S. could match or even exceed the Soviets' largess, but it did not possess the will to do so.

The Soviets were also realists. They knew the U.S. was soured on foreign adventures and lacked the will to oppose their moves in Angola with any degree of vigor.[15] So they felt pretty safe in backing the MPLA. But, having seen the results of the past constant bickering within the MPLA, they would temper their aid with a firm degree of control over their activity. This could be easily accomplished by their surrogates, the Cubans, who had been involved with the MPLA since the mid-sixties.

Given the past history of the MPLA with it succession of feuds and internecine fighting, it begs credulity to think that the Soviets would give massive amounts of aid, with no strings attached, to a group that was noted for its instability. Unlike other nations, the Soviets are not in the habit of blindly throwing aid and cash at a problem. Their help comes with a big string attached—Soviet control. Months after the Soviets cast their lot with

---

[13] Stockwell, J., *In Search of Enemies,* W. W. Norton, New York, 1978, p.67.

[14] Marcum, *The Angolan Revolution, op. cit.,* Vol. II, p.253.

[15] Shultz, R.H., Jr., *The Soviet Union and Revolutionary War,* Hoover Institution Press, Standford, CA, 1989, p.22.

the MPLA, there were still raging feuds within the MPLA. Daniel Chipenda set up offices in Luanda claiming to be the real MPLA. This didn't sit too well with Neto. On February 13, 1975 Neto's followers attacked Chipenda's killing fifteen of them. Chipenda fled from Luanda, taking with him over 2,000 of the MPLA's best trained troops. They promptly joined the FNLA.[16] If anything, Chipenda's split would have convinced the Soviets that the group they were backing still didn't have its act together and would have to be watched and closely supervised.

The loss of such a large number of its trained fighters would obviously affect the ability of the MPLA in any future confrontation with the other two liberation movements and time was against their recruiting, training and replacing Chipenda's forces. Fighters would be needed sooner not later. What, then, could be done about the situation?

From the Soviets' points of view they had few options. They could reverse their decision to support the MPLA. But this would cost them their golden opportunity of bringing Angola into their sphere of influence, as the MPLA was too weak to prevail on its own in Angola. To allow the ripe plum of Angola to fall under the influence of the Chinese because of their help to the FNLA was too much for the Kremlin to stomach. The only other option was to raise the stakes and take more vigorous steps to prop up the weakened MPLA.

There were risks involved, as direct Soviet intervention would wreck the detente between the United States and the Soviets so the use of Soviet forces in Angola to prop up the MPLA was out. But there was an alternative in the person of an ally who was itching to stick his nose into Angolan affairs— Fidel Castro.

Castro is a megalomaniac and one of his most driving ambitions was to be recognized as a leader of importance in the world. He was constantly looking for opportunities to increase Cuban international prestige. The situation in Angola presented just such an opportunity, as Cuba had been involved with Neto and the MPLA for years. The opportunity to rescue his fellow revolutionary proved hard to resist.

The solution was clear: the Soviet Union would supply arms and war material while Castro would send the necessary manpower.

Thus massive aid flowed into the MPLA. Not only had the Soviets been aiding the MPLA since August 1974, a little over four months before the Alvor Agreement, but so had East Germany, Yugoslavia, the Portuguese Communist Party and the naive Scandinavian countries. The aid was so

---

[16] Bridgland, *op. cit.*, p.119.

abundant that the MPLA had more guns than soldiers to shoot them. Obviously, the donors knew that somebody would use these weapons, either an expanded MPLA or somebody else. Given the time-frame of the rapidly changing situation an effective increase in the MPLA's trained manpower situation would evolve after events had passed them by. Thus, it seems logical to assume the weapons were there for use by somebody else—the Soviet's surrogates.

This urgent preparation and arming by the MPLA prior to the Alvor Agreement should have convinced any doubter that the MPLA had no intention of abiding by any agreement signed with the other two contending movements.

Another factor in the political and revolutionary equation in Angola, at the time, was the simple fact that as a minority party, the MPLA could not possibly win free national elections envisioned under the Alvor Agreement. If the envisioned elections had taken place UNITA's Savimbi would have won. On June 16, 1975, Senator Dick Clark (D-IA) asked John Marcum and Douglas Wheeler, two experts on Angola, appearing before the Senate Foreign Relation's Subcommittee on African Affairs, who they thought would win free elections in Angola. Marcum replied, "UNITA first, MPLA second and FNLA third." Wheeler stated, "it is possible UNITA would win . . . perhaps even a slight edge on plurality or majority."[17] A newspaper in Luanda took a nationwide poll in Angola in 1975 to gauge support in the upcoming elections. Its results showed UNITA with forty-five percent, MPLA with twenty-five percent and FNLA with twenty percent of the vote.[18]

The Soviets were no fools and realized the MPLA could not win at the polls. A military solution was the answer to the uncertain ticklish problem of elections posed by the Alvor Agreement. In fact Neto used the respite provided by the Alvor Agreement to mobilize his followers in their stronghold of Luanda to take care of his bitter rival. Fighting in the city between the MPLA and FNLA intensified with the latter being driven out of the capital by mid-July 1975.

The Soviets and their surrogates weren't the only ones that wanted the Marxist MPLA to take power in Angola. Officials in the Portuguese government worked behind the scenes to help them. The most active of these officials was none other than the Portuguese High Commissioner, Admiral

---

[17] ISSUP Bulletin, Pretoria 4/88, p.9; Testimony of John Marcum and Douglas Wheeler, before US Congress, Senate Committee on Foreign Relations, June 16, 1975, p.117.

[18] Matatu, G., "Angola EO Futuro," *Africa,* March, 1975, p.40.

Rosa Coutinho. He devised a scheme to install the Marxist MPLA in power in Angola.[19]

The Alvor Agreement turned out to be just a ploy of Coutinho's to enable the MPLA to buy time to get their act together and mobilize their troops for a military takeover.

To ensure that the MPLA would not be defeated—a reasonable assumption given the fact of the defection of its ablest commander and over 2,000 of its best troops to one of its rivals—Coutinho personally arranged for Cuban troops to be sent to Angola and allowed the Soviet weaponry to be shipped to Angola for use by the Cubans and the MPLA.

Coutinho later admitted that his goal was to ensure that the MPLA succeeded the Portuguese by any means necessary. In a recent Canadian-produced television documentary, he stated: "I knew very well that elections could not be held in the territory. I said at that time that the only solution was to recognize the MPLA."[20]

Why couldn't the elections be held if Coutinho didn't realize that the MPLA wouldn't win them? Obviously, if the MPLA were as strong a political entity as its mythmakers would have us believe, there could have been no reason not to hold elections.

Furthermore, if Coutinho didn't also recognize the military incompetence of the MPLA why did he have to hustle off to Havana and arrange for Cuban troops to prop up the MPLA? If the MPLA were competent enough, why would they need foreign troops?

The stated rationale for using the Cubans in Angola was to save black Angolans from attack by white-ruled South Africa. This myth is entirely false.

For one thing, by mid-1975, the South Africans were not in Angola. They were in South West Africa, in small numbers, fighting the SWAPO terrorist insurgency. The South Africans weren't in Angola, but the Cuban's were. According to Carlos Rafael Rodriquez, deputy prime minister of Cuba, the first "significant" numbers of Cuban troops arrived in Angola in May 1975.[21] By June, the Cubans were building military training centers in widely

---

[19] See the 1988 one-hour television documentary titled "The New Liberation Wars: Angola," produced for public television by Stornoway Productions, 59 St. Nicholas St., Toronto, Ontario, M4Y1W6, Canada.

[20] *Ibid.;* see also: *Kwacha News,* Vol. 3, No. 1, January/February, 1988, p.6.

[21] Binder, D., "Cuba says Africans vote won't affect Angolan aid," *The New York Times,* January 12, 1986, see also: Norval, *Red Star, op. cit.,* p.53.

scattered areas of Angola—centers for launching military operations by the MPLA against the other two movements.

The first South African forces to enter Angola did so on August 11, 1975, when they occupied the Cunene Dam complex just over the border in Angola, which supplies water and electricity to Namibia.[22]

According to the leftist American journalist and author, Tad Szulc, there were 250 Cuban advisors in Luanda in May 1975, rising to 1,500 before the South African intervention.[23]

In July, the MPLA suddenly attacked UNITA, destroying any hope for a negotiated political solution. By mid-July MPLA units had evicted both FNLA and UNITA from the capital, Luanda. The Alvor Agreement for all practical purposes was now a dead letter.

By August, the situation had escalated into a full-scale civil war and the FNLA and UNITA had retired to their tribal areas to build up their forces, acquire weapons and prepare for the ominous future. Under the old theory that "my enemy's enemy is my friend," UNITA and FNLA's fortunes were bound together in an uneasy alliance against the MPLA.

After pushing their opposition out of Luanda, the MPLA also attacked southward to seize the ports of Lobito, Benguela and Mocamedes (now called Namibe). Thus all of Angola's seaports were now in the hands of the MPLA, effectively stopping the other movements ability to use Angolan ports as entry for outside aid. This would affect UNITA more than the FNLA, which had its main bases in Zaire. UNITA was forced to rely on overland or air routes. Material could only come through the north from Zaire and Zambia, or through the south, from the South Africans. Zaire was doubtful because of its close ties with Roberto's FNLA. Zambia, although at first a Savimbi supporter and hostile to the MPLA, did not have the necessary infrastructure to support a massive logistic resupply effort to UNITA.

That left only the South Africans and Jonas Savimbi turned to them for assistance. The South Africans responded, believing they had the assurances of support from the Americans and several black African states, among them Zambia and Zaire.[24]

South Africa's objective in assisting UNITA was to force a military stalemate among the factions which would lead to a negotiated settlement of

---

[22] Statement of Robert Ellsworth, Deputy Secretary of Defense, before the US Congress, Senate Committee on Foreign Relations, Angola Hearings before the Subcommittee on African Affairs, 94th Congress, 2nd Session, January 29, February 3, 4 and 6, 1976, p.83.

[23] Szulc, T., *Fidel: A Critical Portrait,* Avon Books, New York, 1986, pp.708-709.

[24] Bridgland, *op. cit.,* p.169; see also: *Newsweek,* May 17, 1976.

the Angolan civil war.[25] Many still feel, however, that the true goal of the South Africans was to drive north up the coast of Angola, capture Luanda and allow either UNITA or the FNLA to form a government in Angola.

While this view no doubt comfortably reinforces the views of the hate South Africa crowd, it founders on an elementary principle of war—mass. The term mass simply means having enough combat power concentrated at the critical time and place for a decisive purpose.[26] In short, the 2,000 man South African force that crossed the Angolan border at Cuangar on October 14, 1975 was far too small for such an ambitious undertaking. At the time the South Africans had crossed the border there were already close to 4,000 Cubans in Angola and this number would swell three-fold by January 1976. The elements of such a force just don't magically appear out of the sunrise. As Colin Legum, no friend of South Africa, has pointed out: "The mobilization and transport of such large numbers would require at least six weeks from the time the decision was taken. The Russian and Cuban contention that their military intervention was the result of South African intervention is clearly a post facto rationalisation, since they were seriously involved before March 1975, and they had already put their aid program into its second phase by the beginning of October—fully three weeks before the South African army had crossed the frontier."[27]

South Africa had some vital interests in the outcome of the power struggle in Angola. An independent Angola, dominated by a Marxist government, could provide bases and assistance to communist groups such as SWAPO and the African National Congress (ANC) for their attacks on South Africa and Namibia. This is precisely what happened.

South Africa also had economic interests in Angola in respect of the Cunene hydroelectric complex which is of great importance to Namibia. South African capital had invested heavily in the scheme and a Marxist Angola would be unlikely to compensate them for their efforts after taking it over.

South Africa obviously misread the diplomatic situation, especially the weakened condition of the American government's will to pursue and back up its diplomatic action and promises in Angola.

---

[25] Cuban Involvement in the Angolan Civil War, *ISSUP Bulletin* in 4/88, p.4; see also: Moss, R., *The Sunday Telegraph*, February 6, 1977.

[26] Summers, H.G., Jr., *On Strategy*, Dell Edition, New York, 1984, p.175.

[27] Bridgland, *op. cit.*, p.453; see also: Legum, Colin, "The Role of the Western Powers in Southern Africa," in: *After Angola: The War Over Southern Africa*, Rex Collings, London, 1976, pp.21 & 40.

Of course the American action was undercut by the American liberals' assault on the intelligence agencies, those most likely to involved in carrying out secret American diplomacy in Angola. The Church and Pike committees assault and emasculation of the CIA should have alerted the South Africans as to the hollowness of American government assurances and the growing congressional opposition to aiding the Republic of South Africa.

When the South African presence in Angola became public and caused a furor, the United States government tucked its tail between its legs and ran away.

The final ingredient in the Angolan tragedy was provided by the incoming sanctimonious Carter Administration. Nothing illustrates it better than the flip-flop position taken by Carter's UN Ambassador Andrew Young. At the opening of a new Martin Luther King library in Lusaka, Young condemned the Soviets for sending arms into Angola, suggesting that the US should stop selling grain to the Soviets until they quit sending arms to Angola.[29] But, after the Cubans had installed the MPLA in power in Angola, as Carter's UN Ambassador, he would fatuously refer to the Cuban presence in Angola as a stabilizing force.

So the South Africans were left to do the West's dirty work, no doubt hoping for an improvement in their relations with the West. In this they were also to be disappointed.

As the November 11, 1975 date for Angolan independence approached, the FNLA decided it would be in a commanding position to seize Luanda and force the Portuguese to turn over the country to them. Reasoning that whoever held the capital would be in the catbird seat, Roberto launched his drive. Independence day dawned and Roberto's troops, along with two battalions of Zairean forces and a band of mercenaries, were still about 50 kilometers from Luanda.

Cuban/MPLA forces, using "Stalin Organs"—forty-barrelled 122mm rocket launchers—laid a heavy barrage of fire on the FNLA and their allies. This attack by the Cubans showed the phoniness of the FNLA's alleged military prowess. Roberto's soldiers panicked and fled from the scene, totally demoralized.

This disaster, known as the Battle of Death Road, broke the FNLA

---

[28] Bridgland, *op. cit.*, p.154.

and their retreat didn't stop until they had reached their sanctuary in Zaire.

However, the Cuban/MPLA force did not take advantage of the situation by attempting rapid manuevers or pursuit to trap and annihilate the FNLA/Zairean force.

Instead, they cautiously employed conventional Soviet military tactics —advancing methodically, making sure each sector was secure before proceeding further. This slow, steady progress continued until mid-January 1976 when the last FNLA troops cleared out of northwestern Angola.

The Cubans had determined on achieving a military victory for the MPLA. On November 5, 1975, six days before the FNLA launched its ill-fated attack on Luanda, Fidel Castro decided to send more troops to Angola.

His reasoning proved to be sound. By then reports from his troops being mauled by the South Africans in southern Angola had alerted him to the presence of their forces in the civil war. Castro reasoned that once the South African presence became known they would become a lightning rod and attract international condemnation. While they were getting all the abuse his escalation would attract little attention.

He also correctly realized that the shameful American pullout from Vietnam in April of that year had so crippled the American will that the Americans would not support any new foreign adventures, especially in Angola. He was right. Rationalizing his opposition to American aid in Angola, Senator Hubert Humphrey dismissed Angola as a small, faraway country of little concern to the United States, much as Neville Chamberlain had described Czechoslovakia upon his return from his Munich meeting with Adolf Hitler in the thirties.

Castro was right. Condemnation poured down upon the South Africans and Castro was able to pour thousands of his troops into Angola—7,000 by December, up to 12,000 by February 1976.[30] The United States reacted with the Congress passing legislation (the notorious Clark Amendment to the Fiscal Year 1976 Defense Appropriations Bill) prohibiting the use of funds in Angola, except to gather intelligence.

South Africa, with its conscript military, could not afford to match Cuba's escalation and engage in a war of attrition with the Cubans, backed

---

[29] Stockwell, *op. cit.*, pp.231-232.

by the massive logistical depots of the Soviet Union. South Africa's equipment was not as modern as that of the enemies she was facing and there were no Western supporters willing to provide the necessary equipment to continue the war.

Left hanging by the United States and certain black African countries, particularly Zambia and Zaire, failure to give them open support for their Angolan intervention, the South Africans began to withdraw their forces from Angola.

By the middle of February 1976, the Angolan civil war, for all intents was over. The FNLA had ceased to exist as a fighting force; the South Africans had withdrawn; the MPLA's Peoples Republic of Angola was officially recognized by the OAU; and UNITA had scattered into the bush to continue its guerrilla war against new colonial masters in Angola, the Soviet Union and Cuba.

Yet the Cubans remained. There were no South African troops in Angola, so what was keeping the Cubans?

At first it seemed that the Cubans too were going to leave Angola. Castro told Swedish Prime Minister Olaf Palme that Cuba would reduce its forces to 5,000 troops by the end of 1976, and he expected the rest to leave during the following six months.[31] Thus, if these reports were accurate, Cuban troops would have been out of Angola almost one year before South Africa launched her first major cross-border attack on SWAPO facilities in southern Angola. There was certainly no indication when Castro made his statement to Palme that he was anticipating any South African action in Angola. In fact his statement indicates the contrary.

Thus, even if South Africa has become a convenient scapegoat, blaming her for Cuba's continued presence in Angola rests on shaky ground.

If not South Africa, then who, or what, has really kept the Cubans in Angola?

It was the resurrection of UNITA, rising like the mythical phoenix bird from the ashes of the Angolan civil war, that forced the Cubans not only to stay, but to raise their force level to between 50,000 and 60,000 troops.[32] Besides, Castro's ego would not permit him to abandon Angola.

---

[30] Nossiter, B., "Swedes see limited pullout by Cubans," *The Washington Post*, June 3, 1976, p.17; see also: "Castro says Cubans leaving Angola," *The Washington Post*, June 7, 1976, p.6.

[31] Kirkpatrick, J., "Slandering Savimbi," *The Washington Post*, July 4, 1988, p.A21.

This would run counter to the messianic revolutionary mission he has set for himself.

As Dr. Vladimir Ramirez, a psychologist and former Cuban political prisoner and head of the Latin American Study Center in Miami, Florida, points out, "But it is important to understand that Castro doesn't have armies in Africa so that the USSR can keep him in power in Cuba. Rather he tries to keep his power in Cuba to be able to keep armies in Africa . . .

"Castro loves power. He needs power like the addict needs his drug. But power to Castro is not and end in itself, it is an instrument, a weapon to fulfill his messianism and etch his place in history . . .

"Because of the above we can be sure Castro will never give up his presence in Africa. Neither psychologically nor politically can he give up what has always been the meaning of his life . . ."[33]

Cuba entered Angola to protect the MPLA from being tossed out of Luanda by Holden Roberto's FNLA. It has remained because the minority MPLA government cannot rule Angola by itself. The Cuban troops are the Praetorian Guard of the Peoples Republic of Angola and their sole function is to prevent it from being overthrown by UNITA.

The South African incursions into Angola in the late seventies and eighties were aimed at damaging SWAPO bases in Angola and were never designed as a threat to the MPLA regime in Luanda.

The syndicated columnist Georgie Anne Geyer remarked upon the false notion that the Cubans were invited in by the Angolans to protect the Luanda regime: "There is not the slightest historical question that the MPLA, the only Marxist movement of the three, accepted that UNITA would win those elections, and thus moved to bring in Cuban troops and take the capital of Luanda before the elections could be held. They grabbed (not earned) power.

"As a journalist/historian, I am further amazed at the constant falsification of that history to read even in these new agreements that the Cubans were 'legitimately' invited in under a 'request' of the MPLA 'Peoples Government of Angola.' In fact, there was no government at all at

---

[32] Ramirez, Dr. Vladimir, "Castro's Cuba: Socio-Economic Conditions," *American Review,* Institute For American Studies, Rand Afrikaans University, Johannesburg, 1989, p.16.

[33] Geyer, G.A., "But's about Angola," *The Washington Times,* February 13, 1989, p.D2.

that time; indeed, the Cubans' coming precluded the legal formation of such a government."[34]

The real threat to the MPLA's continued hold on power in Angola is from UNITA. It is to counter this powerful threat that Cuban troops will remain in Angola.

22
The Illusion of Peace

In late May and early June 1988, an event was taking place thousands of miles away from Namibia that would have a profound effect upon its future. That event was the May 29-June 2 Moscow summit meeting between Soviet Communist Party General Secretary Gorbachev and U.S. President Reagan.

Gorbachev and Reagan put their stamp of approval on diplomatic attempts to resolve the conflict in southwestern Africa. The diplomatic activity revolved around a series of tripartite talks between Cuba, Angola and South Africa.

The Soviet and U.S. leaders agreed on a deadline of September 29th, the tenth anniversary of UN Resolution 435, for completing a settlement of the regional conflicts in southern Africa.

The summit meeting between Gorbachev and Reagan accelerated to a fever pitch the negotiations that had been first undertaken in London on March 3-4, 1988, under the urging of U.S. Assistant Secretary of State for African Affairs, Dr. Chester Crocker. Crocker had been seeking a place in the history books for the past eight years by brokering a peace treaty in southern Africa.

All parties followed up the London meeting with talks in Brazzaville in the Peoples Republic of the Congo during the second week in May. The big question raised at this meeting was the Caluequque water scheme in southern Angola that the South Africans now occupied. Caluequque provided precious water via pipeline and canals and electric power to Owamboland. The South Africans were reluctant to hand the scheme over to SWAPO's protectors and have them cut off both precious commodities which were essential to Owamboland. The Angolan government, however, promised not to cut off Owamboland's water and electricity. This assurance removed a major concern of South Africa and smoothed the way for it to disengage its troops from continuous potential conflict with the Angolan Army.

The remaining large problem to surmount was the question of Cuban troop withdrawal from Angola.

During the London meeting, the Marxist Angolan government's initial position on the Cuban troop withdrawal proposed a four-year timetable in exchange for an immediate independence of Namibia; South African troop withdrawal within a year, and a halt of all outside aid to UNITA.

The Angolan government's position would allow the last Cuban soldier to leave Angola some three years after the last South African soldier left Namibia. This, coupled with the fact that the Angolan proposal placed no restriction on the amount of Soviet military aid it could continue to receive, led to the impression they were stalling. The Angolans and Cubans obviously wanted the three years without the possibility of outside South African interference so they could attempt to destroy UNITA.

This condition was totally unacceptable to the South Africans. They were pressing for a one-year withdrawal timetable for the Cubans as well. In spite of his overwhelming desire to get a treaty, even Dr. Crocker rejected the Angolan proposal pointing out that American aid to UNITA was not part of the discussions.

The conferees began the next round of talks in Cairo on June 24th. However, a dark cloud appeared over the talks on June 27th as a joint FAPLA/Cuban force launched a ground attack in an attempt to seize the Caluequque water scheme. Apparently the assurances given by Angola during prior meetings that they would not attack the scheme were mere prevarications designed only to keep the peace talks from collapsing.

A follow-up air strike by four Angolan MIG fighter-bombers aimed at the Caluequque Dam wall confirmed the South African suspicions. The attack damaged the dam wall, but it did not collapse. Twelve South African and more than 300 Cuban and FAPLA soldiers died as a result of the fighting at Calueque.

The chief Cuban negotiator in the talks, and a member of Castro's politburo, Jorge Risquet, claimed the attack on Calueque was an "appropriate and calculated response" to alleged unprovoked South African attacks on Cuban positions in southern Angola.[1]

In spite of the Caluequque incident, the peace talks continued, even though Crocker had to work overtime to prevent them from collapsing as a result of the Cuban/FAPLA attacks.

The parties then held the next round of talks in New York on July 11th. Out of this meeting, the negotiators reached for the first time a consensus which could establish a framework for peace in the region. The parties put

---

[1] "SA will withdraw first says Cuban," *Business Day,* July 18, 1988.

Illusion of Peace

this consensus in writing and submitted the document, Principles for a Peaceful Settlement in Southwestern Africa, to their respective governments for approval.

The South African government was the first to give its approval and the other governments soon followed. On July 20th, Cuba, Angola and South Africa announced they had ratified an agreement to withdraw foreign troops from Angola and to grant independence to Namibia as per the terms of UN Resolution 435.

In addition, the sovereignty of the countries that were party to the agreement had to be maintained. The agreement forbade outside interference in the internal affairs of any particular country. The respective countries also had to give assurances that their territories would not be used as staging areas for cross-border acts of aggression against another country.

This meant, in the eyes of South Africa, that Angola would not permit SWAPO to launch guerrilla attacks inside Namibia from their bases in southern Angola. Nor would South African and South West African Territorial Forces be able to chase SWAPO terrorists back across the border and pursue them into Angola.

The South Africans attempted to follow these terms scrupulously, whereas the Angolans were lackadaisical in clamping down on SWAPO. The author personally observed an incident in which SWAPO clearly violated that particular understanding.

On September 27, 1988, while the author accompanied a South West African Police Counterinsurgency Unit patrol in eastern Owamboland, it intercepted a team of five SWAPO terrorists at sundown. The terrorists were waiting for dark so they could launch a stand-off bombardment on the SWATF base at Eenhana. In the ensuing contact and chase, one terrorist was killed. This terrorist was dressed in a brand new uniform of the Angolan Army. His body was taken by helicopter to Eenhana to provide evidence for the Joint Military Monitoring Committee (JMMC) to show that a violation of the July agreement had occurred. What was also fascinating was that, in addition to the dead SWAPO terrorist, the Cuban members of the JMMC were also wearing Angolan Army uniforms. No wonder the Cuban and FAPLA members of the JMMC were a little upset when their decreased comrade was dumped at their feet several kilometers inside Namibia, along with his weapons. No doubt their consternation would have been greater at the time if they knew that an American writer had witnessed the whole scene.

SWAPO's excuse was they couldn't communicate with all their terrorist teams although this team entered Namibia over three weeks after SWAPO leader Sam Nujoma said he would abide by a ceasefire.

SWAPO increased its activity in the period immediately after the South African withdrawal, despite a voluntary undertaking by the SWAPO leader to observe a ceasefire as of September 1, 1988.

According to security force spokesmen there were thirty-seven incidents involving seventy-two SWAPO insurgents that had occurred in the operational area between September 1 and October 10, 1988.[2]

Of those seventy-two, the security forces neutralized a third, with twenty being killed and four captured. During the corresponding period in 1987, only seventeen incidents were reported—a rise a year later of 117%.[3]

In spite of Nujoma's pious assertions of observing a ceasefire, SWAPO was also busy infiltrating political commissars into Owamboland. They were trying to bring the following message to Owamboland: "You'd better support us because we are returning to Namibia with the United Nation's troops."[4] But SWAPO soon toned down their activity because, even though they weren't a party to the negotiations, they were under no illusion that continuation of their activities could cause the peace process in the region to come unstuck. Patience was to be their new byword, because soon the UN would be in a position to help their cause. So for the moment they had to watch their step.

While the agreement provided a framework for future negotiations, major obstacles still remained—the timetable for withdrawing the Cuban troops and an internal solution for Angola's on-going thirteen-year-old civil war. Although resolution of Angola's internal problems was not part of the formal talks, it loomed large in the background of the negotiations.

The Cubans insisted upon a four-year timetable for their troop withdrawal, while the U.S. and South Africa wanted all Cuban troops out within a year. Their departure within that time frame would would coincide with the securing of independence in Namibia. Such reasoning capitalized on past Cuban asertions that they were in Angola to protect it from South African troops located in Namibia. If South African troops were out of Namibia within a certain period of time why should Cuban troops stay longer? Their own self-proclaimed reason for being there—South African troops in Namibia—no longer would exist. Therefore, why stay an extra three years, as the Cubans proposed to do?

[2] *Uniform,* Pretoria, No. 207, p.1.

[3] *Ibid.*

[4] Intelligence briefings and conversations with military and police officials in Namibia, September, 1988.

Illusion of Peace

That was the line of reasoning put forth by South Africa that the U.S. was forced initially to accept.

Even though the ratified document did not address the question of the resolution of the Angolan civil war, it was the United States' position that the internal process of reconciliation in Angola should take place at the same time that the international agreement on foreign troop withdrawal from Angola and implementing UN Resolution 435 was taking place.

Dr. Crocker stressed the United States would not end aid to UNITA until foreign troops were withdrawn and the Soviet Union terminated its assistance to the MPLA.

The understanding reached during the July meeting in New York contained the basis of the final accord signed later in the year.

However, a lot remained to be done and the diplomatic activity did not take a holiday.

Returning to the conference table in Geneva, Switzerland on August 2, 1988, the South African government submitted a set of proposals for peace that would test the sincerity of the other parties to the talks. Three proposals were of major importance to the prospects of peace in the area. The first provided for a ceasefire of all hostilities between the parties to go into effect on August 10, 1988.

The second provided for an immediate start to withdraw both South African and Cuban forces from Angola. As a gesture of goodwill and to demonstrate good faith, the South Africans promised to have all of their troops out of Angola by the first of September.

The South Africans further proposed that a liaison committee be established which would draw up and oversee the mechanisms for the withdrawal of forces from Angola.

Talks were held at Ruacana on August 16, 1988 to address the third point of setting up a liaison committee. The parties agreed that a Joint Military Monitoring Commission (JMMC) would be set up. It would be made up of representatives from FAPLA, the Cuban forces, officers of the SADF and SWATF and mediators furnished by the United States.

Military representatives from South Africa, Namibia's SWATF and a joint Cuban/Angolan delegation formally signed a treaty at Ruacana on August 22, 1988 to formally end hostilities between the two sides. The treaty set up the JMMC and provided for daily meetings of the Commission.

In accordance with the agreements, the South Africans informed the JMMC that they would complete their withdrawal from Angola by the first of September. They were doing this as a gesture of good faith and by so doing seized the diplomatic high ground.

The South Africans beat their own deadline as the last South African troops crossed a pontoon bridge across the Kavango River at Rundu on August 30, 1988.

But the peace that was about to descend was a fragile one.

While the South Africans were demonstrating their good faith, Castro's Cubans were doing just the opposite. In January 1988, with Soviet logistical support, Castro began transporting by air some 9,000-10,000 of his elite troops from Cuba directly into southern Africa, raising the total number of Cuban forces in Angola to over 55,000 men. Scores of Cuba's finest pilots were brought in as well. The Soviets flew in massive quantities of military hardware, including surface-to-air missiles, and other modern equipment such as MIG-23s, to be piloted by Cuban pilots.

In a speech in Parliament on June 20, 1988, South African State President P. W. Botha pointed out that the Cuban build-up might threaten the security of the entire subcontinent: ". . . the Cuban build-up of troops is in direct contradiction to the search for peaceful solutions to the problems of the south-western sub-continent. Since January this year these forces have increased rapidly by some 12,000 troops. Their equipment now includes T-64 and other tanks, MIG-23 fighter aircraft, as well as sophisticated anti- aircraft and radar systems. They have also completed the upgrading of two landing strips in south-western Angola, immediately north of the South West African border."[5]

The Cuban troop deployment posed a serious threat not only to the operational area of northern Namibia, but also raised a serious flanking threat from the west to Savimbi's UNITA stronghold in southeastern Angola. By turning east and attacking UNITA, the Cuban force could not only cut UNITA's supply route from the south, but could possibly capture his headquarters at Jamba. This would scatter Savimbi's forces back into the bush where they would be forced to regroup and start anew the process of guerrilla war as scattered bands of guerrillas.

For a party to a peace conference, the Cubans were acting more as bellicose aggressors than pacifists.

Before March 1988, Cuban deployment in southern Angola had been restricted to a headquarters element at Lubango and regimental deployments at Chivemba-Matala and Jamba (not to be confused with Savimbi's capital). In late March they redeployed to Xangongo, moving their headquarters to Chetequera. Prior to the signing of the tripartite peace accords between

---

[5] Parliamentary speech, June 20, 1988; quoted in: *News from Namibia,* Washington, DC, July 5, 1988, pp.1-2.

Angola, Cuba and South Africa on December 22, 1988, the entire Cuban 50th Division, under the command of General Planas, was deployed at Cahama and points further south to the Namibian border. General Planas' chain of command was not through the head of the Cuban forces in Angola, nor did he consult with the Angolan armed forces. He dealt directly with Fidel Castro in Havana.

Under an atmosphere where one party withdrew his forces while the other increased his, why did the peace talks move forward to a conclusion evidenced by the signing of an accord on December 22, 1988?

Much of the credit was due to Dr. Crocker, the U.S. negotiator. Crocker had been pursuing a peace settlement in southern Africa with the zeal of a Parsifal searching for the Holy Grail. Starting in April 1981, after joining the Reagan Administration, Crocker had been on his quest of negotiating "peace" in the region. As both 1988 and the Reagan Administration were winding down, his efforts increased. As Agence France-Presse stated it in typical dry French manner: "He is very much in a hurry."[6]

From their actions it was obvious the Cuban-Angolan duo were not going to budge. It was up to the non-communists (i.e., the South Africans) to make most of the concessions. The West subjected South Africa to intense pressure, orchestrated by Dr. Crocker and the U.S. State Department. This pressure ran the gamut from no more vetos of UN sanctions against South Africa to threats to refuse to roll over loans or to advance new credits to Pretoria.[7]

Dr. Crocker's pressure, coupled with a growing frustration in South Africa with the antics of the West, contributed to Pretoria's course of action. Western Europe's hostility, the U.S. Congress' acts of economic warfare and the worldwide campaign of ostracism against it, had driven South Africa to turn a blind eye to the double-dealing of the Cubans and Angolans.

For years South Africa had fought against Marxist revolution and inroads into southern Africa at considerable expense to herself. All she has to show for it was the aforementioned abuse and hostility of the world. Therefore, perhaps, she concluded that the best thing to do was pull back, regroup, and shorten and strengthen her line of defenses.

In spite of the dubious prospects that Angola and Cuba would live up to the terms of any peace agreement, South Africa continued to take part in the endless round of talks (twelve since May) which finally culminated in the

---

[6] "A Seriously Flawed Agreement on Angola," *The Freedom Fighter*, Washington, DC, November, 1988, p.1.

[7] "Peace, Miracle or Sellout," *The Washington Times*, December 21, 1988.

signing of the U.S.-mediated agreement in New York on December 22, 1988.

There were actually two agreements signed at the United Nations on that day. One among South Africa, Angola and Cuba to grant independence to Namibia by implementing UN Resolution 435 on April 1, 1989, and the other between Cuba and Angola providing for the redeployment and eventual removal of Cuban forces from Angola.

In general, both agreements would begin various steps to, hopefully, bring peace to the area:

- a general truce among the parties to go into effect immediately upon signing the accords;
- set in motion both the independence of Namibia, and free elections scheduled for November 1, 1988 to elect a constituent assembly which will draft a Namibian constitution;
- provided for the withdrawal of all South African forces from Namibia by the end of 1989;
- respect the territorial integrity and inviolability of the borders of Namibia;
- agreed that their respective territories would not be used by any organization to conduct acts of violence or aggression against the territory of any state in southwestern Africa;
- provided for the withdrawal of Cuban forces from Angola.

In short, South Africa agreed to pull its troops out of Namibia and allow the UN to hold elections in Namibia leading to its independence. All of this would take place in 1989.

In return, Cuba and Angola agreed that the Cubans would eventually leave Angola and that Angola would end its support and training of SWAPO and the ANC.

The timetable of the troop withdrawal for the Cubans was much more generous than that for the South Africans. Instead of all Cuban troops out of Angola by the end of 1989, like the South Africans out of Namibia, the Cubans were supposed to depart in the following manner: 3,000 Cuban troops would leave by April 1, the start up date for implementing UN Resolution 435; by August 1, 1989, all Cuban troops to withdraw away from the Namibian border north of the 15th parallel of south latitude. By November 1st, the date of elections in Namibia, half of the Cubans are to be out of Angola and the rest are to be north of the 13th parallel of south latitude. By April 1, 1990, two-thirds of the Cubans are supposed to be out of Angola; by Ocober 1, 1990, seventy-six percent of the Cuban troops to have left Angola; by January 1, 1991, not more than 12,000 Cuban troops are to be in Angola; and, by July 1,

1991, all Cuban troops are to be out of Angola.

In the end Dr. Crocker got his treaty and with it a world-wide chorus of praise. However, the euphoria it generated could prove to be an illusion because the treaty is seriously flawed. If, as is highly likely, the treaty comes unglued, Crocker, as the architect of the agreement, will have brokered another hollow treaty that didn't promote peace and stability and proved detrimental to Western interests.

Provision 4 of the treaty calls for ". . . the staged and total withdrawal of Cuban troops from the territory of the Peoples Republic of Angola, and the arrangements made with the Security Council of the United Nations for the on-site verification of that withdrawal."[8] Article I of the bilateral withdrawal agreement between Cuba and Angola calls for ". . . the total withdrawal to Cuba of the contingent of approximately 50,000 troops which make up the Cuban forces in the Peoples Republic of Angola, . . ."[9]

But there is a rub, just how many Cubans are in Angola? The U.S. State Depoartment says, 50-52,000; South African intelligence says around 55,000,[10] UNITA says the number is at least 60,000, while the Cubans and Angolans have admitted to only "approximately" 50,000.

UNITA Vice President Jeremias Chitunda has said that between 15-20,000 Cubans have been given dual Angolan-Cuban citizenship, and that most have been issued FAPLA uniforms. (As photos in this book clearly show, the Cubans on the JMMC were routinely wearing Angolan Army uniforms.)

Even though the bilateral agreement between Cuba and Angola promises to withdraw "approximately 50,000 troops," they left themselves a big loophole to weasel out of the deal. Article II states: "The Governments of the Peoples Republic of Angola and the Republic of Cuba reserve for themselves the right to modify or alter their obligations under Article I of this Agreement if blatant breach of the Tripartite Agreement occurs."[11]

Lenin once said, "Promises are like pie crusts, made to be broken." It is well to remember that promises made by Marxist regimes, where lying and disinformation are matters of state policy, are suspect. When you have promises made by one Marxist state to another, they are as reliable as those made between pathological liars.

---

[8] Text of Pacts on Namibia Independence and a Pullout by Cuba, *The New York Times*, December 23, 1988.

[9] *Ibid.*

[10] Interview with South African and Namibian intelligence officials, August-September, 1988.

[11] *The New York Times, loc. cit.*

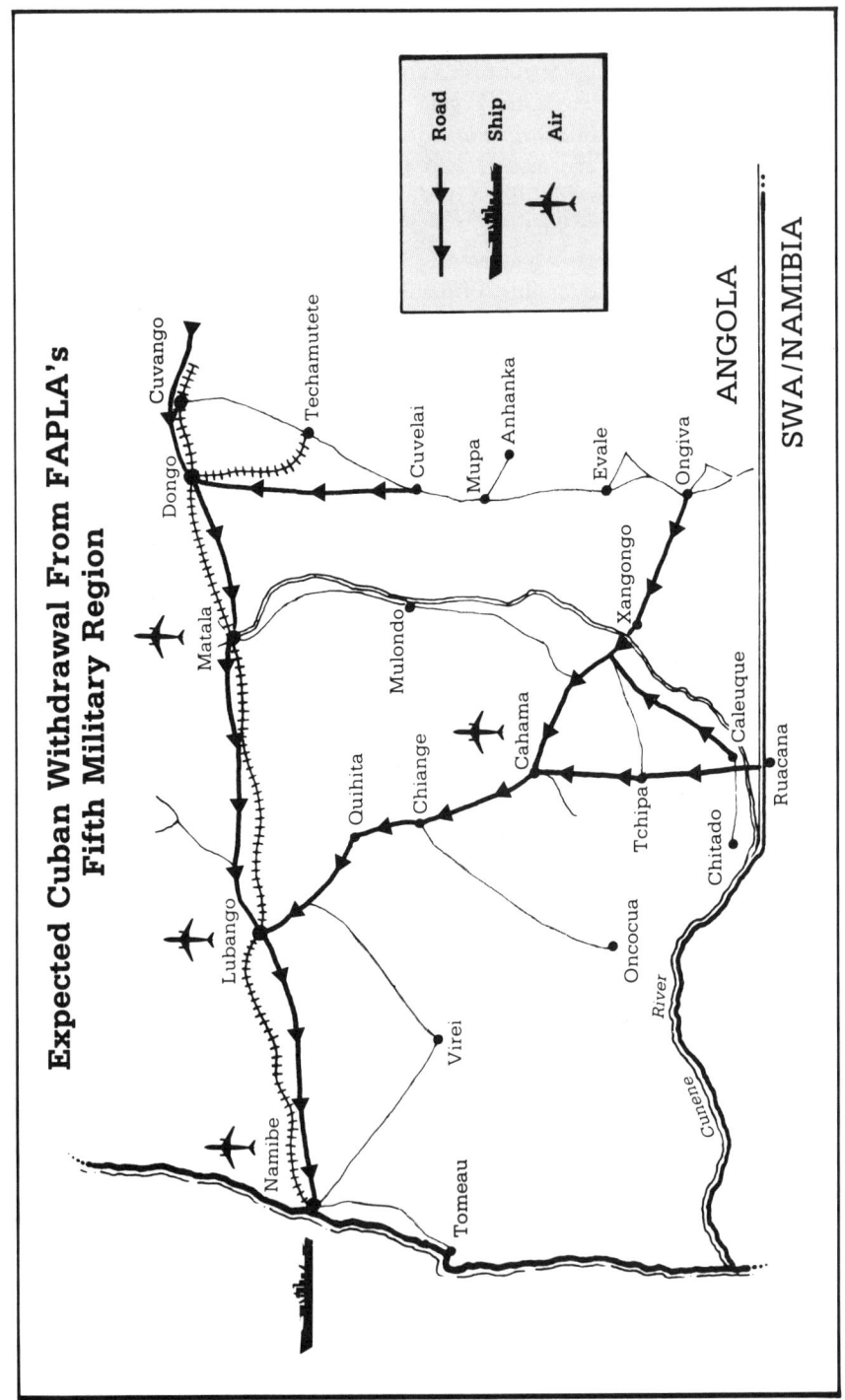

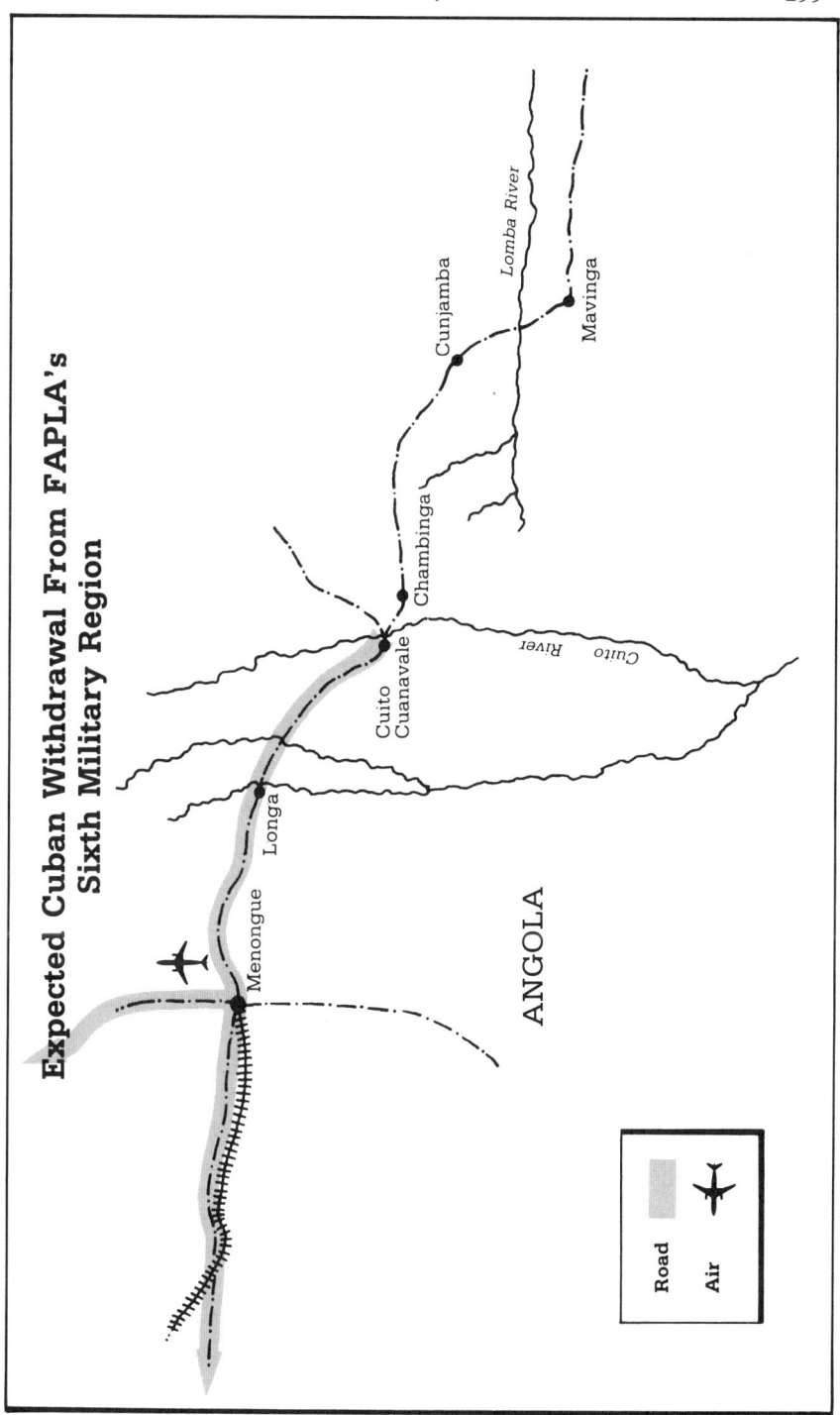

What might constitute a "breach" would obviously be in the eye of the beholder or would be whatever fit the convenience of the moment for the Cubans or Angolans because the fate of the Angolan government really rests in the hands of the Cubans.

Another item that shows the treaty to be a sham is the verification process. While the UN wants to send a 6,500-man peacekeeping force to Namibia to verify the South African withdrawal and to supervise the Namibia elections, it takes a more liberal view of the Cuban pullout. The UN plans to send only a ninety-man unit to Angola to supervise and verify the removal of the 50,000 Cuban troops. The ninety-man team will come from Brazil, the Congo, India, Jordan, Norway, Spain and Tanzania, most of whom recognize and support the Marxist regime in Angola and are on friendly terms with Castro's Cuba. The team will also have to depend upon the good graces of the Angolan government to furnish transportation in carrying out their verification activities as they will not bring their own transport. The head of the ninety-member team is a Brazilian General Pericles Ferreira Gomes. Brazil is a major arms supplier to the Angolan government. If the composition of the group doesn't engender confidence in their zeal or ability to monitor the Cuban withdrawal, General Gomes response left no doubt as to the uselessness of his group when questioned as to how he would verify the Cuban withdrawal. He told *The New York Times*: "When (Angola and Cuba) tell us there are no more troops, we will tell the United Nations they have gone."[12]

The United Nations seems willing to accept the Cuban troop withdrawal on trust, but they want to send 6,500 people to make sure the South Africans leave Namibia.

The South Africans are not pleased with such arrangements. "What we definitely don't like is the fact that 7,500 UN troops and 2,000 UN civilians are allocated to verify the withdrawal of South African forces from Namibia while only 75 UN military personnel are allocated to monitor the withdrawal of 50,000 Cuban troops from Angola," said one South African military source.[13]

"The UN monitoring force in Namibia will have their own transport and other facilities, while the handful of UN personnel in Angola will be depending on Angolan logistics. That doesn't make sense. Angola is a vast

---

[12] UN's Angola Mission to take Cuba at Its Word, *The New York Times*, January 8, 1988.

[13] "S. Africa Asks why UN assigns more 'watchers' for its pullout," *The Washington Times*, January 25, 1989.

Illusion of Peace 257

country. How can 75 men check on the Cuban withdrawal from there? It's farcical."[14]

Since that statement was made, budget constraints forced a reduction in the size of the UN's force in Namibia, but the logic behind the South African comments remains valid.

If the UN's action isn't a double standard what is?

The agreement is flawed and appears doomed to failure. It is well to recall the late Sovietologist Norman Leites' insightful view of Marxist-Leninist attitudes towards negotiated settlements:

"(1) Any agreements between the Party and outside groups must be regarded as aiding the future liquidation of these groups and as barriers against the liquidation of the Party by them . . . Therefore there is no essential difference between coming to an ostensibly amicable arrangement with an outside group or using violence against it; they are both tactics in an overall strategy of attack.

"(2) When an attempt by the enemy, or by the Party to advance by violent means has failed, the conditions for an effective agreement between the Party and the enemy come into existence.

"(3) The Party must always expect outside groups to violate agreements."[15]

SWAPO showed they viewed the December 22, 1988 peace accords as a device to further their goals and provided proof of Leites' admonitions by launching an early morning April 1, 1989, invasion of Namibia.

More than 1,200 Peoples Liberation Army of Namibia (PLAN) terrorists—soon to escalate to 1,800-1,900—armed with AK-47's, light machine guns, 60mm mortars, RPG-7 rocket launchers and SAM-7 shoulder-held anti-aircraft missiles, poured into Namibia in an effort to seize territory and set up bases inside the country. The terrorist assault force consisted of seven major groups of between eighty and 150 each that attacked across the border along a 150-mile front from Ruacana in the west to Nkongo in the east. A second wave of the terrorists followed the initial group until there were in excess of 1,200 SWAPO terrorists in Namibia by the end of the day. Others quickly followed during the next two days.

Why did SWAPO launch a Pearl Harbor-style sneak attack on precisely the date the Namibian independence process began? They launched the attack with the goal of bolstering SWAPO's psychological war campaign in

---

[14] *Ibid.*

[15] Leites, N., *The Operational Code of the Politburo*, McGraw-Hill, New York, 1951, pp.88-90, as quoted in: Dailey & Parker, *op. cit.*, p.149.

Namibia. This was to be done in a series of rapid steps that, to succeed, had to be completed quickly—within seventy-two hours.

The first priority of their assault was to seize areas inside Namibia, proclaim them SWAPO bases, then contact the UN officials in Namibia and place themselves under the auspices of UN monitors—in other words present them with a fait accompli.

From these bases in "liberated Namibia" SWAPO would be in a position to carry out its program of intimidation in Owamboland. This was necessary because their political support inside the country had been lagging and SWAPO needs at least two-thirds of the seats in the new Constituent Assembly in order to have a free hand in writing Namibia's new constitution. Without that free hand SWAPO would find it virtually impossible to force adoption of a pro-Marxist constitution to govern an independent Namibia.

SWAPO also desperately needed these bases to confirm its self-proclaimed image as the liberators of Namibia. It is fatuous to pose as a popularly supported liberator of a country when your so-called liberation forces don't even control any territory in the country you claim to be liberating.

The success of this latest SWAPO offensive would also enhance the terrorists' prediction that they would come to power in Namibia in the wake of the UN troops.

SWAPO's action essentially entailed three risks: (1) it had to be done quickly—within three days—before South Africa could take any effective counteraction; (2) it would jeopardize peace overtures they had made to some of the internal Namibian political parties; and, (3) it could cause the collapse of the whole regional peace plan. Of the three, the first was the crucial risk —the others could easily be taken care of once SWAPO had achieved its goal. Overcoming the major risk would depend upon the success of the PLAN terrorists in achieving their objectives within the prescribed time period.

On paper, they had a good chance to pull it off. The South West Africa Territorial Force (SWATF) had been demobilized and the agreement confined South African army units to their bases. Since the UN was in charge of the operational area as of the day of the attack, their permission would be required for any South African response to the SWAPO invasion. Since the UN troops had not yet arrived, security was the responsibility of the South West Africa Police (SWAPOL), who are policemen, not soldiers. To further disperse the police, and enhance the chances of success of their proposed sneak attack, SWAPO, through its legal internal political entity, scheduled a massive demonstration of its alleged supporters in Windhoek on the same day. Since other parties, particularly the Democratic Turnhalle Alliance

(DTA), were also scheduling demonstrations in the capital at the same time, there would be a need for larger than normal police presence in Windhoek. Cleverly calculating that most police manpower would be diverted to Windhoek for crowd-control purposes, the treacherous attack would be opposed by only a thinly spread and lightly-armed police presence in Owamboland.

SWAPO figured its PLAN terrorists would easily overcome the lightly-armed policemen and establish "bases" while the UN officials kept the South African troops from any retaliatory action.[16]

Unfortunately for SWAPO, the police blunted their attack, and the South Africans, by threatening to tear up the peace agreement and expel the UN from Namibia, received UN permission to remobilize some SWATF units. These units quickly went into action against the invading terrorists now numbering from 1,800 to 1,900 PLAN cadres.

At the end of three days, it was clear that SWAPO had utterly failed with its treacherous gamble, PLAN had suffered huge losses (over 200 killed and many more than that wounded), and was being hunted down by both the police and remobilized SWATF reaction forces from 101 and 201 Battalions. SWAPO's scheme failed because PLAN had utterly failed to carry out its task.

The other two risks SWAPO faced were minimal. Although the attack would break up their peace initiative to the internal parties, that loss would be more than offset by the advantage of being able to intimidate from bases inside Namibia. The least risk was the destruction of the Tripartite regional peace plan agreed to by Angola, Cuba and South Africa on December 22, 1988. Although SWAPO could make a legalistic point by claiming that they weren't a party to the accord, it would be unnecessary as they knew that everyone involved in the process on the side of the West—the UN, South Africa and the United States—would bend over backwards and do anything possible to prevent the peace plan's collapse. SWAPO's little extracurricular invasion might stir up emotions, but the West's pusillanimous desire for peace at any price would not permit it to scrap the accord.

Not only would the West's cowardice not torpedo the peace plan, but it would cause it to turn a blind eye to Soviet, Cuban and Angolan complicity in the attack.

Since Operation REINDEER, over ten years ago, SWAPO bases have been tied in with Angolan Army bases. These FAPLA bases also are home to Soviet and Cuban advisors and their control over FAPLA and SWAPO

---

[16] Hempstone, S., "Nujoma's intimidation trip," *The Washington Times*, April 7, 1989, p.F1.

activities is extensive. SWAPO's logistical system is also integrated with that of FAPLA—again under the watchful eyes of Soviet Bloc advisors.

PLAN terrorists had to move from these bases, pick up their food, ammunition, rockets, mortars, SAM-7 missiles from these integrated supply depots and move south under the watchful eyes of the Soviet, Cuban and Angolan personnel stationed at the bases. For them to claim they didn't know what SWAPO was doing begs credibility. Of course they knew, especially since on the date SWAPO moved south to the attack, they were supposed to be moving in the opposite direction north to the 16th parallel of south latitude as per the December 22nd accord to which both Cuba and Angola were parties.

In addition, the Joint Military Monitoring Commission (JMMC) had ceased to exist on the day before the invasion (March 31, 1989). There were no monitoring forces or posts monitoring movement along the Angolan-Namibian border on the day of the attack. It is interesting to note that the South Africans had long been proposing at least a two-month extension of time for the life of the JMMC, but both Angola and Cuba adamantly opposed any extension of time and insisted upon the JMMC's demise on March 31st. They obviously didn't want any prying eyes observing their marxist comrades-in-arms launching their sneak attack the next day.

There is no direct evidence the UN knew in advance what SWAPO was up to, but the UN did its best to minimize the damage and even half-heartedly tried to help them seize de facto bases in Namibia. The UN hastily admitted that SWAPO did cross the border, but weakly claimed its protege may not have had an "offensive intent."[17] Even after the situation forced the UN to allow the SWATF to use military force against SWAPO, the world body tried to rescue SWAPO. It came up with a compromise plan whereby SWAPO could surrender to hastily flown-in, and no doubt sympathetic UN units, and be interned in UN-supervised camps inside Namibia. This UN scheme was tantamount to giving SWAPO UN-protected bases in Namibia by means of outright UN chicanery.

South African Foreign Minister Botha wisely rejected the UN's devious plan, emphasizing that his government would not allow the guerrillas to remain in Namibia, armed or unarmed.[18]

After a two-day meeting, diplomats from Angola, Cuba, South Africa,

---

[17] *The Washington Post,* April 7, 1989, p.A-16; see also: *The Washington Times,* April 5, 1989, p.A-1.

[18] Claiborne, W., "S. Africa Says Incursions Suspend Namibia Plan," *The Washington Post,* April 8, 1989, p.A-13.

the Soviet Union and the United States, hammered out an agreement whereby SWAPO terrorists would be allowed to pull out of Namibia and return unmolested to Angola.

Not all of the terrorists chose to do so. Those who made the decision to stay were pursued and either killed or captured by the security forces.

And so a fragile, uneasy peace returned to Namibia, but, as syndicated columnist Smith Hempstone pointed out, "But unless the 2,000 guerrillas in the no-go zone return north of the 16th parallel and stay there—they can return to Namibia only if they leave their arms behind—they surely will try again."[19]

SWAPO may succeed the next time. Under the terms of the accord, South Africa must cut its troop presence in Namibia to 1,500 by July 1, 1989, while the Cubans are supposed to withdraw from Angola at a much slower pace. In the meantime, the UN will be in overall charge of security in Namibia and it is highly questionable whether they would intervene militarily to stop a SWAPO invasion.

Why did SWAPO launch such an attack, termed by many diplomatic observers as "ill-advised"? Why not? If SWAPO's gamble had succeeded they could have accomplished four things: (1) given them bases inside Namibia; (2) added credibility and stature to their claim of being liberators of Namibia, as well as friends of the UN; (3) sent a message to Namibia that peace is impossible unless it is on SWAPO's terms; and, (4) might have caused South Africa to cancel the December 22nd Accords. This cancellation would have enabled Cuba to stay in Angola, as she has every intention of doing, but would have put the onus for the breakdown on South Africa.

SWAPO obviously missed the boat on the first two. But it did deliver their no-peace-without-SWAPO message to Namibia and there is still plenty of time remaining for the communists to cook up another reason to keep Cuban forces in Angola.

What did it cost Nujoma: a few hundred dead expendable PLAN terrorists (but then Marxists don't get sentimental over their dead pawns); and some bad publicity for a while but nothing serious because SWAPO still has UN support and recognition. Furthermore, SWAPO hasn't been abandoned by the Soviet Union or the left. SWAPO will just bide their time until this temporary storm blows over and then they will again resume their mischief.

What the SWAPO incursion should tell the West, but it won't, is that there is a king-size question about the effectiveness of the UN in carrying out

[19] Hempstone, *loc. cit.*

the peace plan, conceived during Jimmy Carter's presidency in 1978. Given the UN's past sorry record in Namibia, optimism over the current peace prospects is an exercise in self-delusion.

23
After Independence— Chaos

As Namibia moves towards independence under the terms of UN Resolution 435, what does the future hold? Forecasting the future for anything, much less a newly-independent country, is far from an exact science.

However, an educated guess can be made if it is based upon realistic assumptions. But, until the future arrives, forecasting it remains nothing more than a guess because human beings have an infinite capacity to act in ways least expected of them.

Nevertheless, there are factors and situations involved in the Namibian equation that lead us to say that if such and such happens, then Namibia is likely to follow a certain path. However, if such and such doesn't happen, Namibia will most probably tread a different path.

The pivotal point is the November 1, 1989 elections for a Constituent Assembly to choose delegates to draw up a new constitution for an independent Namibia. There are four possible outcomes, each having a different influence upon Namibia's future.

One possibility is that SWAPO is totally rebuffed at the polls, giving the anti-SWAPO political parties an overwhelming majority in the newly-established Constituent Assembly. With such a majority they could write the Namibian constitution without worrying too much over compromising with SWAPO's Marxist agenda. Such a constitution probably wouldn't differ too much from the one the Multi Party Conference drew up in the mid-1980s.

This scenario would put both SWAPO and the UN in a dilemma. Because the elections are under the sponsorship and supervision of the world body, and SWAPO is its adopted protege, and although the results would be embarrassing to both, they would be hard-pressed to reject the outcome.

The UN plans to sever completely its long-standing recognition and support of SWAPO during the transition period ending in elections for an independent Namibia. They are taking this action, so they claim, to give the appearance of impartiality on their part over the outcome of the elections. This belated action is much like locking the barn door after the horse has gotten out.[1] Ever since the early 1970's, the United Nations has recognized SWAPO and given it much money and support. In fact the United Nations idea of impartiality is such that it gave the UN Council for Namibia $3,935,000 for operating expenses in 1989.[2] The UN's eleventh hour withdrawal of support is almost meaningless and rings hollow as the damage has been done and SWAPO has been linked firmly to the UN in the minds of most Namibians.

SWAPO would risk getting an international black eye from its Western supporters if it rejected the results and returned to the bush to continue its terrorist war—the most likely course of action it would take in such a scenario.

It might also lose its preferred UN status if it returned to its terrorist instincts, although given the makeup of the UN and its long support of SWAPO, it isn't likely SWAPO would fall out of grace with the UN. One thing is sure, if SWAPO felt its survival meant a return to the bush it would certainly do so.

This scenario is least likely to happen given the demographics of Namibia and the cold, hard fact that voting one's tribal loyalty is the first rule of African politics.

The next least likely outcome in the elections is that the voting is so splintered that neither SWAPO or any other political party, or group of parties, commands a majority in the Constituent Assembly. Instead the members are divided among numerous parties and a situation of impotence develops reminiscent of the French Chamber of Deputies in pre-Gaullist France. There so many parties existed and kept squabbling and feuding and forming ever-changing coalitions that for years, the French government accomplished almost nothing of significance.

---

[1] "SWAPO recognition withdrawn by U.N.," *The Washington Times,* February 14, 1989, p.A9.

[2] *435 Watch, Promoting Independence and Democracy For Namibia,* International Freedom Foundation (UK), No. 2, May, 1989, p.4.

Given that there are over forty political parties in Namibia purporting to speak for the 1.2 million people, an innocent observer could conclude that such a splintering effect is possible. If it happened it could certainly paralyze the process of self-government. Again tribal loyalties and demographics dash this scenario to pieces. In point of fact, many of these political parties consist of a few individuals, mostly close friends of the leader who had a disagreement with a pre-existing party he belonged to. He simply left the party, taking his friends and associates, and formed a new splinter party.

The remaining two scenarios are the ones that stand the best chance of happening. One is that SWAPO wins the election, but not by such a margin that it can dictate the writing of the constitution to impose a Marxist one-party state. Under this scenario, they would be forced to negotiate with the other political parties and would not be able to impose their one-party regime in Namibia.

This is the situation that many in Namibia expect will happen.

This scenario is not without danger. For how would SWAPO react if it was forced to share power with the other political parties? A lot would depend upon SWAPO's actions. If it gave up its Marxist program and genuinely entered into a power-sharing arrangement with the other political parties on a basis of mutual respect then the threat of possible problems leading to chaos would certainly diminish.

But even SWAPO taking part as an active member of a pluralistic democratic society will not make Namibia's economic conditions disappear. The problems can be solved but success will require actions and policies that go against SWAPO's long-held positions: an infusion of foreign capital and an economic system based on free enterprise.

That is asking a lot of a political organization that for over twenty years has prided itself on being a true-blue Marxist party. SWAPO has consistently declared publicly that it would "implement socialist economic policies, including the nationalization of industry and mining, with the goal of building a 'classless, nonexploitive society based on the ideals and principles of scientific socialism.' "[3]

The more likely path that SWAPO would take is to enter into a power-sharing arrangement with the other political parties in Namibia but then, in typical Leninist fashion, use that position as a means to subvert and destroy the other political parties.

---

[3] Claiborne, W., "A Free Namibia May Still Have to Rely on S. Africa," *The Washington Post*, December 23, 1988, p.A14.

An independent Namibia is going to face some serious economic problems and have to make some hard choices because of the withdrawal of the South African direct subsidy and its military spending in the country. Foreign investors are not going to rush into Namibia until they are sure that the political climate is stable. Until then the new Namibian government is going to face some belt-tightening which will impose some hardships. Hardships are fertile soil for Marxist-Leninist subversion. Can SWAPO resist such a temptation? Anything is possible. But if not, there is no doubt such subversion could escalate, creating more chaos, to the point that a coup or civil war results. Then SWAPO's enemies would head for the bush knowing they were marked men if they remained where SWAPO could get their hands on them.

A power-sharing situation involving SWAPO and the other political entities in Namibia will only work if SWAPO plays by the rules of the future Namibian consitution and doesn't try to undermine it. This can only happen if they cast aside their Marxist-Leninist program. Only time will tell if this would happen.

The last option is that SWAPO will overwhelmingly win the November elections and to such an extent that it controls the Constituent Assembly. Then it would be able to dictate the writing of the new constitution and will be in a position to write into it its Marxist-Leninist doctrine. There would be no doubt that, under this situation, SWAPO would pay little attention to it political opposition and would impose a one-party state bestowing "scientific socialism" on the people of Namibia. In fact SWAPO spokesman, Daniel Smith, stated in an April 21, 1989, article in the German newspaper *Frankfurter Allegemeine Zeitung* that if SWAPO won the November elections, they would proceed to establish a one-party state and would not necessarily hold further elections.[4]

The reality of the political landscape in Namibia makes the first two situations extremely unlikely. Demographics and tribal loyalties doom them both. Half the population of Namibia are Owambos while ten other ethnic groups make up the other half. Given this fact it is obvious that the Owambos are going to have a major voice in the affairs of an independent Namibia. Their population numbers alone make that point. However, when you add the fact of life of tribalism in Africa to the size of the Owambo population it becomes more apparent that not only will the Owambos have a large say so but they are going to express that by voting for fellow Owambos.

---

[4] *435 Watch, op. cit.*, p.3.

SWAPO is an overwhelmingly Owambo-centered organization. Although its leader, Sam Nujoma, has been out of the country for over twenty years, he is still an Owambo. By this very fact of birth, he and his party have an advantage over the other non-Owambo parties for the votes of his fellow tribesmen.

What about other Owambos running against Nujoma's SWAPO? Few wish to risk the retribution that will follow if they oppose SWAPO and lose. SWAPO has been telling the Owambos for years that they'll be killed if they oppose SWAPO. This fear has been one of the reasons for the lack of Owambo particpation in earlier attempts at self-governing under the Democratic Turnhalle Alliance (DTA) and the Multi-Party Conference (MPC). SWAPO has also been telling the Owambos that they are coming back to Namibia to take power with the UN troops.

SWAPO's unrelenting intimidation tactics have kept many potential Owambos from taking part in past political efforts. This intimidation will continue and even increase with the arrival of the UN.

Intimidation works well in Africa because Africans admire the warrior tradition, which looms large in their heritage. They will gravitate toward the position of strength, as do most people. When you couple this tendency with the fact that losers in Africa often suffer the ultimate loss—their heads—one can see why intimidation can play a decisive role in African politics.

There are parallels in the situation in Namibia today to those preceding the election of Robert Mugabe in Zimbabwe in 1980. Mugabe's powerbase was in the Shona tribe. The Shona tribe, like the Owambos, are the majority ethnic tribal group in Zimbabwe, only more so, comprising eighty percent of the population. Thus the 1980 elections in Zimbabwe turned on who would win the Shona vote Mugabe or Abel Muzorewa.

The British, who had forced this second election within a year on the people of Zimbabwe, were policing the elections. It was their hope that Muzorewa and Mugabe would split the Shona vote and allow the Matabele candidate Joshua Nkomo to become a consensus prime minister.

There was a big joker in the deck, however. Everyone involved knew that Mugabe would do very well in the elections if he were able to use his terrorist network to intimidate the voters in the Shona Tribal Trust Lands. The British assured one and all that they would strictly police the elections and disqualify Mugabe if he attempted to intimidate voters. It was a shallow promise, since Mugabe killed, maimed and terrorized his competition out of the Shona tribal areas and the British didn't lift a finger to stop it. By turning their back on

Mugabe's intimidation tactics, the British tacitly condoned them, paving the way for his ascendency.[5]

A similar situation exists in Namibia although instead of the British making the promises it is the United Nations. The same United Nations that has been funding SWAPO for years and that has declared SWAPO to be the sole authentic representative of the Namibian people.

By their presence in Namibia, the UN forces will add credibility to SWAPO's claims that they are coming to power with the help of the United Nations. In fact the more UN troops they can drag into Namibia the more it reinforces their boast as to how powerful SWAPO is to be able to bring so many troops with them into Namibia. You must remember the vast majority of Owambos live without television or radio coverage such as is experienced in the developed world. All they have seen is that the South Africans and the SWATF were there fighting SWAPO. Now they are gone and SWAPO shows up along with a different variety of soldiers who are not Owambos and are not South Africans. It doesn't take much imagination to see how vulnerable Owambos are to SWAPO's lies. After all, SWAPO had been telling them for some time that the Boers (South Africa's nickname in black Africa) would leave and SWAPO would return along with a different bunch of soldiers. This they have seen happen. Thus what SWAPO has been saying must be true.

While the West may view the UN troops as promoting peace, SWAPO has a more important task for them. They are aids in their psychological war campaign within Namibia. They are status symbols as to the power and prestige of SWAPO. SWAPO needs their presence to give credibility to their claim that they have many and powerful friends who have chased the Boers out of Namibia. This perception, as part of their psychological war is calculated to give the impression that SWAPO is a winner and if you the voter of Namibia know what's good for you, you'll vote for SWAPO.

Much has been made about the size of the two UN peacekeeping forces: one of seventy-five (since increased to almost one-hundred) to verify the Cuban withdrawal from Angola, the other, originally 9,500 (since reduced to 6,100) to verify the South African withdrawal from Namibia. Critics rightfully claim the smaller delegation is too small to oversee the Cuban pullout from Angola. Its size lends itself to Cuban cheating, especially since the United Nations said it would take Cuba's word on the fact that it had withdrawn its forces.

By the same token, the UN originally proposed a 9,500-man contingent

---

[5] Norval, *Red Star, op. cit.,* pp.90-93.

After Independence—Chaos 269

(since reduced) complete with its own transport facilities to check on the South African withdrawal. They obviously won't take South Africa's word on it.

But most critics are overlooking the key point in the UN presence in Namibia and its absence in Angola. SWAPO requires its presence to reinforce its image in Namibia while Angola requires the Cuban presence to enable their Marxist government to stay in power. Thus the fewer outsiders poking their noses into what's going on in Angola, the better Cuba and Angola can simulate the appearance of a Cuban withdrawal.

Why is such a large presence required in Namibia to verify the South African withdrawal? South Africa has few friends in the world and it would lose those if it reneged on its pledged withdrawal from Namibia. If the truth were known, the seventy-five-man contingent assigned to verify the Cuban withdrawal would be more than sufficient to verify the South African withdrawal. The infrastructure of Namibia is such that there are only a few routes out of the country and only a few places inside the country that could support large numbers of troops. Thus watching and counting the South Africans requires few people.

Internal protection of the people is normally a function of the police not the military. If a peaceful situation exists, why do you need soldiers to protect people if both sides have agreed to a cessation of violence? Under UN Resolution 435 the police force in Namibia was not disbanded as was the South West Africa Territorial Force (SWATF). It is large enough to handle the normal peacetime functions in Namibia and protect the people. Why then such a large outside military force?

Sam Nujoma, the head of SWAPO, says ". . . a large United Nations presence is essential to insure free elections in Namibia" and even urged the UN ". . . to consider increasing the force to prevent the Pretoria-controlled security forces from intimidating voters and helping the parties supported by Pretoria."[6] Nujoma was responding to the fact that UN budgetary constraints were forcing a significant reduction in the size of the UN contingent. In fact the size was cut from 9,500 to 6,100 by a unanimous vote of the UN Security Council on February 16, 1989.[7]

Nujoma's reason is nonsense. The SWATF is to be disbanded under the terms of UN Resolution 435, so what Pretoria-controlled security force is he

---

[6] "A Namibian Group opposes UN Cuts," *The New York Times,* January 18, 1989, p.A8.

[7] "UN Security Council Approves Namibia force," *The Washington Times,* February 17, 1989, p.A9; "UN Council Votes Peace Force for Namibia," *The Washington Post,* February 17, 1989, p.A35.

talking about? The 3,000 man police force in Namibia will be dwarfed by SWAPO's over 6,000 terrorists who are suppose to return to Namibia to take part in the independence process. Of course Nujoma is concerned. The reduced number of UN troops seen stumbling around the countryside in Namibia will lessen the image SWAPO has been creating that they have powerful friends in the world who are marching arm in arm with SWAPO to power in Namibia. No wonder Nujoma wants more UN troops. The more there are the more credible becomes his long-repeated claim that the UN will bring SWAPO to power. To a culture that cherishes and admires warriors, the presence of the UN troops from all over the world would tend to reinforce Nujoma's message to the unsophisticated inhabitants of Namibia.

Of a more practical concern to the West is whether the presence of UN troops will guarantee free elections? Or will their presence in Namibia act as it did in the old Belgian Congo over a quarter of a century ago when the UN army became a source of further instability.[8] A better question would be will the UN presence insure an election that is free from intimidation? For it is the presence or absence of intimidation which will determine just how "free" the elections will be in Namibia.

In the United States the thought of gangs of thugs beating, killing and threatening people into voting a certain way is repugnant to all. Yet throughout the world many elections are conducted in this manner, for Africa holds no monopoly on this tactic. Intimidation and terror are stock tools in the Marxist's bag of tricks and SWAPO never blushes at proclaiming itself a true Marxist group.

It is possible, but it stretches credibility, to expect the leopard to change its spots, because for SWAPO to give up intimidation is to throw away its best device for keeping a firm hold on its supporters.

They are already setting up straw men to justify their resort to violence and intimidation by claiming that South Africa is creating "rebel" groups as insurance against a SWAPO electoral victory in Namibia.[9] These alleged groups range from tribal enemies, the Hereros in particular, to 40,000 UNITA supporters purportedly being given false papers to be able to slip into Namibia for whatever reason.[10] The interesting point is that by these

---

[8] Johnson, *op. cit.*, p.516.

[9] "Pretoria Accused of Creating Namibia Rebels," *The New York Times,* January 8, 1989, p.4. Even Jesse Jackson is getting into the act trumpeting the SWAPO line. He claims the South Africans are laying the groundwork for another RENAMO in Namibia. Where did Jackson get his information? He said he based his claim on data he got from SWAPO!—*The New York Times,* January 8, 1989.

[10] *Ibid.*

unsupported accusations SWAPO has laid the groundwork either to blame acts of intimidation on these ghostly groups or to claim that acts of violence they are involved in were merely acts of self-defense against these same groups. (Although these groups don't exist at present, SWAPO activity in the future could lead to their creation, as will be discussed shortly.)

What will the UN most likely do in such a situation? Given the fact of SWAPO's past close association with the UN, they would go through the motions of an investigation, then quietly drop the matter.

Investigating acts of intimidation would not be easy for the UN even if it decided to look into them closely. For one thing, the UN supervisors don't know the area nor the Owambo language. They would be at the mercy of the translators who could be biased either way (pro or anti-SWAPO). Probably the biggest problem they might encounter would be the reluctance on the part of Namibians to get involved in any lengthy bureaucratic-type process. After all, when the elections are over, the UN foreigners will leave and go home while the complaining Namibian must remain to face the wrath of SWAPO. Thus the bulk of the Owambo population will be cowed into silence by acts of intimidation.

The UN, like the British before them in Zimbabwe, will not want their dirty linen aired in public, so if there were widespread intimidation it would tarnish the image of the world body—if that is possible—if its cover-up became widely known. Like the British before them, the UN will turn a blind eye, pretend it didn't happen and forget about it. It will fall back on a long-established characteristc UN double standard: "that whereas the killing of Africans by whites . . . was of international concern and a threat to peace, the killing of Africans by Africans (or of whites by Africans, or of Asians by Africans or all three races by Africans) was a purely internal matter outside the purview of the UN."[11] Such a decision would be supported by the Third World members of the United Nations who are SWAPO supporters anyway.

So the options boil down to the size of the SWAPO victory. But the victory will prove to be a hollow one, for SWAPO must face a very significant problem—governing a country as diverse as Namibia.

SWAPO will find it difficult, if not impossible, to govern Namibia by its own efforts.

SWAPO's base of support is in Owamboland, some 450 kilometers away from the capital Windhoek.

Windhoek is surrounded by enemies of SWAPO, both from an

[11] Johnson, *op. cit.*, p.516.

ideological and cultural basis. The Hereros have been traditional enemies of the Owambos for many scores of years. Most of the Hereros also politically support parties in either the Democratic Turnhalle Alliance (DTA) or their own tribal based, such as South West African National Union (SWANU). They are political opponents of SWAPO.

Most of the whites live in or near Windhoek or in the agricultural areas north of the capital, between it and Owamboland and Kavangoland.

To the south of the capital live the Rehoboth Basters who are also enemies of SWAPO.

As the situation in Angola graphically demonstrates, it is impossible to control a country from just a part of it when you are facing internal armed conflict. In Angola, it is well to recall, the MPLA had the advantage that its original area of support was in the capital and it still holds the capital to this day. Yet by no stretch of the imagination does it control the rest of Angola. SWAPO, unless it were able to transfer the Namibian capital to Oshakati in Owamboland, won't have the MPLA's advantage of having its capital in friendly territory. (Moving the capital to Oshakati, while doing much for Owambo pride, would lessen SWAPO's ability to govern because the town lacks the infrastructure to effectively serve as the capital of the nation. While time and resources could improve the infrastructure problem at Oshakati, diverting scarce resources for such a tribal boondoggle would plunge the rest of Namibia into chaos. Relocating the capital to Oshakati would further isolate the government from the productive areas of Namibia, agricultural, mining and manufacturing, and leave these areas under the influence of SWAPO's opponents.)

SWAPO also lacks the trained manpower to run the government. Although SWAPO can muster over 6,000 terrorists, it takes a different type of individual to be a bureaucrat instead of a terrorist. Although the Namibian Institute in Lusaka has been training SWAPO cadres in governmental administration skills, largely at the UN's expense, their numbers are simply insufficient to take over and smoothly run the levers of government in Namibia.

But, one could ask, what about using the present bureaucrats in the Transitional Government of National Unity? That would be a solution but it ignores two facts: (1) the current bureaucrats are not SWAPO members or supporters; nor, (2) are they Owambos.

No Marxist group taking power is likely to leave its opponents in positions of power in the government they are trying to take over. They want their cadres and party members to take over totally all aspects of the governing apparatus. It would be naive to think SWAPO would be any different. They would not feel secure with a non-SWAPO bureaucracy running their socialist state.

One of their first acts upon assuming power will be to replace all the bureaucrats with their supporters.

This will have both immediate and far-reaching detrimental effects upon Namibia. Government efficiency will fall dramatically right off the bat as the new, inexperienced SWAPO personnel take over. As they gain more experience efficiency may pick up, but it will be offset by the disastrous socialistic schemes that SWAPO says it will impose on the people of Namibia.

Scientific socialism has been a human disaster worldwide, wherever it has been imposed on a society. It is especially harsh on poor impoverished Third World nations. Or it will drive a moderately prosperous Third World country, such as Namibia, into the abyss of poverty, degradation and misery. Given the fragile nature of the Namibian economy SWAPO's dose of Marxism-Leninism would be a fatal blow to Namibia and would be a sure formula for chaos and disaster.[12]

The current crop of bureaucrats are not Owambos and tribal loyalty is strong in African politics.

SWAPO would staff their government of an independent Namibia with loyal SWAPO Owambo people who, at best, would require some time to learn the ropes of administering a national government.

While SWAPO were involved in the mundane tasks of purging and installing their cadres in the governmental structure of the newly independent Namibia, they would have to deal with on-going events that will hasten the process towards destabilization and chaos within Namibia.

One of the first events that would occur when SWAPO takes over and tries to impose a one-party state in Namibia would be a white flight out of the country. This is not such a difficult prediction to make as there have been ample historical precedents in southern Africa in Angola, Mozambique and Zimbabwe. This flight would remove from Namibia, as it did in other countries, the most technologically and managerially skilled workers. Their loss would be a big setback to any economy, but would be especially hard on a fragile economy such as Namibia's.[13]

Marxist rhetoric and politics do not tempt prudent people to invest or participate in ventures that may be nationalized on a moments notice.

Most of the technological and managerial people working in any society,

---

[12] Hempstone, S., "Taking a gamble on Angola," *The Washington Times,* December 23, 1988, p.F1.

[13] Claiborne, *loc. cit.*

ours as well as Namibia's, from a sociological point of view, would be considered as members of the middle class—or the hated bourgeoisie—an object of Marxist scorn and hatred. Why should they remain to be used as scapegoats by a new Marxist regime? Many won't and will vote with their feet by getting out of Namibia taking their skills and expertise with them.

Another initial problem SWAPO will face will be a depressed economy in its own tribal base of Owamboland. The economy of Owamboland for years has benefited from the large presence of South African security force units. The duration and size of the presence has nurtured a growing entrepreneural class that grew up to cater to the mass of soldiers, policemen, administrators and their dependents that were stationed in Owamboland. Numerous small shops and businesses sprang up as a result. Over time Owamboland's economy became enmeshed with that of the security forces and the civic action programs that were part of the counterinsurgency effort. It wasn't only the money spent in pursuing the war by the military, but also the enormous sums that went into civic action programs—schools, roads, water works, etc.—that impacted heavily on the Owamboland economy.

When South Africa pulls out of Namibia that infusion of money into Owamboland, as well as the rest of Namibia, will cease.

The United Nation's presence will be much smaller than the South African was and their stay will be only temporary. Nor will the United Nations be engaged in any programs involving road building, road maintenance, heavy construction, activities that would pump money into the local economy. Thus, the UN will not take up the slack caused by the South African departure. In fact the UN will be forced to buy most of its supplies and equipment from the South Africans, which must gall the hate South Africa crowd.[14]

SWAPO will only exacerbate the problem. In the first place, SWAPO has no money and, indeed, some estimated 16,000 "refugees" will be coming back to Namibia with SWAPO. SWAPO from time to time has quoted the number of refugees at between 55,000 and 60,000 while the South Africans say the figure is closer to 15,000. SWAPO used the inflated figures to get more refugee aid from the UN. The ploy apparently worked, because the UN gave them more than $40 million worth of humanitarian aid between 1977 and 1981.[15] Not all of the refugees are volunteer refugees as many ended up in the SWAPO camps at gunpoint having been abducted and forced to accompany

---

[14] See: Deen, T., "UN proposes reserve peacekeeping stocks," *Jane's Defense Weekly*, February 18, 1989, p.267.

[15] Shultz, *op. cit.*, p.139; see also: Gulich, Thomas, "How the UN Aids Marxist Guerrilla

SWAPO back to Angola. Although SWAPO may count them as refugess to get more UN handouts, they are actually captives as SWAPO did not allow them to go back to Namibia. What is SWAPO going to do with these hijacked Namibians? Their loyalty to SWAPO is certainly questionable and they would be an embarrassment and a potential fifth column if they returned to Namibia to participate in the independence elections.

On the other hand, the genuineness of some of the returning refugees was questioned even by the liberal, pro-SWAPO *The Washington Post*: ". . . several dozen were young, hard-eyed and uncommunicative young men. It appeared likely they were SWAPO guerrillas entering in the guise of noncombatants to begin preparing for an election campaign for a constituent assembly that will form a new government for Namibia, which has been occupied and ruled by South Africa for 74 years.

"SWAPO officials have said privately that SWAPO President Sam Nujoma, who is not expected to return until next month at the earliest, is anxious to establish the presence of combatants to reinforce his contention that the sporadic, 23-year-long guerrilla war that he led was responsible for Namibia's independence.

"The U.S.-brokered regional peace agreement was nearly scuttled on April 1 when an estimated 1,600 heavily armed SWAPO guerrillas crossed the border from Angola and clashed with South African-led counterinsurgency forces. The incursion was viewed as an attempt by Nujoma to create the appearance of a military victory in Namibia.

"South African security sources said they expect the young fighters to return quickly to their homes in the northern Namibian Owambo tribal area, don camouflage fatigues with SWAPO insignia and make themselves visible to bolster SWAPO's chances of winning a two-thirds majority in the election."[16]

To ease the returning refugees return, they are being processed through five centers in Namibia. These centers are being run by the Council of Churches of Namibia (CCN). Since the CCN is an organization closely affiliated with SWAPO, SWAPO will be able to start its politicizing and intimidation in the refugee centers under the benevolent protection of the

---

Groups," *Heritage Foundation Backgrounder*, 1982, pp.8-10; UN Document A/135/178, pp.4-9; UN Document A/AC 109/PV.1173, pp.22-26; UN Document A/135/178, pp.33-34; UN Document A/135/178/Add.I, pp.2-9; LaBarbera, P., "Namibia may have bilked refugee agency of millions," *The Washington Times,* May 24, 1989, p.A-4.

[16] Claiborne, W., "Namibian Exiles Begin to Return Home," *The Washington Post,* June 13, 1989.

CCN who will limit access to the refugees by other groups in Namibia.[17]

Most of the refugees will be returning to Owamboland adding their demands for goods and services to the current residents. What money SWAPO has will be spent in implementing and carrying out its power grab and political policies. There will be precious little left to spend propping up the capitalistic economy that sprang up in Owamboland as a result of their terrorist war.

SWAPO will find themselves facing a full-scale recession in Owamboland which they cannot ignore as it would erode their tribal power base. So they will have to borrow from Peter to pay Paul and divert money being spent on projects in other parts of Namibia to bail out the recession in Owamboland.

This will hurt and depress the areas they diverted the money from. As they shift from here to plug a gap there, before they know it they'll have managed to depress the economy all over Namibia and, at the same time, alienated non-Owambo ethnic groups that weren't too friendly with them in the first place.

Nor can an independent Namibia, especially if it's SWAPO controlled, expect any subsidies from South Africa. During the past ten years South Africa was spending about $1.5 million per day (That works out to over $1 per day per resident of Namibia.) in Namibia. This included direct subsidies to the SWA/Namibian government and all their military spending in fighting the war against SWAPO. Now all that spending is history.

Nor can SWAPO turn to her allies in the Soviet Bloc for financial assistance. They are all having problems of their own and economic assistance has seldom been part of their way of doing things—guns yes, butter no. Only the West can bail them out, but SWAPO's Marxist policies should discourage needed Western investment.

The economic future of a SWAPO-controlled Namibia contains nothing more than a formula for disaster.

SWAPO's policies will also have detrimental politico-social problems as well. Like Robert Mugabe in Zimbabwe, Sam Nujoma has made no bones about his plan to impose a one-party Marxist state upon the people of Namibia.

What will happen to the other political parties in Namibia. A one-party state obviously means only one political party will be permitted to operate in the state. This means the others will have to go. Will the non-SWAPO parties in Namibia meekly accept their fate? Some of the small splinter ones will no doubt realize they are to small to resist SWAPO and either disband, cut a deal with SWAPO or ally themselves with a stronger opposition party. But the

After Independence—Chaos

larger ones, such as South West African National Union (SWANU), which are made up almost entirely of Hereros are not likely to roll over and play dead for their traditional enemies. The very real possibility exists that if push comes to shove, they will resort to arms to settle their differences. They will go into the bush and fight. As mentioned earlier, SWAPO and its mouthpieces, such as Jesse Jackson in the US, have already started accusing South Africa of setting up "rebel" groups to destabilize any SWAPO-controlled Namibian government. Andimba Toivio, secretary general of SWAPO, even went to the extreme of accusing UNITA of providing guerrilla training to several hundred Herero tribesmen loyal to Moses Katjiujonga, the head of SWANU.[18] Toivio's charges are rubbish. UNITA has its hands full fighting FAPLA and its Soviet Bloc advisors and doesn't have the time or the resources to train several hundred people, at considerable expense, to fight in Namibia. Cooking up "rebel" groups in Namibia would wreck South Africa's diplomatic outreach to black Africa and the rest of the world as the stakes are too high to get involved in such high-risk activities.

The complaints, though, do show that SWAPO realizes that taking and hold power in Namibia is not going to be an easy task and it will probably have to be sorted out in terms of blood and bullets.

SWAPO's manpower situation is such that it couldn't resist very well on its own if the other parties formed a united front and took to the bush and fought them. Namibia is a big country and Nujoma's 6,000 terrorists would be hard-pressed to simultaneously protect their power base in Owamboland and try to stamp out rebellion by groups whose strongholds would be many kilometers distant.

Nor could SWAPO turn its back on Owamboland for there are many disgruntled former members of SWATF who were forced out of their well-paying jobs as soldiers by UN Resolution 435, as its terms forced the SWATF to disband. At least 5,000 of these were Owambos who have received extensive military training and would be excellent recruits for any anti-SWAPO guerrilla group in Namibia. SWAPO will have to be worried about this potential "fifth column" in its midst.

Unlike Zimbabwe where Mugabe's tribal base was so overwhelming that he was able to crush his opposition, the Owambos are not an overwhelming tribal majority in Namibia. Geography would hinder them in their attempt to crush a concerted rebellion, especially one involving the Hereros.

[17] *435 Watch,* No. 2, May, 1989, p.1.
[18] *The New York Times,* January 8, 1989.

From a military point of view, the attempt to fight the rebels would be mounted by SWAPO from their powerbase in Owamboland (assuming SWAPO tried to crush their opposition without outside help). It could prove to be a monumental task.

In the first place the terrain between Owamboland and the target area lends itself well to guerrilla hit and run tactics.

The logistical problems would be immense. Where would SWAPO get its supplies from? Shipping them to her through Namibia would pose problems. The only deep water port in Namibia is Walvis Bay which is South African territory.

The rail and road network in Namibia won't ease SWAPO's problems either. The railroads run north from South Africa and the closest rail terminal to Owamboland is Tsumeb, over two-hundred kilometers away. There is only one paved road that runs north from Tsumeb through Owamboland.

Without South African support, SWAPO would be unable to utilize to its advantage the railroads in Namibia to bring in their supplies. Likewise any offensive against rebel strongholds in central Namibia would have to use the lone paved road out of Owamboland as its main supply route.

SWAPO's supply route would depend upon its neighbor to the north. Their supplies would have to come in through the Angolan ports of Lobito or Namibe, travel southward over Angola's crumbling roads to Namibia where it would flow down the one paved road to where SWAPO could mount operations against its enemies.

This fragile route would be easy to attack and cut by rebellious anti-SWAPO guerrillas which would compound SWAPO's problems. They would have to devote more of their scarce resources of men and material to the task of protecting their logistical route. This would drain manpower away from pursuing and fighting their enemies. This, in turn, would diminish considerably SWAPO's ability to contain the rebellion leaving it two options: either give up and make peace with its political opponents or ask for outside help.

Following the first option would in all likelihood permanently cripple SWAPO as a political force in Namibia as it would be an admission of failure.

The second option would escalate tensions in the region and invite South African intervention because the most likely help for SWAPO would come from Cuba. Castro has long indicated a willingness to keep his forces in southern Africa, in spite of any Angolan withdrawal pledge. In September 1986, well over two years before Cuba signed the Angolan withdrawal pact, Castro announced at the Non-aligned Conference in Harare, Zimbabwe that

Cuban personnel would not leave Angola "until there is an end to apartheid and Fascist rule in South Africa."[19]

An independent Namibia, governed by SWAPO, would have the sovereign right to invite Cuban, or any other forces, to enter Namibia to come to its aid.

Castro has boasted that his forces have not only altered the balance of power in Angola, causing the the South African's to agree to implement UN Resolution 435, but that he was ready to invade Namibia to rid it of the South African presence.[20]

A Marxist Namibia would certainly find Cuba more than willing to come to its aid to prop up another Marxist regime, as it did in Angola. It could even retread the same old tired cliches it used several years ago as its justification for intervention—to protect the new regime from the meddling of the hated South Africans, etc.

The presence of South African forces at Walvis Bay would pose a threat to any Cuban expeditionary force in Namibia. The enclave would be a dagger pointing at the heart of the country. From it South Africa could lauch attacks upon the flanks and rear of Cuban and SWAPO forces operating in central Namibia. The South Africans could use the rail and road network leading from Walvis Bay that links with the rest of the road and rail network in Namibia to supply their military effort.

How would the Cubans deal with this problem?

They could assure South Africa that their quarrel is not with them, but with SWAPO's opponents and promise to repect the territorial integrity of Walvis Bay.

Or they could feel Walvis Bay is too big a danger, but too far from South Africa's heartland to be adequately defended and supplied and decide to "liberate" it. In Cuban hands, it would no longer be a threat from their rear, but it would open a more reliable supply route to their forces in central Namibia. Since SWAPO has long claimed Walvis Bay as part of Namibia, they could appeal to their friends in the United Nations and socialist commonwealth for their support in the "liberation" of the territory from South Africa and their further acts of repression in Namibia.

---

[19] Sparks, A., "Gadhafi, Iranian perplex Nonaligned," *The Washington Post,* September 3, 1986, p.4; see also: Goure, L., "Cuba as an Instrument of Soviet International Policy," *American Review,* Institute for American Studies, Rand Afrikaans University, Johannesburg, 1989, p.5.

[20] See: Brooke, J., "Cuba's wider role checks Angola," *The New York Times,* May 17, 1988, p.3; Bodansky, Y., "Cuban strategy: A wild card in Angolan war," *Jane's Defense Weekly,* July 9, 1988, p.24.

South Africa, although basing its claim to Walvis Bay on the niceties of international law, would soon discover its arguments falling on deaf ears. Only force would decide the issue and South Africa's ability to retain Walvis Bay could depend upon the degree of assistance rendered Cuba by their Soviet Bloc comrades. A naval blockade by elements of the Soviet Union, for example, might doom the South African enclave.

Whether such action would cause an escalation of tension between the West and the Soviet Union is problematical. Of course, one would expect there would be the usual protests by the U.S. State Department, but, given the usual cowardice of the West, it is unlikely those protests would translate into open support of South Africa's position vis-a-vis Walvis Bay. The West would leave South Africa twisting slowly in the wind.

The Republic of South Africa would clearly have a national security interest with regard to the presence of foreign troops—especially Cubans—on its northern border, just across the Orange River. They could not allow the Cubans to freely roam around Namibia with impunity or to give support to destabilization efforts within South Africa. A Cuban presence in Namibia would represent a clear and present danger to the stability of South Africa and would be guaranteed to cause an escalation of tension in the region.

As demonstrated earlier in this book, the Cubans were not "legitimately" invited into Angola at the "request" of the MPLA government. In fact, there was no government at all and the action of the Cubans in Angola ensured that there would be no government, as envisioned by the Alvor Agreement, at all.

The Cubans came to Angola and southern Africa over thirteen years ago. They will remain, in spite of American diplomatic activity and their pledge to leave and they will wait for the summons to Namibia to take part in Castro's final fight against South Africa.

Until all Cuban forces are out of the southern African region, there is little hope for a solution to the civil war in Angola and even less for a lasting peaceful solution to the independence of Namibia.

SWAPO's insistence on turning Namibia into a one-party state would be not merely chaotic, but would plunge the country into a bloody civil war. Such an event would be disruptive to the social, economic and political fabric of any nation, let alone a sparsely populated newly-independent desert country like Namibia, where climate and geography have combined to make existence precarious in the best of times.

24
Repairing the Damage

Namibia faces a very uncertain future with the odds leaning towards chaos and instability. However, stability is possible if four conditions are present: (1) political tolerance, (2) protection of individual and ethnic cultural diversity, (3) economic freedom, and (4) non-interference from foreign countries. Given the country's past turbulent history, that is a big order.

The new Namibian government could well profit from the bitter examples of political intolerance and instability that are endemic to sub-Saharan Africa. Given the country's diversity of people, new political institutions must practice tolerance and great flexibility. The type of political system that Namibia eventually adopts must be compatible with the socio-economic system in existence. Some form of representative democracy would have the necessary degree of flexibility to achieve that goal. A one-party overly centralized state would be disastrous to the future well-being of Namibia.

Namibia is a blend of Western and African cultures. The West contributed the theory of individual rights while the African heritage provided ethnic pride and cultural diversity. Both should be protected and respected. Even though the individual is the ultimate base of society and his rights must be paramount, most Namibians cherish the unique ethnic richness of the African culture. Neither should be suppressed for the advantage of the other. Again, a one-party centralized society based on the Marxist-Leninist model would be poison to both cultures.

A flexible, tolerant society and government of the type envisioned by the Transitional Government of National Unity (TGNU) seems to fit the situation in a newly-independent Namibia.

Toleration implies allowing the existence of a loyal opposition. It must be kept in mind, however, that the concept of a loyal opposition is a Western one that is contrary to African traditions. As the history of post-colonial Africa gruesomely shows, in most African countries any opposition was suppressed as soon as possible after gaining independence. In fact the notion of a loyal opposition survives in its pure form in only two countries on the continent: Botswana and South Africa. It may be a forlorn hope that the seeds of self-government and toleration planted in the Namibian political soil in the past decade will survive Namibian independence. If they can survive, opposition in the country need not suffer under the normal African fashion of oppression and dictatorial rule.

Would SWAPO, presuming it either loses the elections or doesn't control the constitution writing process, be willing to admit it was time to give up its military campaign to seize power and enter the political arena?

To do so would be to officially abandon their armed struggle and, in essence, admit defeat, with all the humiliation of now working alongside the very "traitors" and "puppets" they'd been excoriating and fighting in the past.

Would the "Old Guard" present top leaders of SWAPO, who have spent over a quarter of a century in self-imposed exile outside the country, be willing to trade their current exalted status as revolutionaries on the world stage to become mere politicians in Namibia? It would require a monumental change in attitude on the part of Nujoma and his cronies—something they have not demonstrated in the past.

Yet, human beings have an infinite capacity to change, so anything is possible—even a change of long-standing attitudes by the current SWAPO leadership.

Without this monumental change, however, a dark cloud would continue to hang over the future of an independent Namibia, with the real threat of SWAPO returning to its pattern of violence.

Namibia's economy, though prosperous by African standards, is still fragile, given the demographic, climatic, and geographic facts of life in the country. The post-independence economic system must be one that will build on the current system and not tear it to shreds. A Marxist economic system, as espoused by SWAPO, would ensure only the equal misery of all Namibians.

Last, but certainly not least, the outside world, while guaranteeing Namibia's independence, should keep their collective noses out of Namibian internal affairs. This is especially true of the UN.

It should be quite evident by now the United Nations is one of the major problems in insuring a stable future for an independent Namibia. Much has been made of the UN claim to be a neutral party. Far from it, as shown throughout this work, the UN is not only an advocate for SWAPO, but gives it a variety of aid and support.

It is naive to hope that any future stable regime could evolve and enjoy peace and prosperity in Namibia as long as its acceptability depends upon the good graces of the UN. Given the moral corruption and hypocritical degeneracy into which the world body has fallen, the UN is not likely to approve any regime that doesn't mirror its distorted and corrupt view.

From an international body formed after the Second World War to promote international peace, the UN has degenerated into little more than a sanctimonious mutual-protection society of various gangster and beggar states. These states consistently cooperate with the Soviet Union and almost reflexively pursue anti-Western programs.

Since the mid-fifties, beginning with the appointment of then UN Secretary General Dag Hammarskjold, the UN has drifted further and further into an anti-American and anti-Western stance. Hammarskjold's intentions, as historian Paul Johnson tells us, were ". . . to cut the umbilical cord which linked the UN to the old wartime Western alliance, and to align the organization with what he regarded as the new emergent force of righteousness in the world: the 'uncommitted.' "[1]

The "uncommitted," however, have become very committed. Indeed, their commitment is decidedly anti-American, anti-Western and invariably pro-Soviet in its policies.

In 1960, using the occasion when seventeen new nations—sixteen of them from Black Africa—became independent and joined the UN, the Soviets hypocritically called for the independence of all peoples—except those in their Soviet "republics"—and denounced all forms of colonialism—except their own.[2] The Soviets, by this act, threw their support to Hammarskjold's new, emerging anti-Western "uncommitted" members of the UN. As the Sovietologist Alvin Rubenstein notes, "the USSR has taken to bloc politics in the UN with a vengeance, exploiting voting majorities to weaken the West and advocate Soviet proposals and preferred resolutions . . ."[3]

In 1961, the General Assembly established the Special Committee on the Situation with Regard to the Implementation of the Declaration on the

---

[1] Johnson, *op. cit.*, p.494.

[2] See: Rubenstein, A., *Soviet Foreign Policy Since World War II: Imperial and Global,* Winthrop, Cambridge, MA, 1981, p.196.

[3] Shultz, *op. cit.*, p.35.

Granting of Independence to Colonial Countries and Peoples (known as the Committee of 24). This committee has been virulently anti-Western and has most often proposed UN policies and activities that conflict with accepted international practice and even go against the founding principles of the UN itself, further undermining the rapidly declining reputation of the world body.

By the early seventies the rot had set in to the extent that the committee's resolutions and policies became the handiwork of a coalition of communist and anti-Western, Afro-Asian states. So radical and outlandish had it become that both the United States and Great Britain quit the Committee in disgust.

Under the impetus and prodding of the Committee of 24, which considers its resolutions binding on all other UN entities, other UN agencies began to implement its policies. As a result, as described earlier, SWAPO has reaped a treasure trove of UN support. Like a drug addict, it is hooked and virtually dependent upon the UN. To expect the world body to turn its back on the terrorist group it has supported and nurtured for years is an exercise in self-delusion.

Thus we have the sorry spectacle of what should be an exercise in democracy and self-government—a referendum of the people of Namibia— presided over and under the control of a corrupt body whose interest in democracy is wholly rhetorical. The UN is running this show primarily for the benefit of its protege SWAPO, who represents the interests of the people of Namibia about as much as a Mafia family represents the interests of the people of the City of New York.

To add insult to injury, the United States, the model for republican representative democracy in the world, has been a party to this corrupt proceeding.

Bad as this corrupt process is, it totally overlooks a more pertinent point: who gave the UN the moral right to pass judgment on the kind of a government a people may choose for themselves? Given the nature of the regimes that overwhelmingly populate the UN, their moral posturing over Namibia is grotesque.

The UN responds to that question on the shaky presumption that the unfinished business of the League of Nations became the UN's business. But that begs the essential question of whose right it is to decide how a people will be governed: the people themselves or an outside body? From a liberal Western democratic perspective, the question provides its own answer. Yet the UN feels differently on the matter, as evidenced by its lengthy interference in internal Namibian affairs. It is has consistently tried to force the people of Namibia to do its bidding, with the tacit, cowardly acquiesence of the West. It is a formula for continuing chaos and misery in Namibia.

Although it has nurtured SWAPO for years, the UN must resist the temptation to keep "checking up" on the Namibian situation, with or without SWAPO. If SWAPO loses the election the UN can doubtless be counted on to increase its interference in the internal affairs of Namibia.

What can be done so that the flame of liberty and freedom is not snuffed out in Namibia? In an ideal world the most obvious solution would be to get the UN entirely out of the internal independence process in Namibia. Unfortunately, that idea is doomed. Too many political and diplomatic careers would suffer if that happened. So the process will just drift along until disaster and chaos become firmly entrenched in Namibia.

That is the true tragedy of Namibia. For as long as the UN has the final say on Namibian independence that country faces a bleak future. No amount of sanctimonious diplomatic, political or editorial posturing will alter it one iota. The people of that troubled land deserve better.

The hypocrites in the UN have been responsible for enough misery in the country, so what can be done to minimize the damage? If the UN can't keep its nose out of Namibian affairs, the West, in particular the United States, should make sure it does. How? By cutting our monetary contribution to the world body if it doesn't get the message.

The United States must also firmly tell the Soviets that their support of subversion in newly-independent Namibia will not be tolerated. This warning should carry teeth: no trade or loans if the Soviets continue their old ways of subversion. If the free world will let the Soviets stew in their own odious, rotten, socialistic juices, they'll be too preoccupied with their own internal problems to be meddling in other people's business. Without this real threat the Soviets will not be able to resist the temptation to stir up trouble in Namibia. Moscow has made heavy political and financial investments in the past in subversion. To back down on this policy, would put the Soviets in the same basket as the U.S.—not living up to its

[4] Johns, M., "Peace in Our Time," *Policy Review,* The Heritage Foundation, Summer, 1987, p.69.

commitments. The only way to change Soviet behavior is to make the cost of subversion higher than its expected gains. The sure way to do this is to not bail out the Soviets and make the Kremlin use all its own resources to try and keep things together in the workers' paradise.

This will require a change of attitude on the part of the U.S. government away from its "culture of appeasement"[4] to a firm defense of the values and interests of the United States. If the people of Namibia can attain a western-style representative democracy, that is certainly in the interests of the United States. Their fledging efforts should be protected from the assaults of those anti-Western groups such as the UN and the USSR.

Moreover, the United States should also refrain from interfering in the internal affairs of Namibia. By being accomplices in numerous UN actions, America must share the guilt for the UN-induced misery of the people of Namibia over the last ten years. American diplomats will doubtless not be as readily inclined to meddle in Namibian internal affairs as when they were henchmen of the UN, but U.S. policies can easily cripple a fledgling Namibia indirectly and just as destructively. By continuing or escalating the economic war against South Africa, the U.S. will hinder economic development in Namibia. Since Namibia can no more halt its economic dependence on South Africa than Canada can on the U.S., any acts of economic war against South Africa will also affect Namibia, not to mention other independent nations in southern Africa.

If the U.S. is serious in helping newly-independent Namibia become a viable economic entity, it should end its unproductive sanctions campaign against South Africa. Instead it should encourage private investment throughout the southern African region. Investment, not political posturing, will be the salvation of Namibia and the rest of southern Africa.

American meddling, destructive as it may be to Namibia's economic well-being, pales beside the potential destructiveness of Soviet-directed subversion. An independent Namibia can look in that direction for the prime source of looming trouble, especially if the new government is non-SWAPO.

A free and independent Namibia need not fear subversion from its neighbors Botswana or South Africa. In spite of the verbal fog of the left, South African action on the territory of its neighbors has been to strike at terrorist bases operating out of, and often with the protection of, these neighbors. The South Africans have concentrated their attention and actions on the terrorist groups and not on destabilizing or overthrowing the host governments—Angola, Botswana and Mozambique. South Africa's actions were no different than those of the United States when pursuing Apaches into Mexico in the 1880s or chasing Pancho Villa back into Mexico prior to World War I. The presence of American troops in Mexico in both instances was not to overturn the Mexican government or conquer the country, but to take action against forces that had committed hostile acts on American soil who sought immunity from reprisals by fleeing across the international border into Mexico.

It will surely be a Marxist regime that threatens the economic and political future of an independent Namibia. The target will tempt the expansionary and subversive nature of its Marxist-Leninist neighbor. Namibia has far more to fear from communist Angola than it does from its non-Marxist neighbors to the south and east. And well the Namibians should worry, because of the presence of the Cubans, who are a rule unto themselves in Angola.

Fidel Castro, who publicly disagrees with Comrade Gorbachev over the Soviet policy of *glasnost*, fancies himself as the keeper of the flame of pure Marxist-Leninist revolutionary dogma. He has made no secret of his boast that his soldiers are in Africa to liberate Namibia and South Africa for the forces of world communist revolution.[5] He is the loose cannon rolling around the southern African deck. As long as Cuban forces are on the scene, a real danger exists to the security and stability of a free and independent Namibia. The march of the Cuban legions south from Angola would again soak the sands of Namibia with the blood of those seeking their freedom.

Whether Cuban intervention will occur is unknown as there is a slight breeze stirring about the world that is, nevertheless, starting to shake the corrupt foundation of Marxist-Leninist socialism. That breeze is individual freedom and economic liberty. It is stirring even in the heart of darkness itself—the Soviet Union—and has picked up astonishing strength in the People's Republic of China. As the people of these Marxist bodies inhale more and more of its sweet breath, their political systems may become fatally infected with the virus of freedom, with irreversible political and economic consequences.

If this breeze picks up and turns into a gale, the resulting stiff winds of

---

[5] Goure, *op. cit.*, p.5.

change will blow away the odious and absurd ideology of Marxism-Leninism and dump it on the ash heap of history, right where it belongs. When that happens the people of Namibia, and millions of others throughout the world, can peaceably determine their own futures and secure for themselves the blessings of freedom.

Appendix A
United Nations Security Council Resolution 435

Resolution 435 (1978) of 29 September 1978
The Security Council,
1. *Recalling* its resolutions 385 (1976) of 30 January 1976 and 431 (1978) and 432 (1978) of 27 July 1978,
2. *Having considered* the report of the Secretary-General submitted pursuant to paragraph 2 of resolution 431 (1978)[1] and his explanatory statement made in the Security Council on 29 September 1978 (S/12869),[2]
3. *Taking note* of the relevant communications from the Government of South Africa to the Secretary-General,
4. *Taking note also* of the letter dated 8 September 1978 from the President of the South West Africa People's Organization to the Secretary-General,[3]
5. *Reaffirming* the legal responsibility of the United Nations over Namibia,

    1. *Approves* the report of the Secretary-General on the implementation of the proposal for a settlement of the Namibian situation[4] and his explanatory statement;

    2. *Reiterates* that its objective is the withdrawal of South Africa's illegal administration from Namibia and the transfer of power to the people of

[1] United Nations document S/12827.
[2] Thirty-third Year, 2087th meeting, paras. 11-22.
[3] Supplement for July, August and September, 1978, document S/12841.
[4] Supplement for April, May and June 1978, document S/12636.

Namibia with the assistance of the United Nations in accordance with Security Council resolution 385 (1976);

3. *Decides* to establish under its authority a United Nations Transition Assistance Group in accordance with the above-mentioned report of the Secretary-General for a period of up to 12 months in order to assist his Special Representative to carry out the mandate conferred upon him by the Security Council in paragraph 1 of its resolution 431 (1978), namely, to ensure the early independence of Namibia through free elections under the supervision and control of the United Nations;

4. *Welcomes* the preparedness of the South West Africa People's Organization to co-operate in the implementation of the Secretary- General's report, including its expressed readiness to sign and observe the cease-fire provisions as manifested in the letter from its President of 8 September 1978;

5. *Calls upon* South Africa forthwith to co-operate with the Secretary-General in the implementation of the present resolution;

6. *Declares* that all unilateral measures taken by the illegal administration in Namibia in relation to the electoral process, including unilateral registration of voters, or tranfer of power, in contravention of resolutions 385 (1976), 431 (1978) and the present resolution, are null and void;

7. *Requests* the Secretary-General to report to the Security Council not later than 23 October 1978 on the implementation of the present resolution.

Adopted at the 2087th meeting by 12 votes to none, with 2 abstentions (Czechoslovakia, Union of Soviet Socialist Republics).[5]

---

[5] One member (China) did not participate in the voting.

Appendix B
The Windhoek Declaration of Basic Principles

We, the political leaders of the people of South West Africa/Namibia, meeting in the Third Plenary Session of the historic Multi Party Conference, hereby:
- reaffirm the right of our people to national self-determination and independence and our determination to strive for a free, democratic, peaceful, stable and prosperous SWA/Namibia. It is only this goal—the national interest—and this goal alone, which will henceforth guide our actions.
- also reaffirm that Security Council Resolution 435 is at present the only concrete plan on independence which is being accepted by South Africa, the Security Council and the members of the Western Contact Group. Having discussed the many problems confronting our country, in a constructive spirit of frankness, national reconciliation and unity, mutual respect and accommodation, we hereby declare to our people and the world at large that the Multi Party Conference:
- maintains that SWA/Namibia is one and indivisible. SWA/Namibia belongs to all its people who are willing to stay here, build and defend it.
- believes in the concept that All men are created equal and shall have equal rights and responsibilities irrespective of their national origin, race, religion or political views. The people of SWA/Namibia must work together for the common cause of nation-building, and common economic progress.
- takes cognizance of the fact that it may take an indefinite period of time

before Resolution 435 can be implemented, because its implementation is linked to the demand for the withdrawal of Cuban forces from Angola by both South Africa and the USA.
- hopes that the Lusaka Agreement between Angola and South Africa will last to enable a discussion of the wider issues of a Namibia/South West African settlement and peaceful co-existence among the states within the region as a basis for resolving local and inter-state problems as well as a return to normal and peaceful life for the inhabitants of the war-ridden territories.

Our contribution to the resolution of the problems which have given rise to instability and security concerns would be to use the ceasefire agreement in a responsible and constructive manner in order to finally eliminate the causes of social and political confrontation.

An extensive dialogue among the relevant political parties of this country, in a spirit of national reconciliation and the need for a speedy resolution of the independence dispute, and meaningful negotiations with the Government of South Africa and the international community should be considered the primary concern and objective of all the patriotic and concerned leaders and citizens of our country.

Therefore the Multi Party Conference accepts the challenge
- to lead our country to a nationally acceptable and internationally recognized independence.
- to conduct talks and/or negotiations with interested bodies in preparation and implementation of the aforesaid aims, as and when demanded by circumstances. Such talks and/or negotiations will include appeals for the immediate release of Mr. Toivo ya Toivo and Mr. Eliazer Tuhadeleni and all other political prisoners and detainees wherever they might be.
- to conduct investigations regarding the possibility of entering into relations with neighboring and other states with the view to own security and other strategic matters such as cooperation in the areas of health, finance, agriculture and veterinary services, water and energy, physical development, transport, etc. In this connection the issue of Walvis Bay and the borders of SWA/Namibia will be the subject of discussion between the future governments of SWA/Namibia and the Republic of South Africa.
- to draft a permanent constitution
- within the framework of Phase 1 of the Western Settlement Plan
- consistent with the Universal Declaration of Human Rights
- in accordance with the International Covenant of Civil and Political Rights
- which will allay the fears and respect the aspirations, ambitions and desires

Appendix B

of the different groups mentioned in the Covenant above.
- to create an economic order which aims at decreasing our dependence on foreign countries by developing and diversifying our economy mainly through our own efforts and improving the quality of life in our people in all fields—from employment opportunities, health, education and housing to the rural economy. Both the public and private sectors as well as foreign investment must serve this purpose. A sound, healthy and strong economy must be the basis of our economic thinking.
- to pursue a foreign policy based on dignity, independence, peace and friendship and peaceful co-existence with our neighbors and the rest of the world to reserve our right to act as we see best at any particular time and on any particular issue. Our own national interest and the behavior of others toward our country will form the basis of our foreign policy.

Appendix C
Bill of Fundamental Rights and Objectives

PREAMBLE
Independence:
Whereas we, the people of SWA/Namibia, desire *Independence* free from outside domination and direction and wish to constitute our own government; **Peace, Reconciliation:**
Whereas we likewise urgently desire national *Reconciliation* and lasting *Peace;* **Individual Rights:**
Whereas we are united in the belief that all men are born free and equal and endowed by their Creator with human dignity and inalienable *Rights;*
Diversity:
Whereas lasting peace, stability and progress depend on the recognition of and respect for the rights of all in the prevailing cultural, linguistic and religious *Diversity* of our society;
Unity:
Whereas it is the desire of the people to achieve *Unity* in that diversity with common loyalties to a single state;
Purpose and Powers of Government:
Whereas Governments are instituted among men for the *Purpose* of promoting the safety and welfare of the people, from whose consent those governments derive their *Powers* and capacities;
Now Therefore, we, the people of SWA/Namibia, claim and reserve for ourselves and guarantee to our descendents the following Fundamental Rights which shall be respected and upheld by our successive governments and protected by entrenchment in the Constitution.

FUNDAMENTAL RIGHTS
ARTICLE 1
The Right to Life
Everyone has the right to life. No one shall be arbitrarily deprived of his life. The sentence of death may only be executed pursuant to a final judgment by a competent court in respect of the most serious crimes in accordance with the Law. Nothing in this article shall be invoked to prevent the abolition of capital punishment by any future Government should they decide to do so.
ARTICLE 2
The Right to Liberty, Security of Person and Privacy
No one shall be subject to arbitrary arrest or detention. No one shall be deprived of his liberty except on such grounds and in accordance with such procedures as are established by Law.

No one shall be detained for an indefinite period of time without a fair and proper trial by a court.

No one shall be subjected to torture or to cruel, inhumane or degrading treatment or punishment.

No one shall be subjected to arbitrary interference with his privacy, the privacy of his home, correspondence or communications. Everyone has the right to the protection of the Law against such interference.
ARTICLE 3
The Right to Equality before the Law
Everyone shall be equal before the law and no branch or organ of government nor any public institution may prejudice nor afford any advantage to any person on the grounds of his ethnic or social origin, sex, race, language, colour, religion or political conviction.
ARTICLE 4
The Right to a Fair Trial
4.1 In the determination of his rights and obligations in a civil action and of any criminal charges against him, everyone is entitled to a fair and public hearing by an independent, impartial and competent court established by Law: provided that such a court may exclude the press and the public for all or any part of the trial, for reasons of morals, the public order or national security. Any judgement rendered in a criminal or civil action shall be made public, except where the interest of juvenile persons otherwise requires.

Everyone charged with an offense has the right to be presumed innocent until proven guilty according to Law after having had the opportunity of presenting witnesses in his favour and cross-examining those testifying against him. Everyone shall be afforded adequate time and facilities for the preparation and presentation of his defense, before the commencement of and during his trial. Everyone shall have the right of access to legal counsel in the event of charges being preferred against him.

4.2 No one shall be tried, convicted or punished again for an offense which he has already been tried and convicted or acquitted in accordance with the Law.

4.3 No one shall be tried or convicted for an offense on account of an act or omission which did not constitute an offense at the time at which it was committed, nor shall a penalty be imposed exceeding that which was applicable at the time when the offense was committed.

ARTICLE 5
The Right to Freedom of Expression

Everyone has the right to freedom of expression of opinion, conscience and religious belief, including freedom to seek, receive and impart information and ideas through the press and other media. This right shall be limited only by the obligation to ensure that such expression does not infringe upon the right of others, impair the public order or morals, or constitute a threat to national security.

ARTICLE 6
The Right to Peaceful Assembly

Everyone has the right to freedom of assembly for peaceful purposes. No restrictions shall be placed on this right except those which, being necessary for the protection of public order, health or morals or the rights of others, are properly prescribed by law.

ARTICLE 7
The Right to Freedom of Association

Everyone has the right to associate with any other person or group. No one may be compelled or prevented to associate with others. Everyone has the right to form and to join trade unions for the protection of the interests of employees. No restrictions shall be placed on this right, except those which, being necessary in the interests of national security, public order, public health or morals, and the protection of rights of others, are properly prescribed by law.

ARTICLE 8
The Right to Participate in Political Activity and Government

Every citizen shall have the right to participate in peaceful political activity intended to influence the composition and policies of the government. Every citizen shall have the right to form and join political parties and, subject to proper qualification prescribed by law, to participate in the conduct of public affairs, whether directly or through freely chosen representatives. The exercise of the right to participate in political activity shall be limited by the obligation to refrain from any advocacy of ethnic, racial or religious hatred and incitement of discrimination, hostility and violence.

ARTICLE 9
The Right to Enjoy, Pratice, Profess, Maintain and Promote Culture, Language, Tradition and Religion
All ethnic, linguistic and religious groups and all persons belonging to such groups, shall have the right to enjoy, practice, profess, maintain and promote their cultures, languages, traditions and religions, insofar as these do not infringe upon the rights of others or the national interest.

ARTICLE 10
The Right to Freedom of Movement and Residence Everyone lawfully present within the borders of the country shall have the right to freedom of movement and choice of residence subject to the obligation not to infringe upon the rights of others and to such provisions as are properly prescribed by law and in the interests of public health and public order. No citizen shall be arbitrarily deprived of the right to enter the country. Everyone shall have the right to leave the country in accordance with the procedures properly prescribed by law.

ARTICLE 11
The Right to Own Property
Everyone has the right to acquire, own and dispose of movable, immovable and immaterial property, alone or in association to his heirs or legatees. No one shall be arbitrarily deprived of his property. Expropriation shall only be permitted in the public interest and if properly authorized by law. Fair compensation shall be payable in all cases of expropriation.

ARTICLE 12
Enforcement of Fundamental Rights
12.1 The enumeration, in this Bill, of certain specific rights, shall not be construed as denying, limiting or disparaging other rights retained by the people.
12.2 Any legislative, executive or judicial act at variance with the provisions of the Bill, may be declared null, void and of no effect by order of the Supreme Court and any person who may suffer any disadvantage as a consequence of such an act, shall be entitled to legal redress.
12.3 No Fundamental Rights listed herein, may be repealed, excluded or modified in any way so as to affect its substance or intent.
12.4 Where any Fundamental Right is properly limited by legislation, such legislation must have a general character and not be limited to a single case.
12.5 All branches and organs of government shall conduct themselves in all

their legislative, executive and judicial acts in accordance with the principles enshrined in this Bill.

12.6 All persons are entitled to the rights enumerated in this Bill, without distinction on the grounds of race, colour, sex, language, political or other opinion, religion, ethnic or social origin, birth or other status.

12.7 Any person may apply to the Supreme Court by appropriate proceedings to enforce the rights conferred under the provisions of the Bill.

12.8 The Supreme Court shall have the power to make all such orders as may be necessary and appropriate to secure to the applicant the enjoyment of any rights conferred under the provisions of this Bill.

12.9 Any law in force on and continuing in force after the date on which the provisions of this Bill come into operation may be submitted by any government authority to the Supreme Court for a ruling on the compatability of such law with the Fundamental Rights enumerated in this Bill, and if such a law has been so submitted for a ruling, no proceeding based on any provision of such law may be instituted under paragraph 7 of this article until the Supreme Court has given its ruling and a period of six months has elapsed after the date of the ruling.

12.10 For the purpose of the hearing and adjudication of any proceedings contemplated in this article, or otherwise based upon provisions of this Bill, the Supreme Court shall be constituted and sit as a Constitutional Court in accordance with the provisions of the law governing the Supreme Court.

12.11 An independent Parliamentary Commissioner (Ombudsman) shall be appointed by the Parliament for the investigation and settlement through negotiation and mediation by individuals or infringements of their Fundamental Rights, arising into the Supreme Court as contemplated in this article. The Parliamentary Commissioner shall report annually in writing to Parliament and to such organs, of government as are affected by his activities, and shall include in such reports those recommendations he may consider necessary.

FUNDAMENTAL OBJECTIVES

We, the people of SWA/Namibia, further wish to record our determination and to commit our Government to ensure: (a) that every person within our country shall enjoy the opportunity to free and full development of his personality in the exercise of those duties and responsibilities which he owes the community; (b) that the family, as the natural and fundamental group unit of society, is afforded protection by society and the State; (c) that in the exercise of his rights and freedom, everyone shall be subject only to such limitations as are determined by law solely for the purpose of securing due recognition and respect for the rights and freedoms of others and of meeting the just requirements of morality, public order, health and the general welfare and national security of a democratic society; and, mindful of the existence of certain other social goals whose achievement is essential if we are to create the type of national and democratic society which we aspire, hereby require our Government to do all in its power to achieve:

1. the establishment and maintenance of a sound and dynamic economic system capable of providing for the needs of all in our society;

2. the opportunity to work, to exercise free choice of employment and to enjoy just and favorable conditions of work and employment; protection against unemployment; and equal pay for equal work;

3. a standard of living adequate for the health and well being of each person and family unit, including food, housing, medical care and essential social services, and a measure of protection against the consequences of sickness, disability, widowhood and old age;

4. access to education for all the opportunity to attain the highest possible standard of education directed at the full development of the human personality and preparation for gainful employment; that higher education shall be equally accessible to all on the basis of merit; that elementary education shall be free and compulsory; the liberty of parents, and when applicable legal guardians, to choose for their children the type of schools and the direction of education will be protected;

5. the opportunity for all to participate fully in cultural activities, to enjoy the arts, and to share in scientific advancement and its benefits; and protection of the moral and material interests of authors in their scientific, literary and artistic productions.

Appendix D
Namibia Agreement

The Governments of the People's Republic of Angola, the Republic of Cuba, and the Republic of South Africa, hereinafter designated as "the Parties,"

TAKING INTO ACCOUNT the "Principles for a Peaceful Settlement in Southwestern Africa," approved by the Parties on 20 July 1988, and the subsequent negotiations with respect to the implementation of these Principles, each of which is indispensable to a comprehensive settlement.

CONSIDERING the acceptance by the Parties of the implementation of United Nations Security Council Resolution 435 (1978), adopted on 29 September 1978, hereinafter designated as "U.N.S.C.R. 435/78,"

CONSIDERING the conclusion of the bilateral agreement between the People's Republic of Angola and the Republic of Cuba providing for the redeployment toward the North and the staged and total withdrawal of Cuban troops from the territory of the People's Republic of Angola.

RECOGNIZING the role of the United Nations Security Council in implementing U.N.S.C.R. 435/78 and in supporting the implementation of the present agreement,

AFFIRMING the sovereignty, sovereign equality, and independence of all states of southwestern Africa,

AFFIRMING the principle of noninterference in the internal affairs of states,

AFFIRMING the principle of abstention from the threat or use of force against the territorial integrity or political independence of states,

REAFFIRMING the right of the peoples of the southwestern region of Africa to self-determination, independence, and equality of rights, and of the states of southwestern Africa to peace, development, and social progress,

URGING African and international cooperation for the settlement of the problems of the development of the southwestern region of Africa,

EXPRESSING their appreciation for the mediating role of the Government of the United States of America,

DESIRING to contribute to the establishment of peace and security in southwestern Africa,

AGREE to the provisions set forth below.

1. The Parties shall immediately request the Secretary General of the United Nations to seek authority from the Security Council to commence implementation of U.N.S.C.R. 435/78 on 1 April 1989.

2. All military forces of the Republic of South Africa shall depart Namibia in accordance with U.N.S.C.R. 435/78.

3. Consistent with the provisions of U.N.S.C.R. 435/78, the Republic of South Africa and the People's Republic of Angola shall cooperate with the Secretary General to insure the independence of Namibia through free and fair elections and shall abstain from any action that could prevent the execution of U.N.S.C.R. 435/78. The Parties shall respect the territorial integrity and inviolability of borders of Namibia and shall insure that their territories are not used by any state, organization, or person in connection with acts of war, aggression, or violence against the territorial integrity or inviolability of borders of Namibia or any other action which could prevent the execution of U.N.S.C.R. 435/78.

4. The People's Republic of Angola and the Republic of Cuba shall implement the bilateral agreement, signed on the date of signature of this agreement, providing for the redeployment toward the North and the staged and total withdrawal of Cuban troops from the territory of the People's Republic of Angola, and the arrangements made with the Security Council of the United Nations for the on-site verification of that withdrawal.

5. Consistent with their obligations under the Charter of the United Nations, the Parties shall refrain from the threat or use of force, and shall insure that their respective territories are not used by any state, organization, or person in connection with any acts of war, aggression, or violence, against the territorial integrity, inviolability of borders, or independence of any state of southwestern Africa.

6. The Parties shall respect the principle of noninterference in the internal affairs of the states of southwestern Africa.

7. The Parties shall comply in good faith with all obligations undertaken in this agreement and shall resolve through negotiation and in a spirit of cooperation any disputes with respect to the interpretation of implementation thereof.

8. This agreement shall enter into force upon signature.

SIGNED at New York in triplicate in the Portuguese, Spanish and English languages, each language being equally authentic, this 22d day of December 1988.

Appendix E
Angola Agreement

The Government of the People's Republic of Angola and the Government of the Republic of Cuba, designated hereof as the parties,
CONSIDERING
THAT the implementation of Resolution 435-78 of the Security Council of the United Nations for the independence of Namibia will begin on 1 April.

THAT the question of the independence of Namibia and the gateguard of the sovereignty, independence and territorial integrity of the People's Republic of Angola are intimately interconnected and linked to peace and security in the southwest region of Africa.

THAT on the same date of the signing of the present agreement a Tripartite Agreement shall also be signed by the Government of the People's Republic of Angola, the Government of the Republic of Cuba and the Government of the Republic of South Africa which contain the essential elements to achieve peace in the southwest region of Africa,

THAT the acceptance and strict fulfillment of the preceding provisions eliminate the causes which motivated the request by the Government of the People's Republic of Angola—in legitimate use of its rights envisioned by Article 51 of the United Nations Charter—for the sending into Angolan territory of a Cuban internationalist military contingent to insure, together with the F.A.P.L.A. (the Angolan Government army), its territorial integrity and sovereignty against the invasion and occupation of a part of its territory.

TAKING INTO ACCOUNT the agreements signed by the Governments of the People's Republic of Angola and the Republic of Cuba on 4 February 1982 and 19 March 1984, the platform of the Government of the People's Republic of Angola adopted in November 1984 and the Protocol of Brazzaville signed by the Governments of the People's Republic of Angola, the Republic of Cuba and the Republic of South Africa on 13 December 1988, it is thus established.

IN CONSEQUENCE that conditions have been created to begin the return home of the Cuban military contingent present in Angolan territory, after having successfully accomplished its internationalist mission.

THEREFORE the Parties agree to the following:

Article I—To begin a staged redeployment to the 15th and 13th parallels and the total withdrawal to Cuba of the contingent of approximately 50,000 troops which make up the Cuban forces in the People's Republic of Angola, according to the paces and time frames established by the annexed calendar, which is an integral part of the present agreement. The total withdrawal will conclude on 1 July 1991.

Article II—The Governments of the People's Republic of Angola and the Republic of Cuba reserve for themselves the right to modify or alter their obligations under Article I of this Agreement if blatant breach of the Tripartite Agreement occurs.

Article III—Both parties, through the Secretary-General of the United Nations, ask the Security Council to set up verification of the redeployment and staged and total withdrawal of the Cuban troops from the territory of the People's Republic of Angola. With this purpose the corresponding protocol shall be established.

Article IV—This agreement shall come into force as of the signing of the Tripartite Agreement between the Governments of the People's Republic of Angola, the Republic of Cuba and the Republic of South Africa.

SIGNED on the 22nd day of December 1988 at the headquarters of the United Nations Organization in two equally valid copies in Portuguese and Spanish.

SIGNED for the Government of the People's Republic of Angola.

For the Government of the Republic of Cuba.

CALENDAR

Annex to the Agreement between the Government of the Republic of Cuba and the Government of the People's Republic of Angola on the conclusion of the Internationalist Mission of the Cuban Military Contingent;

In fulfillment of Article I of the Agreement between the Government of the Republic of Cuba and the Government of the People's Republic of Angola on the conclusion of the internationalist mission of the Cuban military contingent present in Angolan territory, both parties establish the following calendar for the withdrawal: *Time Frames*

Before 1 April 1989 (date of implementation of Resolution 435) 3,000 troops.

Total length of the calendar as of 1 April 1989: 27 months.
Redeployment to the north:
To the 15th Parallel 1 August, 1989.
To the 13th Parallel 31 October, 1989.
Total Troops to be withdrawn:
By 1 November 1989 25,000 (50 percent).
By 1 April 1990 33,000 (66 percent).
By 1 October 1990 38,000 (76 percent) 12,000 remain.
By 1 July 1991 50,000 (100 percent).
The data base is a Cuban force of 50,000 troops.

Appendix F
Excerpts—
SWAPO Constitution

ARTICLE II
Definition
SWAPO is a national liberation movement rallying together, on the basis of free and voluntary association, all freedom-inspired sons and daughters of the Namibian people. It is the organized political vanguard of the oppressed and exploited people of Namibia. In fulfilling its vanguard role, SWAPO organizes, unites, inspires, orients and leads the broad masses of the working Namibian people in the struggle for national and social liberation. It is thus the expression and embodiment of national unity, of a whole people united and organized in the struggle for total independence and social liberation.
ARTICLE III
Aims and Objectives
B. Now, therefore do declare the basic aims and objectives of SWAPO as follows:
(1) To fight relentlessly for the immediate and total liberation of Namibia from colonial and imperialist occupation;
(2) To unite all the people of Namibia, irrespective of race, religion, sex or ethnic origin, into a cohesive, representative, national political entity;
(3) To foster a spirit of national consciousness or a sense of common purpose and collective destiny among the people of Namibia;
(4) To combat all reactionary tendencies of individualism, tribalism, racism, sexism and regionalism;
(5) To co-operate to the fullest extent with all the genuine national liberation movements, progressive governments, organizations and individuals throughout the world towards complete elimination of the

colonial system of imperialism;
(6) To establish in Namibia a democratic, secular government founded upon the will and participation of all the Namibian people;
(7) To ensure that the people's government exercises effective control over the means of production and distribution and pursues a policy which facilitates the way to social ownership of all the resources of the country;
(8) To work towards the creation of a non-exploitative and non-oppressive classless society;
(9) To ensure that a people's government in an independent Namiba co-operates with other States in Africa in bringing about African unity;
(10) To see that the people's government works in close co-operation with all peace-loving States towards world peace and security.[1]

---

[1] "Constitution of the South West Africa People's Organization," published by the SWAPO Department for Publicity and Information, Provisional Headquarters, Lusaka, Zambia, pp.3 & 4.

Index

Abolishment of Racial Discrimination (Urban Residential and Public Amenities) Bill 83
Action Front for the Retention of the Turnhalle Principles 81
Adams, Brian 159
Adams, Samuel C. 32
Aden 6
Afghanistan 6, 12
African National Congress (ANC) 46, 53, 128, 213, 239, 252
Afrikaans 21, 24, 26, 27, 165
agriculture 7, 19, 20, 30, 31, 32, 35-36, 112, 197, 199, 200
Ahtisaari, Martti 50
Aktur *see* Action Front for the Retention of the Turnhall Principles
Alberts, Donald J. 67
Alexander, Y. 4
Algeria 59, 100, 208
Alvor 233
 Alvor Agreement 233, 235, 236, 237, 238, 280
Amambo, Dimo 62
Amin, Idi 56
ANC *see* African National Congress
Angola 6, 13, 15, 18, 21, 23, 24, 26, 44, 50, 54, 59, 63, 70, 71, 72, 73, 75, 76, 78, 80, 91, 100, 101, 103, 106, 107, 112, 113, 114, 115, 116, 118, 121, 124, 125, 127, 129, 131, 137, 138, 140, 141, 143, 144, 145, 147, 148, 149, 150, 152, 156, 157, 160, 161, 163, 167, 170, 171, 173, 174, 176, 178, 179, 181, 183, 184, 185, 186, 187, 188, 189, 190, 191, 193, 196, 197, 208, 210, 211, 212, 213, 215, 217, 220, 224, 226, 227, 228, 229, 230, 231, 232, 233, 234, 235, 236, 237, 239, 240, 241, 242, 243, 244, 245, 246, 247, 248, 249, 250, 251, 252, 253, 256, 259, 260, 261, 268, 269, 272, 275, 278, 279, 280, 287, 292, 300, 301, 302, 303
Angolan Army (Peoples Armed Forces for the Liberation of Angola) (FAPLA) 127, 141, 144, 145, 146, 147, 148, 160, 174, 176, 177, 178, 180, 183, 187, 191, 213, 214, 216, 217, 218, 220, 221, 223, 227, 245, 246, 247, 249, 253, 259, 260, 277, 302
Angra Pequena 18, 24
apartheid 42, 43, 82, 278
Appolis, Emil 59
Arabia 12
armor 119, 129, 130, 131, 148, 153, 174, 176, 177, 181, 215, 218, 221, 226; *see also* specific names, *e.g.,* T-34 tanks
artillery 137, 138, 170, 217, 200, 221, 223, 224; *see also* specific systems, *e.g.* G5
Australia 2, 3, 100

Babing, Alfred 65
Bagani 112
Bakongo 138, 231
Bantu 21, 23
Barber, Noel 104
Barnard, Bariss, 118, 119, 121, 122
Basters 19, 27, 200, 272
Battalions
 31 (201) 155, 156, 157, 259
 32 137, 138, 140, 179, 180
 33 (701) 155, 156
 34 (202) 155, 156

35 (101)   152, 155, 156, 157, 161,
    162, 163, 164, 165, 166, 170, 259
36 (203)   155, 156
37 (102)   155, 156
41 (911)   155, 156
53   119
61 Mechanized   174, 178, 220
201   123
Beckett, Ian   111
Benguela   238
  Benguela Current   19, 36
  Benguela railroad   229
Bestbier, Frank   131, 132, 133, 136
Bill of Fundamental Rights and
    Objectives   88, 294-299
Bill of Rights, SWA/Namibia   88, 89
Binder, D.   237
Bismarck, Otto von   18, 24
Black, Walter   75, 76
Bodansky, Y.   279
Borrell, J.   232
Botha, Louis   153
Botha, P.W.   92, 94, 95, 187, 250
Botha, Roelf "Pik"   49, 51, 52, 54, 93,
    184, 188, 260
Botswana   18, 57, 100, 211, 213, 282,
    287
Brauer, Hans-Deter   65
Brazzaville   229, 230, 245, 302
Breytenbach, Jan   128, 129, 138
Breytenbach, Breyten   128
Brezhnev, Leonid   7, 64
Bridgland, F.   229, 232, 235, 238, 239,
    240
Brigades (FAPLA)
  11th   147
  11th Mechanized   177, 178
  16th   218, 220
  19th   146, 147
  21st   218, 220, 223
  25th   223
  47th   218, 220
  59th   218, 223
Brooke, J.   279
Buffalo Battalion   *see* Battalions, 32
Buffel (vehicle)   117, 118, 119, 120,
    121, 123, 131, 144, 150
Bukovsky, V.   1, 8

Bushmanland   155, 156
Bushmen   19, 21, 23, 26, 27, 116,
    155, 157, 158, 159, 160, 161, 164,
    170, 179

Cabinet (Namibian)   97, 98, 100
Cahama   174, 175, 176, 251
Caiundo   178
Caluequque Dam   196, 245, 246
Cambodia   6
Canada   45, 237
Cape Colony   18, 24
Cape of Good Hope   11, 13, 15
Cape Town   47, 50, 57, 87, 94
Cape Verde Islands   193
capitalist economy   1, 23, 30, 64
Caprivi Strip   18, 19, 36, 112, 113,
    123, 155, 156, 157, 165, 168, 211
Caprivians   19, 21, 23, 26, 35, 200
Carter, Jimmy (Administration of)
    91, 101, 210, 240, 263
Cassinga   125, 126, 127, 128, 129,
    130, 131, 138, 175, 179, 180, 189
Casspir (vehicle)   117, 188, 119, 120,
    163, 164, 166
Castro, Fidel   235, 241, 243, 246, 250,
    251, 256, 178, 179, 280, 287
Cautir River   223
Cazombo salient   215, 217
CCN   *see* Council of Churches of
    Namibia
Ceylon   11
Chaknovich, Konstantin   215
Chambinga
  heights   223, 224
  River   223, 225
Chetequera   125, 131, 132, 133, 136,
    137, 250
Chiambo   131
Chilton, David   8
China (PRC)   5. 6. 7. 12. 100, 233,
    234, 235, 287, 290
Chipenda, Daniel   231, 235
Chitunda, Jeremias   253
Chitequeta   149, 150
Chivemba-Matala   250
choke point   frontis., 9, 10, 11, 13,
    20

Cilliers, J.K. 104, 105
Citizen Force 153, 177
civic action 104, 107, 116, 162, 163, 195-206, 274
Claiborne, W. 260, 265, 273, 275
Clark Amendment 241
Coetse, Jacobus 24
College for Out of School Training 210
Coloureds 19, 23, 26, 27, 151
Combat Group Serfontein 136, 137
Combat Team Joubert 136, 137
Combat Team Tango 174, 178, 179, 181
Commando 153, 154, 155, 212
Committee of 24 284
communism 7, 8, 9, 12, 13, 14
Communist Party of the Soviet Union 65, 234; *see also* Soviet Union
Congo 228, 229, 245, 256, 270
Congo-Brazzaville 228, 229, 231
Constituent Assembly 56, 79, 80, 81, 82, 233, 258, 263, 264, 266
constitution
   Namibian 294
   SWAPO 63, 65, 305, 305
Constitutional Council 98, 99
containment 4, 5, 6, 12
Conzumbia River 218, 220
Council for Scientific and Industrial Research 163
Council of Churches of Namibia 275, 276
Council of Ministers 83, 84
counterinsurgency 70, 72, 73, 74, 76, 104, 106, 108, 109, 111, 112, 113, 114, 118, 119, 121, 124, 138, 140, 144, 150, 151, 152, 153, 154, 155, 157, 158, 159, 161, 162, 163, 165, 166, 168, 169, 170, 174, 177, 195, 196, 203, 204, 205, 206, 207, 208, 209, 210, 211, 212, 231, 247
Coutinho, Rosa 230, 232, 233, 237
Crocker, Chester 87, 186, 188, 245, 246, 249, 251, 253
CSIR *see* Council for Scientific and Industrial Research
Cuamato 131

Cuangar 239
Cuba 9, 62, 71, 91, 100, 127, 129, 138, 144, 146, 163, 176, 177, 178, 180, 183, 185, 186, 187, 188, 189, 190, 211, 218, 220, 221, 223, 224, 226, 227-244, 245, 246, 247, 248, 250, 251, 252, 253, 254, 256, 257, 259, 260, 261, 268, 269, 278, 279, 280, 287, 292, 300, 301, 302, 303, 304
Cuban Missile Crisis (1962) 6
Cubango River 129, 178
cuca 23, 38, 39, 121, 122, 199
Cuito Cuanavale 214, 216, 217, 218, 220, 223, 224
Cuito River 220, 224
Cunene River 19, 21, 107, 113, 118, 174, 238
Cunjamba 218, 220
Cuvelai 174, 175, 177, 178, 179, 181, 189
Cuzizi River 218, 220

Daily, B.D. 4
DAISY 150
Dala River 225
Damara Council 85, 86
Damaras 19, 23, 25, 155, 200
de Cuellar, Javier Perez *see* Perez de Cuellar, Javier
de Lattre de Tassigny, Jean 212
de Novais, Bartholmeu Dias *see* Dias de Novais, Bartholmeu
De Spinola, Antonio 230
Deen, T. 274
Deibel, T.L. 3, 4, 6, 7, 12
Del Pino, R. 1
Democratic Turnhalle Alliance 77, 81, 82, 85, 86, 96, 204, 258, 267, 272
Denmark 208
detente 1, 5, 6, 75, 235
diamonds 32, 33, 34; *see also* mining
Dias de Novais, Bartholmeu 18
Dombondala Complex 131
Dongo 174
Dorning, W.A. 189
Dreyer, Hans 165, 166
DTA *see* Democratic Turnhalle Alliance

East Bloc   9, 141
East Germany   62, 65, 66, 235
Eastern National Water Carrier   197
economy (Namibian)   3, 8, 30-40, 88, 101
Eenhana   112, 197, 247
Egypt   18, 59, 100
11th Brigade (FAPLA)   *see* Brigades (FAPLA), 11th
11th Mechanized Brigade (FAPLA) *see* Brigades (FAPLA), 11th Mechanized
Ellsworth, Robert   238
energy   11, 13, 245; *see also* oil; power
English (language)   21, 24, 26, 301
Esterhuysen   30, 45
Etale   197
Ethiopia   6, 43
Etosha Pan   196
Euro-Asia   2, 3, 4, 5, 7

FAPLA   *see* Angolan Army (Peoples Armed Forces for the Liberation of Angola)
Fauriol, G.   4
Ferreira, Deon   220, 224, 226
53 Battalion   *see* Battalions, 53
59th Brigade   *see* Brigades (FAPLA), 59th
fishing   11, 24, 32, 36-37, 100, 101
FNLA   *see* National Front for the Liberation of Angola
41 Battalion   *see* Battalions, 41
47th Brigade   *see* Brigades (FAPLA), 47th
France   17, 45, 59, 111, 131, 183, 208, 211, 212, 264
free enterprise economy   4, 11, 30, 36, 195, 199, 203, 265, 276
Frye, Alton   6

G5 artillery system   220, 221, 223
G6 artillery system   220, 221, 223
Gaddis, J.L.   3, 4, 6, 7, 12
Gallieni, Joseph   111
Garoeb, Justus   86
gas, natural   12

Geldenhuys, Jannie   144, 149, 187
geopolitics   5, 11
German (language)   21, 24
Germany   3, 17, 18, 24, 25, 35, 38, 41, 44, 117, 153
  East   *see* East Germany
  West   *see* West Germany
Geyer, Georgie Anne   243
glasnost   60, 287
Gleeson, Ian   125, 136
Gold, Philip   9
Gomes, Pericles Ferreira   256
Gorbachev   60, 245, 287
Gorshkov, Sergei G.   11
Goure, L.   279, 287
Gray, C.S.   1, 2, 3, 4
Great Britain   13, 17, 18, 45, 53, 101, 183, 232, 267, 268, 271, 284
Grenada   6, 184
Greyling, Faan   177
Guinea-Bissau   6, 13, 15, 230
Gulich, Thomas   274
Guyana   6, 100

Haig, Alexander   148
Hamm, Warren C., Jr.   11
Hammarskjold, Dag   283
Hamutenya, Hidipo   62
Harkavy, Robert E.   7
Havana   237, 251
Heartland   2, 3, 4
Heaton, William R.   67
Heitman, H.-R.   189, 221
helicopters   117-125, 127, 128, 129, 130, 138, 140, 208, 209
Hempstone, Smith   259, 261, 273
Hemhombe   137, 140
Hereros   19, 21, 23, 24, 25, 59, 77, 155, 270, 272, 277
Himambe, Dimo   127, 129
horse cavalry   117, 118, 162
Houphouet-Boigny, Felix   93
Humbe   144
Humphrey, Hubert   241

Idi Amin   *see* Amin, Idi
imperialism   1, 3, 4, 5, 7, 14, 306
India   6, 12, 100, 256

Indo-China 6, 12
infantry 118, 119, 133, 153, 159, 218, 223
Institute for Strategic Studies, University of Pretoria 157, 204, 205, 211
intelligence (gathering) 75, 107, 113, 115, 140, 145, 160, 162, 164, 165, 167, 174, 211, 213
International Court of Justice 42, 43
International Law of the Seas Treaty 37
intimidation 48, 53, 60, 69, 76, 93, 114, 152, 267, 271; *see also* psychological warfare
Iran 6, 12, 209
Israel 56
ISSUP *see* Institute for Strategic Studies, University of Pretoria
Ivory Coast 93

Jackson, Jesse 270, 277
Jamba 212, 215, 217, 218, 220, 250
Japan 2, 5, 12, 13, 37
JMC *see* Joint Monitoring Commission
JMMC *see* Joint Military Monitoring Committee
Johns, M. 285
Johnson, Paul 6, 55, 56, 270, 271, 283
Joint Military Monitoring Committee 247, 249, 260
Joint Monitoring Commission 163, 183-194
Joubert, 132, 136, 137
"Juliet" 131, 132, 133, 136, 137

Kalahari Desert 19, 28
Kambode, Jackson 61
Kaokoland 24, 25, 123, 143, 155, 156, 164, 165, 168, 174
Kapuuo, Clemens 77
Katatura 43, 57, 155
Katima Mulilo 112, 201
Katjiuongua, Moses 277
Kaunda, Kenneth 62, 92, 187, 188, 190, 231, 233

Kavango River 19, 21, 24, 36, 107, 112, 156, 165, 167, 168, 197, 200, 250
Kavangos 19, 21, 23, 24, 35, 112, 123, 143, 155, 174, 178, 211, 272
Kenya 233
Kenyatta, Jomo 233
Kerina, Mburumba 59, 61, 63
KGB 15
Khoisan 21
Kirkpatrick, J. 242
Kissinger, Henry 5, 71
koevoet 163, 165, 166, 167
Kozlov, Alexei 14
Kozonguizi, F.J. 59, 89, 91, 93
kraal 114, 115, 116, 120, 122, 165
Kucinski, R. 4
Kwando River 19, 24, 26
Kwanyama 23, 62

labor 33, 59
Labour Party 85, 96
Laos 6
League of Nations 24, 41, 42, 43, 284
Legum, Colin 239
Leister 30, 45
Leites, Norman 257
Lenin, V.I. 13, 14, 64, 65, 66, 67, 68, 149, 253, 265
Leninist socialism *see* socialism
LF *see* Liberation Front
Liberation Front 96
Liberia 43, 100
Lobito 238, 278
Lomba River 214, 218, 220, 221
Louw, M.H. 8
Luanda 61, 67, 146, 147, 210, 227, 228, 230, 231, 232, 235, 236, 238, 239, 240, 241, 243
Lubango 124, 146, 174, 175, 176, 250
Luderitz 26, 37, 38
Luderitz, Adolf 18, 24
Luena 215
Lusaka 61, 62, 92, 93, 94, 187, 188, 189, 190, 240, 306

Lusaka Agreement 91, 189, 190, 191, 193, 292

Machel, Samora 92
Mackinder, Halford 2, 3, 4, 7
Malan, Magnus 30, 45, 127, 148, 186, 188
manufacturing 31, 38, 197, 199
Mao Tse-tung 68, 70, 71, 74, 99, 103, 104, 109, 204
Mapacha 112
Marcum, John 229, 232, 233, 234, 236
Marxist-Leninist socialism *see* socialism
Matabele 267
Matala 174, 250
Matatu, G. 236
Mavinga 214, 216, 217, 218, 220
Max, Alphonse 11
Mbunda 228
McChlachlan, Captain 161
McCuen, John J. 70, 71, 72, 73, 74, 105, 111, 112, 114, 151, 203, 204, 205, 207
Mediterranean 11, 13
Meiring, George 171, 173, 177, 181
Menongue 217
MFA *see* Movement of the Armed Forces
Middle East 12, 15
Mifinawe, Soloman 59
minerals 11, 13, 15, 20, 32-34; *see also* mining
Minguita 140
mining 25, 31, 32-34, 38, 100, 111, 112, 197, 199; *see also* specific names, *e.g.* uranium
missiles, surface-to-air *see* SAM-7, SAM-9
Mocamedes 238
Mongols (Golden Horde) 1, 7, 8, 9, 13, 15
Mongua 147
Monteiro, Ngongo 187
Morris, Robert 9
Moss, R. 239
motorbikes 118, 121, 122, 162
Movement of the Armed Forces 230

Moxico 215, 229
Mozambique 6, 15, 91, 230, 273, 287
Channel 11, 13, 15
MPC *see* MultiParty Conference
MPLA *see* Popular Movement for the Liberation of Angola
Mudge, Dirk 84, 86
Mueshihange, Peter 62
Mugabe, Robert 92, 267, 268, 276, 277
Multi Party Conference 85-94, 95, 96, 204, 263, 267, 291, 292
Mulungushi
conference center 187
Minute 188, 189
Mupa 191
Muzorewa, Abel 267
Mwonga 229

Namas 19, 21, 23, 24, 25, 26, 27, 155, 200
Namib Desert 238
Namibe 18, 19, 278
Namibian Christian Democratic Party 85
National Assembly 81, 82, 83, 84, 85, 97, 98, 99, 100
National Building and Investment Corporation 202
National Council of Churches 208
National Development Fund 100
National Front for the Liberation of Angola 137, 138, 190, 228, 229, 231, 232, 233, 234, 235, 236, 238, 239, 240, 241, 242, 243
National Namibian Front 81
National Party of SWA 85
National Union for the Total Independence of Angola 156, 157, 210, 211, 212, 214, 215-226, 227, 228, 229, 230, 232, 235, 236, 238, 239, 243, 244, 246, 249, 250, 253, 270, 277
Nationalist Party 42, 96
NATO *see* North Atlantic Treaty Organization
naval power 6, 9
NBIC *see* National Building and Investment Corporation

NCDP see Namibian Christian Democratic Party
Ndongo 23, 62
Nel, Gert 138, 140
Neto, Antonio Agostinho 228, 229, 230, 231, 232, 233, 235, 236
Nicaragua 6, 7, 100
Niekirk, Willie van see van Niekirk, Willie
Nigeria 100
911 Battalion see Battalions, 911
19th Brigade (FAPLA) see Brigades, (FAPLA), 19th
Nkomo, Joshua 267
North Atlantic Treaty Organization 3, 5, 13, 181
Norval, Morgan 1, 152, 157, 176, 181, 233, 247, 268
Nossiter, B. 242
NP see National Party of SWA
nuclear arms 6, 13
Nujoma, Sam 57, 59, 60, 61, 62, 65, 66, 184, 193, 209, 248, 259, 261, 267, 269, 270, 275, 276, 277, 282
Nyerere, Julius 57, 231, 233

OAU see Organization of African Unity
Ogandjera 197
oil 7, 11, 12, 13, 111, 209
oil spot strategy 111, 114, 116
Okatope 118, 121
Olifant main battle tank 220, 221, 223
Omauni 130
Okahandja 25, 38, 155
Ombalantu 197
Omega (base) 123, 157, 158, 159, 160
Omepepa 137
Omgulumbashe 60
Ondangwa 112, 113, 118, 121, 130, 136, 144, 152, 165, 197
1 SWA Specialist Unit 155
101 Battalion see Battalions, 101
102 Battalion see Battalions, 102
O'Neil, Bard 67, 68, 104
Ongiva 143, 144, 146, 147, 188, 191, 193

OPC see Owamboland People's Congress
Operation ASKARI 156, 171-181, 183, 186, 220, 221, 228
Operation HOOPER 213, 215-226
Operation MODULAR 213, 215-226
Operation PACKER 213, 215-226
Operation PROTEA 143-150, 156, 163, 171, 173
Operation REINDEER 77, 78, 125-141, 143, 144, 171, 173, 259
Operation SAVANNAH 71, 75, 138, 157, 211, 212
OPO see Owamboland People's Organization
Orange River 18, 19, 24, 25, 27, 33, 280
Oranjemund 38
ore 11, 12, 34; see also mining, resources
Organization of African Unity 51, 56, 59, 148, 208, 242
Oshakati 112, 144, 152, 166, 197, 201, 272
oshanas 196
Oshigambo 197
Oshikango 59
Otjiwarango 112, 113
Ovahimba 25
Owamboland 19, 21, 23, 24, 36, 38, 39, 53, 54, 60, 68, 69, 70, 71, 72, 73, 75, 77, 106, 107, 113, 114, 115, 116, 120, 121, 123, 124, 152, 153, 155, 156, 161, 162, 163, 165, 167, 170, 195, 197, 198, 200, 228, 245, 248, 258, 259, 272, 274, 275, 276, 277, 278
 Central 76, 118, 143, 168, 174, 196
 Eastern 130, 143, 174, 178, 247
 Western 131, 174
Owamboland People's Congress 57, 59
Owamboland People's Organization 59
Owambos 19, 21, 23, 24, 25, 35, 53, 59, 60, 68, 75, 76, 115, 121, 122, 152, 153, 157, 161, 162, 163, 164, 167, 200, 201, 204, 205, 266, 267,

268, 271, 272, 273, 277

PAC *see* Pan African Congress
Palme, Olaf 242
Pan African Congress 46
Parker, P.J. 4
People's Armed Forces for the Liberation of Angola *see* Angolan Army
People's Liberation Army of Namibia 59, 62, 66, 68, 69, 70-71, 74, 76, 77, 107, 191, 204, 205, 209, 211, 258, 259, 260, 261
Perez de Cuellar, Javier 94
Persian Gulf 13
Pestretsov, Nikolai Feodorovich 147
PeuPeu 144
PLAN *see* People's Liberation Army of Namibia
Platt, Nick 187
Podhoretz, Norman 12
Pohamba, Lucas 62
Ponomarov, Boris 13
Ponomorov, M. 226
Popular Movement for the Liberation of Angola 71, 138, 217, 228, 229, 230, 231, 232, 233, 234, 235, 236, 237, 238, 240, 241, 242, 243, 244, 249, 272, 280
Portugal 23, 24, 59, 71, 121, 137, 157, 158, 178, 180, 196, 228, 229, 230, 231, 232, 233, 235, 236, 240, 301, 303
power 32, 39, 112, 113, 118, 119, 120, 238, 239, 145
Pretoria 184, 185, 204, 211, 251, 269
propaganda 13, 67, 69, 148, 167, 183, 208, 209, 210, 227; *see also* socialist propaganda
psychological warfare 8, 69, 72, 74, 104, 107, 143, 257, 268; *see also* propaganda
Pumas 127, 130, 208; *see also* helicopters

Quiteve 174

railways 2, 3, 39, 112, 278
Ramirez, Vladimir 243

Ratel (vehicle) 131, 133, 144, 150, 177
Reagan, Ronald 9, 91, 96, 210, 245, 251
Rehoboth Basters *see* Basters
Resolution 435 *see* UN Security Council, Resolutions
resources 40, 64, 101, 278; *see also* specific resources, *e.g.,* oil
Revel, J-F. 1, 8
Rhodesia 6, 104, 105
Rimlands 3, 7
Rio de Janeiro Treaty 3
Risquet, Jorge 246
Roberto, Holden 137, 228, 229, 230, 231, 233, 234, 238, 240, 243
Rodriques, Alexandre 188
Rodriquez, Carlos, Rafael 237
Romeo-Mike force 163, 164
Rossing mine 33, 34
Ruacana 112, 113, 118, 144, 196, 197, 249, 257
Rubenstein, Alvin 283
Rudolph, Herwig 11
Rundu 113, 201, 220, 250
Rushdoony, R.J. 8
Russia *see* Soviet Union
Rustov, Alexander 8

sabotage *see* intimidation, terror
SADF *see* South African Defense Force
Sagaria, Willibald 91
SAM-7 181, 257, 260
SAM-9 181
SAP *see* South African Police
Savimbi, Jonas 156, 210, 213, 215, 217, 220, 229, 230, 232, 233, 236, 238, 250
Schultz, George 94
scientific socialism *see* socialism
sea lanes 9, 11
seapower 2, 3, 4; *see also* naval power
SEATO *see* South East Asia Treaty Organization
Senegal 100
Sequeira, Sabriaho 187
Serfontein 132, 137

701 Battalion see Battalions, 701
Shafarevich, Igor 8
Shikongo, Silas 61
Shipanga, Andreas 59, 61, 62, 63, 86
Shona (tribe) 267
Shujaga, Toivo 76
Shultz, R.H., Jr. 234, 274, 283
Sieff, Martin 9, 11
Simonstown 13
16th Brigade (FAPLA) see Brigades (FAPLA), 16th
61 Mechanized Battalion see Battalions, 61 Mechanized
socialism 13, 14, 90, 285, 287, 288
socialist
  economy 30, 33, 35, 39, 90, 203, 276, 282
  groups 66, 117, 127, 138, 217, 230, 236, 237, 243, 265, 270, 272; see also specific names, e.g., SWAPO
  leaders 57, 128; see also specific names, e.g., Nyerere
  program 60, 63, 76, 89, 90, 96, 114, 203, 257, 258, 263, 270, 281
  propaganda 227, 266
  regimes 71, 103, 149, 190, 197, 210, 213, 229, 239, 246, 253, 256, 269, 274, 279, 287
  revolution 64, 65, 124, 209, 261, 266, 272
  state 6, 273, 276, 287
  world 1, 20, 100, 208
South Africa 6, 12, 13, 15, 17, 24, 31, 34, 35, 36, 37, 38, 39, 40, 41, 42, 43, 44, 45, 46, 47, 48, 49, 50, 51, 52, 54, 55, 56, 61, 71, 72, 73, 74, 75, 76, 77, 78, 79, 80, 81, 82, 83, 84, 91, 92, 93, 94, 95, 100, 104, 105, 106, 107, 108, 111, 112, 113, 114, 123, 124, 125, 127, 128, 129, 131, 133, 137, 138, 140, 141, 144, 145, 146, 147, 148, 149, 150, 151, 152, 153, 154, 157, 158, 163, 168, 173, 174, 176, 177, 178, 179, 181, 183, 184, 185, 186, 187, 188, 189, 190, 191, 193, 195, 196, 201, 203, 204, 205, 206, 208, 209, 210, 211, 212, 213, 214, 218, 220, 221, 223, 224, 226, 227, 228, 237, 238, 239, 240, 241, 242, 243, 245, 246, 247, 248, 249, 250, 251, 252, 253, 256, 257, 258, 259, 261, 266, 268, 269, 274, 275, 276, 277, 278, 280, 282, 286, 287, 290, 291, 292, 301, 203, 303
South African Defense Force 5, 50, 70, 75, 76, 78, 83, 113, 125, 127, 131, 137, 138, 141, 153, 156, 158, 161, 162, 170, 176, 177, 179, 180, 184, 197, 198, 201, 220, 221, 227, 249, 268
South African Police 163, 166
South East Asia Treaty Organization 3, 5
South West Africa (/Namibia) 17, 18, 19, 22, 24, 25, 39, 41, 42, 43, 44, 45, 46, 47, 49, 54, 56, 59, 60, 65, 77, 79, 82, 88, 91, 92, 93, 94, 95, 98, 100, 153, 156, 171, 173, 184, 188, 189, 199, 205, 237, 250, 276, 291-293, 294, 298
South West Africa Territorial Force 154, 155, 156, 157, 169, 170, 247, 249, 258, 259, 260, 269, 277
South West African National Union 59, 85, 86, 97, 272, 277
South West African People's Organization see SWAPO
South West African Police 166, 258
Southern African Customs Union 39
Soviet Union 1, 2, 3, 4, 5, 6, 7, 8, 9, 10, 11, 12, 13, 14, 15, 20, 36, 45, 63, 65, 66, 67, 71, 100, 101, 103, 128, 138, 145, 146, 147, 148, 149, 156, 177, 178, 179, 181, 209, 211, 212, 213, 217, 218, 221, 223, 224, 226, 229, 231, 232, 233, 234, 235, 236, 237, 239, 241, 242, 243, 245, 246, 249, 250, 259, 260, 261, 277, 283, 285, 286, 290
Sparks, A. 279
spoor see tracking
Spykman, Nickolas 2, 3
State Department see United States State Department
Steenkamp, W. 71. 73, 75, 132
Steward, David 187
Stiff, P. 119

Stockwell, J. 234, 241
strategic areas 9
Suez Canal 11, 13, 18
Summers, H.G., Jr. 239
Supreme Court of SWA/Namibia 98, 298
Surinam 6
SWA Building Society 202
SWA/Namibia *see* South West Africa (/Namibia)
Swakopmund 17, 33, 34, 37, 38
SWANU *see* South West African National Union, 88
SWAPO 23, 30, 33, 35, 41, 44, 45, 46, 48, 49, 50, 53, 54, 56, 57, 58, 59, 60, 61, 62, 63, 64, 65, 66, 67, 68, 69, 70, 71, 72, 73, 74, 75, 76, 77, 78, 79, 80, 81, 82, 85, 87, 89, 90, 91, 92, 93, 94, 96, 98, 99, 103, 104, 105, 106, 107, 108, 112, 113, 114, 115, 116, 117, 118, 120, 121, 122, 123, 124, 125, 127, 128, 129, 130, 131, 132, 133, 136, 137, 138, 140, 141, 143, 144, 145, 146, 147, 148, 149, 151, 152, 153, 154, 155, 157, 158, 159, 160, 161, 162, 163, 164, 165, 166, 167, 168, 169, 170, 171, 172, 173, 174, 176, 177, 178, 179, 180, 181, 183, 184, 185, 186, 187, 188, 189, 193, 196, 197, 198, 200, 202, 203, 205, 206, 208, 209, 210, 213, 224, 227, 237, 239, 242, 243, 245, 247, 248, 252, 257, 258, 259, 260, 261, 264, 264, 265, 266, 267, 268, 269, 270, 271, 272, 273, 274, 275, 276, 277, 278, 279, 282, 283, 284, 285, 286, 289, 305, 306
SWAPO-D *see* SWAPO-Democrats
SWAPO-Democrats 85, 86, 97
SWAPOL *see* South West African Police
SWATF *see* South West Africa Territorial Force
sword of Damocles 94, 185
Szulc, Tad 238

tache d'huile *see* oil spot strategy
Taiwan 6, 12

Tanks, Russian *see* specific tanks, *e.g.*, T-34
T-34 tanks 129, 148, 215
T-54 tanks 176, 177
T-55 tanks 215, 221
T-62 tanks 215
T-64 tanks 250
Tanzania 57, 62, 231, 233, 256
Task Force Delta-Fox 174, 177, 178
Task Force Echo-Victor 174, 179
Task Force Victor 174
Task Force X-Ray 174, 176, 177
Taylor 27
Techamutete 127, 129, 130, 180
Technical College 201
Tedla, Aradom 9
terror 4, 41, 48, 50, 59, 60, 62, 67, 68, 69, 70, 71, 72, 74, 75, 76, 77, 82, 103, 114, 208, 213, 237, 247, 257, 258, 261, 287
terrorist groups *see* specific groups, *e.g.*, SWAPO, PAC, ANC
TGNU *see* Transitional Government of National Unity
Thatcher, Margaret 96
Third World 13, 20, 53, 67, 96, 101, 148, 199, 208, 229, 233, 234, 273
31 Battalion *see* Battalions, 31
32 Battalion *see* Battalions, 32
33 Battalion *see* Battalions, 33
34 Battalion *see* Battalions, 34
35 Battalion *see* Battalions, 35
36 Battalion *see* Battalions, 36
37 Battalion *see* Battalions, 37
Thomas, Wolfgang 39, 40
Thompson, Robert 75, 105, 170, 195, 196
Thucydides 2
Toivio, Andimba 277
Toivo, Herman 57, 59, 91
Toivo ya Toivo 292
tracking 107, 114, 115, 116, 117, 118, 119, 122, 123, 124, 155, 158, 159, 161, 162, 164, 171, 179
Transitional Government of National Unity 30, 95-102, 205, 272, 281
Trinquier, Roger 211, 212
Tsandi 197
Tse-tung, Mao *see* Mao Tse-tung

Turnhalle 44, 47, 48, 49, 77
21st Brigade, (FAPLA) *see* Brigades, (FAPLA), 21st
25th Brigade, (FAPLA) *see* Brigades, (FAPLA), 25th
201 Battalion *see* Battalions, 201
202 Battalion *see* Battalions, 202
203 Battalion *see* Battalions, 203
Tsumeb Corporation Ltd. 34
Tsumeb-Grootfontein-Otavi mining region 34, 174, 278
Tswanas 19, 21, 23, 27, 200, 272

Uganda 56
University of Namibia 201
UN *see* United Nations
UNDP *see* United Nations Development Program
UNESCO 46
United Nations 38, 41, 42, 43, 46, 47, 48, 49, 50, 51, 52, 53, 54, 55, 56, 65, 76, 80, 81, 82, 83, 86, 91, 92, 93, 94, 96, 100, 101, 103, 106, 148, 152, 154, 183, 184, 186, 195, 203, 204, 206, 208, 209, 210, 227, 240, 248, 251, 252, 256, 257, 258, 260, 261, 262, 263, 264, 267, 268, 269, 270, 271, 272, 274, 275, 279, 282, 283, 284, 285, 286, 301, 303
United Nations Council on Namibia 37, 100, 101, 264
United Nations Development Program 46
United Nations General Assembly 45, 46, 48, 49, 51, 56, 61, 65, 80, 101
United Nations Institute for Namibia 65, 90
United Nations, Resolutions
 31/146 65
 33/206 82
 34/92F 46
 435 87, 88, 91, 94, 96, 154, 168, 185, 188, 190, 193, 204, 205, 245, 247, 249, 252, 263, 269, 277, 279, 289-290, 291, 300, 302
 2248 100
United Nations Security Council 43, 44, 45, 48, 49, 50, 51, 80, 96, 101, 183, 185, 253, 269, 289-290, 291, 300, 301, 302, 303
United Nations Security Council, Resolutions
 309 43
 385 44
 431 50
 432 50
 435 55, 79
 566 96
United Nations Trusteeship Council 42
United States 2, 3, 4, 5, 6, 7, 11, 12, 13, 15, 45, 46, 51, 91, 93, 94, 101, 138, 148, 154, 183, 184, 185, 186, 187, 188, 189, 190, 210, 234, 235, 238, 239, 240, 241, 242, 245, 246, 247, 248, 249, 252, 259, 261, 275, 277, 280, 284, 285, 286, 287, 292, 300
United States State Department 87, 148, 185, 187, 210, 217, 251, 253, 280
UNITA *see* National Union for the Total Independence of Angola
uranium 32, 33, 34; *see also* mining
U.S.S.R. *see* Soviet Union

van der Post 27
Vanneman, Peter 14
van Niekirk, Willie 92
Vedder, H. 25
Venter, Al J. 73, 224, 229
Vietminh 212
Vietnam 5, 6, 158, 212, 234, 241
Viljoen, Constand 176, 180, 184
Vogelsang, Heinrich 18
von Bismarck, Otto *see* Bismarck, Otto von
Vorster, John 44, 49, 75

Waldheim, Kurt 43
Walvis Bay 17, 18, 26, 37, 49, 50, 51, 131, 278, 279, 280, 292
Wambos *see* Owambos
"wars of national liberation" 4, 13, 60, 61, 67, 148
Warsaw Pact 12
Weinberger, Caspar 4, 5
Welgemoed, Willie 162, 163

West Germany 17, 45, 184
Windhoek 26, 27, 38, 43, 44, 55, 57, 75, 79, 82, 85, 95, 113, 152, 155, 156, 173, 197, 201, 258, 259, 271, 272, 291-293
  Declaration 88
  Supreme Court 98
World Council of Churches 208, 209
World Island 7

Xangongo 143, 144, 145, 146, 147, 175, 250

Yamazaki, Takio 11
Young, Andrew 101, 240
Yugoslavia 235

Zagladin, V.V. 13, 14
Zaire 138, 228, 230, 233, 238, 240, 241, 242
Zambezi River 18, 19, 24
Zambia 15, 18, 26, 54, 61, 62, 63, 75, 80, 92, 100, 112, 187, 188, 215, 229, 231, 233, 238, 242
Zimbabwe 15, 18, 26, 100, 104, 211, 267, 271, 273, 276, 277, 278

Also By Morgan Norval

Red Star Over Southern Africa

"I wish my colleagues had read this book before they imposed sanctions on South Africa."
**Congressman Dan Burton
(R-IN)**

"It is too bad that Teddy Kennedy, Jesse Jackson and the rest of the Boer-bashers both in and out of government won't take the time to read this important book. If they did, and were honest in their intentions, they would pursue a different course in regards to the tragic events now unfolding in southern Africa."
**Pat Buchanan
Former Director
White House Communications**

*"The true importance of **Red Star Over Southern Africa** is that it provides a sharp contrast to the great majority of information available through the mass media."*
Human Events

Yes! Please send me the latest in foreign policy reading from the Selous Foundation Press.

_____ Copy(ies) of *Red Star Over Southern Africa* at $18.95 plus an additional $2.50 postage & handling for each book. (Overseas orders please add $5.00 postage & handling for each book.)

_____ Amount enclosed: (VA residents please add 4.5% sales tax)

Payable in U.S. funds only

Name _____

Address _____

City _____ State _____ Zip _____

Send check and order form to:
Selous Foundation Press
c/o American Comnet, Inc.
1155 21st St., N.W., Suite 400
Washington, D.C. 20036